The Companies We Keep

Amazing Stories About 450 of Hawaii's Best Known Companies

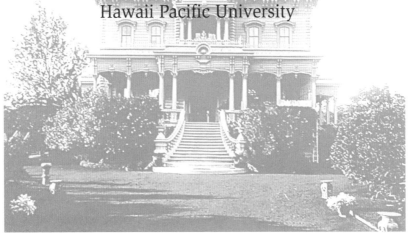

By Bob Sigall
and his students at
Hawaii Pacific University

The Companies We Keep

Amazing Stories About 450 of
Hawaii's Best Known Companies

#1 Hawaii bestseller

© 2008 by Bob Sigall

Fourth Printing

Published by
Small Business Hawaii
6600 Kalanianaole Highway #212
Honolulu, Hawaii 96825
(808) 396-1724

Send comments, new stories and corrections to:
CompaniesWeKeep@Yahoo.com

Visit our web site at: www.CompaniesWeKeep.com

ISBN # 0-9724504-0-8

Cover designed by Debra Castro
Book layout and design by David Walker
Printed in China by Imaging Hawaii

The old Amfac Building was once on the corner of Fort and Queen Streets.

Fort Street in the 1950s, before it was turned into a pedestrian mall. Looking mauka from King Street, Security Diamond is on the left; the Princess Theatre is visible at the top, center; the Kress building toward the upper right; and F. W. Woolworth is lower right. Fort Street was the main shopping district on Oahu until Ala Moana Center opened in 1959.

Table of Contents

What people are saying about *The Companies We Keep*

"If you like to read this column, let me suggest a book you might enjoy: *The Companies We Keep* by Bob Sigall. It's loaded with oddball information about Our Honolulu." **Bob Krauss, *Honolulu Advertiser.***

"One of the most fascinating Hawaii books in a long time." **Perry & Price, KSSK radio**

"*The Companies We Keep* is a fascinating book that, if not on your bookshelf, should be. It's a kamaaina-must-have." *MidWeek.*

"An enlightening and entertaining book, with thousands of intriguing tidbits." *Hawaii* **magazine.**

"People in Hawaii will find it a nostalgic trip down memory lane. It's a Kamaaina trivia lovers delight." *Honolulu Star-Bulletin.*

"History and nostalgia that is thoroughly engaging." *Spirit of Aloha* **magazine.**

"*The Companies We Keep* is a perfect gift for longtime Hawaii residents or someone who has moved to the mainland." *Hawaii Reporter.*

Honolulu in 1852, two years after King Kamehameha III declared it a city.

Companies in the Book

MANY OF THE COMPANIES WE PATRONIZE EVERY DAY HAVE fascinating stories that the public is largely unaware of. One company in Hawaii was the first business west of the Mississippi. Another was founded in Asia 340 years ago. Many survived tsunamis, fires, hurricanes and other adversities to be here today.

Here are the 450 companies and organizations that are in the main two sections of the book. Those sections - **Why Did they Call it Zippy's?** and **Extraordinary Hawaii Companies** are arranged alphabetically. Several hundred other companies can be found in lists such as the Hawaii Business Timeline.

A&W Root Beer
A. L. Kilgo
Aaron's Atop the Ala Moana
ABC Stores
Ala Wai Golf Course
Alexander & Baldwin
Alexander Young Hotel
Aloha Airlines
Altres Global Business Services
American Savings Bank
Amfac
Andy's Drive-In
Angelo Pietro
Anheuser-Busch
Anna Miller's
APCOA
Apartment Appearance
Arakawa's
Arby's
Arirang Korean Barbecue
Assaggio
ASSETS School
Aston Hotels and Resorts
Auntie Pasto's
Ayuthaya II Thai Restaurant
Baci Bistro

Ba-Le
Bank of Hawaii
Barnes & Noble
Baskin-Robbins
Bea's Drive-In
Benetton
Benihana
Da Big Kahuna
Big City Diner
Big Island Candies
Big Save Super Markets
The Bistro
Black Mountain Coffee
Blue Moon Builders
Bob's Big Boy
Body & Soul
Borders Books and Music
Boulevard Saimin
Brennecke's Beach Broiler
Brent's Restaurant
  & Delicatessen
Bubbies Homemade Ice
  Cream & Desserts
Buca di Beppo
Buena Sera
Burberry's

Burger King
Buzz's Original Steakhouse
Byron's Drive Inn
C. Brewer
C&H Sugar
C. S. Wo
Cafe Laufer
Cafe 100
Cafe Sistina
Carol & Mary
Castle & Cooke
Central Pacific Bank
Central Union Church
Chamber of Commerce of
 Hawaii
Charley's Taxi
CHART
Chef Mavro
Chez Michel
Chiang Mai Thai Cuisine
Cholo's
Chosun Korean Restaurant
Chun-Hoon Supermarket
Cinnamon Girl
City Mill
Coco Palms
Columbia Inn
Compadres Bar & Grill
Consolidated Amusement Co.
Cornet
Costco
Crabtree & Evelyn
Crazy Shirts
Da Big Kahuna
Daiei
Dairy Queen
Damien Memorial High
 School
Dana Labels
Dave's Hawaiian Ice Cream
Del Monte Fresh Produce

Denny's
Diêm Café
Dillingham Corp.
Dole Food Company
Don The Beachcomber
Dot's In Wahiawa
Downing Hawaii
E.K. Fernandez
Ed and Don's
Edelweiss
Edo Japan
Eki Cyclery
Elephant & Castle
Ethel M's Chocolates
Ethel's Dress Shoppe
Ezogiku
Famous Amos Chocolate
 Chip Cookie Company
50th State Fair
Finance Factors
First Hawaiian Bank
Fisher Hawaii
Flamingo Restaurants
Flora-Dec Sales
Flowers by Jr. Lou and T
Following Sea
Foodland
Fook Yuen Seafood Restaurant
Fujiya Restaurant
Furusato Japanese Restaurants
GBC
GEM
The Gap
Garden Island Newspaper
Gay & Robinson
Gaylord's
Gee...a Deli
Genki Sushi
Germaine's Luau
Gibson's Discount Store
Gordon Biersch

Grace's Inn
Grove Farm Company
Gucci
Gyotaku
Gyu-kaku
HOPACO
HPM
Hakone
Hakuyosha Hawaii
Haleakala Dairy
Halekulani Hotel
Hailimaile General Store
Hallmark Cards
Hama Yu Japanese Restaurant
Han Yang Restaurant
Hana Gion
Hanahauoli School
Hanohano Room
Hardware Hawaii
Harry's Music Store
Hasegawa General Store
Hauoli
Hawaii Business
Hawaii Hochi
Hawaii National Bank
Hawaii Medical Service
 Association
Hawaii Pacific University
Hawaii Sugar Planter's
 Association
Hawaii Visitor's and
 Convention Bureau
Hawaiian Airlines
Hawaiian Brian's Billiards
Hawaiian Electric Company
Hawaiian Eye Center
Hawaiian Moving Company
Heald College
Hee Hing
Heidi's Bistro & Deli
Helena's Hawaiian Food

Hilo Hattie - The Store of
 Hawaii
Hilo Macaroni Company
Hilton Hawaiian Village
Hoku's
Holiday Inn
Holy's Bakery
Honolulu Advertiser
Honolulu Sake Brewery and
 Ice Co.
Honolulu Star-Bulletin
Honsador Lumber
Hotel Hana-Maui
Hudson's Bay Company
Huli-Huli Chicken
Hungry Lion
Hyatt Regency Waikiki
Hygienic Store
Hy's Steakhouse
Ideta
Iida
Ilikai Hotel
I Love Country Cafe
Imari
Indigo
Iolani School
Irifune
Ito En
J. C. Penney
JTB
Jack in the Box
Jamba Juice
Jameson's By The Sea
John Dominis
Jolly Roger Drive In
Jose's Mexican Restaurant
K•B Toy & Hobby Stores
KC Drive Inn
KCCN
KFC
KGMB

KGU
KHNL
KHON
KITV
KKUA
K-POI
KSSK
KTA Superstores
Kahala Mandarin Oriental
Kahi Mohala
Kahn Galleries
Kamaka Hawaii
Kamehameha Garment Co.
Kamehameha Schools
Kanemitsu Bakery and Restaurant
Kapiolani Health
Kawara Soba Takase
Keiki Kani Music Studio
Kemoo Farms
Ken's Pancake House
Kenny's Coffee Shop &
 Restaurant
Keo's Thai Cuisine
Kiibo
Kim Chee
Kim Taylor Reece
Kincaid's Fish, Chop & Steak
 House
Kinko's
Kintaro Restaurant
Kmart
Kobayashi Travel
Kobe Japanese Steak House
Koehnen's Interiors
Koiso Sushi Bar
Ko Ko Ichiban Ya
Kozo Sushi
Kramers Mens Wear
Kua Aina Sandwich Shop
Kuakini Medical Center
Kuhio Grill

Kumon Math and Reading Centers
Kyotaru
Kyo-ya
L & L Drive Inn
Lahainaluna School
La Mariana Restaurant & Bar
Lapperts Ice Cream
Leahi Hospital
Le Guignol
Leilehua High School
Leonard's Bakery
Lex Brodie's Tire Company
Liberty House
Like Like Drive Inn
Liliha Bakery
Linekona Elementary School
Lion Coffee
Lodge at Koele
Longhi's
Longs Drug Stores
Love's Bakery
Lung Fung
L'Uraku
Lyn's Delicatessen
M's Coffee Tavern
McDonald's
McInerny
McKinley Car Wash
McKinley High School
Magoo's Pizza
Maguro-ya
Makiki Christian Church
Malolo Beverages and Supplies
Manago Hotel
Manele Bay Hotel
Maple Garden Restaurant
Mariposa
Marriott International
Masu's Massive Plate Lunch
Matson Navigation
Matsumoto Shave Ice

Matteo's Italian Restaurant
Maui Divers
Maui Land & Pineapple
Maui Memorial Medical Center
Mauna Kea Beach Hotel
Meadow Gold Dairies
Mid-Pacific Institute
Ming's
Moanalua Gardens
Molokai Ranch
Mongolian Bar-B-Que
Moose McGillicuddy's
Morton's of Chicago
Mountain Apple Company
Murphy's Bar and Grill
Musashiya
NAPA Auto Parts
Naniwa
Natsunoya Tea House
Neiman Marcus
New England Financial
New Otani Kaimana Beach
 Hotel
Niblick
Ninniku-ya Restaurant
Nordstrom
Ohelo Road
One Fas Lube
Onjin's Café
Orange Julius
Otsuka's Furniture and
 Appliances
Our Lady of Peace Cathedral
Outrigger Canoe Club
Outrigger Enterprises
Pacific Business News
Pacific Club
Paesano
Papa John's Pizza
Parker Ranch
Patti's Chinese Kitchen

Pearl City Tavern
Pearl Country Club
Pegge Hopper Galleries
Perry Boy's Smorgy
Pescatore
Pizza Bob's
Pleasant Holidays
Pohai Nani
Pomare
Prada
Primo Beer
Punahou School
The Queen's Medical Center
RadioShack
Red Dirt Shirt Company
Reyn's
The Ritz
Robert's Hawaii
Ronnie's Ice Cream Parlor
Rosie's Cantina
Royal Hawaiian Hotel
Royal School
Roy's
Ruth's Chris Steak House
SIDA Taxi
SPAM
Safeway
St. Andrew's Priory School
St. Francis Healthcare System
Saint-Germain Bakery
Saint Louis School
Sam Choy's
Sam Sato's
San Souci
Sarrento's Top of the "I"
Schuman Carriage
ScooZee's
Sears
Sedona
Servco Pacific
7/Eleven

Sheraton Moana Surfrider
Shirokiya
Singha Thai Cuisine
Sizzler
Small Business Hawaii
Sorabol Restaurant
SPAM
Spencecliff
Spindrifter
Spot's Inn
Star Markets
Starbucks
State Farm Insurance
Straub Hospital and Clinic
Strawberry Connection
Suehiro
Suisan
Sure Save Super Market
Surf News Network
Sushi Sasabune
Swiss Inn
TCBY
Taco Bell
Tai Sei Ramen
Tamarind Park
Tamashiro Market
Tasaka Guri Guri
Tedeschi Winery
Ted's Bakery
Telecheck
Teshima's Restaurant
Tesoro
Tex Drive In and Restaurant
Theo. H. Davies & Company
3660 on the Rise
Tiffany & Company
Times Supermarket
Ting Hao Mandarin Seafood
 Restaurant
Todai Restaurant
Tony Group
Tori Richard

Tower Records
Town & Country Surf Shops
TOYS "R" US
Trader Vic's
Tripler Army Medical Center
Turtle Bay Resort
The Ultimate You
Verbano Ristorante Italiano
University of Hawaii
Verizon
Victoria Ward
Louis Vuitton
Volcano House
W Hotels
W & M Bar-B-Q Burgers
Waikiki Lau Yee Chai
Wailana Coffee House
Waioli Tea Room
Waipahu High School
Waldorf School
Wal-Mart
Waltah Clarke's Hawaiian
 Shops
Warren's Boarding House
Watumull's
Wigwam
Wilcox Health System
The Willows
Wisteria
Wo Fat
Alan Wong's
Won Kee
Wyland Galleries
Y. Hata
Yick Lung
Young Brothers
Young Guns
Young Laundry
Yum Yum Tree
Yummy Korean B-B-Q
Zippy's

Preface to the fourth edition

Thank you for purchasing this fourth edition of **The Companies We Keep**. Roughly 150 updates and changes were made in this and each of the two previous editions. Several companies have closed or sold since the first edition, such as Columbia Inn, Masu's Massive Plate Lunch, Kyoya, Grocery Outlet, McCully Chop Suey, Kilgo's, Kam Bowl, and Wisteria.

I felt the book would do well, but I never dreamed it would be a bestseller. It's spent months in the top ten and was #1 for three weeks. It was also named **Outstanding Business Publication of 2005** by Small Business Hawaii.

As this fourth edition goes to press, I'm hard at work on a new book, tentatively entitled **In the Company of Aloha**. This second book will also contain dozens of amazing stories about Hawaii people and companies. I appreciate all the readers of **The Companies We Keep** who suggested stories I could include in a future book.

In the Company of Aloha is due in late 2007 or early 2008. For more information, see page 400.

The Liliha Theatre in 1936 on Liliha Street where the H-1 Freeway is today. Realtor Rick Ornellas remembers that Joe Perry was the bow-tied manager of the Liliha Kiddie Club, where he went for many Saturday matinees.

The corner of Kalakaua Avenue and Kapiolani Blvd. prior to 1960 shows the Kau Kau Korner, built in 1935, where Hard Rock Cafe is today. It became Coco's in 1960. The Honolulu Convention Center is now across the street.

Kalihi Valley. Mark Twain once described Kalihi Valley as the most enchanting valley in all the islands. A hundred years ago, Kalihi Valley was a quaint, rural area with chickens, pigs and farms.

Jimmy Chong, who grew up in the valley recalls riding a horse to King and Kalihi Streets. He'd tie the horse to trees and brush about where the KFC is today, across from Farrington High School, then catch the streetcar into town.

When he returned in the afternoon, he'd find his horse where he left it, and ride back home in Kalihi Valley.

Introduction

"**Y**OU ARE KNOWN BY THE COMPANY YOU KEEP," a 2,500 year old Aesop Fable tells us. If that is the case, then Hawaii can be known by the companies we have kept in the islands with our patronage. This book is about Hawaii's home grown companies and the ones that have come here. The book contains hundreds of interesting stories and facts about those companies. The companies we visit every day often have fascinating backgrounds that are not publicly known.

- Meadow Gold, for instance, was originally a butter made by Continental Creamery.
- Bank of Hawaii was founded with a downtown parade of gold coins taken out of the predecessor of First Hawaiian Bank.
- The Hawaiian Moving Company was once a Monday night dance show that moved from disco to disco each week and taught viewers "the moves."
- Zippy's got its name from the Zip Code.
- L&L Drive-Inn evolved from a drive-up milk depot owned by L&L Dairy in 1952.
- Telecheck started at a Hawaii Boy Scout leader's meeting when they decided to keep a file on people who bounced checks.
- Shirokiya's roots go back to 1662, when Tokyo was called Edo. The name literally means "white tree store."
- The Charlie Chan detective stories were based on real life Honolulu detective Chang Apana. The first novel – *The House Without a Key* (now a restaurant at the Halekulani Hotel) was named because Honolulu residents did not lock their doors.

In researching this book, we have found companies that survived great challenges and natural disasters. City Mill, for instance, burned down in its first six months and again 20 years later. The 1960 Hilo tsunami swept Café 100 and the house behind it, with the owner's family, 300 feet away.

The companies we've kept in Hawaii have often overcome great challenges to be here today. This book salutes them and is an attempt to honor their extraordinary effort and innovation.

What is a Hawaii company?

Early on, we ran into an interesting dilemma in deciding which companies to include and which to leave out. Where should we draw our line? Our initial idea was to only look at companies that were started in Hawaii and are still owned here.

But then we thought: What about Longs? They seem to epitomize the Hawaii company, yet they have always been headquartered in California. How could we leave them out?

What about Liberty House? They were a tradition in Hawaii, for over 150 years, but were owned, when we started the book, by JMB Realty of Chicago. Macy's has taken them over. How could we leave them out?

Most of our newspapers, radio and TV stations are no longer locally owned.

We arrived at the decision to focus on home grown companies, but give some mention to the companies that have come to or left the state.

Companies and beyond

The book includes an inside look at the stores, hotels, banks, restaurants, newspapers, TV and radio stations, airlines, theatres, artists, manufacturers, hospitals, and travel companies that we patronize every day.

So what are schools doing in a book like this? Many schools are actually corporations, and interestingly, the very first corporation in Hawaii was Punahou School.

We have expanded a little beyond profit-making companies to include interesting stories we've found about schools, clubs, non-profit organizations, churches, and even a couple of places because we found so many amazing, little-known stories about them.

- McKinley High School, for instance, was originally the Fort Street English Day School in 1865. It moved to Princess Ruth's Palace, where Central Middle School is today, and became Honolulu High School. Today it honors President William McKinley, who supported Hawaii's Annexation, but was assassinated before the current campus was built.
- Alexander Hume Ford founded the Outrigger Canoe Club and is credited with reviving the forgotten sport of surfing.
- Makiki Christian Church on Pensacola street was modeled after the Kochi Castle in Japan, which was built in 1603.
- Pearl City was Hawaii's first planned community in 1890 and

was founded by B. F. Dillingham as a stop for his train. Until World War II, Pearl City was a weekend and summer retreat for Hawaii's wealthy.

- The Pacific Club was once the British Club. It now occupies the home where Princess Kaiulani was born.

Many of the stories are brief. Others take 2–5 pages. The focus has been on what the public is likely to find interesting about the companies they patronize every day. We have not attempted to include complete histories or information about these companies.

How this project developed

This book grew out of an assignment given to the students in my graduate-level Integrated Marketing class at Hawaii Pacific University. The idea was to give the students a task that would force them off campus and get them to meet some of the business leaders in the state.

Specifically, they were asked to find out how well-known companies in Hawaii chose their names, slogans, and logos. After three semesters of reading their reports, it was obvious they had uncovered so many interesting stories that they should be published.

With that objective in mind, the assignment continued for another three years. The students researched over 150 companies, about a third of those in the book. Why did we pick the particular companies that are in the book and not others? One answer is that these are the companies the students wanted to interview.

The author added to the list with interviews of companies he knew to be interesting. Did we miss some great stories? Undoubtedly. We invite you to let us know about those stories so that we can update future editions of the book.

Given that over 150 people helped write this book, it is inevitable that errors were made despite the efforts of the team to check them for accuracy. For any errors that survived to publication, we apologize.

Part of the problem is that source materials are often inaccurate. Several errors were found in published newspaper reports. This is compounded with companies themselves having an inaccurate account of their own history, particularly when the company is old and no one is around from the early days.

The book contains over 3,000 facts. Sources include the companies themselves, their staff, customers, web sites, brochures and other documents. Books, magazines, and newspaper articles were also referenced.

If you know of great stories we missed, errors or omissions, email them to us at **CompaniesWeKeep@Yahoo.com**. We'll include some of them on our web site, which can be found at **www.CompaniesWeKeep.com.**

In the main section of the book, **Extraordinary Hawaii Companies**, students are credited immediately after the company they interviewed. In other sections, it was deemed to be a distraction to credit them there. A list of all the students who contributed to the book can be found on page 401.

An Overview of the book

The book has six main sections:

- **Hawaii Business Timeline**. Hawaii's rich business history spans several centuries. A timeline gives it an interesting perspective.

- **Why Did they Call it Zippy's?** This section provides brief information on 250 companies and organizations, such as what their name means or why it was chosen. It also has brief tidbits on many of these companies.

- **Extraordinary Hawaii Companies**. Fascinating stories about companies, organizations and places in Hawaii will be found in this in-depth section.

- **Behind the Scenes at Hawaii's Radio and TV Stations**. Many of Hawaii's more colorful characters have shared their broadcasting stories in this section.

- **Making the Grade at Hawaii's Schools and Universities**. Some of the best stories in the book involve Hawaii's schools and their amazing tales.

- **Games, Lists and Fun Stuff**. This book is meant to be fun and a lot of it can be found in this section. There are over 15 games and lists in this section. Half a dozen more can be found in other sections of the book.

Since it first came out, *The Companies We Keep* has spent months on the *Honolulu Advertiser* non-fiction bestseller list, including three weeks in a row at #1.

A Special Mahalo:

To my wife, Lei, for her love, support, and editing.

My father, Sol Sigall, who got me started in my first business in the 8th grade.

My mother, Martha Sigall, who gave me an appreciation of history and encouraged me to do my best.

Julie Percell for inspiring me with stories of Arakawa's and Liberty House.

Rich Budnick, my mentor in self-publishing.

All my students at HPU who researched companies for the book.

HPU Student Book Team: Amy Ashizawa, Kathleen Severini, Irena Deisinger, Monisha Sivadason, Jamie Chang, Stacy Tritt, Cheryl Goh, and Yvonne Mia.

The Pau Hana Pumpers: Dean Kaneshiro, Wanda Nakamura, Herb Hamada, Mel and Theo Fujiyoshi, Brian Walthall, Van Lee, Brian Hayashibara, Helen Gillmor, Craig and Karen Arakawa, Byron Yogi, Ken Shiroma, Val Ahina, Kathy Yasukochi, Noreen Louie, Fritz Ventura, and the staff at CHART.

Sam Slom and the Board of Small Business Hawaii.

DeSoto Brown and the staff of the Bishop Museum.

Luella Kurkjian and the staff of the Hawaii State Archives.

Barbara Dunn and the staff of the Hawaiian Historical Society.

The staff of the Hawaii State Library system.

The Aiea Pearl City Business Association.

Junior Achievement of Hawaii.

Andy Poepoe, Jane Sawyer, Lora Noda and the staff of the U.S. Small Business Administration, the Small Business Development Center, and the Women in Business Committee.

Darryl Loo, Cheri Kishimoto, Clyde and Irene Kobayashi, and the Kaimuki Monday night volleyball folks. Steve Katona, for suggesting the name of the book.

Mel Ah Ching, Lowell Angell, Elizabeth Bailey, Randy Brandt, Frellie Campos, Pam Chambers, Jed Gaines and Barbara Campbell, Glenn Goya, Ron Jacobs, Lola Lackey, Kitty Lagareta, Dennis Kondo, George Mason, Manny Menendez, Tom Moffatt, Bill Ogawa, Michael W. Perry, Rod Romig, Bob Sevey, Bill Sewell, Jim Sattler, Harry Soria Jr., and Lori Wong.

Your support made a huge difference. Thank you all.

Mahalo to Our Sponsors

Many individuals and companies have come forward to support the publication of this book and we wish to thank:

Sam Slom and Small Business Hawaii

Jack Schneider of J.S. Services

Barbara Campbell and Jed Gaines

Dale Evans of Charley's Taxi

Barron Guss of Altres Global Resources

Sol and Martha Sigall

Dedication

THIS BOOK IS DEDICATED TO ALL THE entrepreneurs who have saved for years, mortgaged their homes, borrowed from their relatives and gone out on a limb to start a business, and survived such adversity as recessions, depressions, tsunamis, hurricanes, fires, high taxes and unnecessary government regulations, to work 80-hour work weeks to provide the clothes we wear, the food we eat, the homes we live in, and all the accoutrements that make up the good life we now lead.

The quality of our lives today is due to the risks you have taken. I salute you.

A military Sikorsky flies over Honolulu Harbor in the 1930s.

Hawaii Business Timeline

SOME OF HAWAII'S WELL-KNOWN COMPANIES, organizations, and products had their beginnings long, long ago. Some, such as Shirokiya, existed for 300 years before opening in Hawaii. Most are listed by their current name, along with some key historical events.

1262   Budweiser beer first brewed in Budweis, Czechoslovakia
1555   A Spanish ship probably arrives in Hawaii (first contact)
1609   Kikkoman Shoyu first brewed in Japan
1662   Shirokiya founded in Edo, Japan
1670   Hudson's Bay Company founded (North America's oldest company, later opens a branch in Hawaii)
1758   Kamehameha the Great is born on the Big Island

Kamehameha I

1776   U.S. War of Independence
1778   Capt. Cook arrives and names the "Sandwich Islands"
1795   King Kamehameha conquers Oahu
1805   Hawaii's first western style economy is based on sandalwood trade
1810   King Kamehameha unites all the Hawaiian Islands; Queen Kaahumanu is his favorite of 20 wives.
1815   Russians build a fort at Honolulu Harbor (torn down in 1857)
1819   Prince Liholiho ascends the throne as Kamehameha II
1820   First American Protestant missionaries arrive, the first mango tree is brought to Hawaii by Don Francisco de Paula Marin. It is planted near Vineyard and River streets.
1825   King Kamehameha III (Kauikeaouli), sugar grown in Manoa, Warren House, Hawaii's first hotel opens.
1826   C. Brewer
1830   Cowboys (paniolos) arrive from California and Mexico
1831   Lahainaluna School
1832   Jardine, Matheson & Company (China)
1835   Koloa Sugar Company

1836 First English newspaper west of the Rockies, the *Sandwich Isles Gazette* is published, Royal Hawaiian Band founded

1837 Hotel Waikiki, Tiffany & Company, Queen Victoria rules Britain until 1901, Honolulu streets begin to be laid out

1839 Chiefs' Children's School (Royal School)

1840 Original Iolani Palace is built

1841 Punahou School

1842 Kawaiahao Church, Our Lady of Peace Cathedral

1843 Queen Emma Summer Palace, Lord George Paulet seizes islands for England. Admiral Thomas restores monarchy

1845 Theo. H. Davies, Alexander Cartwright standardizes the rules of baseball

1846 Saint Louis School, Washington Place built

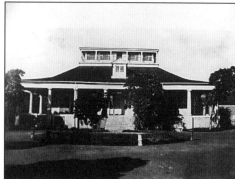

The original, modest, Iolani Palace was built in 1840

1847 Parker Ranch, The Thespian - first theatre in Hawaii opens; first monkeypod trees brought to the islands

1848 St. Anthony Schools, Great Mahele, Royal Hawaiian Theatre

1849 Liberty House/Amfac, California Gold Rush, Lihue Sugar Plantation

1850 McInerny, Chamber of Commerce of Hawaii, Molokai Ranch, Kualoa Ranch, King Kamehameha III declares Honolulu a city, whaling becomes mainstay of Hawaii's economy, Honolulu Fire Department

1851 Castle & Cooke, Love's Bakery, The Pacific Club

1852 New England Financial, Lewers & Cooke, Honolulu Iron Works, first Chinese laborers arrive, Beaver Grill (closed in 1973)

1853 Foster Botanical Garden, Kauai Coffee Company

1854 King Kamehameha IV (Alexander Liholiho) and Queen Emma, Louis Vuitton

1855 May's Market, first in Hawaii to specialize in groceries (closed in 1956)

1856 *Honolulu Advertiser*, Grove Farm Company, Burberry

1857 McInerny, Carlsmith Ball Wichman & Ichiki

1858 First Hawaiian Bank, Macy's

1859 The Queen's Hospital

1861 U.S. Civil War drives sugar prices up

1863 Iolani School, King Kamehameha V (Prince Lot), Heald College

1864 Grove Farm Plantation, Lion Coffee (Ohio)

1865 McKinley High School (Fort Street English Day School)

1866 Volcano House, Leprosy patients sent to Kalaupapa

1867 St. Andrew's Priory

1868 First Japanese workers arrive in the islands

1869 YMCA of Honolulu, Puunui Dairy (Hawaii's first)

1870 Alexander & Baldwin

1871 Original Royal Hawaiian Hotel built downtown, Kapiolani Park dedicated

King Kamehameha V, Lot Liholiho Kapuaia

1872 King William Lunalilo

1873 Fireman's Fund Insurance Companies, Father Damien goes to Kalaupapa, Barnes & Noble

1874 King David Kalakaua (reigns until 1891)

1876 Reciprocity Treaty with U.S. allows for duty-free sugar exports

1877 Hamakua Sugar

1878 Goodsill Anderson Quinn & Stifel, Falls of Clyde built, first Portuguese laborers arrive from the Madeira Islands, Liliuokalani pens *Aloha 'Oe*

1879 Friends of the Library (Honolulu Library and Reading Room), the ukulele first produced in Hawaii, Chinese Christian Church of Honolulu, James Campbell and John Ashley drill and discover Oahu's underground aquifer

1881 Fort Street is Hawaii's first paved street

1882 *Honolulu Star Bulletin*, Matson Navi-

Fort and Hotel Streets about 1879

gation, Wo Fat, Iolani Palace is built, Congress passes Chinese Exclusion Act

1883 Verizon Hawaii (Mutual Telephone), Benson Smith Drug Company

1884 Moanalua Gardens, Kamehameha Schools, Maui Memorial Medical Center, Sans Souci Hotel, Kiewit Pacific, Waikiki Seaside Hotel

1885 Sugar becomes basis of Hawaii's economy, first substantial Japanese immigrants arrive

1886 Yat Loy, Coca-Cola, Sears

1887 C. Q. Yee Hop

1888 *Honolulu Magazine* (*Paradise of the Pacific*), Haleakala Ranch, Maui Soda & Ice Works, Harris United Methodist Church, Case Bigelow & Lombardi

OR&L trains were in operation by 1890.

1889 B.F. Dillingham starts Oahu Railway & Land Co., Honpa Hongwanji
Mission, Gay & Robinson

1890 Kapiolani Health, Pioneer Federal

1891 Hawaiian Electric, Bishop Museum, Queen Liliuokalani ascends the throne

1892 Hawaiian Historical Society, Del Monte, Hawaii Sugar Planter's Association, Yokohama Specie and Sumitomo Banks, Kobayashi Travel

1893 Schuman Carriage, Hawaiian Monarchy overthrown

1894 Salvation Army of Hawaii, Kaneshige Jewelers (Maui)

1895 Walker-Moody Construction

1896 Musashiya, Title Guaranty, S. H. Kress (1931 in Hawaii)

1897 Bank of Hawaii, Hilo Medical Center, Meadow Gold

1898 U.S. Annexation of Hawaii, Honolulu Brewing & Malting Co., Moanalua Golf Club (Hawaii's first), Hawaiian Trust, Molokai Ranch

The Haleiwa Hotel opened in 1899.

1899 City Mill, Haleiwa Hotel, Princess Kaiulani dies at age 23, K-Mart, Von Hamm-Young, Diamond Head Lighthouse, McBryde Plantation, first automobiles on Oahu

1900 Yick Lung, Young Brothers, Maui News, Kuakini Health System, Leahi Hospital, McCabe Hamilton & Renny, Iida's, Chinatown fire

1901 Moana Hotel, Dole Food Company, King Edward VII (England), Primo Beer, Honolulu streetcars (through 1941), Pioneer Inn, Nordstrom, Retail Merchants of Hawaii, Hosoi Mortuary, Marconi invents wireless telegraph

1902 Dillingham Construction, Alexander Young Hotel, Young Laundry, The Garden Island newspaper, Hawaii Visitors and Convention Bureau, undersea cable brings telephone service from mainland, Hauoli, J.C. Penney, Honolulu Symphony, Wright Brothers fly at Kitty Hawk, N.C.

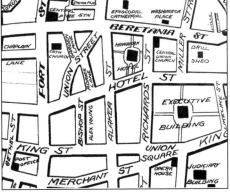

Bishop Street was just a block long in 1902

1903 E. K. Fernandez, Honolulu Medical Group, Y. Hata, first group of Korean workers arrive

1904 The Gas Company, First Federal Savings and Loan, Wing Coffee Co., Tesoro Petroleum, Waikiki Aquarium, Oahu Market

1905 Thayer Piano, Hygienic Store, I. Kitagawa & Co (Hilo), Kaimuki Zoo, Territorial Legislature establishes five counties: Kauai, Oahu, Maui, Hawaii and Kalawao (Kalaupapa)

1906 C&H Sugar, Hakuyosha, D. Uchida Coffee Farm (Kona), Dole Cannery in Iwilei, Coldwell-Banker, Kohala Ditch, Commercial Club

1907 Halekulani Hotel, Suisan (Hilo), Neiman Marcus, University of Hawaii, Tripler Hospital, Fort Shafter, first picture brides (14,000 through 1923), first large groups

The Dole Cannery opened in Iwilei in 1906

27

of Filipino immigrants arrive (120,000 through 1934)

1908 Mid-Pacific Institute, Outrigger Canoe Club, Chun Kim Chow, Honolulu Sake Brewery and Ice Company, Ameron Hawaii, Pacific Fleet arrives at Pearl Harbor, Schofield Barracks founded

1909 C. S. Wo, Arakawa's, Sacred Hearts Academy, Maui Land and Pineapple, Kemoo Farms, Kula Hospital

1910 Hasegawa General Store (Hana), Ishigo Bakery & Store (Honomu), Sugai Kona Coffee, Hallmark Cards, King George V crowned

1911 Eki Cyclery, First Insurance (originally Home Insurance), Solo Papaya introduced from Caribbean

1912 Hawaii Hochi, JTB, Duke Kahanamoku wins Olympic Gold, Ben Bridge jewelers, Edwin Armstrong invents AM radio receiver

1913 Hawaii State Library opens on King Street, Prada (Milan)

1914 Watumull's, The Blue Print Company, Panama Canal opens, Hilo Macaroni Company

1915 Kemoo Farm, Diamond Head Theatre, Uyeda Shoe Store

1916 KTA Super Stores (Big Island), Borthwick Mortuary, Waiahole ditch, Sueoka Market (Kauai), Kamaka Hawaii

1917 Consolidated Theatres, Ah Fook's Super Market (Maui), Girl Scout Council of Hawaii, HOPACO, Armed Services YMCA, Kohala Hospital, U.S. enters World War I

1918 Hirano Store (Glenwood), Washington Place becomes the Governor's residence

1919 Servco Pacific, Aloha United Way, Fujikami Florist, Andrade, A&W Root Beer, Junior Achievement, AIG Insurance

1920 Fisher Hawaii, Grace Pacific, M's Coffee Tavern, Fukuda Seed, Ebisuzaki Fishing Supply (Hilo), first commercial radio station (KDKA in Pittsburgh, PA)

1921 Straub Clinic and Hospital, Territorial Savings and Loan, RadioShack, HPM Building Supply, Diamond Bakery, Natsunoya Tea House, Gucci, Seaside Restaurant (Hilo)

Waialae Avenue in 1920.

1922　KGU, KGMB (radio), Cades Shutte Fleming & Wright, Liberty Bank, State Farm Insurance Company, KB Toys, Dole purchases island of Lanai for $1.1 million, Diamond Parking Service, Waioli Tea Room

1923　Valley Isle Motors, Shriner's Hospital, Hawaii Tribune-Herald, Cornet Stores (1957 in Hawaii), Ala Wai Golf Course, Arthur Murray Dance Studios, Hotel Lanai, McCully Bicycle & Sporting Goods, Church of the Crossroads

1924　St. Francis School, W. T. Haraguchi Farm (Kauai)

1925　American Savings Bank, International Savings, Big Save Markets, Honolulu Stadium (torn down in 1976), NAPA Auto Parts, People's Cafe

1926　Kaimuki Dry Goods, Kanemitsu Bakery, Safeway, Aloha Tower built, Orange Julius, Kona Hotel

1927　St. Francis Healthcare System, Maryknoll Schools, Star Markets, Royal Hawaiian Hotel (Waikiki), Haleakala Motors, Malolo Beverages and Supplies, 7-Eleven, Lanai Community Hospital, Honolulu Academy of Arts, War Memorial Natatorium, Outdoor Circle eliminates billboards, Charles Lindberg's first solo flight across the Atlantic, Philo Farnsworth transmits the first television image

1928　Pacific Insurance, Kona Inn, Kahua Ranch (Kohala), Ala Wai Canal completed, Sumida Watercress Farm, first Lei Day

1929　Hawaiian Airlines (Inter-Island Airways), KC Drive Inn, Waikiki Lau Yee Chai, Koehnen's Interiors (Hilo), H. Hamada Store, Gump's, Dutch Girl Pastry Shoppes, Teshima's Restaurant (Kona)

1930　Victoria Ward Ltd., Hawaiian Bitumuls, Chock's TV & Appliance, R.M. Towill Corporation, Holy's Bakery (Kapaau), first aloha shirts were made about this time

1931　Thalia Massie case, Hygienic Dairy, Maluhia Hospital

1932　Kalapawai Market, Stewart's Pharmacy and Restaurant,

1933　Sure Save Super Market (Big Island), Gouveia Portuguese Sausage Factory, Okahara Saimin Factory, Sam Sato's (Maui), Honolulu Civic Auditorium opens (closed in 1974), Edwin Armstrong invents frequency modulation (FM)

1934　Stanley Ito Florist, Hawaii Motors (Hilo), 9th Avenue Bakery

1935　Kau Kau Korner, Chun-Hoon Supermarket, Honsador Lumber, first Pan American China Clipper flight (to Hawaii from San Francisco), *Hawaii Calls* first broadcast from Moana

Hotel, Sekiya's, Otsuka's Furniture & Appliance (Kauai)

1936 Kamehameha Garment Company, Kahala Sportswear, Honolulu Freight Service, Security Diamond and Conrad Jewelers, Hawaii's first traffic light at Nuuanu and Beretania

1937 Carol & Mary, Kodak Hula Show, Beretania Florist, SPAM, Krispy Kreme doughnuts

1938 Charley's Taxi, HMSA, Longs Drug Stores, Wilcox Health System, Ritz Department Stores, Kaimuki Super-Market, Dairy Queen, The Pocketbook Man

1939 Fletcher Pacific, Island Insurance, Spencecliff, Tamura Super Market, Easy Music Center, Ming's, Honolulu Sign Co., Kramers Mens Wear, Pearl City Tavern, Fukuya Delicatessen, Fronk Clinic, Kona Community Hospital, Kona Trans

The Kau Kau Korner preceded Coco's and the Hard Rock Café on the corner of Kalakaua and Kapiolani. Its sign was the most-photographed in the world.

1940 Barbecue Inn (Lihue), Tropics Restaurant, Naniloa Hotel, Dot's in Wahiawa, Elsie's Fountain & Diner (Hilo)

1941 Columbia Inn, Robert's Hawaii, Jack in the Box, Pearl Harbor attacked, U.S. enters World War II

1942 Battle of Midway, 1,300 Japanese-Americans volunteer for the 100th Infantry Battalion, Ethel's Dress Shoppe, Yamashiro Farm, Mauna Loa erupts

1943 House of Hong

1944 The Willows, Wahiawa General Hospital, Waikiki Yacht Club, Summer Fun initiated

1945 World War II ends, Kuhio Grill, House of Adler, Watanabe Florist, Kaiser Permanente, Baskin-Robbins, Moiliili Community Center, KHON radio

1946 Aloha Airlines (Trans-Pacific Airlines), Architects Hawaii, Helena's Hawaiian Food, Kilgo's, Ross Sutherland, Heide & Cook, Aloha Shoyu, World Wide Tours and Travel Service, Harry's Music Store, Café 100 (Hilo), Seaside Restaurant (Hilo), Shishido Manju Shop (Maui), Sweet Leilani

Florist, The Oasis, Hotel Hana, Aloha Week, KPOA radio station, Smith's Tropical Paradise, Hilo tsunami kills 159

1947 Outrigger Hotels, McKinley Car Wash, Tamashiro Market, Hula Records, Torkildson & Katz, Ka Lei Eggs, KULA and KIPA radio stations, Friends of the Library Book Sale, Highway Inn, Garden House, Bell Telephone invents the transistor

1948 Foodland, The Drive-in, St. Germaine Bakery, Tripler Hospital moves to Moanalua Ridge, Wailana Coffee House (Kapiolani Drive Inn), Maui Bowling Center, McDonald's

1949 Times Supermarket, Queen's Surf, Hawaii Stationery, six month dock strike, National Memorial Cemetery of

"The Drive-in" opened in 1948 where Daiei is today.

the Pacific at Punchbowl dedicated, Yori's Happy Valley Tavern (Maui), Koa Trading Co. (Kauai), Redondo's Sausage Factory, Forty Niner Cafe

1950 Liliha Bakery, Tin Tin Char Sut, Aloha Tofu Factory, Trade Wind Tours, Flamingo Restaurants, Leong's Hawaiian Cafe, Taniguchi Store

1951 Matsumoto Shave Ice, Ben Franklin, Kelly's Coffee Shop, Valley Isle Produce, Young's Fish Market, Foremost Dairies Hawaii, Kahului Shopping Center, KIKI radio

1952 First TV broadcast by KONA (now KHON), KGMB TV, Leonard's Bakery, Hawaiian Sun, Slipper House, Wisteria, Surfrider Hotel, Frank Young's Chevron Station,

Craig's Bakery, Hamura's Saimin Stand (Kauai), L & L Dairy, Kawamata Farms

1953 KAIM, Finance Factors, Canlis Charcoal Broiler, Crouching Lion Inn, Coco Palms Resort, Friendly Market Center (Molokai), Timmy's Gym, Denny's, Wahiawa Tire Center, Fujiya Ltd., Like Like Drive Inn, first section of H-1 Freeway opens (called the Mauka Arterial)

1954 KITV, Central Pacific Bank, Hardware Hawaii, Hicks Homes, W&M Bar-B-Q Burgers, Alex Drive Inn, McDonald's, Pacific Poultry (created Huli-Huli chicken in 1955).

1955 Hilton Hawaiian Village, Princess Kaiulani Hotel, Reef Hotel, Waikiki Biltmore, Bonded Materials, Chaminade University, BYUH, La Mariana, Waltah Clarke's, *Hawaii Business* magazine, Stadium Bowl-O-Drome, Frankie's Drive-in, Tasty Broiler, Lanai Sportswear, Democrats take power for the first time in the Territorial Legislature

1956 Outrigger Reef Tower, Tori Richard, Waikikian Hotel, Tahitian Lanai, Scotty's Drive-Inn, Waikiki Shell opens, Kalihi Bowl, Ed & Don's, Boulevard Saimin, KFC

1957 Daiei, McCully Chop Suey, Pali Highway tunnels open, Fred's Produce, Andy's Drive-Inn, Paradise Cruise, Hilo Seaside Hotel, Hyatt Hotels, Marriott International, Elliott's Chuckwagon, Kauai Veterans Memorial Hospital

1958 GEM, Maui Divers, Wigwam, Sizzler, American Trust Company of Hawaii

1959 Ala Moana Center, Aston Hotels, Kyo-ya, Reyn's, City Bank, Pleasant Holidays, Chuck's Steak House, Nishimoto Trading Co., Chunky's Drive Inn, Kilani Bakery, Jolly Roger, K-POI, Dee Lite Bakery, Hawaii becomes 50th State, William Quinn elected Governor, Hurricane Dot

1960 Hawaii National Bank, Coco's, KNDI, 35-foot Hilo tsunami, Princess Kaiulani Fashions, Hawaiian Host, Molokai Drive Inn, Chaney Brooks & Co., Hawaiian Rent-All, Kona Seaside Hotel, Hy's Steak House, Tower Records, SMS Research, Pacific Health Research Institute, Smitty's Pancake House, Marian's Catering

1961 Rainbow Drive-In, Wholesale Motors, Trader Vic's, Perry

Boys' Smorgy, Violet's Grill, Chart House, Royal Contracting

1962 Buzz's Original Steakhouse, KHNL TV, Jade Food Products, Taco Bell, Wal-Mart, John Burns elected Governor, Daniel Inouye and Hiram Fong, U.S. Senators; Spark Matsunaga, Thomas Gill, U.S. Congress, Arizona Memorial dedicated

1963 *Pacific Business News*, Castle Medical, KUMU and KZOO radio stations, Hee Hing, Kenny's Burger House, Hino Hairstyles and Wig Salon, King's Bakery, Pfleuger Honda, Noh Foods, International Innkeepers, Polynesian Cultural Center, Merrie Monarch Hula Festival

1964 Ilikai Hotel, Benihana, Lex Brodie's Tire Company, Crazy Shirts, Holiday Mart, Pagoda Hotel, Arby's, Maile Restaurant, Pohai Nani, Stuart Anderson's Cattle Company, Service Printers, Tahiti Nui Restaurant (Hanalei), Suda Store (Kihei)

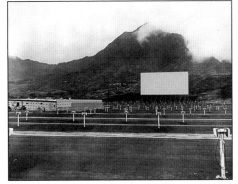

The Kailua Drive In opened in 1965.

1965 Hawaii Pacific University, Hilo Hattie, ABC Stores, Orchid Isle Auto Center (Hilo), Mauna Kea Beach Resort, Kona Village Resort, Ruth's Chris Steak House, Wholesale Unlimited, first Aloha Friday

1966 KCCN, Zippy's, *This Week* magazine, Flora-Dec Sales, Lihue Fishing Supply, Gibson's, Ito En

1967 Patti's Chinese Kitchen, Pearl Country Club, Fast Food (Wahiawa), Menehune Mac, Pomare, Magoo's Pizza

1968 Ezogiku, The Patisserie, Tex Drive In & Restaurant, *Hawaii Five-O* premieres, Momyer Chiropractic

1969 Altres, Tihati Productions, Anna Bannana's, Ideta, Vintage Wine Cellar, Kaya Fishing Supply, Huggo's Restaurant (Kona), Communications-Pacific, Prudential Locations Hawaii, tourism replaces agriculture to becomes the #1 factor in Hawaii's economy

1970 Kozo Sushi, Kinko's, Trattoria, Kahala Mall, Crabtree & Evelyn, Habilitat, Waimea General Store

1971 Town & Country Surf Shop, Sheraton Waikiki Hotel, Dia-

The Oceania Floating Restaurant opened in 1972 next to the Hawaii Maritime Center.

mond Head Plumbing, Ken's Pancake House (Hilo), Down to Earth, Borders Books & Music, Starbucks

1972   The Bistro, Oceania Floating Restaurant, Royal Hawaiian Heritage Jewelry, GBC, Heidi's Bistro, Kim Chee Restaurant, Pearlridge Center, Kaahumanu Center, Slim's Power Tools, Kobe Japanese Steak House, Singha Thai Cuisine

1973   Hawaiian Graphics, Clean-N-Rooter, Anna Miller's, Jose's Mexican Restaurant, The Bull Shed (Kauai), Jameson's By the Sea, Turtle Bay Resort, Apartment Appearance

1974   Small Business Hawaii, Matteo's, Eggs 'n Things, Elena's, Roy Sakuma Ukulele Studio, Hula's Bar & Lei Stand, Tedeschi Vineyards, Pizza Bob's, King Tsin, Cutter Group, Mutual Publishing, George Ariyoshi elected Governor

1975   Famous Amos Chocolate Chip Company, Hawaiian Eye Center, Hale Koa Hotel, Bobby McGee's Conglomeration, Mongolian Bar-B-Que, Aloha Stadium, Polynesian Orchids and Anthuriums (Big Island)

1976   Spindrifter, Longhi's, Costco, Horatio's, Yum Yum Tree, The Running Room, Surf News Network

1977   Local Motion, Mekong Restaurant, Big Island Candies, Tony Group, Cane Haul Road, Wally's Garden Center, Dickens English Pub

1978   Wyland Galleries, Grace's Inn, Morton's of Chicago, Hawaiian Bagel, Professional Image, Tanaka of Tokyo, Institute For Human Services

1979   Hawaiian Moving Company, John Dominis, CHART, Marsh

Company, Steamers, Lion Coffee (in Hawaii)

1980 Angelo Pietro, Keo's Thai Cuisine, Moose McGillycuddy's, The Wave. Hungry Ear Records (Vinyl Donut)

The Wave Waikiki

1981 Sam Choy's, Rosie's Cantina, TCBY, J.S. Services, Cookie Corner, GUESS?

1982 Auntie Pasto's, Swiss Inn, Gee ... a Deli, Windward Mall, J.S. Services, Hungry Lion, Battery Exchange Hawaii, Kukui Grove Center, Hurricane Iwa

1983 The Ultimate You, Brennecke's Beach Broiler (Kauai), Mauna Lani Bay Hotel, Sanford Saito, DDS, Pegge Hopper Gallery, Chun Hoon Supermarket closes

1984 Strawberry Connection, Compadres Mexican Bar and Grill, Ba-Le, Kahn Galleries, Papa John's Pizza

1985 Bubbies, Kona Brewing

1986 Yummy Korean Bar-B-Q, Hale Vietnam, Hyatt Waikoloa, Commercial Data Systems, John Waihee elected Governor

1987 Old Lahaina Luau (Maui), Salerno Restaurant, Murphy's Bar & Grill, Ted's Bakery, Fabric Impressions (Hilo)

1988 Café Sistina, Roy's

1989 I Love Country Cafe, Cost-U-Less (Hilo)

1990 The Lodge at Koele, Pescatore (Hilo), Jamba Juice

1991 Manele Bay Hotel, Assaggio

1992 Body & Soul, Hurricane Iniki struck Kauai on Sept. 11th

1993 Maui Tacos; Dole Cannery, Pearl City Tavern and GEM close

1994 Da Big Kahuna, HomeWorld, Cinnamon Girl

1995 Horatio's at Ward Center becomes Kincaid's, Arakawa's closes, David Paul's Lahaina Grill, Cookie Corner, Cafe Laufer

Fort Street was named for the Fort that stood where Nimitz Highway is today. It was built by Russian sailors in 1815 and torn down in 1857. Fort Street was Hawaii's first paved street in 1881. Here are inside and outside views.

Why Did They Name it Zippy's?

COMPANIES AND ORGANIZATIONS ARE OFTEN NAMED for their founders, children, or location. Others honor a grandparent, a pet, a film, or song. Sometimes it has meaning in a foreign language. Here is how some of the companies that do business in Hawaii got their names.

A&W Root Beer .... Roy Allen invented root beer in Lodi, California, in 1919 and, with Frank Wright, launched A&W Root Beer. They opened the nation's first drive-in in Sacramento, serving their root beer in frosty mugs.

A. L. Kilgo .... A. L. (Aubra Laura) Kilgo started this Sand Island hardware store in 1946 as a military surplus store. It grew from a Quonset hut to 7 acres and 125 employees. Former Mayor Frank Fasi credits Kilgo's with breaking the hold the Big Five held over the pricing and availability of building materials.

Aaron's Atop the Ala Moana .... Named for Aaron Placourakis, co-owner of the Tri-Star Group. Formerly Nicholas Nickolas. Tri-Star also owns Sarento's Top the of the I, Sarento's on the Beach (Maui), and Nick's Fishmarket Maui.

ABC Stores .... Founded by Sidney Kosasa as Mister K stores. They shifted to a name that was easier to remember.

Ala Wai Golf Course .... Originally the Territorial Fair Grounds Golf Course, it grew from a single hole in 1923 to become the most played 18 hole golf course in the state.

Alexander & Baldwin .... Founded by Samuel Alexander and Henry Baldwin, boyhood friends from Lahaina.

Aloha Airlines .... Formerly Trans-Pacific Airlines (TPA) - The Aloha Airline, and affectionately referred to as *The People's Airline*. The name was changed in 1958.

Altres Global Business Services .... Altres is short for Alternative Resources for Business.

AMFAC .... Short for American Factors, this was originally H. Hackfeld and Company. During World War I, a more patriotic name was chosen when German companies were forced to sell.

Angelo Pietro .... Named for an Italian fairy tale about Peter the Angel. Kunihiko Murata established the first Pietro restaurant in 1980 combining the best of Italy and the distinct and delicate flavors of Japan. Today there are over 20 in Japan, one in Korea, and one in Honolulu. Pietro's Original Shoyu Dressing sells over 15 million bottles a year and is the top-selling dressing in Japan.

Anna Miller's .... T h i s Pearl City restaurant with a Pennsylvania Dutch theme and a fantastic strawberry pie is named for founder Stanley Miller's grandmother. Few know that it has 20 sister restaurants in Japan. Miller opened six in California (now closed) before opening in Hawaii in 1973. He later franchised in Japan, then sold them. He also owns Bravo downstairs (formerly the Round House).

APCOA .... An acronym of the Airport Parking Company of America. It began at the Cleveland, Ohio airport in 1949 and has been in Hawaii since 1956. Now called the Standard Parking Corporation, they are Hawaii's largest parking management company.

Arby's .... Forrest and Leroy Raffel created this fast food business in Ohio "based on something other than hamburgers" in 1964. They came up with Arby's, which stands for R.B. (Raffel Brothers). Today there are over 3,000 Arby's worldwide including seven in Hawaii.

Arirang Korean Barbecue .... Hilo restaurant (and several other bars and restaurants in the islands have used this name). *Arirang* is the Korean national song, like *Waltzing Matilda* is for Aussies, and *Santa Lucia* is for Italians, but the word has no meaning in Korean.

Assaggio .... Italian restaurants in Hawaii Kai, Mililani, Kailua and Ala Moana Center. Assaggio means to "taste, sample, or try" in Italian.

ASSETS School .... Founded at Pearl Harbor in the 1960s, the name originally was an acronym for Armed Services Special Educational Training Society School. Children of military families were served at the private K-12 school, which moved off base in the 1970s and now accepts non-military children who need an alternative educational environment.

Ayuthaya II Thai Restaurant .... This Hilo restaurant is named for the former capital of Siam, before Bangkok. Ayuthaya prospered for 400 years until it was destroyed by the Burmese in 1767. Ayuthaya was named for the city of Ayodhya, which was one of the largest and most magnificent of Indian cities. Siam officially became Thailand in 1949. "Thai" means "free."

Baci Bistro .... Kailua restaurant. The name means "kisses" in Italian.

Ba-Le .... Ba-Le means "Paris" in Vietnamese. Vietnam was once a French Protectorate.

Barnes & Noble .... Chares M Barnes sold books from his home in Wheaton, Illinois in 1873. His son, William joined G. Clifford Noble in New York in 1917. Leonard Riggio bought it in 1971 and expanded to 900 stores in 49 states. It has become the "World's Largest Bookstore."

Bea's Drive-In .... Owner Bea Miyasato had to change Donald Duck Drive-in's name when Disney objected.

Benetton .... Luciano Benetton and three of his siblings began a small fashion company in Italy in 1965 making sweaters. They now have 5,000 stores in 120 countries.

Big City Diner .... Lane and Murphy Muraoka picked this name because Kaimuki used to be the end of the Big City. Past that, Hono-  lulu turned into sparsely popu- lated farms. The farmers referred to all the lights and traffic in Kaimuki as the "Big City." In 2002, Big City Diner opened a second restaurant in Kailua.

Big Island Candies .... Famous for its choco- late covered shortbread cookies, founder Allan Ikawa says he almost went bankrupt in previous businesses, but a friend told him a samurai never gives up. He founded Big Island Candies in 1977 with the intention of making the finest mac- adamia nut chocolates and cookies found anywhere in the world. Big Island Candies is the gift of choice from Hilo.

The Bistro .... In the 1970s, The Bis- tro, on Kapiolani near Keeaumoku, was the top French res- taurant in town. Karl Diebold ran the kitchen and Michael Pirics, the dining room and bar. They are still fondly re- membered for their French onion soup and cheesecake. Michael manages a restaurant today in Western Samoa and Karl divides his time between Mexico and France.

Black Mountain Coffee .... It is named for the mountains behind Poipu, Kauai. Fishermen in the area call it Black Mountain because it is often shrouded in clouds.

Founder Dennis Okihara says the strong, smooth coffee is a result of hand picking and sun drying the beans.

Blue Moon Builders .... It was incorporated in June 1987, a "Blue Moon" month (there were two full moons that month). Owner Michele Harris says her dad, Bill Sewell's previous company, Waialae Builders, suffered the Yellow Page dilemma of being dead last in the phone books for years. He suggested she choose a name for her company that started with an A, B, C or D. When the company was founded, a TV show called "Moonlighting" was big. It was about a detective agency named "Blue Moon Detective Agency." Harris feels that was a catalyst for the decision.

Bob's Big Boy .... Bob Wian created the double-decker hamburger in Glendale, California in 1937. He named his restaurant for a chubby young customer he affectionately called "Big Boy."

Body & Soul ....

Hawaii's top cosmetics company was founded by Tao Miller in 1992 when he was just 21. Born in Sweden, Tao moved to Pahoa as a teenager. After graduation from high school, he moved to Honolulu and found himself promoting Nars Cosmetics before starting Body & Soul. Tao was named the Small Business Administration's Honolulu Young Entrepreneur of the Year four years later, in 1996. Body & Soul uses beautiful vintage designs from the 1930s and 1940s. Its packaging is known for its keyhole die cut allowing you to see the drawing of a girl named Gigi inside. Body & Soul is sold all over the world.

Brennecke's Beach Broiler .... Named for a favorite body-surfing beach in Poipu, Kauai.

Brent's Restaurant & Delicatessen .... Brent Brody started this Kailua restaurant in 1996. Brent learned the business from Nate and Temma Libling in L.A. when he was 14.

Bubbies Homemade Ice Cream .... This ice cream parlor's name means "grandmother" in Yiddish and is named for founder Keith Robbins' grandmother. Founded in 1985, the slogan is "shouldn't you be licking something?"

Buca di Beppo .... "Buca" means basement in Italian and "Beppo" is slang for Giuseppe or Joe. Joe Micatrotto is president of this chain with 69 restaurants in 25 states including one next to the Consolidated Ward Theatres.

Buena Sera .... A restaurant in Kailua, Buena Sera means "good evening" in Italian.

Burberry's .... Thomas Burberry perfected a method of weaving gabardine wool that was both lightweight and waterproof in 1856. He turned it into the world's first raincoat. The military adopted it as their trench coat during World War I.

Burger King .... James McLamore and David Edgerton founded Insta-Burger King in 1952 in Jacksonville, Florida. "The Whopper" was developed in 1957. "Have it Your Way" never got them to #1, but $9 billion in annual revenues is a pretty good second.

Byron's Drive Inn, Byron II .... These restaurants are named for a son of founder Andy Wong. His brother, Orson, also had restaurants named for him. Both names mean "bear," which Wong believed lent strength to a business.

C. Brewer .... Named for sea captain Charles Brewer, this 1826 business is Hawaii's oldest at over 175 years.

C&H Sugar .... C&H originally stood for California and Hawaiian Sugar. With the decline in Hawaiian sugar, they have had to buy sugar from other places and because of that, C&H is just C&H.

Café Laufer

Marlies Von Laufer was the former partner of owner Cyrus Goo. They founded their Waialae Avenue restaurant in 1995 as a European-style cafe, featuring coffee and delicious pastries, wonderful soups, and sandwiches, all served on fine china.

Cafe Laufer owner Cyrus Goo, with some of his fabulous creations behind him.

Carol & Mary .... Carol Singlehurst and Mary Afong founded this clothing store in 1937, downtown.

CHART .... Acronym for Comprehensive Health and Active Rehabilitation Training. CHART is a multi-disciplinary physical rehabilitation clinic specialized in returning injured individuals back to work. CHART pioneered the idea of using active rehabilitation instead of the then-common passive treatments of immobilization, traction, and strict bed rest for lengthy periods. Frieda Takaki runs this King Street facility, near Ward Avenue, that was established in 1979.

Chef Mavro .... James Beard Award winner George Mavrothalassitis has shortened his name for this King Street restaurant that fuses Hawaiian and French cuisine. He was formerly the chef at La Mer.

Chez Michel .... Michel Martin was born in Nice, France in 1907. He came to Hawaii and opened his first restaurant in Wahiawa in 1942. He quickly became famous for his French onion soup, duck l'orange, and frog legs. In 1959, he moved to the Colony Surf in Waikiki, and sold that in 1970 to open in Eaton Square. Michel raised the standard for customer service in Honolulu. At 96, he is now a partner in the Patisserie.

Chiang Mai Thai Cuisine .... A town in Northern Thailand gives this Moiliili restaurant its name.

Cholo's .... This North Shore restaurant's name means "gangster" in Spanish.

Chosun Korean Restaurant .... This Kapiolani Boulevard restaurant is named for the former Korean capitol, before Seoul.

Chun-Hoon Supermarket .... Chun (last name) Hoon (first name) was a peddler who came to own vegetable farms on the military bases and little grocery stores all over Oahu. He bought the home of Hawaii's first Chinese millionaire, Chun Afong, on Nuuanu and School streets, and his children started a retail store there in 1935. It was one of Hawaii's top markets for almost 50 years until it closed in 1983.

Chun Hoon (1873-1935)

Cinnamon Girl .... Jonelle and Reid Fujita started this clothing store in 1994 that has the same name as a Neil Young song. "Jonelle wanted to use the word 'cinnamon' and I thought 'girl' would be a great addition" Reid said. It originally was a kiosk at Aloha Tower Marketplace and then opened in Ward Warehouse, Waikiki, Maui, Ala Moana, Pearlridge, and Las Vegas. Jonelle's Aunt Shirley taught her to sew, and her first creations were for her dolls.

Compadres Bar & Grill .... This Ward Warehouse restaurant's name means "friend" in Spanish.

Costco .... Sol Price pioneered the concept of discount warehouse membership shopping in 1976 when he opened the Price Club in San Diego. In 1983, James Sinegal left Price Club employment to start his own discount warehouse club, Costco, in Kirkland, WA. Ten years later, the two stores with similar names merged. The philosophy is to "stack it high and sell it cheap." Their 350 plus stores generate an average of $100 million each in annual sales.

Crabtree & Evelyn .... Cyrus Harvey Jr. founded The Soap Box in Cambridge, Massachusetts in 1970. Two years later, he renamed it for 17th Century English horticulturists George Crabtree and John Evelyn.

Crazy Shirts .... In 1964, Rick Ralston and "Crazy Arab" opened Ricky's Crazy Shirts in the International Market Place, creating the first designer T-shirts.

Daiei .... It was formerly called "Shufu no mise Daiei Osaka Honten" meaning "big, prosperous store in Osaka for housewives."

Dairy Queen .... Dairy Queen founder J.F. "Grandpa" McCullough invented soft-serve ice cream in 1938. McCullough thought of the cow as the "Queen of the Dairy Business" and his soft frozen product as the "Queen of Dairy Products." The result was the name Dairy Queen. The first store opened in Joliet, Illinois in 1940, and today, there are over 5,600, including eight in the islands.

Dana Labels .... Named for founder Harold Haines' daughter, Dana, a flight attendant for United Airlines. Dana married a pilot and had twins in 2003.

Dave's Hawaiian Ice Cream Factory ...... Jack Leong loved ice cream so much he started his own ice cream business. Begun in 1982, Jack studied how to make ice cream in the library. The top seller is green tea, and the second is lychee. Guava and Poha Berry also do well. Dave is the founder's youngest son, and he now runs the company.

Del Monte Fresh Produce Hawaii .... The Hotel Del Monte in Monterey, California lent its name to a coffee blended for the hotel in 1886. Five years later, the Oakland Preserving Company used Del Monte as a brand name for its premium canned fruits. Del Monte eventually became the company name and a major competitor to Dole.

Denny's.................................Harold Butler opened Danny's Donuts in Lakewood, California in 1953. He expanded into sandwiches and changed the name to Danny's Coffee Shop. By 1959, he had a chain of 20 coffee shops, and he changed the name again to Denny's Restaurants. He chose Danny and Denny because they were familiar names. Now there are 1,600 Denny's including six in Hawaii.

Diêm Café ....Named for the owner's daughter. Diêm means "beautiful" in Vietnamese. Ngon Kim Trinh opened in 1989 on South King Street and is now in the 99 Ranch Market food court.

Downing Hawaii ....This Waialae Avenue surf shop is named for the family of famed surfer George Downing, who constructed the first surf board for huge waves.

Ed & Don's Candies..............................Brothers Ed and Don Maier have their names on this company, founded in 1956, although Don was never really involved, but their mother, Martha, was. Ed & Don's opened a candy store in Ala Moana in 1959 and, a year later, introduced 14 flavors of ice cream for 20 cents a scoop. In 1985, Ed sold the business to his top client Vladimir Grave, CEO of the Oritz Corp., which provides high-quality food products to Japan. Today, Ed & Don's sells its fine chocolates and candy to Guam, Fiji, Japan, Taiwan, and Hong Kong.

Edelweiss ....This Kamuela restaurant has the name of a small white flower that grows in the Alps.

Edo Japan ....This restaurant in Kaahumanu Center and Lahaina Cannery Mall carries the previous name of Tokyo. *Edo* means "mouth of the river" or "door to the creek." *Tokyo* means "eastern capital"

Eki Cyclery ....Founded by Tochi Eki in 1911, it is Hawaii's oldest bicycle shop.

Ethel M. Chocolates ....Formerly at Ala Moana, this chocolatier honors Ethel Mars, who founded

Mars candy with her husband Frank in 1911. Her son, Forrest, came out of retirement to launch Ethel M. Chocolates in 1979. Forrest created M&M's in 1941, named for Mars and former Hershey President Bruce Murrie.

Ethel's Dress Shoppe .... Named for Ethel Hong who opened a dress shop downtown in 1942 with her husband Herbert.

50th State Fair .... The 50th State Fair was once called the 49th State Fair in anticipation that Hawaii would be the 49th state admitted to the Union. The fair dates to 1930 when the Chamber of Commerce held an exhibition of Hawaiian products at the old National Guard Armory downtown. Over 30,000 attended. Succeeding fairs were held at Sand Island, Magic Island, and McKinley High School.

The Honolulu Jaycees took over sponsorship in 1937. In 1949, in anticipation of Statehood, it was called the 49th State Fair. Concerns that Hawaii's ethnic mix was incompatible with that of the United States caused the U.S. Senate to delay our nomination, but opponents realized they could not let Alaska in but not Hawaii. When Alaska was admitted to the union as the 49th State and Hawaii as the 50th in 1959, the fair's name was changed to the 50th State Fair. Held over four weekends, an average of 150,000 people come for the rides, entertainment, and musical acts each year.

Fisher Hawaii .... Founded in 1920 as an office equipment and printing company by Hy Holloway and Geoffrey Fisher, it was originally called Multigraphy, List and Letter Co. It was renamed Fisher Hawaii in 1933.

Flora-Dec Sales .... Florist and decorative supplies can be found at this Nimitz store that first opened in 1966. It's also a favorite stop for craft makers.

Flowers by Jr. Lou & T .... Junior and Lou Kawamura are husband and wife, and they run this Moiliili florist shop with their son, T.

Following Sea .... This former Kahala Mall store was named for a state of perfection in sailing – when the waves are driving you forward, and the wind is at your back. It could also be used to wish someone well. Sailors might wish you "fair winds and a following sea." "Kalapana had a song called *Following Sea* and it triggered it for me," says owner Pam Ross. The first store opened in 1973. In 1984, it moved to Kahala Mall. At one time, there were two in Southern California. Ross closed the stores in 2002 and focused on her other store, Ohelo Road.

Fook Yuen Seafood Restaurant .... This McCully Shopping Center restaurant's name means "fragrant garden" in Chinese. Honolulu used to have a Fook Yuen Jewelry store.

Fujiya Restaurant .... This Maui eatery could be named for Mt. Fuji, or it can mean that "our company is the best."

Furusato Japanese Restaurants .... Furusato means "sweet home town" or your "native village" in Japanese.

GBC .... You might think GBC stands for General Box Company, since they have the largest selection of packaging materials in stock, but GBC is the founders' initials – George and Bertha Chu. GBC started in March of 1972 as a wholesaler of Hawaiian souvenirs. They sold that part of the business in 1982 and have concentrated completely on packaging products and services since then.

The Gap .... Don and Doris Fisher opened the first Gap store in San Francisco, California in 1969. In the last 30 years, they have grown to become the leading international specialty retailer offering clothing, accessories, and personal care products in 4,200 Gap, GapKids, BabyGap, Gap Adult, GapBody, Gap Outlet, Banana Republic, and Old Navy stores worldwide. They employ 165,000 and have sales of $14 billion. Gap bought Banana Republic in 1983, then a two-store safari and travel clothing company with a thriving catalog business. Old Navy grew out of the value-priced Gap Warehouse in 1994.

Gay & Robinson .... Kauai's last remaining sugar plantation was started in Makaweli in 1889 by cousins Francis Gay and Aubrey Robinson. The family bought Niihau in 1864 for $10,000.

Gaylord's .... This Lihue restaurant is named for sugar baron Gaylord Wilcox and is in his former estate, Kilohana.

Genki Sushi .... Genki means "good in health," "in a good mood," "happy" or "fine," and is used to answer the question, "how are you?"

Gibson's Discount Store .... Three of Hawaii's top business people joined together in 1966 to turn their Family Fair Store in Mapunapuna into part of a mainland chain. George Fukunaga from Servco, Dan Yonemori from Shopping Basket, and John Kunihisa from the Ben Franklin stores in Hawaii believed being part of a 250 store chain would strengthen their buying power and allow them to lower prices 10-15%. The chain was founded in Texas by H. G. Gibson Sr. Gibson's empire has crumbled, and the only stores remaining in the chain are in the Majuro Islands.

Gordon Biersch .... Named for founders Dan Gordon and Dean Biersch. They have 12 brewery restaurants in five states and have annual revenues of $50 million

Grace's Inn .... Takashi and Yoko Kiyozuna named their restaurant for their daughter, Grace.

Grove Farm Company .... Once the largest sugar plantation on Kauai, it was founded in Lihue in 1856 and named by Judge Herman Widemann for a shady grove of kukui trees that grew near his home. George Wilcox bought it in 1870. Today the company owns the Kukui Grove Center, Kauai's largest shopping center, a golf course, and develops real estate. Punahou graduate and AOL founder Steve Case bought Grove Farm in 2000.

Gucci .... Guccio Gucci opened a luggage and saddlery store in Florence, Italy in 1921. The company's trademark striped webbing was inspired by a saddle girth.

Gyotaku

Former Kyotaru executives started this company in 2001. Gyo means "fish," and taku means "impression." Gyotaku refers to the Japanese art of making prints from fish. The *kanji* for "taku" could also mean "fish on the table."

Gyu-kaku .... This Kapiolani yakiniku restaurant's name means "bull's horns." It is part of a chain with 450 restaurants in Japan.

Hakone .... These restaurants in the Hawaii Prince Hotel Waikiki and the Maui Prince Hotel are named for a famous mountainous resort area west of Tokyo. Those wishing to enter Tokyo (then Edo) had to pass through a difficult customs office there. Many inns and hot springs thrived nearby for travelers awaiting approval.

Hakuyosha Hawaii .... Haku means "white." Yo means "western ocean." Sha means "company." The laundry service business was imported from western countries.

Haleakala Dairy .... Founded in 1888 as Haleakala Ranch, this venerable Maui institution once owned Haleakala Crater. Milk was sold in glass bottles capped with small cardboard discs until the 1950s. Kids collected and

played games with these "milk covers," and Haleakala Dairy continued to give them out for promotional purposes. Some of these advertised POG, their Passion-Orange-Guava drink. In the early 1990s, kids called the milk caps POGs, and collecting and playing with them became a craze. William Gladstone's company printed over 100 million POGS in 1993. "Every company and organization, it seemed, wanted their own POG. The energy of the people then was unbelievable. People could not get enough of these things," Gladstone recalls.

Haliimaile General Store .... Maui's only upcountry three star restaurant has a Hawaiian name that means "maile vines strewn." It is also the former name of the Iolani Palace grounds.

Hallmark Cards .... This franchise with several in the islands was founded in 1910 by Joyce Clyde "Mr. J. C." Hall. Their 700 artists, photographers, designers, stylists, and editors form the largest creative staff in the world. Together, they produce over 14,000 different designs yearly and sell more than 10 million greeting cards a day in 20 languages.

Hama Yu Japanese Restaurant .... These are restaurants in Kona and Waikoloa. In Japanese, hama refers to a "sandy coast or beach," and yu means "play." Hamayu literally means "play at the sandy beach." There is also a flower called hama-yu. Known for its beautiful white flowers, hama-yu plants live in sandy soil by the ocean. Dozens of restaurants in Japan use this name, wishing that they could be elegant and yet tough enough to survive and thrive.

Han Yang Restaurant .... This Kalihi restaurant carries the former name of Seoul, Korea. The people of Korea call themselves the Han, and the river that runs through

Seoul is also the Han.

Hana Gion .... This is a Wailea, Maui restaurant. Hana means "flower" in Japanese, and Gion is a district of Kyoto known for its geisha.

Hanahauoli School .... Hanahauoli means "joyous work" in Hawaiian and was founded in 1918 by Sophie and George Cooke. The elementary school of 200 children produces independent and resourceful individuals who develop a love of learning. Among the school's interesting traditions, is one in which each student leaves a stepping stone on the campus.

Hanohano Room .... Atop the Sheraton Waikiki Hotel, hanohano means "glorious, magnificent or honored" in Hawaiian.

Hardware Hawaii .... Dana and Mary Lundquist founded Hardware Hawaii in 1954. Its stores are now in Kailua, Kaneohe, and Mapunapuna.

Hasegawa General Store .... The Hana store famous for stocking almost everything was founded in 1910 by Saburo Hasegawa. For those who had just made the 2-1/2 hour drive on the Hana Highway, around 600 turns and over 59 bridges, the store was a welcome rest stop. To the 2,100 local residents, the store supplies their basic food and household needs. The original store burned down in 1990 and moved to the old Hana theater. In 1966, singer Paul Weston recorded a song entitled "Hasegawa General Store" and put Hana on the map.

Hawaii National Bank .... Hawaii National was the second Chinese Bank after Liberty Bank, which has merged into American Savings. Hawaii National Bank was founded in 1960 by K. J. Luke in Chinatown.

Hawaiian Brian's Billiards .... Pool hustler Brian Hashimoto started this place on Keeaumoku Street in 1985. He has another one in Anchorage, Alaska. Hawaiian Brian played professionally for many years and is known across the United States.

Heald College .... In 1863, 20 year-old Edward Payson Heald founded this school in San Francisco. It now has 12 campuses in Honolulu, Oregon, and California.

Hee Hing .... The Lee Family has owned this Kapahulu restaurant since 1966. The name means "a joyous event."

Heidi's Bistro & Deli .... Heidi is the daughter of founder Micki Mortensen, who is Swiss. Their logo is a little alpine girl in a dirndl.

Hilo Hattie - The Store of Hawaii .... This was the stage name for Clara Haili Nelson, a very popular entertainer in Hawaii from the 1930s throught the 1970s.

Hoku's
This Kahala Mandarin restaurant's name means "stars" in Hawaiian.

Holiday Inn
The Wal-Mart of the hospitality world was founded in Memphis, Tennessee in 1952 by Kemmons Wilson. It was named after the 1942 Bing Crosby and Fred Astaire movie *Holiday Inn*. Wilson and partner Wallace Johnson invented motel franchising, and today, there are four Holiday Inns in Hawaii and over 1,000 in 70 countries.

Holy's Bakery .... This Kapaau (North Kohala) bakery was founded by Yoshio Hori in 1930. The sign maker misheard his last name and made the sign "Holy's Bakery." Daughter Margaret said he decided to keep it.

Honsador Lumber .... Founded in 1935 as the Honolulu Sash and Door company.

HOPACO .... An acronym of the Honolulu Paper Company, it was founded in 1917. It is now owned by Idaho-based Boise-Cascade, a lumber and paper company.

HPM Building Supply .... HPM is short for Hawaii Planing Mill. When it opened in 1921, it was a small lumber mill. Today, it provides a complete assortment of building supplies in Hilo, Kona, and Waimea.

Huli-Huli Chicken .... Ernest Morgado and Mike Asagi founded Pacific Poultry in 1954 and sold chickens under the Ewa brand. In 1955, Morgado marinated some chickens in a teriyaki sauce his grandmother created and broiled them for a group of farmers. The farmers loved them. Morgado offered the chicken to groups for fund-raisers. The chicken was barbecued between two grills. The cook would shout, "huli," Hawaiian for "turn," when one side was cooked. That led Morgado to call it Huli-Huli Chicken. Since then, non-profit groups have raised millions of dollars selling Huli-Huli Chicken, and the Guinness Book of World Records credits Morgado for the largest chicken barbecue ever: 46,386 chicken halves at a 1981 Iolani School fund-raiser.

Hygienic Store .... The Hygienic Store got its name from the Hygienic Dairy of Kahaluu. The store has been there since 1905.

Hy's Steakhouse .... Hy Aisenstat started Hy's in Calgary, Canada in 1955. There are now seven Hy's in Canada and one in Hawaii.

Imari .... Two island restaurants carry this name, one in Waikoloa and the other in Honolulu on Keeaumoku. A place famous for its porcelain, Imari is located in the northern part of Kyushu Island, Japan.

Indigo .... Indigo is a very dark blue. The owner of this Nuuanu Avenue restaurant, Glenn Chu, says he chose it for many reasons. It is his favorite color, and also the color of the 6th Chakra. It alludes to Indochine, India and Indonesia. The "Ind" in *Hindu* and all these words comes from the Indus River, which means water or stream. Chu once owned RoxSan Patisserie, a fine French restaurant in Ward Center, and Hajibaba's, the popular Moroccan restaurant in Kahala. Indigo's Eurasian cuisine is a distillation of all his experiences of Eastern and Western cuisines, combined with his finely developed sense of taste, and interpreted through the principles of balance and harmony in traditional Chinese cooking.

Iolani School .... Founded in 1863 as a school for boys in Lahaina called Luaehu ("many and colorful"), it moved to Oahu in 1870. Queen Emma bestowed the name Iolani, or "Heavenly Hawk" on the school for her husband, Alexander Liholiho Iolani, Kamehameha IV. "Iolani" can also refer to the Supereme Being. Dr. Sun Yat-Sen, the Chinese nationalist who overthrew the Manchu dynasty, attended Iolani School.

Irifune .... A Japanese restaurant on Kapahulu. Iri means "to enter." Fune is a "ship." Irifune here means "an incoming ship" or the place where ships enter. There are many port cities called Irifune throughout Japan.

Ito En .... The first company to successfully develop canned green tea was founded in 1966 as the Frontier Tea Corporation in Shizuoka City, Japan. In 1969, they bought the name Ito En from another tea company. Ito En opened its first branch office outside Japan in 1987 in Honolulu, when they bought S & S Saimin. They still carry S & S products, but island residents are probably more familiar with their Aloha Maid brand and its top-selling iced tea drink.

JTB Hawaii .... Japan's first travel agency opened in 1912 under the name Japan Tourist Bureau. The company was renamed Japan Travel Bureau in 1945 after the war. In 1952, they opened an office in New York City. They now have 66 overseas offices and 316 branches in Japan. The Hawaii offices are in Honolulu, Kona, Maui, and Kauai. JTB handled more than 500,000 visitors to Hawaii in 1997, almost one quarter of the state's Japanese tourists. They employ over 12,000 people  and have revenues of over $1.7 billion annually. "Oli Oli" on their tour buses means "joyful" in Hawaiian.

Jamba Juice .... Jamba means "to celebrate" in an African language. It started out in 1990 as the Juice Club in California.

Jameson's By the Sea .... Owner Ed Greene named his restaurants in Kona and Haleiwa for Jameson's Irish Whiskey.

Jose's Mexican Restaurant .... Ina Martinez started this Kaimuki eatery in 1973 and named it for her husband, Jose. It is now owned by brothers Richard, Frederick and Mark Martinez. Sisters Linda and Yolanda own Jose's Restaurante Mexicana y Cantina in Restaurant Row. The family at one time owned La Paloma on Kapiolani.

K•B Toy & Hobby Stores .... K•B Toys, with several branches in the islands and 1,300 stores in 50 states, dates back to a 1922 wholesale candy business known as Kaufman Brothers. During the 1940s, a toy wholesaler who purchased candy from Kaufman Brothers, offered his toy company in payment for his debts. Wanting to diversify due to the shortages of key ingredients for the production of candy during World War II, Kaufman Brothers agreed to assume operation of the company and changed the company's name to K•B Toy & Hobby Stores.

Kahala Mandarin Oriental...................... It was local developer Charlie Pietsch who partnered with Conrad Hilton to build a hotel equal to the Royal Hawaiian but not in Waikiki. A Hilton executive wanted to call it the Waialae Hilton until Pietsch challenged him to spell *Waialae*. The word Kahala can refer to the hala or pandanus tree, or to the kahala fish.

Charlie Pietsch

Kahi Mohala .... This Ewa mental health care provider's name means "a place to blossom, open, and shine."

Kahn Galleries .... Art lovers on Kauai are fond of Kahn Galleries, established by Marty and Carole Kahn in 1984. Artist Roy Tabora, one of the most critically acclaimed seascape artists, has his paintings at their Coconut Market Place, Hanalei, Kauai Village, Kilohana, Koloa, and Waikoloa (Big Island) galleries.

Kanemitsu Bakery and Restaurant .... Shigeo Kanemitsu founded this Molokai institution in 1926. "He's still around," says manager Blossom Poepoe, "and is 90." Kanemitsu is famous for its Molokai Bread and makes 600-700 loaves on an average day. "The bread has been all over," Poepoe says, "to all the islands, the mainland, and Europe." Old-timers remember that "Kane," as he is called, used to have a fish market, bowling alley, and night club all in the same building in the 1940s and 1950s.

Kawara Soba Takase .... This is a Lahaina restaurant whose name means "by the river" or "porcelain that is used for a roof." Soba is a brown buckwheat noodle. Takase is a Kyoto district and a river famous for its beautiful fall scenery.

Keiki Kani Music Studio .... "Keiki Kani" in Hawaiian refers to the sound of small bells ringing or the high sound of children's voices. Camilla Corpuz Yamamoto runs

57

this leading Leeward music studio. Their students' ages range from newborn through adult.

Keo's Thai Cuisine .... Laotian-born Keo Sananikone popularized Thai food in Hawaii. Bon Appétit voted Keo's "American's Best Thai Restaurant."

Kiibo .... This Lihue restaurant's name means "tom boy" and was the nickname of the owner's sister.

Kim Chee .... The first of nine Kim Chee restaurants opened in Kaneohe in 1972 by Hee-Joo Chun. She picked the name because kim chee is the most well-known and popular Korean dish. Korean restaurants were somewhat rare back then and Kim Chee was well-received. Chun's son, Henry, opened Kim Chee II in Kaimuki in 1975. Daughter Su-Young Kim opened Kim Chee III on King Street a year later. Other siblings and in-laws opened up others, using the same secret recipes.

Kim Taylor Reece .... Hawaii's foremost fine art photographer is color-blind and was discouraged from pursuing a career in art. "Change majors or be a starving artist," he was advised. Instead, he turned his condition to an advantage, capturing the mystery and magic of hula kahiko in sepia-toned black and white. Kim has been publishing his art prints since 1983 and has won 15 Pele Awards and numerous others. His gallery is at Sacred Falls.

Kinko's ....

Kinko's is the nickname of founder Paul Orfalea, who has curly, red hair. Orfalea founded Kinko's in 1970 in Santa Barbara, California. "Paul's Copies" was 100 square feet and featured a single copy machine, offset press, film processing, and school supplies. Kinko's today has 1,200 retail locations in the U.S., Japan, the Netherlands, Canada, Great Britain, Australia, China, and South Korea.

Kintaro Restaurant .... This is a Kapaa, Kauai restaurant. Kin means "gold" in Japanese, and taro means "boy." Kintaro means "Golden Boy." Kintaro was a hero in a 10th century Japanese folk tale.

Kobe Japanese Steak House .... Kobe is a city in Central Japan.

Koiso Sushi Bar .... This is a Kihei restaurant. Ko means "small" or "little." Iso refers to a rocky coast or beach that is good for fishing. There are many fishermen's wharves or seafood restaurants named Koiso or Oiso (which means big coast) in Japan.

Ko Ko Ichiban Ya .... This is a Maui restaurant whose name means "our restaurant is the best." Koko means "this place." Ichiban is "the best" or "number one."

Koloa Sugar Company .... The first commercial sugar plantation in the Hawaiian Islands was established in 1835 by Ladd & Company. It merged with Grove Farm in 1948.

Kozo Sushi .... Ko means "little or tiny." Zo means a "little boy." A long time ago, Japanese retailers had an internship system (in a sense, they were more like slaves). They hired young boys (mostly from poor families) with no salary, and those young male interns were called "kozo." Kozo Sushi was launched in 1970 in Osaka, Japan and has been in Hawaii since 1980. Today, they have more than 2,500 stores in Japan and six in Hawaii.

Kramers Mens Wear .... Samuel R. Kramer Naval Uniforms was founded in 1939 upstairs in the Pantheon Building on Fort Street. Kramer altered military shirts and pants so that they would fit right and look sharp. When he moved into a retail space on the ground floor, he expanded to civilian clothing as well, and became well known for superior customer service. Today, son Jeffrey, manages the company's Big and Tall shop on Ward Avenue.

Kua Aina Sandwich Shop .... Kua Aina, in Hawaiian, means "outlying land." They have restaurants at Victoria Ward Centers, Haleiwa, and eight in Japan.

Kumon Math and Reading Centers .... Toru Kumon developed the Kumon Method of learning 40 years ago in Japan.

Kyotaru .... Kyotaru purchased Columbia Inn in 1986. Kyo refers to Kyoto and can mean "capital" as it was the old Japanese capital. Taru means "barrel or a big wooden container to keep wine." The Waimalu Kyotaru changed its name to Gyotaku.

L & L Drive-Inn .... The name came from the L & L Dairy, owned by Robert Lee Sr. from 1952-59 and named for himself and his son Robert Lee Jr., who now owns Pizza Bob's, Rosie's Cantina, and Steamers.

Lappert's Ice Cream .... This company is based in Hanapepe, Kauai and is named for Walter Lappert, who made his first gallon in 1983. It is his picture, with an ice cream cone that hangs in their stores on Kauai, Maui, and Oahu. His former wife, Mary Pratt, directs the operations and maintains the high quality standards that have made them famous. Walter Lappert passed away in 2003.

Leahi Hospital .... Established in 1900 as the "Honolulu Home for the Incurables," its initial focus was the treatment of tuberculosis. After moving from Chinatown to Kaimuki in 1902, it was renamed Leahi Home in 1906. In the 1960s, Leahi Hospital broadened its services to include long-term care and adult and children's psychiatric inpatient services. Leahi is the Hawaiian term for Diamond Head.

Le Guignol .... This restaurant on King and Victoria Streets is named for a famous French glove puppet. Guignol, his shrewish wife Madelon, and colorful friend Gnafron were created by Laurent Mourguet over 100 years ago in Lyons. Their humorous performances still entertain young and old today.

Leonard's Bakery .... Frank Leonard Rego Sr., who went by his middle name, started his Malasada Manor in 1952. His mother, Mary, suggested they sell malasadas, and Lucky Luck pitched them in TV commercials. Malasada means "badly cooked."

Lion Coffee .... Hawaii resident James Delano came upon the distinctive logo and artwork of the former Lion Coffee of Toledo, Ohio. Founded in 1864, Lion pioneered selling roasted beans in sealed bags. The lion head logo was so popular that families cut them out and collected them. By the mid-1890s, Lion Coffee roasted a million pounds a week.

Lodge at Koele .... A four-star resort in the cool hills above Lanai City, its name means a "small land area farmed by a tenant for the chief" in Hawaiian.

Longhi's .... Bob Longhi brought 50 insurance people from Washington, DC to Maui in 1976 for a business meeting. He met the owner of Captain Jack's Pub Tiki in Lahaina and ended up buying him out. "I came for three days and never left," says Longhi. Longhi's opened another branch in Wailea in 2000 and above Morton's in Ala Moana Center in 2003. The space is uniquely designed. "There are no 90 degree angles. We have curves, high ceilings, fans instead of air conditioning; flowers, and a view of the ocean. It's designed to create negative ions, which puts our customers into a higher, energized space."

Lung Fung Restaurant .... Lung Fung means "dragon and phoenix." Dragons represent males, and the phoenix represents females. Chinese consider them lucky and use them to congratulate people who have a new baby.

L' Uraku .... This was a Kapiolani Blvd. restaurant whose name meant "heavenly place."

Lyn's Delicatessen .... This former Ala Moana Center restaurant, famous for its pastrami sandwich, is named for founder Calvin Chun's daughter, Lyn. Lyn is Patti's sister, of Patti's Chinese Kitchen.

Magoo's Pizza .... Gilbert Sakaguchi opened the first Magoo's Pizza in 1967. At his girlfriend's suggestion, he named it after a Hollywood, California pizzeria. Initially a take-out/delivery operation, they have shifted their University restaurant (where Mama Mia's used to be) to casual dining. It serves 120 beers on draft - the most in the state. Surprisingly, Magoo's has 20 franchises in the Philippines and one in Dubai.

Maguro-ya .... Goro Obara's Waialae Avenue restaurant's name means "tuna house." *Sumotori* Konishiki visited Maguro-ya in a VISA Card TV commercial.

Malolo Beverages and Supplies .... Malolo means "flying fish" in Hawaiian. Founder Chow Chang started this company in 1927 as Malolo Soda Works and was inspired by Matson's first White Ship, the Malolo.

Manele Bay Hotel .... Manele is a native soapbury shrub. Its brown and black seeds are used for making leis. This is the sister hotel to Lanai's Lodge at Koele. Bill Gates was married there. It sits above Hulopoe Beach, which was named America's most beautiful shore.

Mariposa .... This Neiman Marcus restaurant name means "butterfly" in Spanish.

Marriott International .... John Willard Marriott was born in 1900 in Marriott Settlement, Utah. In 1927, he and his wife Alice opened a small root beer stand in Washington, D.C. His first hotel came in 1957. Today, Marriott International has nearly 2,100 hotel properties in 50 states and 59 countries. The Ilikai, Ihilani, and six other hotels in Hawaii are managed by Marriott.

Masu's Massive Plate Lunch .... Masu is Paul Masuoka. He credits then KCCN DJ Dave Lancaster with adding "massive" to the name during an ad campaign. He and James Grant Benton would sample that day's special and play it up on the air. Founded in the early 1970s as Livingston Food Service, the business focused originally on catering.

Plate lunches were the sideline but soon took over. For under $7, they had a variety of mixed plates with steak, baby lobster tail, fried chicken, shrimp tempura, baked Spam, shoyu hot dog, rice, and crab potato salad. They weighed in at 3 pounds and easily fed two. Masu's closed in 2007.

Matteo's Italian Restaurant .... Matty Jordan, who was Frank Sinatra's touring chef, opened up restaurants in Hollywood and Honolulu when Sinatra stopped touring. Matteo is a variation on his name, created for the restaurant.

Maui Land & Pineapple
Maui Land & Pineapple was founded in 1909. Its two major subsidiaries are Maui Pineapple Company and Kapalua Land Company. It owns 28,700 acres on Maui.

Maui Memorial Medical Center .... Maui Memorial began in 1884 as Malulani Hospital. Malulani means "protection of Heaven." Queen Kapiolani placed the hospital under the direction of the young Princess Liliuokalani and the Franciscan Sisters. Mother Marianne, Sister Renata, and Sister Antonella, who also founded St. Francis Hospital, took formal charge of the new hospital. In 1952, a new 140-bed Central Maui Memorial Hospital, dedicated to Maui's fallen veterans, opened its doors. In 1998, the name of the facility was officially changed to Maui Memorial Medical Center. Now state-run, it has 196 beds and employs nearly 700 people. In 2000, there were 11,698 admissions, with 1,644 births, and a total of 58,560 patient days.

Mauna Kea Beach Hotel .... Laurence Rockefeller built this "Grand Dame of the Kohala Coast" in 1964 at the request of the governor of Hawaii. Many consider Kaunaoa Bay, where the world-renowned resort is located, to be the island's single most picturesque beach

Meadow Gold Dairies .... "Meadow Gold" was the winning entry in a 1901 employee contest to name Continental Creamery's new butter.

Mongolian Bar-B-Que .... Gigi and Frank Lau started this restaurant in 1975 as a healthy alternative to traditional Chinese food at the Chinese Cultural Plaza. The style of cooking developed in the 13th century when Gengis Khan extended the Mongol Empire from the Pacific Ocean to the Danube River in central Europe. His soldiers would put their metal shields over open fires and cook meat and vegetables on them, searing the flavor into the food. The Lau's closed in 2003.

Moose McGillycuddy's

Bullwinkle's opened in Waikiki in 1980 but soon was challenged by the owners of the cartoon character. In 1983, they kept the moose logo but changed the name. You can find them today in Waikiki, Lahaina, Las Vegas, and California.

Morton's of Chicago .... Arnie Morton and Klaus Fritsch, former Playboy Club executives, founded this Windy City style restaurant in 1978. Morton saw his restaurant as a "comfortable saloon." The Ala Moana Center restaurant is their 63rd.

Mountain Apple Company .... Founder Jon de Mello named his music recording business for the mountain apples that once fell on the roof of his Tantalus home.

Murphy's Bar and Grill .... Don Murphy opened his downtown establishment in 1987 on Merchant Street. Murphy is a big supporter of University of Hawaii athletic programs and other community groups. His Pigskin Pigout and other events raise hundreds of thousands of dollars anually. The site Murphy's occupies has hosted a bar or restaurant since the 1870s when King Kalakaua was a frequent patron. Much of the building's bricks were once ship ballast from the mainland.

NAPA Auto Parts .... NAPA is an acronym for National Automotive Parts Association, founded in 1925.

Naniwa .... Naniwa is a restaurant at the Sheraton Kauai Resort, and there is a Naniwa-ya at the Food Court at Ala Moana. Naniwa is the former name of Osaka and means "old town," according to hotel concierge Heike Fujita. Osaka was the Japanese capital before Kyoto. "Nani" means "hard or difficult," while "wa" means "surf or wave." Naniwa means "hard to travel by ship." Osaka (Naniwa) was an old port city that had traded with China since the 5th century. The ocean near Osaka was dangerous because of its big waves, and many ships were wrecked in the area.

New Otani Kaimana Beach Hotel. .... Kaimana means "diamond," referring to the hotel's location at the foot of Diamond Head. The Sans Souci area was a favorite hangout of Robert Louis Stevenson who enjoyed the shade of the hau tree at the McInerny residence over 120 years ago. The hotel opened in 1964.

Niblick .... This restaurant, formerly at the Ko Olina Golf Course and Resort carries an old term for a golf club, specifically a pitching wedge. The original equipment that was used to play golf included mashies, spoons, cleeks, and niblicks.

Ninniku-ya Restaurant .... This Waialae Avenue restaurant's name means "garlic house or restaurant."

Ohelo Road .... This Kahala Mall store is named for the Ohelo berry which grows in volcanic soil on Maui and the Big Island. Owner Pam Ross says, "My dad used to say that out of the mud comes the lotus and out of volcanic ash comes the ohelo berry. He was talking about me because I was a difficult child. He wanted me to know that I would turn out just fine. I guess I did."

One Fas Lube .... Donald Fasone rearranged his last name to get the name of this oil change business in Salt Lake where Costco once was. Donna McLaughlin, who runs the company with her husband

John and several members of the family, says her father thought One Fas was a catchy, clever use of their last name. Their logo is Mr. Oily. He donned a sombrero and became Señor Oily when John and Donna won the Compadres/Ward Centre South Pacific Chili Cookoff a few years ago.

Onjin's Café .... OnJin Kim, who used to own Hanatei Bistro in Hawaii Kai, opened this Kamakee Street cafe.

Orange Julius...................................... Julius Freed opened a fresh orange juice stand in downtown Los Angeles in 1926. Real estate broker Jas Hamlin suggested adding crushed ice and various natural food powders. Customers found it delicious and would often say, "give me an orange, Julius."

Otsuka's Furniture and Appliances .... Brothers Wallace Y. Otsuka and Jay J. Otsuka went into business selling Studebaker automobiles in 1935. After World War II, they added general merchandise, furniture and appliances. Automobiles were eventually phased out and the company concentrated on furniture and appliances. Today it is the largest furniture store and the largest appliance store on Kauai, with 42 full-time employees.

Our Lady of Peace Cathedral .... The United States' oldest, continually used church can be found on the Fort Street Mall, where it was built in 1842. Father Damien was ordained there.

Outrigger Enterprises .... Roy Kelley took over the lease of the old Outrigger Canoe Club, next to the Moana and Royal Hawaiian Hotels, when it expired in 1963. He liked the name and applied it to his growing hotel chain.

Pacific Club

Founded in 1851 as the British Club, the name was changed at Annexation. Princess

The "British Club" on Alakea and Hotel Streets, about 1880.

Kaiulani was born at the current site, which used to be her father's home.

Paesano .... This name of this Manoa restaurant is Italian and means "fellow countryman."

Papa John's Pizza .... John Schnatter started making pizzas in a broom closet in the back of his father's tavern in Jeffersonville, Indiana in 1984. The pizza was well-received, and the first Papa John's restaurant opened in 1985. That first store has grown to more than 2,600 restaurants with sales of over $1.7 billion.

Perry Boys' Smorgy .... Founded in 1961 in Fresno, California by Coleman Perry, the first of three in Hawaii opened at the Reef Hotel in 1964. It rode a wave of popularity for the Swedish *Smorgasbord* that started in the U.S. in the late 1950's. *Smorgas* means "open sandwich," and *bord* is the Swedish word for "table." *Smorgasbords* developed in the 18th century and consisted of a number of small dishes from which you could take your pick: fish, meatballs, salads, vegetables, and desserts. At one time, there were as many as 20 Perry's Smorgys in California and Hawaii.

Pescatore .... This Hilo restaurant's name means "fisherman" in Italian. It was founded in 1990.

Pohai Nani .... Pohai Nani opened in 1964 and is operated by the Evangelical Lutheran Good Samaritan Society, the largest non-profit operator of senior communities in the United States. They have over 240 facilities in 25 states. In Hawaiian, Pohai Nani means "surrounded by beauty."

Pomare

Pomare is a Tahitian royal family name. It was first given to Tu around 1790 because the flu caused him to cough at night. "Po" means "night" and

Pomare, King of Tahiti.

"mare" means "cough." Jim Romig founded Pomare-Tahiti Sportswear as it was originally called in 1967. Pomare is the parent company of Hilo Hattie.

Prada .... Mario Prada founded this Milan, Italy, company as a manufacturer of leather bags in 1913. Granddaughter Miuccia Prada moved the family business into women's and men's wear in the last 20 years. Her distinctive trademark is a surprising combination of materials and understated luxury.

Primo Beer .... For almost 100 years Primo was Hawaii's favorite beer. Primo  was first brewed in 1898 by the Honolulu Brewing & Malting Co. Production resumed in 1934 after Prohibition ended, under the name Hawaii Brewing Co. "Hawaiian Champagne," as it was affectionately known, was the first U.S. beer to be sold in aluminum cans in 1958. Primo captured an astounding 70 percent of the Hawaiian beer market in the late 1960s and early 1970s. The brewery ran 24 hours a day to keep up with demand. Stroh Brewery bought Primo from Schlitz and production moved to the mainland. Microbreweries sprang up, sales dropped, and Stroh ended Primo production in 1998.

RadioShack .... Brothers Theodore and Milton Deutschmann opened the first RadioShack Store in 1921. A "radio shack" was a term for the small wooden structure that housed a ship's radio equipment. The store supplied the needs of radio officers aboard ships as well as "ham" radio operators. They later moved into stereo equipment, citizen-band (CB) radios, and introduced the first mass-produced personal computer: the TRS-80 microcomputer. Today, they have 7,200 stores and sales of $5 billion.

Ronnie's Ice Cream Parlor ....
This Pearlridge ice cream parlor and restaurant honored Ronnie Hope by her children, Ed, Jamie, Andy, and Clint. Ronnie was the first female to own a radio station in Hawaii (KINE) and helped launch the Hoku awards.

Rosie's Cantina ....
Bob Lee, who also owns Pizza Bob's and Steamers, named this North Shore

Ronnie Hope owned KINE.

restaurant from the lyrics of the song *El Paso*. ("Out in the West Texas town of El Paso, I fell in love with a Mexican girl. Night time would find me in Rose's Cantina; music would play and Felina would whirl.") He changed Rose's to Rosie's.

Ruth's Chris Steak House .... Ruth Fertel was looking for a way to raise money to send her sons to college. She mortgaged her house and bought Chris Steak House in New Orleans in 1965, later changing the name to Ruth's Chris Steak House. Their Restaurant Row, Beach Walk and Lahaina locations are part of more than 80 restaurants in the U.S.

Safeway... In the small farming community of American Falls, Idaho in 1915, M.B. Skaggs bought his father's grocery store. Low profit margins attracted shoppers, and by 1926, 428 Skaggs stores were operating in 10 states. That year he bought out the 322 rival Selig store chain and renamed his grocery empire Safeway.

In the 1930s, Safeway introduced produce pricing by the pound, open dating on perishable items, nutritional labeling, and even parking lots. Today Safeway operates more than 1,650 stores across the U.S. and Canada.

St. Francis Healthcare System ....
Pope Pius IX named the Third Franciscan Order of Syracuse, New York for St.

St. Francis of Assisi

Francis of Assisi. Mother Marianne Cope brought six other sisters to Hawaii to help Father Damien and ran his ministry on Molokai after he died. They founded St. Francis Hospital in 1927.

Saint-Germain Bakery .... The bakery was named for St. Germain's Chapel in France and picked because Japanese could pronounce the name easily. It was founded in 1948, and now has over 120 stores in Japan, two in Thailand, and 11 in Hawaii, including Dee Lite Bakery, which was bought in 1990. Dee Lite was founded in 1959 by Herbert and Sue Matsuba.

Sans Souci Hotel .... One of the earliest hotels in Hawaii, the Sans Souci, built by Allen Herbert, opened in 1884. Sans Souci means "without a care" in French and was the name of Russian Czar Frederick The Great's Palace.

Sarento's Top of the "I" .... This restaurant at the top of the Ilikai is named for Aaron Placourakis' father, Sarento Nickolas. Sarento's offers superb regional Italian cuisine with a Mediterranean flair and spectacular views. Sarento's on the Beach offers their award-winning cuisine to Maui residents and visitors.

Schuman Carriage .... Gustave Schuman opened his business in 1893, six years before cars hit our shores. He sold carts, carriages, wagons, and surreys. Schuman returned from the 1903 World Expo with one of the island's first automobiles, a Pope Tribune. In 1904, a shipment of Model T's arrived and were advertised as cheaper to maintain than a horse. When Central Union Church moved from Richards and Beretania Streets to its present Punahou Street location in 1922, Schuman Carriage moved in and occupied the ornate site until the State Capitol was built three decades later.

ScooZee's .... Scoozee means "excuse me" in Italian, but owners Marlene Among and Richard Swartz say they named the former Ward Center restaurant for their nephew "Z."

Sedona .... This Ward Center retail store is named for the Northern Arizona town of Sedona, known for its majestic mountains and magnetic vortices with spiritual and healing powers.

Servco Pacific .... Servco had its humble beginnings as a two car service station that Peter Fukunaga opened in Waialua in 1919. When he moved his Waialua Garage company to Wahiawa in the 1920s, he offered $25 to whomever came up with the best new company name. An Army Air Corps sergeant suggested Service Motor Company because "service was the heart of the company policy." Cars and trucks are Servco's specialties with Toyota, Lexus, and Suzuki dealerships. Servco has an insurance division, sells educational products through Education Works, and owns the Easy Music Center. Their employees contribute to numerous charities and foundations.

7-Eleven .... 7-Eleven was once open from 7 AM to 11 PM. It was founded in Dallas, Texas in 1927 as an ice company and then began selling milk, bread, and eggs as a convenience to customers. Today, their 21,000 stores sell $10 billion in goods annually.

SIDA Taxi .... Acronym for State Independent Driver's Association. It closed in 2003.

Singha Thai Cuisine .... Chai Chaowasaree named his restaurant after Thailand's famous Singha Beer. Chai's Island Bistro at Aloha Tower Marketplace combines Hawaiian Regional Pacific Rim Cuisine with some of the island's hottest musicians in nightly performances.

Sorabol Restaurant .... This Keeaumoku Street restaurant is named for the Korean Royal Palace in Seoul. The word "Seoul" is derived from Sorabol and means "the center of everything." The name of the capitol was changed to Seoul in 1948 when the Republic of Korea was established. For several centuries before that, it was called Han Yang. A Korean restaurant in Kalihi bears that name.

SPAM .... The "miracle meat in a can" was originally called Hormel Spiced Ham when it came out in 1937. Competitors' products soon captured the largest share of the market and Hormel decided it needed a catchier name. It offered a $100 prize won by Kenneth Daigneau. SPAM quickly recaptured the market. It does not stand for spiced ham or shoulder of pork and ham as some believe. Could a mere luncheon meat win wars and save lives? Former Russian Premier Nikita Kruschev credited SPAM with the survival of the Russian Army during World War II. Beef was rationed during the war but not SPAM, and American and Hawaii families in particular embraced it.

SPAM – the luncheon meat that won World War II.

Spindrifter .... Jolly Roger bought Reuben's at Kahala Mall and hired a consultant to come up with possible names. "Spindrift" is the spray that comes off the bow of a ship. Biff Graper says it was chosen because it was a single word and was uplifting. Spindrifter closed in the late 1990s and a Barnes & Noble bookstore occupies the site.

Spot's Inn .... This restaurant on Dillingham is named for the family's seven-year-old Dalmatian.

State Farm Insurance .... In 1922, G. J. Mecherle started an automobile insurance company that would only sell to farmers in the state of Illinois. The State Farm Mutual Automobile Insurance Company used an old Model T, a Cornucopia or Horn of Plenty, and a fire hat in its emblem. The image of Father Time holding a scythe was rejected. The jingle "Like a Good Neighbor, State Farm is There" was written in 1971 by Barry Manilow.

Suehiro .... "Sue" means "end, edge, or further" in Japanese. "Hiro" means "expansion." Its fan logo is the symbol of further expansion in the future and long-lasting prosperity of their business. However, that did not keep them from selling to Gyotaku in 2001.

Sure Save Super Market .... One of the Big Island's oldest family-owned businesses started in 1933 as Okuyama Meat Market. Tomohide Okuyama founded the company and 20 years later, his son Tom shifted gears into the supermarket business in 1953. Grandson Carl moved Sure Save into Wiki Wiki convenience stores in 1978.

Surf News Network .... Founded by "Surfer Joe" Teipel in 1976 as a way of providing local surfers with accurate surfing condition information. Now owned by former employee, Gary Kewley, SNN has a team of reporters all over the islands who call in regular reports. These go into Surf Reports on over 22 radio stations on Oahu, Kauai and Maui, KHON and KITV television stations, the Internet (www.SurfNewsNetwork.com) and the Surf Line (596-SURF).

Sushi Sasabune .... "Sasa" means "bamboo leaf," and "bune" or "fune" is a "boat." Sasabune is a "bamboo leaf boat." In Los Angeles and at 1417 South King Street, the patron has to trust the chef to choose their sushi. They credit Yohei Hanaya with creating sushi 300 years ago using fish from Tokyo Bay (when it was still called Edo), which he sliced and put on bite-sized, vinegared, rice balls.

TCBY .... TCBY was founded by Frank and Georgia Hickingbotham in 1981. The story is that Georgia offered Frank frozen, peach-flavored yogurt, which he thought he would not like. However, on one occasion, he decided to try it. "This can't be yogurt," he exclaimed. The Hickingbothams decided to go into the frozen yogurt business, opening their first "This Can't Be Yogurt" store in Little Rock, Arkansas. TCBY later became "The Country's Best Yogurt" and has 3,000 stores in 70 countries.

Taco Bell .... Glen Bell left the service in 1946 and opened Bell's Drive-In, a hot dog stand, in San Bernardino, California. Bell liked Mexican food and soon started Taco Tia, then El Tacos, and finally Taco Bell in Downey in 1962.

Tai Sei Ramen .... The name of this restaurant on Beretania Street is similar to Suehiro, referring to growth and expansion in the future. It is also the name of a village in Hokkaido.

Tamarind Park ....

This acre on the corner of King and Bishop Streets is named for the tamarind tree that Bernice Pauahi Paki's parents, Abner and Konia, planted outside their home on the day she was born, Dec. 19, 1831. Her husband, Charles Reed Bishop, cut the tree down after she died of breast cancer in 1884. The stump is preserved in the Kamehameha School Chapel.

Bernice Pauahi's parents planted a tamarind tree here on the day she was born in 1831.

Tasaka Guri Guri .... Founder Jokichi Tasaka originally called his snack shop Tasaka Goodie Goodie but many immigrant Japanese could not pronounce it properly. They called it Guri Guri and that became the name. The 80 year-old company once sold mochi, manju, senbei, and other Japanese snacks at its shop, but today the pineapple and strawberry 'guri guri' (similar to sorbet) is all they sell.

Tedeschi Vineyards .... Napa vintner Emil Tedeschi founded this Ulupalakua winery in 1974. The winery produces red, white, and sparkling wines. A cottage built for King Kalakaua and Queen Kapiolani in 1874 is used today as their tasting room.

Ted's Bakery .... Ted Nakamura started the business, famous for its chocolate-haupia pie, in 1987 with his brother Glenn. Ted calls the mixing of leftover chocolate and haupia a mistake. However, it sold well, and now half of their orders are for this pie.

Tesoro .... Tesoro means "treasure" in Spanish. Robert V. West Jr. founded this oil company in Texas in 1964.

Tex Drive In and Restaurant................. The Ernest Texeira Family started a small fast food shop in the plantation town of Honokaa in 1968 and expanded it into an affordable family restaurant. Ada Pulin-Lamme bought the business in 1994 and began working with the visitor industry to bring a steady stream of tourists. Tex Drive In was selected to be the official Hamakua Visitor Center because of its prime location on Highway 19. In 2001, a second location was opened in Pahala as well as a gift store at the Honokaa site. They now sell nearly 60,000 malasadas monthly, and on a clear day you can see Maui's Haleakala.

3660 on the Rise .... The name of Russell Siu and Gale Ogawa's restaurant on Wilhelmina Rise at 3660 Waialae Avenue came from a contest in Honolulu Magazine.

Ting Hao Mandarin Seafood .... This Hilo restaurant's name means "top or the best"

Todai Restaurant .... Located in Waikiki and 26 other locations in seven states, Todai means "lighthouse" in Japanese.

Tony Group .... The Tony Group is in the islands because of asthma. Tony Masamitsu was a civilian working for the U.S. Army near Tokyo, Japan in the 1960s. He became a Honda dealer there in 1967, selling power equipment, motorcycles, and later small cars from a showroom that initially was only 8 by 8 feet. His son, Stan, had childhood asthma and missed half the school year because of the severity of symptoms. When the family made a trip to California and Hawaii, they noticed that Stan's asthma disappeared here. They soon moved to Hawaii for Stan's health and opened Hawaii's first exclusive Honda dealership on 7-7-1977. Tony retired, and Stan took over as president. The Tony Group recently consolidated their multiple dealerships into one supersite in Waipio. "Honda made motorcycles before cars," Stan points out. "The first cars they designed were made from motorcycle parts. Both Honda and the Tony Group had very humble beginnings."

Tori Richard .... Mortimer Feldman founded this company in 1955 and named it for two of his children, Victoria and Richard. It's grown to become one of the world's premier resort wear designers.

Tower Records .... Tower Records was founded in Sacramento, California in 1960 by Russ Solomon and named for the nearby Tower Theatre.

Town & Country Surf Shop .... This shop was named because its Pearl City shop was half way between Honolulu and the North Shore. T&C founder Craig Sugihara only wanted to make enough money to be able to surf, when he opened in 1971. He and his wife, Linda, now have seven stores on Oahu.

TOYS "R" US .... Charles Lazarus returned from World War II and turned his father's bicycle repair shop in Washington D.C. into the Baby Furniture and Toy Supermarket. He soon realized that baby furniture was a one-time purchase and focused on toys in 1957, changing the name to TOYS "R" US. Today they have 1,450 stores worldwide and sales of $11 billion.

Turtle Bay Resort .... The Del Webb Kuilima Hotel was built in 1973. Bob Hope, Jane Russell, Barbara Eden and Connie Stevens came for the opening ceremonies. Del Webb also built Sun City and the Flamingo Hotel in Las Vegas for gangster Bugsy Siegel. "Kuilima" means arm in arm, or to hold hands. The hotel is now known as the Turtle Bay Resort.

Ultimate You .... This Ward Center women's clothing store was named by a psychic. Owner Kelsey Sears was thinking of naming her store the Ultimate Woman, but a psychic told her to put the word "you" in it instead.

Verbano Ristorante Italiano .... Verbano is another name for Lake Maggiore in the Piedmont district of Northwestern Italy. They have three restaurants on Oahu: South King Street, Waialae Avenue in Kaimuki, and Pearlridge.

Verizon .... Verizon is a combination of the Latin word *veritas*, and horizon. *Veritas* means "truth" and also connotes certainty and reliability, and horizon signifies endless possibilities.

Louis Vuitton .... Louis Vuitton, a trunk-maker in Paris, built up his legend around travel by creating luggage, handbags, and accessories that were as innovative as they were elegant and practical, in 1854.

W Hotels .... Diamond Head is one of 20 U.S. locales to have a hotel with the name "W," which stands for "whatever you want, whenever you want it," and "warm, wonderful, witty, wired, and welcome."

W&M Bar-B-Q Burgers .... Wilfred and Myra Kawamura opened in 1954 on 9th and Waialae but have moved next to City Mill. Myra's Bar-B-Q sauce is their secret.

Wal-Mart .... Sam Walton began his retail career as a J. C. Penney management trainee and later leased a Ben Franklin store. His first store soon grew to 15 under the Walton 5 & 10 name. After Ben Franklin management rejected his suggestion to open discount stores in small towns, Walton and his brother, James "Bud" Walton, opened the first Wal-Mart Discount City in Rogers, Arkansas in 1962. Today, Wal-Mart Stores, Inc. is the world's largest retailer with $218 billion in sales. The company employs more than 1.3 million people in its 4,300 stores. More than 100 million customers per week visit Wal-Mart stores worldwide.

Warren's Boarding House .... William Warren built Hawaii's first hotel and restaurant on Hotel near Bethel Street in 1825. Hotel Street got its name from Warren's.

Watumull's ....
Jhamandas Watumull founded this local retailing giant in 1914.

Wigwam .... T h e first Wigwam store in Hawaii opened in 1958 in Dillingham Plaza in Kalihi, where Savers is today. They had eight stores in

Jhamandas Watumull

the islands at one time and 35 in Washington, California, and Arizona. Pay Less Drug Stores bought out the Wigwam chain in 1971. A wigwam is an American Indian dwelling, and the chain took that name because the first store in Seattle, Washington began in a tent.

Wilcox Health System .... Wilcox Memorial Hospital was founded in 1938 on Kauai by community leaders George Norton Wilcox and Dora Rice Isenberg. The hospital opened with seven doctors and 19 employees. Today, they serve more than 90 percent of Kauai's population and employ more than 600 people. Wilcox Health System's two largest components are Wilcox Memorial Hospital and Kauai Medical Clinic, which provide direct in-patient and out-patient health care. In 2001, Wilcox merged with Kapiolani Health and Straub to form Hawaii Pacific Health.

Wisteria .... The wisteria is a vine with purple flowers. The Asato family of KC Drive Inn bought this restaurant on King and Piikoi Streets in 1971. At one time, there was another restaurant in the Kaneohe Bowl.

Wo Fat .... Wo Fat means "peace, prosperity, and harmony," says 1973-1978 owner Ted Wong.

Won Kee .... This restaurant is in the Chinese Cultural Center. Its name means "prosperous shop."

Yick Lung .... Crack seed manufacturer Yick Lung was founded in 1900 and closed in 2003. Its name means "profitable enterprise."

Young Guns .... This gun shop in Mapunapuna got its name from its original location on Young Street.

Young Laundry .... Young Laundry was Hawaii's first commercial laundry. It was established over 100 years ago in 1902 as the in-house laundry for the Alexander Young Hotel on Alakea and King Street. An artesian well on the property supplied 3 million gallons of water a day.

Alexander Young

Yum Yum Tree

This restaurant's name may have been inspired by the 1963 movie *Under the Yum Yum Tree* starring Jack Lemmon. Vi's Pies in California inspired their recipes.

Yummy Korean Bar-B-Q .... Peter Kim left the gridiron for the restaurant business. Kim graduated from Kaiser High School, played football for the University of Hawaii, the University of Alabama, and the Tampa Bay Buccaneers. An injury sidelined his kicking career. His borther-in-law, Ken Choi owned Yami Korean Bar-B-Q in Waikiki, and taught him the business. In 1987, Kim founded Yummy Korean Bar-B-Q. He now also owns Chow Mein Express, Lahaina Chicken, Bear's Kitchen and Mama's Spaghetti House – 14 on Oahu, one on Maui, and the latest, in Nagoya, Japan. Bear's Kitchen is named in honor of his former Alabama coach, Paul "Bear" Bryant.

Zippy's .... Zippy's was founded in 1966, three years after the Zip Code came out in 1963. Initially, they were going to call it Zip Drive Inn. The name Zippy's was designed to convey that they served fast food.

E-mail your stories to CompaniesWeKeep@Yahoo.com or visit our web site at www.CompaniesWeKeep.com.

Hawaii's flag has the United Kingdom's Union Jack in the corner. It's made up of three crosses: St. Andrew's, representing Scotland, St. George's, representing England, and St. Patrick's, representing Ireland.

Consolidated opened Hawaii's first drive-in theatre in 1948 where Daiei is today.

Extraordinary Hawaii – Companies –

Amazing stories about Hawaii companies

The stories and accomplishments of companies in Hawaii are nothing short of extraordinary. In this chapter, you will learn:

- How Bank of Hawaii was founded with a parade of gold coins through downtown Honolulu in 1897.
- Why Lex Brodie says "Thank you very much."
- Which dairy L&L Drive-Inn is named for.
- How Pearl City came to be Hawaii's first planned community in 1890. It was built by B. F. Dillingham, and was a weekend and summer retreat for Oahu's wealthy until World War II.
- How Tripler come to be painted pink.
- How Iolani Palace came to have electricity four years before the White House, and before any building in California.
- How Consolidated Theatres supported what may have been Hawaii's first successful racial discrimination lawsuit.
- How two queens, two Japanese emperors, and the Pope were involved in the founding or naming of four Hawaii hospitals.
- What Hawaii got from the United States in exchange for Pearl Harbor.
- Which hotel has kept a fire continuously burning in its fireplace since 1888.
- Where the plate lunch came from and how macaroni salad came to be on it.
- How residents from one Okinawan hamlet founded 72 Hawaii restaurants. *And much more!*

ABC Stores

How can a company have three stores in the same block, and 37 in one square mile *and* succeed? ABC Stores may be the only company in Hawaii that has done that.

ABC stumbled onto it accidentally. They opened a store near one that was soon to close. While both were open, they noticed sales did not drop at the one that was closing, and sales at the new store matched sales at the older one.

One cannot help but notice that ABC stores are everywhere in Waikiki, many within 50 to 100 feet of each other. This gives little room for competitors to gain a foothold and gives ABC a winning formula for convenience in the market.

Sidney Kosasa founded ABC Stores in 1965. He had worked in his parent's Honolulu grocery store as a child. In 1942, he earned a degree in pharmacology from the University of California at Berkeley, and in 1949, he and his wife Minnie opened a drug store called Kaimuki Pharmacy.

There are 65 ABC Stores including this one at Ala Moana Center.

On a trip to Miami Beach, Sidney saw that tourists favored convenience over price. They bought groceries and drugs as well as souvenirs, resort apparel, and cosmetics. He foresaw that Waikiki would become a major tourist attraction like Miami and had the idea to open convenience stores for the tourists.

This idea was the genesis of the first ABC Store at Kalakaua and Beachwalk, which opened in 1965. They sold souvenirs, drugs, cosmetics, resort apparel, Hawaiian gifts, and anything else tourists needed.

Sidney picked the name ABC Stores because it was easy to remember. ABC Stores employs over 800 people. There are a total of 65 ABC Stores with 37 in Waikiki, and others in Honolulu, Maui, Kauai, Kona, Guam, and Saipan. The first ABC Store in Las Vegas opened in 2002. Almost all the ABC stores are open 365 days a year from 7 AM to 1 AM.

—Researched by Shih-Wei (Amelia) Chen

Alexander & Baldwin

Of the five sugar producers that dominated Hawaii's economy (and politics) for half a century, the sole entity still growing sugar today is Alexander & Baldwin, Inc.

A&B was founded in 1870, on Maui, by two childhood friends from Lahaina: Samuel T. Alexander and Henry Perrine Baldwin. Their parents were missionaries and they were sent to Punahou School. Alexander earned a degree on the mainland, and returned to Maui in 1862 to teach at Lahainaluna School.

Baldwin had just set to work earning funds for college. Alexander was hired to manage the Waihee Sugar Plantation, and he added Baldwin to his staff. By 1870, they started growing sugar cane on

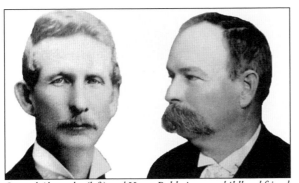

Samuel Alexander (left) and Henry Baldwin were childhood friends in Lahaina in 1843.

their own 12 acres of land near Makawao. Adding to their landholdings, they soon had 500 acres. This first plantation eventually became the largest plantation in the state, with 37,000 acres. It was known as the Hawaiian Commercial & Sugar Company (HC&S).

Baldwin married Emily Alexander, his partner's sister. Alexander had married the former Martha Cooke in 1864. Baldwin served in the legislature from 1887 until 1903. He presided as A&B President until his death at age 68. Alexander died at age 67 while on safari in Africa. His gravesite near Victoria Falls was recently rediscovered in 2002.

By 1876, the partners had concluded they had to bring water from the rainy windward slopes of Haleakala to irrigate their east Maui fields. The initial Hamakua Ditch, 25 miles across gulches and ravines from mountains to the coast, grew into a complex system of ditches, flumes and tunnels known today as the East Maui Irrigation System. In 2003, the EMI System was recognized as an engineering landmark.

To get their raw sugar to the C&H Sugar refinery in Crockett, California, the plantations invested in ocean shipping. Matson Navigation Company operated both cargo and passenger vessels, and was instrumental in developing Hawaii's tourism industry, buy owning or building four hotels in Waikiki.

During the World War II, four of Matson's vessels were used by the military to transport troops. Of Matson's many freighters conscripted into war service, fifteen were destroyed, along with 65 of the company's loyal employees. In 1964, A&B began to buy out Matson's other owners and five years later, Matson was wholly owned by A&B. Today, it is focused on ocean transportation and related services. The 'C&H' used to mean California and Hawaiian but, with the decline of Hawaii's sugar production, C&H turned to other sources. A&B sold all of its interest in C&H in 2005.

The third leg of A&B's stool is property development and management, which began in the late 1940s as an effort to develop a community of homes and commercial sites to serve HC&S plantation employees and retirees. Nicknamed 'Dream City' by dreamer Frank Baldwin, the community, now a suburb of Kahului, comprises nearly 4,000 homes and multiple commercial sites. On Kauai, A&B developed homes for its McBryde Sugar plantation employees, and Hawaii's largest coffee estate, Kauai Coffee Company, which A&B still owns.

The founders' children and grandchildren, in their respective times, played important roles in the businesses of A&B. Today, Alexander's great granddaughter, Maryanna Gerbode Shaw, serves on the A&B Board of Directors as does Baldwin's great-grandson, Charles Garfield King. A&B celebrated its corporate Centennial in 2000, marking 130 years of business in Hawaii. More than 2,000 employees work for this publicly traded company that is moving forward into its second century.

— Researched by Madeleine Wadelius and Patty Hsu

Alexander Young Hotel

When it opened in downtown Honolulu in 1902, the Alexander Young Hotel was the finest hotel in the entire Pacific Basin. Spanning the entire city block from Hotel to King Street and fronting Bishop Street, the Alexander Young was a marvel.

The Alexander Young Hotel built Bishop Street, then just one block long, in 1902.

Young was a native of Scotland. He arrived in the islands in 1865 and became a partner in the Honolulu Iron Works and several sugar companies. He was a member of the Cabinet under Queen Liliuokalani and President Sanford Dole.

The Alexander Young Hotel surpassed the Royal Hawaiian Hotel, built 30 years earlier and then declining, on Hotel and Richards Streets. The site was chosen because an artesian spring, which produced 300,000 gallons of water a day, existed there.

The five story hotel with Roman and Renaissance architecture was called "one of the most luxuriously furnished and completely equipped hotels west of New York." It had 192 guest rooms, and a dozen retail stores.

The Alexander Young Roof Garden, seen here about 1905, was the "in-spot" for dining and dancing until WW II.

The Alexander Young Roof Garden became the "in" spot for dining and dancing in Honolulu. As many as 1,000 people could enjoy the cool night air and unparalleled vista from high above Bishop Street.

The Alexander Young Hotel's candy shop may have been the first to make chocolate-covered macadamia nuts in the 1930s. The bakery was known for having beautifully decorated cakes and was particularly famous for its lemon crunch cake.

The in-house laundry later moved out and today is Hawaii's oldest. Young Laundry and Dry Cleaning traces its roots to 1902 as well.

In the old days, Fort Street was the main mauka-makai downtown thoroughfare. Alexander Young built Bishop Street, naming it for Charles Reed Bishop who owned a home on several acres around what is now Bishop and King Streets. Bishop Street was initially only one block long. It took another three decades to extend the street from the docks to Beretania.

Alexander Young and his son Archibald formed a partnership with Conrad Von Hamm who married Young's daughter Ida, forming the Von Hamm-Young Corp. The business brought the first automobiles, gasoline stations, refrigerators, and radios to Hawaii and was one of the largest and most influential in the middle of the 20th century. In 1964, the firm became The Hawaii Corp. or THC, Hawaii's first conglomerate. Ten years later, it disappeared in what was then Hawaii's largest bankruptcy.

After World War II, tourism focused on Waikiki and the Alexander Young Hotel gradually came to contain only offices, by about 1970. It was torn down in 1981 and was replaced with Tamarind Park and the Pacific Trade Center Pauahi Tower.

Aloha Airlines

In 1946, right after World War II, Ruddy Tongg founded Trans-Pacific Airlines. Stories abound that Hawaiian Airlines, formerly called Inter-Island Airways, bumped him and a couple of traveling companions in favor of caucasian travelers, and they were so upset that they started their own "local" airline.

Dr. Hung Wo Ching recalls the poor treatment he received flying from Kauai as a boy aboard Inter-Island. He had to sit in the stairwell and was drenched from the waterborne takeoff of the Sikorsky plane.

Race was a much more important factor 50 years ago than it is today. Many Asians had moved off the plantation, but found it hard to get good jobs or loans from banks. From the beginning, Trans-Pacific Airlines hired locals and created a feeling of *ohana* among its employees.

The airline faced stiff competition from its Hawaiian Airlines rival. Hawaiian fought Trans-Pacific Airline's bid to be a certified carrier for years until President Truman granted it in 1949.

Former CEO of Aloha Airlines, Hung Wo Ching.

Trans-Pacific Airlines survived its early years because its employees worked extra tasks without pay and sometimes waited to cash their checks until money was in the bank. Peacetime had left former military DC-3 aircraft in Hawaii available for civilian purchase. TPA was able to buy three of these "pre-owned" planes for as little as $25,000 each.

Tongg picked the name Trans-Pacific Airlines because he initially had an interest in flying routes to China. However, the communist revolution in 1949 put an end to that.

The airline became popular and known for its friendly and efficient service. The marketing department used the company's initials, TPA, to create its first slogan – "The People's Airline." The slogan was immensely popular and people started referring to the airline as "The People's Airline" instead of Trans-Pacific Airlines.

In the 1940s, the planes carried the words Trans-Pacific Airlines - The Aloha Airline. In the 1950s, it was called TPA Aloha Airlines. In 1958, the new CEO, Dr. Hung Wo Ching dropped the TPA in favor of Aloha Airlines. He said the friendliness of the staff came from their Aloha Spirit. He saw tourism growing and wanted a company name that would appeal to them. Bow-tied and sporting a crew cut, Hung Wo Ching took Aloha Airlines from being a struggling newcomer into a profitable jet age. The venerable 16 passenger DC-3's lasted 15 years but were eventually replaced in 1969, with Boeing 737 "Funbirds" that could hold 118.

Merger talks between Aloha and Hawaiian have begun and ended several times without result. In 1970, Hawaiian CEO John Magoon backed away from a proposed merger at the last minute. In 2002, it was Aloha's turn to step back from an attempt to combine the two into one inter-island airline.

"The People's Airline" celebrated its 55th anniversary in 2002, showing that ingenuity, determination, and pulling together is a winning combination for the long haul. From the free-wheeling days following World War II to the high growth years following Statehood, the story of Aloha Airlines closely mirrors the story of the State of Hawaii.

—*Researched by Suda Ngamviali*

Trans-Pacific Airlines became federally certified on June 5, 1949.

Altres Global Business Services

William Guss founded Altres Global Business Services in 1969 as Labor Services, Inc. Altres is short for Alternative Resources for Business. Guss' family was originally from the state of New York. When his wife developed kidney disease, they moved to Hawaii looking for a warmer climate.

"He came to retire," said son and now-president and CEO, Barron Guss. "But, he got tired of beachcombing. He worked for Kelly Services and got the idea to open Labor Services, providing temporary laborers for construction, offices, and the dock yards."

The advantage of temporary laborers was that companies could avoid all the red tape and paperwork in hiring short-term workers. Guss promised to provide workers on one hour's notice.

The original location of Altres was on Kalakaua Avenue and Uluniu Street in Waikiki near where the Hyatt Regency is now. "When we needed laborers," Guss continued, "dad would raise a flag outside the building. The surfers would see it, and those wanting work would come in."

William Guss founded Altres in 1969 as Labor Services, Inc.

Barron Guss worked for his father in the early days of the business and took over as president in 1993. "Dad made us work for others. When we needed people, he sent us out. I worked for Frito-Lay, a bike shop, and many others. It gave me a real appreciation for work and choices in my life. Dad was a great mentor; more like a business partner. I realized I was 'getting it' when I stopped getting yelled at."

Over the years, Guss launched several other businesses, including Pacific Logistics, Employee Management Corporation, and Factor One Funding Resources. These companies were combined into Altres in 1993. Altres has ten offices in California, Arizona, and Utah in addition to Honolulu, Kona, and Hilo. It employs over 10,000 people. Altres has revenues of over $140 million a year and is growing by 20 percent a year.

Employee leasing is a relatively new industry. "Basically, Altres is the employer for some 200 businesses. They work at the Colony

Surf, Denny's, the Willows, or Diamond Head Grill, but are technically employees of Altres," Guss continued. "We have one payroll instead of 200, one HMSA account, and one employee handbook. It brings efficiency to the workplace and allows companies to focus on their core strengths."

CEO Barron Guss has expanded Altres to California, Arizona, and Utah.

Altres is an innovator in Hawaii. In 1972, they were one of the first businesses to be computerized. All their offices are connected today with fiber-optic cable. "It allows us to use an intercom between offices here and on the mainland. It lowers the barriers to communicating."

Guss is also an inventor. He patented a radio frequency time and attendance device. In the past, workers had to punch a time clock or swipe a card. Guss created a device that attached to an employee's key ring so it wouldn't be forgotten. It contained a microchip the size of a grain of rice. Workers only needed to walk within three feet of the reader for the PBX System and operators to instantly know who was in or out.

American Savings Bank

American Building and Loan was founded in 1925 by a prominent Mormon family from Utah - Floyd S. Bradshaw, his father John F. Bradshaw, brother-in-law Wesley R. Beckstead, and J. Mark Clark.

According to Sara Medeiros, who worked for parent company Hawaiian Electric Industries, American Building and Loan's early customers were members of the Latter Day Saints Church. Mormon missionaries had purchased 6,000 acres in Laie around 1830 with the original aim of establishing cotton and tobacco farms. Large groups of prosperous church members made frequent trips to Hawaii, using the territory as a jumping off point for mission work in the Pacific as well as a place to meet and relax.

Mergers in the 1930s with another Utah bank, Mutual Building and Loan, founded in 1922, created American Mutual Savings and Loan. Its head office was in Utah, and new offices were built at 915 Fort Street, the same site occupied today by American Savings' corporate offices.

During the war years, American Savings branches were established in Kaimuki, Hilo, and many mainland cities. Its customer base in Hawaii included individual accounts largely held by residents of Japanese and Filipino ancestry. Very few people had cars in those days, so American's agents visited the homes of customers to pick up deposits.

In the 1970s, American Savings bought Kauai Savings, Maui Savings and Loan, and Pacific Savings and Loan. In 1986, Hawaiian Electric Industries purchased American Savings for $113 million. The acquisition of First Nationwide Bank's Hawaii branches in 1990 allowed American Savings Bank to extend its network of branches. This led to the acquisition in 1997 of Bank of America's Hawaii branches and its current ranking as the third largest bank in the state.

Before 1984, when Hawaiian Electric Industries purchased the bank, all loans were approved in Utah. Loan papers had to be sent there for management approval.

Today, American Savings has 50 branches throughout the islands. Connie Lau is American Savings Bank's president and CEO.

Amfac

Sea captain Heinrick Hackfeld started what would become American Factors (Amfac) in 1849. Hackfeld was one of many prominent Germans who heard about Hawaii and came to seek his fortune.

The first store, H. Hackfeld and Company, was on Queen Street near Nuuanu Avenue and sold dry goods, hardware, cookware, and other products. Hackfeld and Company imported and sold merchandise to whaling crews and bought whale oil and bone for export to Germany. A second store was later opened on Kauai, and the company soon had six ships

H. Hackfeld and Company *was taken off the building and* American Factors *was put on in 1918. A newer Amfac Building took its place in the 1960s.*

transporting goods between Germany and Hawaii.

Hackfeld and Company helped finance one of the first sugar plantations in the islands, Lihue Plantation, founded by W. L. Lee. The Lihue Plantation was the first to use a ditch irrigation system to move water from wetter areas. Captain Hackfeld left Hawaii for good in 1863 to manage his European business, and the company prospered in Hawaii without him.

During World War I, the Alien Property Act forced Hackfeld to divest their U.S. assets, and they were sold for $7.5 million. In an act of patriotism, the new management renamed the retail side Liberty House and the sugar company became American Factors. In 1966, the name was shortened to Amfac.

In 2001, Amfac/JMB sold the Liberty House chain to Federated Department stores, parent company of Macy's, for $200 million.

At its peak, Amfac was the biggest of the Big Five and grossed over $2 billion annually. That figure would still make it the biggest company in Hawaii today.

Andy's Drive-In

One of Hawaii's top restaurateurs, Andy Wong's first business was a tavern – Leon's at Kailua – in 1955. The 27-year-old called himself a barkeep, says daughter Lori Wong.

While many business owners opened branches of their restaurant in different neighborhoods, such as Zippy's, Ba-Le or L & L, Wong had 17 different restaurants and few knew they were all related. "He thought it was too boring to do the same thing. Multiple restaurants also gave him flexibility with lessors, since he never knew when he would lose a lease," Lori Wong recalls.

Andy's Drive-In opened in 1957 on Oneawa Street in Kailua.

Andy's Drive-in opened in 1957 in Kailua.

Internet Radio Hawaii founder Robert Abbett remembers Andy's for its shrimp burgers and cheese burgers with secret sauce.

"Whenever I meet somebody who grew up in Kailua, they always tell me their favorite Andy's Addiction," Lori Wong muses. "Oyster burgers, shrimp burgers. The Little Red Hen – Henny Penny Chicken. When my brother Byron visited us, he often headed straight to Andy's for a slush shake."

A year later, Wong opened Andy's Ebb Tide and, in 1959, opened

Joe's in Waikiki. The Coral Reef at Ala Moana Center followed in 1960.

He named restaurants for himself (Andy's Drive-In, Andy's Ebb Tide, Andrew's, and Wong's Okazu-ya), his sons (Byron's Drive-In, Byron II, Orson's Bourbon House in Kailua, Orson's Restaurant in Ward Warehouse), and his wife Marian, who he teasingly called a Fishmonger's Wife.

Big Ed's, where ScooZee's was, was a Jewish deli named for his landlord, Ed Hustace, who was tickled to have his name on a restaurant.

"Several of his restaurants were firsts for Hawaii. Orson's Bourbon House in Kailua was Hawaii's first New Orleans style restaurant," says Lori Wong, "Joe's at Waikiki was the first to serve pasta in the islands, in 1959.

"Dad thought restaurants needed strong, masculine names – bear names – to succeed. When mom gave birth to Orson in 1970, dad wanted to name him Boris, which means 'bear.' Mom wanted to name him Scott and refused to leave the hospital with Boris. They compromised on Orson Scott Wong. Orson also means 'bear.'"

Byron works for the Mandarin Oriental Hotel in Hong Kong and Orson lives in Los Angeles.

Andrew Wong was born Yip Yau Wong. How did he get the name Andrew? "Dad used to say he went to the bank and drew

Restaurateur Andy Wong had 17 different restaurants over the years.

and drew and drew."

Wong collected menus from all over the world and styled Hawaii restaurants on those he liked elsewhere. Orson's Seafood Restaurant in Ward Warehouse was modeled after Scoma's famous seafood restaurant at Fisherman's Wharf in San Francisco. Byron II was styled after the House of Lords in Las Vegas.

Wong's Okazu-ya in Ala Moana Center (1966) sounds like a clash of cultures, but Lori says her dad wanted an Okazuya. And it was a gift to his wife, Marian, who managed it.

Andy Wong died in 1985, at 57, of cancer. "On his death bed he asked for a chili burger," Lori recalls. "I take one to his grave occasionally, along with a miniature Johnny Walker."

Lori and Marian Wong continued the tradition and opened several restaurants, notably Oinks at Ward Center, Fishmonger's Wife and Orson's Chowderette at Ala Moana, the Chinese Chuckwagon, and they moved Andrew's to the Executive Center.

On his grave at Diamond Head Mortuary, it says "Andrew Wong. Restaurateur."

Anheuser-Busch

The best selling beer in Hawaii traces its roots to 1262 and the town of Budweis, Czechoslovakia, now called Ceske Budejovice. Over the centuries, Budweis exercised the brewing rights given by King Otakar II. The resulting Budweiser beer became so renowned, the town counted imperial courts and royalty among its customers. It became known as the Beer of Kings. (Budweiser in America is called the King of Beers).

According to Denisa Mylbachrová, Public Relations Manager for Budweiser Budvar, the name "Budweiser Beer" has been used since 1262 when the city was established. Budweiser was not a particular company brand, but designated any beer brewed in the city of Budweis. Since 1925, the company Budweiser Budvar, n.c. has had the right to the name "Budweiser Beer."

Anheuser-Busch traces its American roots to the Bavarian Brewery established in St. Louis, Missouri in 1852. German immigrant Eberhard Anheuser acquired the Bavarian Brewery in 1860.

Adolphus Busch married Anheuser's daughter, Lilly, in 1864 and went to work at his father-in-law's brewery. Busch took over when Anheuser died and built the brewery into an industry leader. He was the first to use pasteurization and refrigeration and the first to bottle beer extensively. These techniques allowed him to market his products nationally while most of his competitors sold locally.

The company introduced Budweiser in 1876. It was America's first national brand and soon earned a reputation for quality. It became the world's best-selling beer brand. Twenty years later, in 1896, Busch developed Michelob, a beer for "connoisseurs." Prohibition, which began in 1919, and the depression were Busch's greatest challenges. August A. Busch Sr. and Adolphus Busch III focused on keeping their workers employed and the company solvent. They introduced new products, including soft drinks, ice cream, baker's yeast, refrigerated cabinets, and trucks.

When Prohibition was repealed in 1933, the company shifted back to its core business – beer. August A. Busch Jr. gave a surprise gift to his father in celebration - a team of Clydesdale horses.

Today, the Budweiser Clydesdales travel 100,000 miles a year to appear in parades, festivals, and rodeos. Six teams of eight horses are stabled around the country. One used to be based in Hawaii.

Anheuser-Busch sells over 100 million barrels of beer a year and brews more than 30 different beers including Budweiser, Michelob, Red Wolf, O'Doul's, Tequiza and Kirin. It operates ten theme parks (including Busch Gardens, Sea World, Water Country USA, Discovery Cove, and Sesame Place). Over 200 employees work for Anheuser-Busch in Hawaii.

Apartment Appearance

The world's premier home cleaning service was founded by Hawaii resident Jed Gaines in 1973. His seven person teams cleaned the homes of 75 Hawaii residents annually, and his senior team was flown all over the world to clean the homes of such celebrities as Henry Mancini, Norman Lear, and Marcia Mason.

An average home would take 2-4 days for his "domestic engineers" to clean, while mansions would often take 2-3 weeks. The cost could top $50,000. What made them so special? Their work was thorough and deep with a staff of highly trained professionals. Every fixture would be taken apart and cleaned. Every book in a book case would be cleaned. All the natural wood would be oiled. Windows would be cleaned, as would sills, tracks, frames, and screens. Tracks would be lubricated.

Appliances would be moved and cleaned under and behind. "You wouldn't believe what we'd find when we pulled appliances from the walls," Gaines said. "Often we found papers that had fallen and were scorched. I'm sure we prevented some fires from deteriorated electrical wiring, and avoided flooding from corroded pipes that were on the verge of bursting."

"Spring cleaning was once an American tradition," Gaines says. "The whole family would pull together and thoroughly clean everything. But, with our busy lives, that tradition has been lost. Apartment Appearance took on that task. Interestingly, there were often noticeable health benefits. We often found that people's allergies were reduced. With deep cleaning, there was a feeling of renewal and many people reported feeling better mentally and physically."

Gaines closed the business in 1997. He had already shifted gears in 1990 when he created the non-profit Read Aloud America. Their mission is helping adults and children discover the joy and enrichment of reading and being read to. His Read Aloud Program (RAP) has reached over 120,000 adults and children in 56 of Hawaii's public schools.

Arakawa's

Small stature is not necessarily a disadvantage. Okinawan immigrant Zempan Arakawa turned it into an advantage.

Arakawa grew up in Onaha Village, Okinawa, the second son in the family. "The first son had to remain and take care of the family," said Goro Arakawa "but my father came to Waipahu at age 19 to seek his fortune and to avoid conscription in the army."

Weighing in at only 96 pounds, he was too small to cut cane. Instead, he was assigned the job of being a water boy to the larger plantation workers at the Oahu Sugar Company.

Zenpan and Ruth Arakawa founded their Waipahu store in 1909.

"Arakawa got to know all the workers and what they needed," says marketing maven Julie Percell. "He ran errands for them. This understanding proved useful when he went into retail a few years later."

He took sewing lessons and learned to make work clothes and *kau-kau* (food) bags as a sideline. "He was moonlighting," says Goro. "In 1909, there was a long strike by the Japanese workers and strikers were kicked out of plantation housing. His five-year contract was up. He didn't want to go back and didn't."

In 1909, Arakawa and his wife, Tsuru (Ruth), opened their first store, Arakawa Shoten, on Waipahu Street. He sold *kau-kau* bags and sewn *tabis* (footwear). The *kau-kau* bags, containing the worker's lunch, were carried into the field. Soon thereafter, he expanded into clothing for the workers and dresses for the women.

His understanding of worker needs helped steer him into the general merchandise business. He made tabis and moved the string from the middle to the side for a more comfortable fit next to the big toe. Goro remembers sewing them like crazy as a kid.

"Dad popularized palaka. It wasn't invented in Hawaii, but he made it famous. Originally blue and white – woven, not printed – we carried 15 different colors and five or six styles." Reporter Susan Kim called palaka the "pattern of the islands." Palaka is the Hawaiian transliteration for "frock," which is an outer garment, according to the late University of Hawaii English professor Alfons Korn.

"Dad tried to accommodate every need. There was no transportation, except for the train. So, for emergencies, Dad bought a Model T and ran a taxi service. We opened the first hotel in Waipahu on the second floor of the building for single men and actors performing at the theatre next door."

Waipahu Depot Road about 1920.

"Dad borrowed money and invested in pineapple in the 1920s, and the depression wiped him out. I think his partners took off, but dad sent me with an envelope to Mr. Cable every month. I remember when he told me that this was the last payment for the pineapple investment."

"When World War II started, we took down the Arakawa Shoten sign and replaced it with Arakawa's Store." Soon after the war, the government condemned Depot Road to widen it. Arakawa's building was torn down. "We moved into the old Magoon Theatre, which had closed due to competition from the Waipahu Theatre. The Waipahu Theatre opened in 1930 and showed talkies. Silent movies were shown at the Magoon Theatre. "You had to walk down a narrow pathway between the buildings to get to us,"

Goro continues. Arakawa's became known as "the big store in the little lane."

The country store became well known for the friendliness of its staff and for having everything a home needed. Furniture, appliances, kitchenware, toys, sporting goods, sundries, clothing, and dry goods would hang from the ceiling, walls, and clutter the aisles. One of their slogans was "if you don't know what you're looking for, you'll find it at Arakawa's."

"Our logo and advertisements all said 'Waipahu' under our name," Goro continues. Our identity was tied to Waipahu. When people thought of Waipahu they thought of Arakawa's. We had many opportunities to open stores in Kapahulu and Kalihi, but we always decided to stay where we were.

"We decided to expand the Waipahu store and get people to come to us. We'd run ads that said 'only 10 minutes from Hickam.' We wanted to make it seem like a pleasant outing. Of course you had to drive like hell to get here in 10 minutes!

"A nephew had a tape recording of animal sounds, and one was a rooster," Goro recalls. "I felt it conveyed that country feeling we embodied, so we used it in all our radio and TV ads. 'Arakawa's on historic Depot Road...cock-a-doodle-do...in Waipahu' we'd say. It was attention-getting. People would smile and joke. We'd say, 'when we crow ... it pays to listen.'"

Arakawa's even had rooster crowing contests live on KCCN radio from their parking lot. "People would come out in rooster costumes and compete for prizes. A *haole* nun from Canada won one year," Goro recalls. "A Portuguese guy was so good, we used him in the ads. Everyone thought it was a real rooster."

Zenpan retired in 1955, and four of his sons (Kazuo, Takemi, Shigemi and Goro), two of his daughters (Leatrice and Joan), and their husbands (Sei Kaneshiro and Horace Taba) took over. "Dad pointed to the four of us brothers (another worked elsewhere) and told us to always work together. 'A single chopstick can be easily broken,' he told us. 'Two would be harder to break. Three would be much harder. Four would be practically impossible.' It's a Japanese proverb."

"My grandfather imbued his ten-member family with a 'united we stand, divided we fall' philosophy," says David Arakawa, who is now Honolulu Corporation Counsel. "He held family meetings whenever major decisions had to be made, such as expansion or land purchases."

David and Cosmo Arakawa model palaka vests and pants in this Arakawa's ad.

In 1959, Zenpan was recognized as Father of the Year by the Honolulu Chamber of Commerce. He also received the George Washington Honor Medal from the Freedom Foundation of Valley Forge.

The family closed the store in 1995 after 85 years in business. "We saw the handwriting on the wall," Goro says. "Wal-Mart and Costco were changing the retail landscape. We were all in our 70s, and retail is a younger person's game."

Karla Brom of the Rainbow Collection said, "Arakawa's closed with dignity and style. It was a very well planned and classy event."

"Hardly a week goes by that someone doesn't tell me how much they miss Arakawa's," Goro says.

Hundreds of years from now, people will trace their roots to the *issei* (first generation Japanese emigrants) who moved to Hawaii and worked the plantations. On Oahu, Arakawa's will always be an integral part of that story.

Assaggio

In Italian, "assaggio" means "to taste, sample, or try." It is also the name of a cheese and is the name of four restaurants on Oahu: In Kailua, Mililani, Hawaii Kai and Ala Moana Center.

Thomas Ky, a native of Vietnam, founded Assaggio in 1991 with his wife Siri. Ky left Vietnam in a crowded fishing boat 20 years before and spent nine months in a Malaysian refugee camp and five years in a New York foster home before moving to Hawaii.

They started Salerno Restaurant in the McCully Shopping Center in 1987 with four others who had worked at Castagnola's in Manoa. George "Cass" Castagnola trained many of our Italian chefs.

Salerno's was a resounding success. Ky wanted to expand, but his partners did not. Ky then sold his interest in Salerno in 1991 and opened the first Assaggio.

In 1992, he opened Paesano, which means "villager" or "fellow countryman," in Manoa where Castagnola's used to be. Billy and Nila Rattanasamay, who are related to the founders, run Paesano.

Assaggio has won the Hale 'Aina award for best Italian restaurant since 1997. Nila credits customer service, hard work, fresh ingredients, and quality control as the keys to their success.

—Researched by Joy Crawford

Aston Hotels and Resorts

Andre Tatibouet's parents started the 14-room Royal Grove Hotel in 1948 in Waikiki. Andre worked in the hotel and later at the Outrigger Hotels.

He started building the Pacific Beach Hotel in 1959 when he was just 19 years old. The banks required he add kitchenettes so the rooms could be sold as apartments if it failed. The kitchenettes became a signature item in his hotels, appealing to budget-minded travelers. Andre operated under the name The Hotel Corporation of the Pacific from 1959 until 1986 when he started looking for a better name.

Tatibouet noticed that many hotel names ended in "ton" like Sheraton and Hilton. He wanted a name that would be at the beginning of the alphabet so it would appear early in the yellow pages and other lists. "A __ ton." He went through all the letters, "b, c, d, e...Afton...Agton...Ahton..." looking for something interesting. Nothing fit until "s." "Aston" had a nice ring, he thought, and "AST" also happened to be Tatibouet's initials.

Sam Slom says, "Andre Tatibouet is one of the most creative, innovative hoteliers in Hawaii history. He has also been a community leader and has lent his name and resources to making Hawaii a better place. He understands business - big and small - and has had a major influence on our community."

Today, Aston is owned by Resort Quest and manages 32 condominiums and hotels in Hawaii.

—Researched by Kathryn Acorda

Auntie Pasto's

A little spaghetti joint, a place where people could get great quality pasta at reasonable prices, in a place everyone could feel at home – that was the idea owner Ed Wary had in 1982 for Auntie Pasto's.

Wary broke all the rules on his road to success. He picked a location without parking which meant problems for customers but lower costs for the restaurant.

Costs of doing business in Hawaii are high – rent, shipping, state-mandated employee benefits, and taxes. Therefore, he felt he had to find ways to cut costs. One way to do this was to have huge menu signs on the walls, instead of printed ones. There is no host or hostess. He bought ten-ounce glasses and served wine, beer, soda, and even milk in them. Going with the bare essentials lowered his costs dramatically.

Wary sees himself as the director of a play, not a restaurateur. He sets the stage, checks the lighting, costumes, servers, and makes sure they have their lines right. How customers are affected through their senses is critical to Auntie Pasto's. Sight, sound, smell, touch, and, of course, taste, were taken into account when the restaurant was created. At the beginning of each meal service, garlic is grilled so that the aroma can waft out onto the street. The place is intentionally loud because Ed wants people to feel free to talk and laugh.

Many Caesar salad affectionados know that Caesar Cardini created the salad in Tijuana, Mexico in 1924. Auntie Pasto's uses his original recipe, given to Ed by Caesar's granddaughter Felicia. That is why Ed calls it the "Original Caesar."

Many of the recipes come from Ed's mother who lives in New England. When she visits Hawaii each winter, she spends time in the kitchen preparing soups, casseroles, and stuffed pastas.

The name Auntie Pasto's was a clever play on words, Wary felt. However, when he tried to register it, he found there were seven restaurants with the same name on the mainland. He had to get permission from all, and one initially resisted. The logo uses an elementary school font.

In 2000, Wary opened a second Auntie Pasto's on Kapahulu. He has licensed four more on the mainland and opened two Dixie Grills. Wary also owns Eddie's Burgers & Frozen Custard on Waialae Avenue and a California vineyard.

—Researched by Natalie Mei Lau

Bank of Hawaii

Bank of Hawaii could be the largest company in Hawaii founded by a competitor's disgruntled customers. The Bank of Bishop & Company, the predecessor of First Hawaiian Bank, denied sugar producer Castle & Cooke a loan and bounced a $54 check in 1896.

When their financial situation improved, Charles M. Cooke, his five sons, Peter Cushman Jones, Joseph Ballard Atherton, and several others showed up at the Bishop & Company bank on December 17, 1897 with a wheelbarrow and withdrew all of their funds in gold.

The group loaded the gold coins into the wheelbarrow and paraded up and down the streets of downtown Honolulu, finally stopping two blocks away, on Fort and Merchant, which became the site of the first Bank of Hawaii.

In a touch of irony, the building chosen for the bank's third location, on the Ewa-mauka corner of King and Bishop Streets, was formerly the home of First Hawaiian Bank founder Charles Reed Bishop and Bernice Pauahi, called "Haleakala."

Peter Cushman Jones was the bank's first president. Joseph Ballard Atherton was vice-president; his son, Edwin Jones was cashier; and Clarence Hyde

Peter Cushman Jones was a founder and first president of Bank of Hawaii.

Cooke was secretary and receiving teller. With the exception of P.C. Jones, the Bank's officers were in their early twenties, and the new bank soon became known as "The Kindergarten Bank."

Bank of Hawaii added branches around the islands, and in 1934 had the distinction of being the first in Hawaii to be robbed. The Paia, Maui branch was held up by two brothers from Lahaina, David and George Wong. Both were captured a few hours later with the $979 they had stolen. The next bank robbery in the islands didn't occur for another 20 years.

Maui-born Wilson P. Cannon, Jr. served as Bank Of Hawaii president from 1974 to 1980 and was one of the most beloved in the community. Cannon wore aloha shirts daily when other bankers wore coats and ties. He also spent much of his time outside the bank, serving on various non-profit committees.

Anna Derby Blackwell, a granddaughter of Charles M. Cooke, fondly remembers calling him one day. "I was writing a story for the *Honolulu Beacon* and phoned him. 'Willy,' I said,

Wilson Cannon joined the bank in 1941 and became president in 1972.

and then sang 'There's a longing in my heart for the Dear Old Valley Isle.' What's the next line? I can't remember!

" 'And the spirit in my heart will never die,' he sang back, and we finished the song together. 'Thank you very much,' I said. 'You're welcome!' he replied, and we hung up.

"Later, the day the story appeared, we met at a cocktail party. Cannon said there had been a banker from New York in his office at the time, and he was kind of surprised when I started singing into the phone!"

Bank of Hawaii ran one of the longest and most memorable ad campaigns in Hawaii history, featuring Ben and Gloria

Haleakala – Charles and Bernice Pauahi Bishop's home on King near what is now Bishop Street became Bankoh's third location in a touch of irony since Bishop was their competitor.

Tamashiro as Harry and Myra. They made more than 60 commercials over five years. "Ben came in to read for a commercial in 1985," said former Bankoh advertising director Janice Flick. "The woman he was supposed to read with didn't show up. Ben said his wife, Gloria, was outside in the car, and they had practiced together. We brought her in just so we could see Ben read his part.

"The chemistry between them was so superb, they were both hired. They were so honest, so down to earth," said Starr Siegel advertising executive, David Koch. "The bank had ten to 15 different messages to deliver, from their investment services to their Access Card, and Harry and Myra worked for all of them."

"Everyone seemed to be having fun with the ads," Ben said. "Perhaps, I liked best the comment of a woman who stopped me recently while I was on my usual early morning four-mile walk through Manoa Valley. Gushing over Harry, she said 'You are so representative of us!' That could be a fitting reflection of a boy from the country."

—Researched by Salig Chada

Baskin-Robbins

Most baby boomers remember when they were kids that ice cream came in just three flavors: chocolate, vanilla and strawberry. Every now and then, a sherbet or other flavor would pop up, but three was often it.

After World War II, two brothers-in-law, Burt Baskins and Irv Robbins, opened an ice cream store with 31 choices, one for each day of the month. Started in 1945, the store was originally named "Snowbird." The next year, the name was changed to Baskin-Robbins. When the first franchise opened in Hawaii in Puck's Alley in the 1980s, the wait for service was often 45 minutes.

Today, there are 5,600 Baskin-Robbins stores in over 60 countries, and sales top $1 billion a year. They've developed nearly 1,000 flavors of ice cream. There are 30 Baskin-Robbins in Hawaii.

—Researched by Emily Huang

Benihana

Benihana may be the most successful Japanese restaurant in the U.S., having prepared over 100 million meals. It began as a four-table Japanese restaurant on New York's West Side in 1964.

The company says that when the first Benihana opened, Japanese cuisine was unknown in the United States, and the idea of having a chef prepare a meal at your table was completely unheard of. Blending exotic Japanese dishes with a dazzling chef performance may have been a radical idea, but it was the recipe for success at Benihana.

By bringing Japanese food into the mainstream and pioneering its "eatertainment" style of presentation, Benihana has also paved the way in America for the popularity of other Japanese cooking styles and food products.

Yunosuke Aoki, a popular Japanese entertainer, and his wife Katsu opened a small coffee shop in Tokyo after World War II. A red flower, the benihana, sprouting around the neighborhood, gave the restaurant its name. Aoki combined good food with entertainment. The eldest son, Hiroaki, also grasped the important lesson of offering guests something out of the ordinary, and he couldn't help but inherit his father's appreciation for "theatrics."

Hiroaki moved to the U.S. in 1960 and adopted the name Rocky. Rocky scraped together enough money to finance his first four-table restaurant on New York's W. 56th Street.

Food would be prepared right at the table "teppan-yaki" style. *Teppan* meaning "steel grill" and *yaki* meaning "broiled" with dazzling effects by highly trained chefs. Rocky also believed that because the restaurant was near Broadway, the showmanship of the chefs was extremely important. Beef, chicken, and shrimp would be the stars of the menu, all prepared "hibachi-style," an American-style term for "teppan-yaki" cooking.

Guests at the communal tables would place their orders with the chef and watch in amazement as these items were sliced, diced, and flipped into the air. The timing in cooking was critical. These different ingredients had to be ready to serve to the guests simultaneously.

In 1964, Benihana of Tokyo was only serving one or two customers a day. Aoki family members moonlighted at other restaurants just to pay the bills. However, six months after the restaurant opened, an enthusiastic review by Clementine Paddleford, legendary restaurant critic of the New York Herald-Tribune, reversed the trend for good. New Yorkers flocked to Benihana, and Rocky Aoki suddenly found himself in the position of having to turn dining guests away. Aoki expanded, opening in Waikiki in 1971. Today there are over 75 Benihanas worldwide.

Da Big Kahuna

It began in an unlikely location on the fringe of the Mapunapuna industrial area, and moved to the Airport Retail Center in 2007. Big Kahuna has become an icon in Honolulu. The new location still has the little green shack feel, with surfboards, bamboo, thatched roofing and a reputation for friendliness and an aloha spirit. Like most successful 'holes in the wall' it is known far and wide among locals, military and tourists.

Their pizzas and sandwiches are constantly making the trek to outer islands and into the Pacific rim area. Its popularity is attributable to its owner Kelly Suchotzki, who started the business in 1994. "No compromising on quality or quantity" is her promise to customers and it shows.

Their motto "da buggas are loaded" is consistent. Pizza and bread dough is made from scratch, and baked daily for the massive sandwiches. They've sold 5 million garlic cheese balls - their signature dish. The balls are baked to order in garlic butter and smothered in cheese. Big Kahuna is an island favorite.

— Researched by Raquel De La Garza

Big Save Supermarkets

The Kawakami family dates the history of its Big Save Supermarkets to much earlier than 1925 when their first store opened in Waimea, Kauai. They trace their roots to Fukuoka Prefecture in Kyushu, Japan and to Fukujiro and Kiyo Kawakami, simple rural farmers.

Japan at the turn of the 20th century was a poor country, struggling to catch up with the west after 200 years of isolation under the Shogunal feudal regime.

Their eldest son, Fukutaro Kawakami, emigrated to Hawaii around 1904. Once in Hawaii, he saw the opportunities America offered and worked to bring his brothers Sakuichi and Saburo (called "H.S.") here. Fukutaro sent H.S., who was just 12 at the time, to Mid-Pacific Institute, to get an American education.

H.S. worked at the Kunikiyo Store on Fort Street to support

himself while at school and was inspired to go into retailing upon graduation in 1922. He returned to Kauai and worked at the Makaweli Plantation store for three years and then opened his own store in Waimea around 1925. He founded the store with $1,000 he had saved, and received a $2,000 loan from Fukutaro and $1,000 from close family friends.

Business prospered with H.S. and Fukutaro working together, and soon they opened stores in Lihue and Kapaa. In 1933, Fukutaro opened a 20 by 40-foot store in Hanapepe, naming it the N. F. Kawakami Store for his son Norito (the late First Circuit Court Judge Norito Kawakami) and himself.

In 1955, Alexander & Baldwin built the Eleele Shopping Center and N. F. Kawakami opened a grocery/variety store there. It was the first "cash and carry" store on Kauai. Soon after, Lihue and Kapaa branches opened, the latter in partnership with Minoru Furugen.

In 1958, N. F. Kawakami, H. S. Kawakami, and Minoru Furugen were consolidated into one corporation, Big Save, Inc. In 1984, H. S.'s son Charles Kawakami took over and expanded the family business and diversified into neighborhood mini marts.

Big Save today includes Big Save Supermarkets, Kauai Kitchens, Resort Gift Shops, Menehune Food Marts, Subway Sandwiches, a Shell Super Service and Mini Mart, and the Kauai Kookie Kompany. The company employs over 500 people in its various ventures.

"We're still a local community-oriented company," says Charles Kawakami, "and our base of business is the local population. We view the tourists as the topping on the cake. We must always take care of the local people."

Borders Books and Music

First opening in Waikele in 1994, Borders Books and Music has reshaped the way bookstores do business in Hawaii. From small cramped stores to a spacious place to relax and read, Borders has transformed the industry in Hawaii. A second store at Ward Center opened in 1995.

Tom and Louis Borders opened the first store in Ann Arbor, Michigan in 1971. The Ann Arbor store was so successful that the Borders brothers decided to open more stores in suburban markets. The concept worked. Borders was a hit everywhere it opened.

In the early 1990s, Borders began selling music in addition to books. As the inventory and the company expanded, competitors and investors took serious notice, and the Borders brothers decided to go national. At the same time, large book chains started emulating the Borders concept.

Borders is now one of the nation's leading book and music retailers with nearly 300 stores.

—Researched by Larson Kiyabu

Boulevard Saimin

Toshiaki Tanaka was the oldest of eight children. When his father passed away in 1956, he had to feed his brothers, sisters, mother, and his own three kids. The family florist shop at Dillingham Boulevard and McNeil Street was undependable, so he started a saimin shop inside with just $200.

"My grandma knew a couple that were retiring," says daughter Joan Watanabe, "and they gave my dad the recipes for their saimin. The Nomiyama's gave us their secrets. And that's why it's so good. It's all made from scratch."

In 1960, the lease was up and they moved to their current site at 1425 Dillingham. "We were the first tenant in the building, and expanded four times. Mom was always concerned but dad felt we should take the chance. The area was pretty undeveloped back then. I remember there was a park where Popeye's Chicken is now."

"Originally we just served saimin, but dad liked the teri beef at Rainbow Drive-In and so we added that to the menu. The top seller is the Boulevard Special Saimin that comes with two shrimp tempura."

McDonald's kingpin, Roy Kroc, came into the shop many years ago with several men in black suits to have saimin. A couple of months later, McDonald's started serving saimin locally. Was Boulevard Saimin the inspiration for McDonald's saimin? Maybe!

Toshiaki retired about ten years ago. "Do you want this gold mine?" he jokingly asked his three daughters. "Joyce was on the mainland, but Lynn Yagi and I took over," Joan continued.

Patsy Mink could often be found at Boulevard Saimin, as could Senator Inouye, Governor Waihee, Loyal Garner and the Cazimeros. "People often get off airplanes and make a bee-line to Boulevard Saimin on the way home. They're so hungry for our saimin."

Buzz's Original Steakhouse

Former Canlis maitre d' Buzz Schneider opened Buzz's Steak and Lobster in 1962 in Waikiki. He left the restaurant to his partners, and a year later, bought out the Lords of Lanikai restaurant where he started Buzz's Original Steakhouse Kailua in 1963.

The restaurant was successful, and Buzz decided to expand to Aiea in 1965. In 1975, they moved to their present location at Kuahao Place in Pearl City. Buzz Schneider sold out to his first wife Barbara in 1986 and retired to the Big Island.

If you look closely at Buzz's logo, you can see six paddlers in a canoe under the name. This is because many paddlers worked at Buzz's.

John Reuben McIntosh, who founded the Yum Yum Tree, based his Reuben's chain on Buzz's, liking its simple menu and casual setting.

—Researched by Dan Izawa

C. Brewer

Hawaii's oldest company and the oldest operating American corporation west of the Rocky Mountains, C. Brewer traces its beginning to 1826 – over 175 years ago. The company was founded by James Hunnewell, second mate aboard the Thaddeus, which brought the original missionaries to Hawaii in 1820.

Hunnewell returned to Hawaii in 1826 with 50 barrels of merchandise and rum. He established a trading business on Fort Street on an acre-sized lot that had four thatched roofed huts on it.

Honolulu then was a dry and dusty town with mostly grass huts. Wooden buildings were few and far between, and the streets were more like paths. However, Hunnewell felt Hawaii was the crossroads of the Pacific. He would bring in coffee, tea, sugar, chocolates, pork, beef, spices, hardware, candles, and other goods the islands needed. He would also sell sandalwood and furs from the West Coast to China.

Being first was not easy, but eventually the business grew and Hunnewell amassed a considerable fortune. His $5,000 investment grew to $67,000.

Hunnewell was a founding trustee of Punahou School. Hunnewell Street nearby is named in his honor. He returned to Charleston, Massachusetts and left the business to his second in command, Henry Pierce.

Hunnewell lived until 1869, overseeing a shipping business that spread around half the globe, from Boston to Honolulu and foreign ports. Pierce soon involved sea captain Charles Brewer in the business, and the two were a strong team.

Under Brewer, the store supplied whaling ships, but when oil was discovered in Pennsylvania in 1859, whaling in Hawaii died out. Sugar cane became the dominant force in Hawaii's economy. The passage of the 1876 Reciprocity Treaty, which allowed duty free sugar exports to the United States, solidified sugar's importance to Hawaii. While over 150 companies rushed into the sugar business, eventual control went to the Big Five (C. Brewer, Castle & Cooke, Amfac, Alexander & Baldwin and Theo. H. Davies), which dominated the industry for almost 100 years.

Competition from cheaper foreign growers eventually doomed sugar production in Hawaii, where costs were high, and the Big Five scrambled into other ventures. C. Brewer moved into diversified agriculture with macadamia nuts, coffee, and guava taking the lead.

Recently, President J.W.A. "Doc" Buyers moved the headquarters to Hilo, transforming the publicly owned company into a private one. The new company, called C. Brewer Enterprises, focuses on the wellness industry. They envision long-term care facilities for older people, growing healthy crops, and developing a wellness school.

C. S. Wo

"Many people think our family name is Wo," President Robert "Bub" Wo, Jr. told us. "But Wo is not a Chinese surname. My grandfather's name was Ching Sing Wo. Ching was his surname. Wo was his first name. My dad, Bob Wo, Sr. was a Ching. We changed the family name to Wo in the 1950s."

Founder Ching Sing Wo

Ching Sing Wo grew up on Kauai, saved his money, and opened up a general merchandise store on King and Smith Streets in 1909 named C.S. Wo and Brother. Ching Sing Wo retired in 1948 and turned the business over to his sons, Jim and Bob Wo, who had just graduated from college. They focused the business on furniture. "Dad wanted us to be best at one thing. If not, we'd have probably stayed a mom and pop store." The company name shifted to C. S. Wo and Sons.

A year later, a major challenge faced the company. A dock strike in 1949 shut down shipping to Hawaii for six months. C. S. Wo could not bring in furniture, so they bought timber and started manufacturing their own furniture here in Hawaii. "That worked for a while, but Hawaii really didn't have the raw materials and skilled labor needed."

In 1957, while Japan was still recovering from World War II, Bob Wo, Sr. launched a joint venture with a company there. The new company was called Teakwood Holdings. "They took U.S. designs to Asia and made the furniture to our specifications. With the advent of containerized shipping, it became easy to bring them into the state."

In 1967, manufacturing moved to Taiwan and later Singapore. Costs had risen in Japan, and they had priced themselves out of the market. Teakwood Holdings and its marketing arm, Universal Furniture, were the first to recognize Asia's potential, and that realization made them one of the top ten largest furniture manufacturers in the world.

Income from Universal Furniture, which was bought out by an even larger company, allowed the Wo's to ease the transition to the third generation. Instead of turning the company over to three families, Bob Wo's five sons stayed with the company, and Jim and Bill's sons were bought out.

First C.S. Wo and Brother store on King Street downtown. Ching Sing Wo wears the white suit.

Bob and Jim, who had desks five feet apart for almost 40 years, moved their office off-site so staff would have to go through Bub Wo, Jr. who became president and CEO of the neighbor island stores. Wendell Wo became vice president in charge of C. S. Wo Gallery, Furnitureland, and Z-Interiors.

Mike Wo became vice president over HomeWorld, Slumberworld, and La-Z-Boy Furniture Gallery. Bennett Wo became vice president of Sleepland USA and distribution operations. Scott Wo, who earned a Ph.D in economics became overseer of the company's investment portfolio with his father. Bob Wo Sr. became chairman and handles long range planning.

"Was BJ Furniture named for brothers Bob and Jim Wo?" "It has lots of meanings," Bub Wo Jr. replied. "It could have been Bob and Jim. Or, it could have been for my mother, Betty Jane. Jim's wife is Juanita. We also had a dog named BJ, but he came later. BJ is ambiguous. It has lots of meanings."

Bub got his name from his aunt. "With two Roberts, it was confusing. My auntie suggested Bub and it stuck."

As the big box retailers started moving to Hawaii, C. S. Wo put their own superstore together to fend them off. The result, in 1994, was HomeWorld. However, while it was a success in keeping big box furniture retailers out, it was not a hit with the public.

The third generation now manages the stores. From left: Bub, Wendell, Michael, Bennett and Scott Wo.

Unlike many family-owned businesses that were slow to change, C. S. Wo was bold. HomeWorld refocused on mid-priced goods, while C. S. Wo Gallery, representing the upper end of the market, was resurrected.

C. S. Wo today operates under seven different divisions: C. S. Wo Gallery; HomeWorld; Furnitureland, with lower to mid-priced lines; Sleepland USA; Slumberworld; Z-Interiors, with low to mid-priced contemporary furniture, and La-Z-Boy Furniture Gallery.

Their 17 stores on Oahu, Maui, and the Big Island gross over $50 million a year. Former store names, including BJ Furniture, the Marsh Furniture Mart, Scandinavian Gallery, and Basic Concepts, have been retired.

Café 100

Café 100 got its start in the trenches of Italy during World War II, where Richard Seiji Miyashiro, serving in the 100th Infantry Battalion, learned to cook. After the war, in January 1946, Richard opened Café 100 as a memorial to the men of the 100th who did not return home.

Café 100 survived the April 1, 1946 tidal wave with little water damage, but the 1960 tidal wave was more destructive. "It demolished us completely," said daughter Gloria Kobayashi. "We lived in a house in the back. The tidal wave picked up the house and deposited it a block away. We were all inside."

Many businesses in Waiakea Town were damaged or destroyed by the 1960 tidal wave including Suisan, KTA, I. Kitagawa (now Kamaaina Motors), and Sure Save.

"Dad bought Naomi's Fountain after the tsunami," Kobayashi continued. "Mrs. Higa, the former owner, had made a dish called a Loco Moco, which was a bowl with rice, a hamburger patty, an egg, and gravy. Loco Moco's were actually invented by the Lincoln Wreckers baseball team who were named because they used to hang out at the Lincoln Grill. They wanted something cheap and filling. The name 'loco moco' was chosen because it rhymed."

Café 100 has patented and refined the Loco Moco and now makes over 20 different varieties.

Café 100 founder Richard Miyashiro named his café for his compatriots in the 100th Infantry Battalion who did not come home.

Café Sistina

"In Italy, we have a great passion for food," says Sergio Mitrotti, owner of Café Sistina. He learned to cook from his grandmother, mother, and aunts.

Sistina is named for the Sistine Chapel at the Vatican, and Mitrotti has beautifully painted the walls and ceiling with large frescos from the Chapel. Above the bar is a breathtaking scene of God and Adam touching fingers, 35 feet long.

Sergio received a Masters of Arts degree and began working as a graphic artist. "Art," he believes, "is feeling with your eyes, and food is feeling with your mouth and taste buds."

He moved to America when he was 33 years old and opened a clothing store in Beverly Hills with his brother. The store provided Italian clothing to the cast of shows and movies such as *Miami Vice* and *American Gigolo*.

Even though he was busy with the store, he often found himself cooking for parties. His food won rave reviews, and he was encouraged to pursue it professionally.

Café Cambio on Kapiolani Boulevard, was Sergio's first restaurant. It was named after a famous restaurant in Turin, Italy. After his divorce in 1988, he moved to the First Interstate Building and opened Café Sistina, a marriage of food and art.

—Researched by Nunzio Taranto and Yvonne Mia

Castle & Cooke

Few families have had as much positive impact on the islands as the Castles and Cookes. The company and descendents of the founders have been involved in dozens of companies, schools and communities.

Castle & Cooke started, owned, or supported the Ewa Plantation, Waialua Sugar Company, Kohala Sugar, Dole Foods, Hawaiian Tuna Packers, Standard Fruit, the Lodge at Koele, and the Manele Bay Hotel. They founded or supported the Hawaiian Chiefs' Children's School (now Royal School) and Punahou School. They built Mililani Town and Royal Kunia.

It all started when Samuel Northrup Castle and Amos Starr Cooke arrived in Hawaii in 1837 as lay members of a missionary group from Boston. Castle was the bookkeeper of the depository. Cooke and his wife started and ran the Chiefs' Children's School for its first ten years, educating the children of royalty.

In 1850, Cooke joined Castle at the depository where the mission had lost financial support from the Commission Board in Boston. Castle and Cooke formed a partnership and opened a downtown store and sold "ink powder, quills, whiffle trees, hooped skirts, corsets, blasting powder, hair tonic, spelling books, cod fish, sewing machines, kerosene, and Dr. Jayne's celebrated family medicines," according to company documents.

One day a rumor spread that Castle & Cooke was getting into

the liquor business, which was unheard of for missionaries. A missionary delegation was quickly sent to investigate. Castle not only admitted to having alcohol on hand but also led them to a storage room and pointed it out. "There it is in the leaky cask," Castle said defiantly. "If you doubt my word, taste it." One of the missionaries touched his finger to the seepage on the side of the cask and winced as he licked his finger and confirmed Castle's admission.

"Why don't you take the whole cask as evidence," Castle suggested. "Be sure to return it to us as we are holding it for transshipment to Boston. It contains the preserved body of Captain Blank who died in Micronesia." The delegation fled the premises.

Sugar was beginning to be the mainstay of the economy, and in 1858, the company made its first investment. Later, investments were also made in sailing vessels to carry sugar to the mainland.

Tremendous amounts of water were required for sugar production. Castle & Cooke built the Wahiawa reservoir in 1904. Waialua, Kohala, and the Ewa plantation were a few of their sugar ventures.

Amos Cooke died in 1871. Castle continued with the business with help from J. B. Atherton. Atherton later married one of Cooke's daughters, and when Castle died in 1894, became company president.

Castle & Cooke took over management of James Dole's Hawaiian Pineapple Company when the Depression caused sales to drop.

The Big Five were the most powerful companies in Hawaii when sugar cane dominated the economy, but they were all forced to diversify as its influence waned. Castle & Cooke turned to real estate, fresh fruits and vegetables, and hotels. They owned Hawaiian Tuna Packers, Castle & Cooke Terminals and several other companies.

Mililani Town and Royal Kunia are two of its Hawaii developments, and there are many more on the mainland. In 1991, Castle & Cooke changed its name to Dole Food Company and Castle & Cooke became Dole's real estate subsidiary.

Castle & Cooke owns 98% of Lanai and turned the island into one of the world's leading tourist destinations, building the Lodge at Koele in 1990 and the Manele Bay Hotel in 1991. David Murdock took Castle & Cooke private in 2000.

Beyond the accomplishments of the company, Samuel Castle, Amos Cooke, and their descendents helped found or played substantial roles with the Oahu Railway & Land Company, Honolulu Rapid Transit, Bank of Hawaii, Gasco, Lewers & Cooke, Molokai Ranch, Castle High School, Hanahauoli School, the University of Hawaii, Castle Medical Center, The Waikiki Aquarium, and the Honolulu Academy of Arts. Foundations started by the families have donated millions to worthy causes in the state.

—Researched by M. J. Quenga

Central Pacific Bank

In the early 1950's, much of life in Hawaii was controlled by the large landowners that ran the Island's plantation-based agricultural economy. Bishop Bank (now First Hawaiian) and Bank of Hawaii reflected the interests of this dominant economic minority who controlled 90% of Hawaii's capital assets. For the many immigrant-laborers struggling to leave the plantations to make a better life for their families, it was nearly impossible to obtain financing for starting a business or buying a home.

A group of young *nisei* World War II veterans of the 442nd and 100th Battalions, and Military Intelligence Service, including Daniel K. Inouye, Sakae Takahashi, Elton Sakamoto and others, refused to accept the social inequities and economic status quo of the post-WW II period. They started meeting regularly at Ala Moana Beach Park with their 50-cent plate lunches to plan the materialization of their new dream – creating a bank that would serve all of the people of Hawaii. The name "Central Pacific Bank" was an extension of Pacific Bank, a Japanese-managed bank that was shut down when the war started.

Owning not much more than their dream and the "Go For Broke" spirit that earned them the distinction of true heroes during WW II, this group of young nisei veterans turned to the community for support. To their surprise, the grassroots campaign to raise capital was met with such overwhelming support throughout the state, that $1 million was raised in the first effort.

The next hurdle was to convince the State Bank Examiner, at a hearing required by statute, that a need existed for a new bank. The principal argument was that the Chinese community, which represented 10-15% of the total population, had two banks – Liberty Bank and American Security Bank. The Japanese community, which represented 40% of the total population, had none.

The three Japanese-managed banks that operated before the war were all shut down by the Office of the Alien Property Custodian after the bombing of Pearl Harbor.

In dire need of a qualified bank manager, the founding fathers of Central Pacific Bank embarked on a frustrating search that eventually extended to the mainland. Just when the situation became bleak, they had a stroke of luck in meeting an advisor from Sumitomo Bank (of Japan). Touched by the valiant efforts of the group, Sumitomo Bank agreed to "loan" someone to help the fledgling bank in Hawaii. Kazuo Ishii, who had just established the Sumitomo Bank of California a year before, arrived in Hawaii in May 1953. He quickly assembled a local management team and established an operating system for the bank. His temporary assignment eventually turned into being the first President and CEO of Central Pacific Bank. The Bank finally opened for business on February 15, 1954 on the corner of King and Smith Streets, and was the first bank to open in Hawaii since 1935.

The first year of business generated over $5 million in deposits, $6.4 million in assets, and a very small profit. Central Pacific Bank has been profitable every year since then, attaining $33.3 million in net income, $1.6 billion in deposits, $2.0 billion in assets and 24 branch offices in 2002. The bank started paying dividends to its shareholders from the third year of operations and has never failed to do so ever since. The Sumitomo "connection" was so successful that the next 2 CEO's of the Bank were seasoned executives from the Sumitomo Bank, Ltd. system – Yoshiharu Satoh and Joichi Saito.

It wasn't until January 2002 that the first non-Sumitomo executive was recruited to take over the reigns as CEO of Central Pacific Bank. Clint Arnoldus, a highly regarded 28-year banking veteran in the industry was selected over 300+ candidates for the position. In a period of one year, the new CEO took the bank to unprecedented levels - listing its stock on the prestigious New York Stock Exchange, increasing shareholder value significantly, establishing top-notch trust, investment and asset management services, increasing brand awareness through bold marketing initiatives, and being recognized by the American Banking Association's Banking Journal as the 23rd best performing bank in the nation. From it's humble beginnings, conceived under the trees at Ala Moana Beach Park nearly 50 years ago, the "people's bank" has grown to be the third largest commercial bank in Hawaii.

Wayne Kirihara, CPB spokesman, points out that "for those loyal supporters who invested their $35 per share in this venture 50 years ago, with the multiple stock splits that have occurred over time, they would now be holding 70.4 shares of stock for every one share they originally purchased. This is about a 5,200% return on their investment based on today's CPB stock price."

Central Union Church

In 1833, The American Seamen's Friend Society established the Seamen's Bethel on the Honolulu waterfront to give sailors from whaling and trading ships a place to go besides saloons.

A split in 1852 led to the creation of the Bethel Union Church and the Fort Street Church, whose English Day School eventually became McKinley High School. After a waterfront fire destroyed the Seamen's Bethel in 1886, the two merged again to form Central Union Church on Richards Street, on what is now the grounds of the State Capitol across from Washington Place.

Central Union Church on Richards and Beretania Streets, now the grounds of the State Capitol. When it moved to its present site in 1924, Schuman Carriage moved in.

Thirty years of growth caused Central Union's then-pastor, Dr. Albert Palmer, to look for a bigger location. He picked the former residence and dairy farm of prominent businessman B.F. Dillingham and his widow, Emma, a member of the church.

The 8-acre site at Punahou and Beretania streets was called "Woodlawn" by the Dillingham family. The church, designed in traditional New England style, was completed in 1924.

A dozen Honolulu churches, schools and organizations trace their roots back to the Seaman's Bethel Church, including Mid-Pacific Institute, La Pietra, The Fort Street Chinese Church, Palolo Chinese Home, and Kuakini Medical Center.

The Chamber of Commerce of Hawaii

On October 15, 2003, the Chamber of Commerce celebrated 153 years of existence, making it Hawaii's oldest business organization. It was involved in most of the major events that shaped the Kingdom, the Territory, and the State of Hawaii.

It all started in 1850, in the store of Starkey, Janion and Company, which later became Theo. H. Davies & Company, where merchants, sugar growers, ship owners, attorneys, and others met to draft a constitution. The annual dues were $25.

The Chamber's first role in Hawaii was helping to create a common monetary system in the Kingdom. Originally, the early Hawaiians paid in goods and services. Whalers and traders landing in Hawaii came from many countries and carried coins of different sizes and denominations. By 1850, more than 50 different gold coins and 100 different silver coins were in circulation.

Individual merchants determined the relative value of each coin. A particular coin might be more or less valuable at neighboring stores. The result was chaos. One of the Chamber's first acts was to determine a fixed rate for the different coins. In 1859, a table was established that was based on the exchange rates of gold coins used by San Francisco merchants.

The Chamber played an important role in eliminating tariffs on trade with the United States, making Hawaii's sugar competitively priced. The price Hawaii paid for the 1876 Reciprocity Treaty was the promised use of Pearl Harbor for the U.S. Navy. Forty years later, in 1907, it was a Chamber survey that paved the way for dredging the shallow Pearl River, as it was then called, and building a naval station there.

Robert Crichton Wyllie was one of the main founders of the Chamber of Commerce of Honolulu in 1850.

In the wake of a bubonic plague epidemic in 1899, the Chamber saw public health as one of its key issues and lobbied for the filtration of water, better sewage treatment, and the systematic destruction of garbage. When a fire destroyed 38 acres in Chinatown in January 1900, and left 4,000 people homeless, the Chamber raised funds to compensate the victims and worked to secure federal assistance from Congress.

The Chamber of Commerce of Hawaii has, through the years, helped to create important organizations that today are independent, such as the Hawaii Sugar Planters Association (1892), the Retail Merchants of Hawaii (1901), the Hawaii Visitors Bureau (1902), the Aloha United Way (1919), and just before Pearl Harbor was bombed, the Blood Bank of Hawaii (1941).

The Chamber also supported the founding of the Hawaiian Statehood Commission, Crime Stoppers (1981), and the Mental Health Association (1937). In 1945, the Better Business Bureau and the Tax Foundation of Hawaii became independent agencies.

Cultural programs of the Chamber included the 1935 launch of the famous radio program, *Hawaii Calls*, which was produced by the Hawaii Visitor's Bureau. The Merrie Monarch Festival developed out of a Chamber of Commerce promotion to help Hilo recover from the 1960 tsunami.

The Chamber can also be thanked for keeping Hawaii free of rabies and snakes through its support of a Territorial Board of Agriculture and Forestry.

Chamber President Jim Tollefson says that "the evolution of business in Hawaii has involved adaptation, adjustment, innovation and profound change in the way we do business and view business. In order to remain vital, vigorous and relevant, the Chamber continues to reinvent itself so that we provide essential value, offer products and services, and function in ways that are fresh and relevant for our members."

—Researched by Elie Sauma

Charley's Taxi

Charley's Taxi is Hawaii's oldest taxi service. "We may even be Hawaii's oldest transportation company," said President Dale Evans. "My dad started Charley's in 1938."

Today, Charley's is recognized as the premier taxi company in Hawaii. By focusing on training for its drivers and insisting on a code of behavior, uniforms, and late model vehicles, Charley's is able to deliver excellent, consistent service to visitors and local people alike. Charley's has won awards from the Hawaii Hotel

Association, the Honolulu City Council, and the Hilton Hawaiian Village for setting new standards in the taxi industry.

Charley's Taxi has over 400 drivers and carries two million passengers a year. It is the only taxi company in the United States to provide 24-hour Japanese-speaking dispatch service. "It is costly to do that, but having a separate dispatch for Japanese clientele is one of our specialties," Evans says.

Local residents may not know that Charley's runs the Medicab program. This provides door-to-door taxi service for the elderly and disabled. The drivers come to the door, and escort the customer to the cab; they drive them to their destination, escort them to the doctor's office, or back home. For this, the drivers charge the normal fare plus three dollars — much cheaper than hiring an aide.

Charley was Hana-born Charles S. Morita, who founded Charley's Taxi in 1938 with his wife, Helen Hifumi Hirahara. Charley's parents, immigrants from Japan, worked on a plantation in Paia, Maui. Charley's sister ran Paia Liquor Store, and his half-sister, Mrs. Koja, was the blind vendor at the Kahului Airport for decades until the 1980s.

During World War II, Charley added a car rental business called Charley's U-Drive at Schofield Barracks. Charley also opened a photo studio during the war called Chick's Photo Studio, which was more successful than the taxi and car rental business. They had a studio on Alakea Street, and the soldiers and sailors used to wait in long lines to have pictures taken to send back to their families. "Dad ran the photo studio, and Mom ran the taxi and car rental," Dale continued.

On Friday and Saturday nights in the 1940s and 1950s, some of the cab drivers gathered together between fares to play music at their stand on King and Richards Streets, where the Kamamalu Building now stands.

A young, Roosevelt High School (class of 1955) boy used to attend these jam sessions. He had a great voice, and listeners rewarded him when he sang. That young man was Danny Kaleikini, and he was encouraged by the applause and tips to pursue a professional career. Eddie Kamae and the Kalima Brothers also got their start at these jam sessions.

When Charley and Helen were divorced in 1957, he went to work at Aloha Motors. Helen took over the taxi and U-Drive business. She was very gutsy, going into other businesses, such as a service station, travel agency, and bus company. Helen ran the taxi cab company until 1997 when she turned the reins over to daughter Dale. "Mom was active in the business until she was 89. She came in most days at 6 AM and took calls until about four in the afternoon. Older people are valuable. Their memories are long." Helen turned 90 in 2003.

Entrepreneurs run in Helen's family. Helen's parents were *Issei* who came to work on the plantation and saved to buy property in the Moiliili area to run a dairy. After a while, they moved the dairy to Kaimuki. They worked hard and saved to buy property in Waianae and Palolo.

Helen's brother, Tom Hirahara, was also a remarkable business-man. During his World War II travels in the 100th Battalion, he saw how the farmers around the United States formed co-ops to sell their produce. When Tom came home, he suggested that the pikake growers in the 22nd Avenue area in Kaimuki form their own co-op. Tom became known as the Pikake King, making commercial growing very popular for the lei and flower shops.

"Tom was always thinking of other businesses to enter," said Evans. "He used to raise bees and had his own honey plant. Tom also raised orchids commercially in the 1950s and invested in more real estate in Waianae. One of Tom's daughters, Linda, and her husband, Craig Sugihara, own Town & Country Surf Shop. I guess they are entrepreneurial like her father."

Dale's sister, Momie Bradley, and her husband, Sonny Bradley, own Bradley, Hawaii, which builds some of the fastest canoes in the islands. Their boats win most Molokai to Oahu canoe races.

Charles Morita was a key industry leader to spearhead an open taxi system focused on the consumer and not on a limited number of cab licenses. During World War II, the license (medallions) were worth more than the cars.

Charley, Lester Irish of Irish Cabs, and Hanford Harrison of Harrison Taxi in Waikiki worked with Mayor Johnny Wilson and the city to have "fixed taxi stands" where the taxi drivers answered telephone calls from customers located within one mile of the taxi stand. Cabs worked at these taxi stands and were not allowed to cruise. This is why Honolulu does not have a taxi medallion system where the customers are hostage to the taxi drivers.

Charley's Taxi President Dale Evans was named Small Business Person of the Year by Small Business Hawaii in 2004.

City Mill

City Mill had to overcome a lot of hardships to survive the last 100 years according to Steven Ai, grandson of founder Chung Kun Ai. "Six months after opening in 1899 there was a bubonic plague in Hawaii. A fire got out of control and burned most of Chinatown, including City Mill, in 1900."

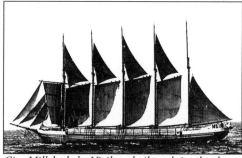

City Mill had the Vigilant built to bring lumber to Hawaii. It was the fastest five-masted schooner in the Pacific at the time.

C.K. Ai, who had borrowed money from friends to start City Mill, had no insurance. He had to go back to his friends for money a second time. "He had a 'never give up' attitude," according to granddaughter Carol Ai May. "It took him through many crises. Twenty years later, City Mill burned down a second time, but fortunately, this time he was insured."

Not many companies overcame such obstacles, but times were different then. City Mill built its own ship, the Vigilant, in 1920 to bring lumber to its store in Hawaii. It was the largest five-masted schooner in the Pacific. It carried two million board feet of lumber. Each board had to be loaded by hand.

During the depression, City Mill owed $750,000, and the banks considered foreclosing. In today's dollars, that is equivalent to about $11 million. C.K. was 65, but he persevered. In 1940, at age 75, the debt was paid off.

City Mill started off as a lumber and rice mill in 1899. One of the original coral mill stones is embedded in the parking lot next to Nimitz Highway. In 1950, when they moved from Chinatown, Nimitz Highway was closed for the grand opening ceremonies.

Since then, City Mill has added eight retail stores and 35,000 new items to its inventory.

City Mill used this large coral ring to mill rice in its early days. It's now embedded in the parking lot at their Nimitz Hwy store.

The Coco Palms Resort

The area encompassing the Coco Palms Resort was the home of Kauai's last reigning queen, Queen Deborah Kapule, in the mid-1800s. It had been the ancestral home of Kauai's *alii* since the 13th century.

Originally opening on January 25, 1953, the Coco Palms Resort had been Kauai's oldest operating hotel until Hurricane Iniki closed it. It had 24 rooms, two guests, and four employees when it opened. Under the visionary promotional eye of Grace Buscher Guslander, the resort grew to include 416 rooms by 1970. In August 1985, Wailua Associates acquired the Resort.

Lyle Guslander had been general manager of the Moana Hotel, according to Bill Sewell, a chief purser with Matson. "Guslander first built and operated the Maui Palms Hotel, and I was among the first visitors to his first new 'gamble,' for which many thought he was mad. From there, he built the King Kamehameha Hotel in Kailua-Kona," said Sewell who stayed there on his honeymoon in 1960 and was given the top suite, complimentary. "He then met Grace Buscher who had control of the Coco Palms on Kauai. They formed a partnership and later married."

Within the resort is the famous 2,000-tree coconut grove, which is the largest of only three similar groves in the entire state of Hawaii. The grove was originally planted with coconut tree nuts imported from Samoa by Mr. William Lindeman in 1896.

Grace was well known for her ability to embellish and create myths, stories, and facts surrounding her resort. Under Grace Guslander's expanded interpretation of the Hawaiian practice of *akua* or "replenishment," many noteworthy people took part in the planting of new coconut trees. Some of these included Hawaiian Olympic swimming champion, Duke Kahanamoku, The Von Trapp Family Singers, Bing Crosby, and a Japanese prince and princess. These and many other trees were marked throughout the property with name plaques.

The Coco Palms Resort achieved early exposure and fame in the 1961 Elvis Presley movie, *Blue Hawaii*. Virtually the last 20 minutes of the movie was shot on the grounds of the Coco Palms.

The ceremonial torch lighting ceremony "Call to Feast," which took place every evening at 7:30 PM for 40 years until September 11, 1992 when Hurricane Iniki struck the Island of Kauai, was featured in the film. This torch lighting ceremony was the original such event, copied in recent years by many other resorts and hotels in Hawaii. An additional favorite scene for movie watchers and visitors alike was the conch shell-blowing doorman greeting them at the entrance.

The wedding ceremony, portrayed in the final scene where Elvis crooned *The Hawaiian Wedding Song* to Joan Blackman as they rode their flower bedecked double hulled canoe through the lagoon to the Wedding Chapel, is credited with creating a high demand for weddings at the Coco Palms Resort. Prior to its closing in 1992, the Resort hosted over 500 wedding ceremonies annually.

Metro Golden Mayer (MGM) Studios donated the Wedding Chapel to the Coco Palms in the mid-1950s after constructing it for the film *Miss Sadie Thompson*, which starred Rita Hayworth. The Blue Hawaii wedding scene has been replayed over the years by thousands of couples exchanging vows at the Coco Palms Resort. Kauai's former mayor, Maryanne Kusaka was married at the Coco Palms.

Even with the property closed to overnight guests, on average one or two weddings take place weekly, either on the lagoon or next to it, as couples desire the *Blue Hawaii* wedding with its famous songs from the movie sung for their own ceremony. A Kauai tour operator, Hollywood Movie Tours, stops daily with a van of tourists interested in seeing the grounds, lagoons, and coconut grove.

The Wailua area in which the property is located is culturally, spiritually, and historically significant. This is because it is in very close proximity to three of the most important historical *heiaus* on Kauai.

Nearby is the beginning of the legendary walk of the *alii* spirits on their path up the mountainside and around-the-island King's Trail. The Royal Bell Stone, significant as the blessing place for Kauai's rulers prior to their births for more than 1,000 years, is less than one mile from the corner of the property.

There are also important ancient burial sites throughout the area including the grounds of the property. In fact, some believe the proper translation of Wailua is "spirits."

Coco Palms had a long and glorious history of strong traveler demand and had consistently maintained the highest occupancy records in the state of Hawaii during its operational heyday. The Coco Palms Resort on Kauai had been one of the best known resort properties in all of Hawaii.

—Researched By David Cisan, Kapaa, Kauai

Columbia Inn

Brothers Frank Kaneshiro and Fred "Tosh" Kaneshiro planned to open a restaurant on Beretania Street on a Monday in 1941. The date they picked was December 8th. They hoped it would be a good day to launch their new venture.

"They were in the restaurant cleaning the dining room, getting ready for the Monday opening when the bombs were dropping," says Tosh's son, Gene. "They were able to open a week before Christmas per the Provost Marshall's approval and operated during daylight hours throughout the war."

"The Columbia name sounds patriotic and American, but it came from Colombian Coffee bags," Gene Kaneshiro continues. "My dad used to say that good coffee and good restaurants go together."

In 1964 Columbia Inn moved to the "Top of da Boulevard" - 645 Kapiolani, next to the newspaper building. Interestingly, the site they occupied had been the Times Grill since 1939. The Times Grill was the predecessor of Times Supermarkets.

"The Teruya's, who opened Times, and my dad and uncle were both from the hamlet of Oroku Aza in Okinawa," says Gene Kaneshiro. "Ushi Takara, who owned the American Café next to the Alexander Young Hotel in 1922, trained many individuals from that hamlet. They learned a trade and later opened their own restaurants in Hawaii. At one time we counted 72 restaurants from people of that hamlet."

"There has been over 250 restaurants since the 1920s started by Okinawan's in Hawaii. Zippy's, Flamingo, Like Like Drive Inn, Shiro's, Wisteria and KC Drive Inn to name but a few. Most sold American food, because that is what people wanted."

"Tosh" Kaneshiro was a big Dodger fan, and L.A. banners adorned Columbia Inn. Back then the place was open 24 hours, and Waikiki entertainers used to come by after their shows. Reporters and editors from the two daily papers were also regulars. Frank and Tosh

Honolulu Advertiser cartoonist Harry Lyons drew Tosh Kaneshiro returning from the 1966 World Series in which the Dodgers lost to Baltimore.

passed away and the business was sold to the Kyotaru Company.

The restaurants did well in Hawaii, but the parent company in Japan filed for bankruptcy, and the Kapiolani site was sold to Servco in 2001. The Waialae Avenue restaurant in Kaimuki closed in 2007. A group of Kyotaru managers led by Tim Jones turned the Pearl City restaurant into Gyotaku.

—Researched by Vicky Yu-Chi Wen

Consolidated Amusement Company

The history of theatre in Hawaii preceded motion pictures by more than 75 years. The Thespian on the corner of King and Maunakea Streets was Hawaii's first theatre, opening in 1847. *The Adopted Child* and *Fortune's Frolic*, a double-bill, was the first performance, and admission was $1.

A second theatre, the Royal Hawaiian Theatre, opened in 1848 at Hotel and Alakea Streets, where the courthouse now stands. *She Stoops to Conquer* was the first stage production there. Shaped like a Quonset hut, it sat 200 people.

Other theatres opened in the following decades, including the Varieties, Buffum's, and The Honolulu Music Hall on King and Mililani Streets, where the post office parking lot is today.

The Royal Hawaiian Theatre was possibly the inspiration for the Royal Hawaiian Hotel being so named. Both occupied the same block on Hotel Street from 1871 until 1881 when the Theatre was torn down.

Consolidated founder Joel Cohen got into the theatre business in 1899.

Edwin Booth, brother of John Wilkes Booth's (assassin of President Lincoln), was an actor in Hawaii in the 1850s. In 1884, sugar baron William Irwin rebuilt the Honolulu Music Hall and renamed it the Opera House. It was a magnificently ornate theatre. In those early days, drama companies, circuses, minstrels, and burlesque artists came to Hawaii, performed for a few weeks, then returned to the mainland.

It wasn't until 1897 that the first movies were publicly shown in the islands, according to Robert Schmidt. That first movie was

Comedian Ernest Hogan won one of Hawaii's first racial discrimination lawsuits with the support of Joel Cohen.

shown at the Opera House and was probably a ten minute film.

Joel C. Cohen, who would later found the Consolidated Amusement, got into theatre in 1899. Cohen rented the Orpheum Theatre for 6 months at a cost of $600. His Orpheum Company had 14 directors, including Prince David Kawananakoa, Prince Jonah Kuhio, and Gus Schuman. The Orpheum Theatre was on Fort Street above Beretania and was later replaced by the Princess Theatre. Kukui Plaza's Diamond Head tower is there today. Vaudeville acts performed to enthusiastic audiences, and business boomed.

Later in 1899, however, a bubonic plague hit Honolulu. If ships put in, they could not leave. By happenstance, one of the greatest black comedians of all time stopped in Honolulu on the way back to the mainland from a tour of Australia. Ernest Hogan and his troupe had the ship stop 30 feet from the dock. Half the town had come down to greet them.

Cohen tried to negotiate a series of performances. He offered $650 a week and lodging for the troupe. Hogan demurred. He then reconsidered. "Let me see the color of your money, mister," he shouted.

This might not have been the first time "show me the money" was uttered, and it probably was not the inspiration for the movie *Jerry McGuire*, but it got Cohen racing to the bank. He returned with $5,000 in gold coins that he set on a table.

Hogan hesitated, moved forward, backward, and finally came off the ship. Cohen put them up in the Orpheum Theatre where they put on performances for four weeks to packed houses.

The Hawaii Theatre had the largest neon display in the islands.

127

When it came time to leave, the Canadian-Australian Line refused the black troupe passage because of their race. Cohen suggested they sue and offered to pay the legal costs and split any amount recouped. Thirty separate suits were filed, and after the shipping line lost the first three, they settled for $15,000 in gold. Hogan's com-

The Lihue Theatre, and many others, had clubs and special weekend matinee programs for kids.

pany performed for a total of 14 weeks in Hawaii and left rich men.

In 1914, Joel C. Cohen acquired the assets of the Honolulu Amusement Company, which had started in 1911. Lowell Angell, who is writing a book about the history of theatres in Hawaii, believes they owned the Bijou, which stood where the current Hawaii Theatre now stands; the Liberty, built in 1912; Empire, built in 1909 on Hotel and Bethel Streets; and the old Hawaii Theatre on Hotel Street between Fort and Bethel. This earlier Hawaii Theatre had been built in 1910 as the Savoy.

Lowell Angell describes the Bijou as looking like a big barn. "It had a flat floor, no décor whatsoever, and could probably hold 900 to 1,000 people. J. Alfred Magoon, who later became partners with Cohen, built it in 1910."

Consolidated Amusement was first incorporated in 1917, but the major event for the chain was the opening of the new Hawaii Theatre on Bethel Street in 1922. The Hawaii Theatre replaced the Bijou and was to be called the New Bijou.

People line up for the Pot Luck show at the Princess Theatre in 1940.

The Hawaii Theatre was designed for motion pictures, vaudeville, symphonies, and stage productions. It was the finest theatre of its day in the islands. "The pipe organ was the grandest the city had ever seen," says Angell. "It had four levels of keyboards. When the Waikiki Theatre opened, the Hawaii's pipe organ was moved there." When the Princess Theatre was torn down, Angell and long-time organist Johnny De Mello saved that organ from the wrecking ball. "We disassembled it and moved it to the Hawaii Theatre, where it is today," continued Angell.

The Hawaii Theatre's neon marquee, built in 1936, covered the front and wrapped around the Pauahi Street side of the theatre. In its time, it was the largest neon display in the islands.

Consolidated continued to buy or open theatres and by 1930 owned the Empire in Honolulu, Kaimuki, Kalihi, Palama, Princess and New Pawaa, which later became the Cinerama. They began showing talking pictures regularly in 1929.

The Great Depression did not slow them down. In the years leading up to World War II, they bought the Palace Theatre in Hilo, opened the Waipahu, Lihue, the Empire in Hilo, the Kapahulu, Liliha, Wahiawa, Kewalo, Toyo, Varsity, Hilo, and Kohala theatres.

The Waikiki Theatre, built by C.W. Dickey, opened in 1936 and seated 1,335 people. With paper maché and concrete coconut trees, bougainvillea, cereus, and papaya along the walls, and a blue sky ceiling with stars and moving clouds, it was like being outdoors. The screen had a rainbow arch over it, and it was flanked by coconut trees with fronds that swayed. The 14 member Usherettes Glee Club often sang before shows.

The Drive-in was built in 1948 and torn down in 1962. Holiday Mart, then Daiei occupied the site. This 1955 photo shows Ala Moana Center under construction and no Magic Island.

That same year, a Pot Luck Show was instituted every Saturday night at the Princess Theatre downtown. "Pot Luck did not refer to food," says former General Manager Art Gordon. "It was a surprise combination of vaudeville acts, short features, and movies. People lined up hours in advance. It was the most popular show in town, and it continued until World War II."

Angell describes the Pot Luck shows as a sort of Hawaiian Amateur Hour. "After the last movie, as I recall, they had local entertainers, singers, and dancers perform. Many famous local entertainers got their start there."

In 1938, the Toyo Gekijyo (Oriental Theatre) was built on College Walk, where Saint Louis College used to be. Architect C.W. Dickey based the design on the Toshogu Shrine of Ieyasu Tokugawa in Nikko, Japan. During the war, the Toyo's name was changed to Aala Theatre. In 1952, the former name was restored to the Toyo.

"During the Depression, Consolidated and others built theatres in nearly every neighborhood," says Angell. "All the military bases had theatres, and Schofield Barracks had five. Even though we were poor, we flocked to the theatres. The advent of television in the 1950s changed all that."

In 1948, Consolidated opened the state's first outdoor drive in, initially called The Drive In, where Daiei is today. It became the Kapiolani Drive-in after the Kam Drive In opened in 1962. "The Drive In was huge," says Angell. "The entrance was on Kapiolani Blvd. near Kaheka St., and the exit on Kalakaua Ave. near Makaloa St. It could hold 750 cars."

Consolidated was purchased by Pacific Drive In Theatres of California in 1959. Pacific Theatres was founded by William Forman in the 1940s and is now run by his grandson Jerome.

The Hilo Theatre, which opened in 1940, had the distinction of being the only theatre in the United States to be hit by a tidal wave...twice. The tsunami of 1946 did little damage to the theatre, but the 1960 tsunami destroyed much of the interior. With those two major tsunamis, and two minor ones in 1952 and 1957, Consolidated decided to close the theatre. "Ironically there have been no major tsunamis since then," points out Bishop Museum

The Hilo Theatre has the distinction of being the only theatre in the U.S to be hit by tsunamis twice.

Collections Manager DeSoto Brown. "The Hilo Theater building stood empty until 1965, when it was finally demolished."

Art Gordon, who was Consolidated's general manager from 1970 until 1985 had an interesting association with Toei Films of Japan. "We were the largest importer of Japanese films in America, bringing in 40 to 60 films a year. They played at the Toyo, Kuhio, Liberty, Cinerama, and some California theatres."

Gordon would fly to Tokyo two to three times a year to screen films. "I'd watch four a day and pick the ones I thought local audiences would like. The *issei* generation liked heavy drama," Gordon continued. "Sad stories that made you cry. The *nissei* liked samurai films. The *sansei* generation wanted karate films."

"Whoever came up with the English names of these films obviously didn't understand the language well. I complained that the names were not very attractive, and they began sending me scripts, asking me to come up with English titles. I even got involved in the English subtitles because they were often poorly done as well. Pretty soon, I added Hong Kong and Taiwan to my travels. My staff thought, 'There he goes again!' "

Many people questioned why Consolidated let its flagship Hawaii Theatre get rundown. "The Bishop Estate would never give us more than a 2-year lease," continued Gordon. "We could not invest money on renovation under those circumstances and sadly, had to walk away."

Thirty years ago, before multiplexes, first-run movies would be shown often at only one theatre in town. If you wanted to see that particular movie, you had to go to the theatre that played it. When *The Sound of Music* came to Hawaii in 1965, for instance, it played for over a year at the Kuhio Theatre.

Premiere of The Sound Of Music at the Kuhio Theatre in 1965. It played at the Kuhio for over a year, attesting to the enduring popularity of this classic film.

The end of an era occurred in November 2002 when Consolidated closed its Waikiki Theatres. Most theatres are now multiplexes.

Consolidated Theatres has been the leader in Hawaii since its founding at the beginning of the century. Today, it operates 102 screens in 14 theatres on Oahu, Maui, and the Big Island. Theatre historian Lowell Angell believes theatres have souls. "Millions of people have laughed, cried, and been amazed in them."

Timeline of the Consolidated Amusement Company

Here are theatre opening and closing dates and some important highlights of Consolidated's history:

1899 Joel Cohen's first performances at the Orpheum Theatre.
1914 Cohen and Magoon acquire the Honolulu Amusement Company (founded in 1911), owning the Liberty Theatre (built in 1912, closed in 1984), Empire, Bijou, and the old Hawaii Theatre (formerly the Savoy).
1917 Consolidated Amusement is incorporated.
1922 (New) Hawaii Theatre opens on Bethel Street.
1925 Purchased the Princess Theatre on Fort Street (built in 1922 where the Orpheum had been; closed in 1969).
1927 First successful American talking film, *The Jazz Singer*, starring Al Jolsen.
1930 Waipahu Theatre (sold in 1970). Acquired the Palace Theatre in Hilo (built in 1925, closed in 1982), and the Palama Theatre (sold in 1985).
1931 Lihue Theatre.
1933 Acquired the Empire Theatre in Hilo.
1935 Wahiawa Theatre (closed 1977).
1936 Waikiki (closed in 2002), Kapahulu (closed in 1980), Liliha Theatre (closed in 1962).
1937 Kewalo Theatre (closed in 1966).
1938 Toyo Theatre (closed in 1984).
1939 Varsity Theatre (made into twins in 1985).
1940 Kohala, Hilo Theatre (closed in 1960 by tidal wave).
1945 Kuhio Theatre (closed in 1995).
1947 Concession stands open in theatres.
1948 The Drive-in Theatre (later named Kapiolani Drive-in Theatre, closed in 1962).
1954 First Cinemascope with stereophonic sound at Kuhio Theatre.
1958 Cinerama installed at the Princess Theatre.

1959   Consolidated purchased by Pacific Theatres of California. Purchased the Kaimuki Theatre (built 1901, closed in 1982).

1962   Kam Drive-in (closed in 1998). Pawaa renovated into the Cinerama Theatre.

1965   Kailua Drive-in (closed in 1992).

1966   Hawaii's first swap meet at the Kam Drive-in.

1970   Waikiki Twin Theatres (closed in 2002); Aikahi Theatre.

1976   Pearlridge 4-Plex; Kuhio Theatre made into twins; buys and turns the Toho into the Kapiolani Theatre (built in 1964; closed in 1996).

1977   Took over the Maui Theatre in Kahului.

1980   Waiakea Kai Tri-plex; Asian Cinema House.

1981   Hualalai Tri-plex; Plantation Cinema, Kauai.

1984   Koko Marina.

1985   Prince Kuhio (Hilo).

1986   Kahala Theatres; took over Marina Twins.

1987   Pearlridge West.

1999   Mililani Town Center; buys IMAX Theatre (closed in 2003).

2000   Temple Valley.

2001   Ward 16-plex.

Cornet

Joseph Cornet was a Belgium-born merchant who escaped Europe just before World War I. His first venture, an Arkansas farm was a dud. Not to be deterred, he opened a soft drink stand and later the first Cornet 5-10-25¢ Store in Covina, California in 1923.

By 1929, he had six Cornet stores, but when the depression started, he sold all but the original store. He could not find a buyer because of a large chain store across the street.

To compete, Joseph Cornet became a discounter and found it was a winning formula. He built up a chain of 138 stores in nine western states and retired to Hawaii in 1956 but continued to open new stores.

Cornet's first store in Hawaii, in the Aina Haina Shopping Center, opened in 1957. In 1958, a second store was opened in the Kaneohe Shopping Center, and soon after, opened in Wahiawa, Waianae, and Kailua.

The variety store competed with such stores as F. W. Woolworth and Kress. However, by the 1990s, sales dwindled, and the stores closed after a 35 year run in the islands.

Crazy Shirts

Rick Ralston came to Hawaii from California in 1962. The 20 year-old had just $80 in his pocket. However, he brought an airbrush and an idea. Rick began airbrushing T-shirts and sweatshirts on the sidewalks of Waikiki. In those days, T-shirts were considered to be underwear, but Ralston adorned them with surfing scenes, hot rods, and monsters. Customers stood in line for them.

In 1964, Ricky's Crazy Shirts opened in the back of the International Market Place, occupying a vacant space until a "real tenant" could be found. "Crazy" came from a friend, "Crazy Arab." Two years later, the business incorporated as Crazy Shirts. The newspapers called it the "passing fad of the summer."

Crazy Shirts opened in Ala Moana Center in 1970, and embroidered as well as screen-printed shirts were added. The Waikiki Trader Corp. bought Crazy Shirts in 2001. It now operates 40 Crazy Shirts stores in Hawaii, Guam, California, Nevada, Louisiana, and Florida.

—Researched by Suherman Manurung and Penny Ho

Daiei

Hurricane Popcorn creator, Mark Doo, was in Japan in 2000 with the Hawaii Food Manufacturers Association and visited a Daiei in Yokohama. "It looked just like the ones here in Hawaii," Doo said. "It had the same lay out and even the same linoleum floors. From the inside, it was impossible to tell I wasn't in Hawaii."

Isao Nakauchi started Daiei in 1957 in Japan under the name of *Shufu no mise Daiei Osaka Honten* which means "big and prosperous store in Osaka for housewives." The original target was a Japanese housewife looking for reasonably priced products. Daiei wanted the housewives to know that it was there for them.

In 1970, the store name was simplified to Daiei, Incorporated to broaden their appeal beyond Osaka housewives. "Dai" means "big" and "ei" means "prosperous."

The logo was a combination of a circle, triangle, and square and represents incompleteness. The founders and decision-makers created this image to symbolize imperfection in regards to product fulfillment and customer service. Daiei felt that that service was a constant evolution.

In 2006, Don Quijote bought Daiei's four Hawaii stores, although it carries much of the same merchandise.

—Researched by Mikio Watanabe

Dillingham Corp.

Benjamin Franklin Dillingham was only 36 years old when he had a vision: a train that would connect downtown Honolulu's harbor and factories to Pearl Harbor, Waianae, around Kaena to Haleiwa, and then on to Kahuku. The idea, as so many great ones are, was first ridiculed. "Dillingham's Folly" it was called. The former sailor, who came to the islands around 1865, proclaimed that the railroad would be built and in operation by his 45th birthday.

Benjamin Franklin Dillingham proposed building a railroad on Oahu when he was just 36 years old. It was operational by his 45th birthday.

The pineapple and sugar growers loved the idea and funded it. By 1889, the Oahu Railway & Land (OR&L) trains were in daily operation. OR&L eventually built 72 miles of track to Kahuku, where it joined the Koolau short line to Laie. It transported general freight and supplies to the plantations and allowed many workers to visit Honolulu from then distant areas. The first automobiles did not reach Oahu until 1899.

By 1930, the company had 170 miles of track, 24 locomotives, 1,400 freight cars, and 35 passenger cars. The railroad was instrumental in enabling the sugar plantations to ship their product to the mainland, says former CFO James Pollock.

In 1902, B.F.'s son, Walter, founded Hawaiian Dredging and Construction. Their first job was developing Honolulu Harbor in 1902. By 1903, they opened the entrance to the Pearl River Lagoon and dredged the main channel to Pearl Harbor. In 1909, they built Pearl Harbor's Drydock #1.

The OR&L terminus was across from Aala Park. Punchbowl is in the background.

In the 1920s, 1930s, and 1940s, the company restored Kawaihao Church and constructed 28 air bases in the Pacific. They dredged the Ala Wai Canal, which was completed in 1928. Much of today's Waikiki and

Walter Dillingham's Hawaiian Dredging and Construction opened Pearl Harbor for ships, built the Ala Wai Canal, and Ala Moana Center.

Ala Moana areas were filled and constructed by Dillingham.

Since those early days, the company has expanded throughout the Pacific Basin and the world and has become a builder of all types of construction. Dillingham crews served and supported the United States in World War I, World War II, Korea, Vietnam, and Desert Storm.

"Walter Dillingham was a very caring and interesting individual," Pollock continued. "He was shrewd in business but had a great relationship with employees at all levels. He remembered and took an interest in their spouses and kids and lives away from work."

The advent of the automobile and truck eventually spelled doom for the Oahu Railway, but Hawaiian Dredging and Construction's business soared.

In 1959, they built Ala Moana Center, then the largest shopping center in the world. They also built almost half of the large office

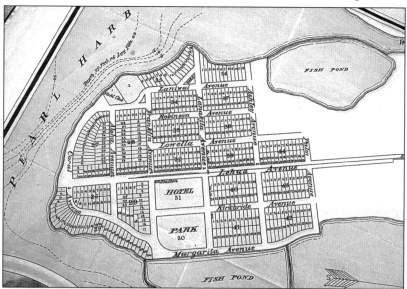

Dillingham built Pearl City in 1890, and until World War II it was a retreat for the wealthy of Oahu, who owned homes on the water.

136

buildings, hotels, and condominiums in the 1960s and 1970s.

In 1961, Oahu Railway & Land and Hawaiian Dredging & Construction were merged to form the Dillingham Corporation.

Dillingham was the third largest Hawaii business in 1982 when it was sold to a mainland investment company for $348 million. It employed over 12,000 people and had sales of over $1.6 billion.

Dillingham has completed over 200 projects since World War II, including roads and bridges, airports, runways, dams, industrial facilities, tunnels, water treatment, and residential, commercial, and government buildings. They helped build BART in San Francisco and the Metros in Washington, D.C. and Atlanta.

"Dillingham wasn't in the Big Five," Pollock continued, "but it was bigger than most of them. We could and did build almost anything in the world." No other company in Hawaii has had the impact of the Dillingham Corporation.

Dillingham Blvd. in Honolulu is named for Benjamin Franklin Dillingham. Son, Walter, built La Pietra, a mansion at the foot of Diamond Head, modeled after an Italian villa where he was married. The home is now La Pietra – Hawaii School For Girls.

Pearl City

Ben Franklin Dillingham was the father of Hawaii's first totally planned community. Originally a stop for his Oahu Railway & Land Co. train on the way to the sugar plantations, Pearl City was created in 1890. Dillingham held a contest to name the city and its main street, Lehua Avenue. Before that, the area was referred to by its *ahupuaa* district name of *Manana*, meaning "the place where two lava flows converge."

Pearl City's name probably came from the Pearl River that connected Pearl Harbor and the ocean. Before it was dredged in 1909, pearl-bearing oysters could be found in the harbor. but agricultural runoff ruined them.

The first Pan American Clipper sea planes landed at Pearl Harbor in 1935.

Dillingham sold 100 lots on the peninsula extending into Pearl Harbor for $44. Included in the price was guaranteed train passage to town for ten years at 10 cents a ride. There were a few dusty roads, but the first cars to appear in the area would not come for another 10 years.

Pearl City School (now Lehua Elementary) opened in 1907, but older students initially attended McKinley High School, then Farrington High School when it was built in 1936. Two years later, Waipahu High was built. Pearl City High did not open until 1971.

The first Pan Am Clippers landed at Pearl Harbor in 1935, and the mooring site on the peninsula is still marked.

In its first 50 years, the city was a retreat for the wealthy who came on weekends and in the summer to relax, party, and sail. The Dillinghams, Cookes, Dowsetts, Spauldings, Atkinsons, and many others had country estates at the tip of the peninsula. Carole Lombard and "Thin Man" William Powell honeymooned there in the 1930s.

The Pearl Harbor Yacht Club closed when World War II broke out and was later relocated to Waikiki. World War II ended the era of weekend retreats for the wealthy. Train service ended in 1947. Today, Pearl City is firmly middle class.

Dole Food Company

Food canning was developed around 1800 by Nicholas Appert to supply Napoleon's invasion of Russia. Canning came to America in the 1820s and expanded greatly with the gold rush of 1849 and the miners' need for portable food. The Civil War in 1861 relied heavily on canned food as have all wars since.

Christopher Columbus's crew was offered pineapple in 1493 when they anchored in the Caribbean. The fruit soon became a sensation in Europe. It was the most highly prized exotic fruit for three centuries. However, pineapple needed a warm climate to grow, and slow shipping caused most of

James Drummond Dole founded the Hawaiian Pineapple Company in 1901.

it to spoil in transit.

James Dole thought pineapple could be grown and canned in Hawaii, and then shipped anywhere in the world. He founded the Hawaiian Pineapple Company (HAPCO) in 1901. James Dole's second cousin, Sanford Dole, who was part of the group that overthrew the monarchy in 1893 and was the first elected Governor of the Territory, recommended not using the family name because of the political baggage.

Many thought Dole's idea was crazy. The *Honolulu Advertiser* called it a "foolhardy venture" that was certain to fail. However, Dole's first crops were met with enthusiasm on the mainland, and soon he could sell as much as he could grow.

Canning allowed the "royal fruit" to survive long shipment times.

The original cannery was in Wahiawa near the fields but moved in 1907 to town. The OR&L trains made the move possible. Dole expanded his acreage, and by 1915, pineapple was Hawaii's second-largest industry after sugar cane.

In 1922, Dole decided that growing in scattered patches of land was not smart and sought a large, contiguous area. The result was the purchase of the island of Lanai for $1.1 million.

In 1927, the cannery needed a larger water tank. Architect C.W. Dickey suggested that it be made in the shape of a pineapple. The tank stood 80 feet above the cannery and held 100,000 gallons. It was 50 feet long with a 22-foot crown and weighed 30 tons. It cost $16,500 to build. Lit at night and visible from as far away as Waikiki Beach, it quickly became a Honolulu landmark.

During the great depression, sales fell. However, James Dole had an inspiration. Pineapple juice could be squeezed from the pineapples rather than thrown away. Dole turned to the engineers at American Can asking them to invent a can opener that did not take the whole top of the can off. The result: the punch can opener.

Pineapple juice sold well, but Dole's debt remained a problem. The banks were willing to help, but James Dole lost control of the company to Castle & Cooke. Dole remained as a figurehead president with a token salary.

Lex Brodie worked at the cannery in 1945 and became the assistant cannery superintendent in 1952. "Jim Dole was a wonderful man," Brodie recalls. "I would brief him when he came each summer. He would spend all day talking with people about their families and kids. He remembered it all and would ask people about their sons in college or how their mothers were doing. He was well loved by the employees."

In 1957, the company decided to make, instead of buy, cans. "American Can had us over a barrel. We felt they were holding us up." Lex Brodie argued for hiring the best can makers available, but the vice president figured they had all the talent they needed.

"When the harvest came in, the cans were of poor quality, but we had to use them," Brodie recalls. "Some would bulge, and others would burst. We had to go through the cannery each night and pull them." Dole didn't want the press to know, so they trucked the cans at night, covered, to Kapalama and barged them off Lanai, and dumped them in 2,000 feet of water. "We did this weekly for months," Brodie said.

Some of the cans generated gas and floated to the surface. "They ringed the island of Lanai, landed in Lahaina and some even made it to windward Oahu," says Brodie. "We had to send out crews each day to pick them up. The papers never got wind of it, except for a two-inch article that appeared citing 'mystery cans' floating ashore on Oahu."

"When the vice president returned from a mainland trip. I had to tell him we had lost $6 million. He put his head down

The Dole Pineapple, built in 1927, was a Honolulu landmark. Lit at night, it was visible from Waikiki.

on the table. A couple of days later he asked me to sign a letter of resignation. I refused, and he cried for 20 minutes. One of us had to take the fall for this. He ranted and raved and fired me." Of course, if this had not happened, Lex Brodie's Tire Company might never have been formed!

"When I left Dole," Brodie continues, "the International Longshore and Warehouse Union – ILWU - threw me a thank you banquet at their headquarters. Four hundred people came. They knew I was a fisherman and covered one table with fishing gear – rods, reels, you name it. When I was Cannery Superintendent we never once had a serious grievance. The union knew they could call me 24-hours a day. We spotted problems before they happened and fixed it. They appreciated that."

In 1961, four years after James Dole's death, HAPCO was renamed Dole Pineapple Company and later Dole Foods Company. It is ironic that the Dole name never adorned the company until after James Dole died in 1957. He is buried in Makawao, Maui, near Maui Pineapple Company's fields.

Today, Dole Foods is the largest producer and marketer of fresh fruit and vegetables in the world, doing business in over 90 countries and employing over 40,000 people. Its annual sales are around $5.1 billion.

Castle & Cooke Inc. spun off Dole as a separate company in 1995. It is based in Westlake Village, California. Dole is the third-largest private landowner in the state with 123,000 acres.

Working at the Cannery in Iwilei was the summer job for several generations of Hawaii's youth until its closure in 1993. The Dole Pineapple was taken down in 1997 and will not be replaced. However, if you look closely, the shadow of the pineapple-shaped tank remains on the side of the Dole Cannery shopping complex.

—Researched by Fehmi Gumusel.

Don the Beachcomber

The *Honolulu Advertiser* called him a tropical tramp who converted a bamboo shack, a few dollars of rum, and a couple of coconuts into a million dollar business. Born Ernest Raymond Beaumont Gantt in Louisiana, he spent two years travelling around the world before finding a job as a bootlegger during prohibition in 1932. When it was lifted, he opened a 400-square foot Don's Beachcomber restaurant off Hollywood Blvd. His rent was $30 a month.

His rum drinks and South Seas atmosphere caught on, and soon he opened another in Chicago. Many of his customers, knowing about his bootlegging business, called him Don, and he decided to change his name to Donn, and the business became Don the Beachcomber.

An affectionado of fine Jamaican rum, Gantt invented over 50 original tropical drinks, including the Zombie, Vicious Virgin, Missionary's Downfall, and Scorpion. Trader Vic (Bergeron) and Donn both claim to have invented the Mai Tai, although Bergeron appeared to have dropped that claim.

After service in World War II, Gantt moved to Hawaii in 1947 and opened a Beachcomber restaurant across from the Royal Hawaiian Hotel on Kalakaua Avenue, where the International Market Place is today. Few in Honolulu remember that it was Donn who, in 1954, with architect Pete Wimberly, came up with the idea for an International Pacific Village and Market Place, drawn on a brown paper bag.

Don the Beachcomber moved to the International Marketplace when it opened, and one of its renowned features was the Treehouse for Two. High up in the old banyan tree, the Treehouse for Two was Donn's office as well as a comfortable, private place for VIPs to enjoy a unique setting for dinner.

Donn brought Martin Denny to Hawaii to work at his restaurant. His band, with John Kramer on bass, Augie Colon on percussion and birdcalls, Arthur Lyman on vibes, and Denny on piano, performed on and off there for 10 years.

Donn died in 1989. Duke Kahanamoku's replaced his Waikiki restaurant in 1961. His last wife, Phoebe Beach, and Arnold Bitner recently published a book about Donn and his colorful history: *HAWAII Tropical Rum Drinks & Cuisine by Don the Beachcomber.*

Dot's In Wahiawa

Dot has never owned Dot's in Wahiawa. Her sister, Marian Harada, started it and named it for her.

"My mom, Shio, and sister, Marian, first started Sukiyaki in 1935. It was a restaurant and bar on Kilani Street and Cane Road," Dorothy Harada, now 82, says. "In 1938, they opened a skating rink where Dot's is now, called the Wahiawa Amusement Center.

"Locals were not familiar with roller skating so they hired GI's from Schofield Barracks to show people how to do it."

It was an outdoor roller rink," recalls nephew Mel Sakaba. "It could hold 700 people, if you can imagine that! We had many variations of skating, such as moonlight, couples, and waltzes."

"I wanted to go to school to become an executive secretary," Dorothy continues, "but my older sister said no. She was the eldest of seven. She said she was going to open a drive in, and I would manage it."

Dot's Drive-in opened in 1940, replacing the skating rink. "The skating rink was where the parking lot for the restaurant is," says

Sakaba. "That was over 60 years ago, and very few of the people parking here today know that tidbit of history."

In 1950, the drive-in became a restaurant and nightclub. "The nightclub could hold 400 and was packed six nights a week. We had local entertainers and brought in troupes from Las Vegas and Japan. We even had some exotic dancers. The most popular was Diane Ross, who had a monkey that undressed her."

In the 1950s and 60s, Dot's in Wahiawa was the finest place for dining and entertainment in Central Oahu. There was

Dot Harada still works at 82. Dot's was once a skating rink, drive-in, night club, and the top restaurant in central Oahu.

nothing to rival it.

Marian's at Haleiwa opened in the 1960s where Jameson's is today, and Marian's Catering was also started. "The catering is the largest source of revenue today," says Sakaba. "We cater weddings, anniversaries, and everyday, we do Germaine's Luau." At 82, Dot stays busy. "I work as a bartendress at the Luau."

E. K. Fernandez

Hawaii's first circus, carnival, rodeo, Wild West show, bull fighting, and ice show were all due to Edwin Kaneikawaiola Fernandez. King David Kalakaua, a close friend of E. K. Fernandez's mother, put on a weeklong birthday luau for him when he was a year old. It was an auspicious beginning for Hawaii's top entertainer.

E. K. Fernandez got started in 1903 when he brought Hawaii's first motion picture camera from Germany for the huge sum of $1,000. With it, he filmed island people and showed movies on a bed sheet in his parent's back yard.

His back yard shows caught on, and he was nicknamed Keiki Kii Oni Oni – the Moving Picture Kid. E. K. Fernandez next took his shows to plantations around the islands. People would bring their own wooden boxes to sit on – a "box seat".

E.K. Fernandez ran for the Territorial Legislature in 1911 and served nine terms through 1929. While in office, he brought the first sound pictures to the islands in 1913 in tent shows.

In 1915, he traveled to the World's Fair in San Francisco. He purchased a steam-powered merry-go-round called a Flying Jinny, which he introduced at the Maui County Fair. Later that year, he staged his first circus featuring human performers and animals including the 400 pound bear, "Alice Teddy."

The E. K. Fernandez Show traveled to the island plantations, and since air service was more than a decade away, all the equipment, personnel, and animals had to travel by boat. It would take two months to tour the Big Island.

During World War II, with its nightly blackouts and curfews, E. K. Fernandez put buildings up at Aala Park where there were daily shows and rides. He also brought entertainers to the military clubs in the islands.

Mari Peros, a supervisor at Liliha Bakery, remembers going to the E. K. Fernandez circus at Aala Park. "We would take the train in from Waipahu. The terminal was just across the street from the park. My favorites were the midgets, a husband and wife. They were so cute I wanted to pinch them."

After the war, E. K. Fernandez shows traveled to China, Hong Kong, Singapore, Guam, Japan, and Canada. For a while, he even had an amusement park in China. In 1956, E. K Fernandez introduced "non-violent bullfighting in Hawaii" at the old Honolulu Stadium, but it did not last long.

E. K. Fernandez died in 1970, and his son Kane and wife Linda took over and expanded the company. "I started out working for Kane as his 'operations field manager' which translates to driving trucks, setting up carnivals, hiring and firing, operating rides and games, etc.," says Linda. "With the advent of Fun Factory we separated our efforts differently. Kane ran the outside business, E.K. Fernandez, and I ran the inside business, Fun Factory Inc. I became president of Fun Factory, Inc in 1980."

Outdoor entertainment had its drawbacks, they realized, and rain was one of them. One particularly rainy year got them thinking about an indoor entertainment company, and the Fun Factory was born. Today, there are more than 18 Fun Factories in Hawaii and in 8 states on the mainland.

After steering the company for 30 years, Kane Fernandez died in 2001. After Kane's death, Linda became the CEO and President of Fernandez Entertainment, Inc., the holding company of E.K Fernandez Shows and Fun Factory, Inc.

Son Scott Fernandez was managing the carnival business at the time of his dad's death. "I asked him to be my partner in the outside business and promoted him to CEO," Linda continues. "Scott accepted and together we are building our businesses and seeking new opportunities in our new partnership."

Here are some interesting facts about Fernandez Entertainment:

- Some rides cost $1 million and may contain more than 5,000 light bulbs.
- They have more than 200 full time employees with another 800 working part time.
- They own over 200,000 square feet of canvas tenting.
- During a dock strike, they had to fly the elephants back to the mainland - one elephant per plane!

At E. K. Fernandez's funeral in 1970, Eddie Sherman said in eulogy, "as long as there is a circus or carnival operating in Hawaii, as long as there is laughter and the joy of little children, E.K. Fernandez will never be forgotten."

—Researched by Holly Kaneko

Eki Cyclery

Tochi Eki founded Eki Cyclery in 1911, and it is Hawaii's oldest bicycle dealer. He came from Yanai City, Japan at age 18 and first worked in Hawaii clearing land for Oahu Country Club. When the club opened, he worked as a waiter and earned $25 a month. He sent $15 of it to his parents in Japan and of the $10 left, managed to save $160 in 3 years to open a one-room bicycle shop at 681 South King Street.

"We originally sold motorcycles," says Jayne Kim, the founder's granddaughter, who now operates the business with her husband Howard Kim Jr. "But grandpa phased them out because they took up too much room and were noisy. Tochi was a quiet, peaceful man of few words. He was honest, intelligent, and active in the community."

In 1911, there were more horses than cars in Hawaii. Bicycles were the preferred mode of transportation. Delivery people and students in particular rode them.

The store faced a great challenge in World War II when bicycle manufacturers all switched to making ammunition. All they had was the inventory on hand. Their solution? Rent bicycles for 50 cents per hour.

Son-in-law Shuichi Arakawa took over the leadership of Eki and moved the store from Alapai Street near the bus barn to Ala Moana Center in 1966. In 1987, they relocated to 1603 Dillingham Blvd.

"We have the biggest selection of bicycles in the islands in one store," Jayne says. "We also have bicycles from the past on display here. We have a 1950 Panther and a 1952 Schwinn American, for instance, both restored to their original luster. We're a museum retail showroom!"

Frank V. Schwinn and Toichi Eki outside his first store, which opened in 1911.

The word "Eki" comes from a Chinese character; one side translates into "horse" and the other into "measurement." Together it means "station." When Eki was founded, horses were the predominant means of transportation in the islands. Eki was the perfect station for bicycles.

"*Cyclery* is an old word. Many have trouble spelling it," Jayne continues. "We've thought of changing it. Someone suggested Eki Bike, which would be a palindrome – reading the same forward as backward. But we haven't done anything yet."

Elephant and Castle

Many Pearl City residents remember this restaurant in Waimalu on Kaahumanu Avenue, but few know how it got its unusual name.

"There is an old English story about a young Spanish princess who traveled to England to marry a prince," says owner Emilio Quiton. "This was to tie the royal houses of England and Spain together and was a common practice at the time.

"She was called *La Infanta de Castile,* which meant 'princess from Castile,' a province of Spain. But people in England could not understand this phrase and heard it as 'Elephant and Castle.'"

"Today, there are several pubs in England with that name, and

I used to work at one in Portland, Oregon when I was fresh out of college," Quiton continued. He and the owners of that one opened up the one here in Hawaii, but it closed in 2006. "We we're a fish and chips English pub, but we made a great prime rib, too!"

Ezogiku

The most northern of the four major Japanese islands, Hokkaido, which means "the road to the northern ocean," used to be called Ezo, which means "the land of barbarians," since it was far north of the capitol city of Kyoto.

A particular type of chrysanthemum only grows in Hokkaido (Ezo). The Japanese word is "kiku," and as many know, the chrysanthemum is the royal family's crest. The throne is called the Chrysanthemum Throne. *Kiku* is sometimes pronounced and spelled *giku* when it is connected to other words. Ezogiku is named for the Hokkaido chrysanthemum.

There are several areas in Japan that are famous for their ramen: Kyushu (in the southern part of Japan), Tokyo, and Hokkaido. Each of them has a different style or taste.

The founder of Ezogiku, Kenichi Mitsui, liked the taste of the miso ramen he had when he visited Sapporo, Hokkaido. He found a ramen technician, Tomoji Onishi, and they opened the first restaurant in 1968 in the Wasada University district of Tokyo.

In 1974, Ezogiku opened in Hawaii. There are now seven restaurants in Hawaii and branches in Vancouver and Seattle.

—Researched by Effie Lin and Miho Mahler

Famous Amos Chocolate Chip Cookie Company

Los Angeles talent agent Wally Amos worked for the William Morris Agency with Simon & Garfunkel, the Supremes, and other musical acts in the 1960s. He began baking chocolate chip cookies at home as a therapeutic exercise after a difficult day at work. Amos gave them out to friends and associates and soon became known as the Cookie Man. His cookies were the hit of the town.

When his agency ran into difficulties, he decided to open the world's first chocolate chip cookie store. Friends Helen Reddy, Marvin Gaye, and others invested $25,000, and in 1975, the Famous Amos Chocolate Chip Cookie Company opened on the Sunset Strip.

It was instantly a hit, and Amos became the "face that launched a thousand chips." His Panama hat and aloha shirt became his corporate logo and are now enshrined in the Smithsonian Museum.

The business grew, and Famous Amos Chocolate Chip stores opened all over the country. The growth, however, may have been too explosive. Start-up costs for new stores were expensive and preceded revenues. Amos took in investors to stem financial losses.

The business changed hands several times and Amos eventually found himself without any ownership in the company he had founded. To his dismay, he learned he had no right to use his name or likeness in another business. "I became the man without a name," Amos said.

However, Wally Amos' business loss was the seeds of his spiritual gain. His book, *Man With No Name*, was all about how he turned adversity into opportunity.

Famous Amos believes that "each person in this world is a jewel in a crown of unequaled beauty." Amos has written 10 books and speaks all over the country. The Lanikai resident's latest book, *The Cookie Never Crumbles* is a cookbook, offering recipes for life, "specifically recipes for the successes you can whip up in your own life, if you have the right ingredients!" Wally and his wife Christine opened a Chip & Cookie store in Kailua in 2005.

Finance Factors, Ltd.

In the early 1950s, a concerned group of Hawaii businessmen saw a need. Families needed homes, but there was a severe shortage of affordable home loans available throughout the islands. In 1952, Fong Choy, Daniel Lau, Clifford Yee, Hiram Fong, Mun On Chun, and L. Q. Pang formed Finance Factors, Ltd.

Finance Factors opened its first office on the corner of King and Smith Streets in April of 1952 with only nine employees. Today, the company has a network of 15 branch offices and has become one of the largest financial institutions in the state. The company has seven branch offices on Oahu, two on the Big Island, one on Maui, one on Kauai, and loan cen-

Hiram Fong and five partners founded Finance Factors in 1952.

ters in Kahului, Kailua-Kona, and Guam.

The Finance Factors Family consists of four main operating companies: Finance Factors, Finance Insurance, Finance Realty, and Finance Investment. Finance Factors concentrates on mortgage loans, FDIC insured savings accounts, and certificates of deposit. Finance Enterprises is a holding company and parent to the four operating companies.

The company name comes from the traditional meaning of the word factoring—an extension of credit based on the value of a company's receivables. Although the company never actually did any factoring, the name remains today.

In 1967, the company's 15th anniversary, a new logo was created using six diamonds positioned together to make up a six pointed star. This new symbol represented the six members of the Family of Companies.

All of the founders have been successful, prominent individuals in the local community. Hiram Fong was in the Territorial legislature for 14 years and served as its speaker for six. He was also a U.S. Senator from 1959 to 1977.

Daniel Lau fought during World War II and received the distinguished Purple Heart award. During battle, Lau learned the value of dedication, loyalty, discipline, and fighting for what you believe in.

What started out as a company with $200,000 in cash and nine employees in 1952 has become one of Hawaii's big players in the local lending market with 15 branch offices and 139 employees.

—Researched by Marcus Lindstrup

First Hawaiian Bank

Until oil was discovered in Pennsylvania in 1859, whale oil was used in America for lubricants and lamps. A substantial whaling industry thrived in Hawaii during the 1840s and 1850s, and Honolulu was a major port for supplies. Without a bank in town, sailors turned to general merchandise stores, but they were not really adequate.

Local businessmen Charles Reed Bishop and William A. Aldrich seized this opportunity and opened the Bank of Bishop & Company in 1858. They set up shop near Honolulu's waterfront. The deposits at the end of their first day in business were a respectable $4,784 (about $85,000 in today's dollars).

Bernice Pauahi married Bishop in 1850.

Bishop had come to Hawaii 12 years earlier. The New York native sailed for Oregon in 1846 when he was 24 years old. The long and unpleasant trip around the tip of South America was punctuated by a stop in Honolulu, and Bishop decided to get off. This seemingly small detail in the history of the world was destined to change the face of Hawaii forever.

Bishop met and fell in love with Bernice Pauahi Paki, daughter of Maui *alii* Abner Paki and Konia Kaoleioku, the granddaughter of King Kamehameha the Great. Abner Paki was the captain of Honolulu Fort and later a Supreme Court Justice. Her parents wanted Bernice to marry Prince Lot Kapuaiwa, who became Kamehameha V, but she loved Charles Bishop.

In 1850, despite the Paki's objections, the couple married in the home of Amos and Juliette Cooke at Royal School on the Palace grounds. Only six attended the wedding.

Bernice Pauahi and Charles Bishop had 34 wonderful years together until she died tragically from breast cancer at age 53 in 1884. Pauahi left 434,300 acres of Kamehameha lands for the education of the children of Hawaii. Though rich in land, her estate was cash poor. It was her husband's money and management that established the Kamehameha Schools.

Samuel Damon bought Bishop & Company in 1895, and Bishop retired to California. In 1925, the bank moved its downtown branch to its present site, on the corner of King and Bishop Streets, and built a new 75,000 square foot building. Honolulu's first "skyscraper" was built next to the existing building in 1962. It was 18 stories (225 feet high)

Charles Reed Bishop, above, and William Aldich founded Hawaii's first bank in 1858, when whaling ruled the economy.

and the first downtown building taller than Aloha Tower.

One of the most respected members of the business community in Honolulu was John Bellinger who was one of the youngest bank presidents in the country at age 45 in 1969. Bellinger started work as a teller in 1942 for $115 a month. Bellinger considered himself to be "a local boy running a local bank."

Bishop & Company's name changed several times (Bishop First National Bank of Honolulu, First National Bank of Hawaii) and in 1969, became First Hawaiian Bank.

When Bellinger passed away in 1989 at age 66, another local boy who had worked his way up through the ranks, Walter Dods, became president. Dods came up through the marketing department and positioned First Hawaiian as "The Bank that Says Yes."

In 1998, First Hawaiian merged with BancWest Corporation, which was bought by BNP Paribas of Paris, France in 2001.

—Researched by Seung-Koon Seo

The First Banks

The history of banking began around 2000 to 3000 BC in Babylonia. Temples and palaces provided safe places for the storage of valuables. Initially, deposits of grain, cattle, agricultural implements, and precious metals were accepted. The Lydians (now Turkey) created the first coins around 2000 BC.

Flamingo Restaurants

Steven Nagamine bought the old Olympic Grill in 1950. "It was on Ala Moana Boulevard where Restaurant Row is today," said daughter Sandy Chong. "Dad planned to keep the name, but a funny thing happened. My parents went to Detroit to buy a car with my Uncle Larry Akamine. They bought a big Chrysler and drove it to the West Coast, where it would be shipped to Hawaii.

"They stopped in Las Vegas, and the Flamingo Hotel's logo caught their eye. It was busy and profitable," Chong continued. "Back in Hawaii, Uncle Larry suggested they change the name of the restaurant to Flamingo's. It caught on. People liked it right away. The logos were similar, and people asked all the time if we we're related," Chong continued.

Nagamine was a big promoter of his new restaurant. Every day for the first month, he walked around downtown passing out menus. He also cashed paychecks for dockworkers. "Dad was a go-getter," Chong continued.

Perhaps the key to their success was that they sold complete meals initially for 35¢. Customers would get a fruit cup, soup or salad, entrée, drink, and dessert. They also put out a relish tray with green onion stalks, because "dad loved green onions, carrots, and olives.

Daniel, Thelma and Steven Nagamine outside the original Flamingo restaurant on Ala Moana Blvd.

"We're famous for our double-crusted banana pie. We sent 12 to San Francisco this week. People don't care how much it costs. Last week we had an order sent to Arkansas."

Flamingo moved to Kapiolani Blvd in 1960. They bought the former Elliott's Chuck Wagon in 1966. House Speaker Calvin Say used to be a busboy at the Flamingo Chuck Wagon. Flamingo restaurants opened in Pearl City in 1981, Kaneohe in 1986, and Waipahu in 1990.

Steven died in 1993. His wife, Thelma, is still active. Son Daniel is the president. Daughter Jean is vice president, and daughter Sandy manages the Kaneohe restaurant.

Foodland

Maurice J. Sullivan left his native Ireland in 1927 for New York with seven dollars in his pocket. He got a job with the A&P Tea Company, the country's largest grocery chain. Within a few years, he became a manager.

World War II brought him to Hawaii where he was in charge of a commissary. Sullivan became friendly with the Lau Kun family who had a wholesale food business and owned Lanikai Store. After the war, Sullivan was hired to manage the store.

"In those days, clerks waited on customers. At May's Market (1855 to 1956) on Beretania Street, they must have had 20 clerks," Sullivan recalled. Having seen the first A&P supermarket in Buffalo, New York in 1935, Sullivan thought it would work in Hawaii.

Foodland opened its Aina Haina store in 1953.

He borrowed $10,000, and the Lau family put up the same. In 1948, they opened Foodland Super Market on Kapiolani Boulevard and Harding Avenue in Hiram Fong's Market City shopping center.

"I persuaded Theo. Davies and Amfac," Sullivan said, "the two biggest grocery wholesalers, to give me enough merchandise to stock our store with the promise that I would pay them one week after we opened." Sullivan also talked the newspapers into giving him advertising on credit.

Hundreds of shoppers appeared in response to the full-page ads on May 6, 1948. The crowds were so large that the front doors had to be locked, allowing only a few people in at a time. The store had to be closed several times to restock the shelves. Sullivan opened a new store every year for ten years after that. The chain now includes 29 Foodland and Sack N Save stores, and employs 2,000.

"The biggest reason people flocked to the store was our low markup," Sullivan said. His philosophy was to "treat your customers well and they will come back."

Sullivan passed away in March of 1998, and his daughter, Jenai Sullivan Wall, became chairman and CEO.

Over 400,000 residents hold Foodland's Maikai cards. *Maikai* means "excellent" in Hawaiian; excellent savings, excellent service, and excellent rewards each time the card is used.

—Researched by Siriporn Chaiwilai

GEM

Retail guru Glenn Kaya brought GEM to Hawaii in 1958. "It started in Denver in 1957," Kaya said. "GEM stood for Government Employee Mutual, and you had to be a member to come into the store. The idea was that membership caused a sense of belonging. With membership, we knew who our customers were and where they lived. Our marketing was direct mailing to our members."

That was one part of the formula. The other was that GEM leased out space to businesses that ran its various departments. GEM did not have any investment in inventory. The businesses carried most of the risk.

"Many of Hawaii's well-known companies were GEM departments. ABC Stores, Wong's Drapery, C. S. Wo, Mid-Pacific Lumber, Kim Chow, and Hauoli were all GEM tenants." says Kaya.

"We went into the pharmacy business ourselves and had to kick out Sidney Kosasa's drug department. Sidney owes me a lot of thanks for that because ABC is huge today!"

"There were 40 to 50 GEMS at its peak," Kaya said. "Denver and St. Louis were the first and second stores in 1957, and the next year, we opened Honolulu. Kansas City, Los Angeles, and Minneapolis soon followed."

Kaya was working in a local furniture store in the late 1950s when Harold Toplin walked in one day. "Harold was from Los Angeles and we were talking and found we were both University of Michigan graduates. He asked me to join their enterprise."

"There were no Asian managers of stores here at the time, and Harold gave me that opportunity. We opened the Kapalama GEM first, then Ward Avenue where Sports Authority is now, in 1961 or 1962, and later in Waipahu."

Kaya oversaw five stores in the Bay area and five in Hawaii. He was offered the role of company president. "I turned it down. The company headquarters was in Kansas City, and I was walking the street there and passed a guy with orange pants and a strange shirt. I thought to myself, 'what am I doing here?' "

GEM was part of a wave of socio-cultural change that swept Hawaii after World War II. "Stores were closed on Sundays when we first opened," Kaya said. "We were instrumental in getting that changed." Seibu of Japan bought GEM, and in 1993, decided to focus on its Southeast Asian businesses, and closed GEM.

The Garden Island

Kauai's leading newspaper, *The Garden Island*, was first printed in 1902 by Sometaro Sheba in English and Japanese versions. Sheba had been working as manager of the Hanamaulu store. He quit his job, and got hold of a printing press that had been sitting idle since the Malumalu Industrial School had closed in 1898. With the help of some friends, Sheba began turning out a weekly newspaper in Kapaia.

A photograph of the 12th issue of the paper shows the front page news included reports of new babies, a Republican victory celebration, visits to Honolulu, reports of illness, and a suggestion that your livestock be clipped at Waimea stables.

Subscription rates for the paper were $1 per year. Advertising rates were one dollar per month or five dollars per year.

Sometime later (it is not known just when) the company divided, and the Japanese version of the paper became known as Shuho Sha. It was printed on the old, original presses, and the printing was quite a feat for it reportedly took two men six hours to turn out 800 copies on the creaking and groaning presses.

The Garden Island also remained in Kapaia and got newer equipment, but type was still hand-set with the work being done by young ladies. For reasons also unknown, despite Sheba's earlier editions, 1904 is listed as the official date of beginning publication. The newspaper eventually moved from Kapaia to a cottage on the spot where the Lihue Hotel was later built. In 1911, the cottage burned down, and the shop moved to the Rice family carriage house, now the site of Yoneji's Store, where it remained until 1904 when the building on the east side of Kuhio Highway was erected.

In 1922, a young upstart who had been sending in news he created from his imagination while working at Makee Plantation at Kealia, walked into the office of then-editor Kenneth C. Hopper. He came to tell the editor that he thought the sports news was lousy. The upstart was Charles J. Fern, who was hired as a sports writer. Fern rose to become editor and later publisher of *The Garden Island*.

Charlie Fern became a powerful figure in the community. He added a radio station (KTOH, now KIVM) and a print shop (now Printing Services Inc.) to the firm. In 1964, after more than 50 years of *The Garden Island* being a once-a-week publication, Fern announced that the paper would be published twice weekly on Wednesdays and Saturdays.

In 1966, Fern decided to retire to Honolulu, and *The Garden Island* newspaper, the radio station, and the print shop were sold to Hagadone Publications, a subsidiary of Scripps League.

Today, *The Garden Island* is a daily paper owned by Pulitzer Publishing, which also owns the *Kauai Times*. Cynthia Schur is the publisher, and Rita De Silva is editor.

Gee ... a Deli

This hidden Kailua treasure was well worth finding. It was off Kuulei and behind McDonald's. "A lot of people asked if we we're related to Ghiradelli Chocolate from San Francisco, which is pronounced similarly, but we're not," said owner Doug Izak.

"Gee...a Deli was started in 1982 by an ER doctor at Castle Medical Center, Bernard Sherman, because he wanted a place to eat," Izak says. Izak worked for Sherman and bought the deli in 1985.

Izak brought in exclusive products from the mainland. "The best roast beef, pastrami, and corned beef. No one else in Hawaii had them." The menu covered a 40-foot wide wall with each sandwich named for someone.

"The joke was, if you eat it 100 times, we'd name it for you," Izak says. "John Dilks, who ordered turkey with smoked cheddar every day, had the Dilkswich named for him."

Randy Robbins was a 27 year-old instrument maker who died of cancer. "We sent him a turkey, roast beef, ham and cheddar sandwich at Castle Hospital and named the sandwich in his memory."

Doug Izak and Don Shideler prepare to install their sign in 1985.

The Gorga Sub was named for Bob Gorga, who, while hiking with Doug on Kodiak Island, Alaska, fell from Barometer Mountain 1,500 feet and lived. Doug, Bob, and another person had just arrived at the summit when Bob slipped. "He couldn't dig in and stop," Doug recalls. "He fell into the clouds."

Doug spent hours in panic looking for him, but his friend got the Coast Guard and they sent 40 guys who found him halfway down the 3,000-foot mountain. "He had hit his head, but had no broken bones. He's a miracle guy," Doug says. "The hand of God must have caught him and sat him down. He was in rehab for two years and had to learn how to walk, talk, and write all over again. He's now a special education teacher in Michigan.

"Lots of famous people have eaten here. Golfer Scott Simpson brought Bill Murray in one day. One of my boys, Bobby, who had seen *Caddyshack* said 'Scott. You brought your caddy!'" San Francisco 49er Steve Young was here as was sailor Dennis O'Connor. But the group that got my daughters to seventh heaven was the Red Hot Chili Peppers. They all freaked out."

In 2005, a fire burned down Gee...a Deli and Doug Izak decided to take a well-earned vacation.

Germaine's Luau

Germaine's Luau is named for Marcia Germaine. It was originally at Sea Life Park and later at the Hale Koa Hotel before moving to a private beach near Barber's Point. Zippy's owns the luau today.

The term "luau" goes back to at least 1856 when it was used by the *Pacific Commercial Advertiser*. Formerly a feast was referred to as a *paina* or *aha aina*. The *paina* describes a small dinner party as compared to the *aha aina*, which refers to a large banquet type gathering or feast.

Traditionally, feasts were held for social enjoyment or to communicate with and seek the help of, or to appease the gods. In pre-missionary Hawaii, both special religious occasions and personal milestones were observed with feasting. Food in early Hawaii was very often scarce and precious. What food they had, they shared with each other.

Today, the observance of the religious significance of the *aha aina* has all but disappeared, and a feast, as it is hosted and celebrated in contemporary times, has become essentially a purely social affair.

Hakuyosha Hawaii

Hakuyosha Hawaii is the Hawaii division of Hakuyosha Company of Japan, founded in 1906. It is regarded as the pioneer of dry cleaning in Japan. Hakuyosha is one of the finest and most highly respected cleaners in the world with over 1,200 outlets internationally. In addition, Hakuyosha's laboratory is generally acknowledged as Japan's pre-eminent garment-care testing and research center.

Hakuyosha Hawaii has been providing quality cleaning services in Hawaii for 30 years. Their 200 skilled employees in 16 locations work hard to make "Clean Living" a way of life for thousands of Hawaii's residents.

Haku means "white." *Yo* could have many meanings including "western ocean." The laundry service business was imported from western countries. *Sha* means "company or western style buildings."

—Researched by Miho Mahler

Halekulani Hotel

One of Hawaii's finest hotels began in the home of Robert Lewers in 1907. Lewers had moved into Waikiki and built a two-story cottage on the beach in the days when Waikiki's population consisted of more ducks than people.

Local fishermen who Lewers had welcomed to rest under a giant hau tree next to the house gave his home the name Halekulani – "house befitting heaven." Edward Irwin leased the property from the Lewers family and opened the Hau Tree Hotel in 1907.

Haleiwa Hotel proprietors Juliet and Clifford Kimball purchased the hotel and its five acres of prime ocean-front property in 1917 and renamed it the Halekulani Hotel. In 1929, the Lewers' home was torn down and replaced with a main building that had a distinctive high-pitched roof that caught the gentle trade winds. Over time, 37 bungalows were built around it.

One of the greatest movie detectives of all time, Charlie Chan, had a special relationship with the Halekulani Hotel. Mystery writer Earl Derr Biggers based his famous detective on real life Honolulu Police Department detective Chang Apana. Apana grew up on the Big Island and joined the Honolulu Police Department in 1902. He spoke English, Chinese, and Hawaiian, and was comfortable with all ethnic groups.

Biggers noticed that people in Honolulu did not lock their doors and named his first Charlie Chan novel, published in 1925, *The House Without a Key*. Kimball soon applied that name to a cottage on his property.

In a 1931 newspaper interview, Biggers said that "sinister and wicked Chinese were old stuff in mystery stories, but an amiable Chinese acting on the side of law and order had never been used up to that time."

When we think of great fictional Hawaii detectives, younger readers probably think of Steve McGarrett of *Hawaii Five-O* or Tom Selleck of *Magnum P.I.* Charlie Chan was the original and ruled the 1930s and 1940s. Biggers wrote six Charlie Chan novels, and 47 movies were made with the sagacious detective. Later in his life, Detective Chang Apana enjoyed signing his name as "Charlie Chan

Apana."

In 1983, the low-rise Halekulani was remodeled, but much has been retained including the original eucalyptus floors of the Main Building, which were carefully restored. One can still dine in the House Without a Key and enjoy the sunset.

Today's Halekulani is faithful to the spirit of the former, preserving the charm of the property while maintaining and enhancing its level of comfort. Halekulani's reputation as a five diamond oasis of tranquility in Waikiki has brought this unique property to its current status as one of the world's top luxury resorts.

—Researched by Kyung-Hee Ma

Harry's Music Store

Harry Yoshioka started a little appliance store on Waialae Avenue in 1946 just after World War II. Kaimuki was at the outskirts of Honolulu then and was served by a trolley line until 1941.

"We sold a lot of refrigerators, washing machines, toasters, rice cookers, and the first TV sets in the state," says nephew Alan Yoshioka.

"Back in those days, 25 years BC (before cable), we installed antennas on people's roofs," Yoshioka continued. I was usually the kid sent up on the roof to move the antenna until the best reception came in.

"We also sold musical instruments and records. Back then, they were 78 RPMs. Elvis' first records were 78s. We were getting a lot of competition from appliance stores, so Harry decided to focus just on music." Today, Harry's has the largest selection of musical instruments, sheet music, accessories, and books in the state.

Harold Chang, who played with Martin Denny (*Quiet Village*) and Arthur Lyman (*Yellow Bird*), runs Harry's drum department. "All the professional musicians come in here," Chang says. "Don Ho, Genoa Keawe, Melveen Leed, and Jake Shimabukuro, for instance, all come in. Gabby Pahinui used to put on concerts in the store, trying out our guitars.

"Country stars Hank Williams Sr., Dolly Parton, Jerry Vaughn, and Patsy Cline have all been in here. Daniel Ho used to work here in our keyboard department.

"Keola Beamer walked in with long hair and barefooted 30 years ago." Chang recalls, "He wanted to teach classical guitar. 'Why don't you play Hawaiian music?' I asked, knowing his family's musical inclination. He said he had grown up with it and was tired of it. He wanted to focus on classical. He taught here for three years and paid his way through the University of Hawaii. Of course, just a few years later, he and his brother were playing their beautiful slack key Hawaiian music at the Territorial Tavern and their records were at the top of the charts."

Harry Yoshioka passed away in 1999 at age 90, and his nephews Clayton and Alan Yoshioka play on.

Hauoli

Many locals remember the Hauoli stores in Kaneohe and Pearl City. Doo Wai Sing started Hauoli, which means "happy," in 1902 as Yat Loy Co. which means "welcome" in Chinese. Yat Loy was a general merchandise store downtown. The brick building is still there on Bethel and King Streets. They sold dry goods and clothing for infants, kids and adults.

"My grandfather employed a cook and ate at the store," said grandson Mark Doo. "He rarely left the place. My dad, James Doo, worked for him and took over when he died." Doo wanted to get into discounting and became one of the concessions at GEM. He sensed that retailing was moving away from downtown where it had traditionally been.

"Ala Moana opened and downtown petered out," said Mark Doo. "But dad was very successful in GEM, and soon he opened the Pearl City Hauoli store in 1969, and then Kaneohe in 1973."

Hawaii Business

In 1955, Joe and Ethel Murphy started *Hawaii Engineer* magazine. The territory's economy was booming and the fledgling magazine broadened its scope just before Statehood and re-named itself *Hawaii Industry* magazine.

Jetliners began bringing in record numbers of tourists and construction was flourishing. In 1964, the Murphys renamed their publication again to *Hawaii Business and Industry*. In 1969, it settled for good on *Hawaii Business*.

PacificBasin Communications bought the magazine in 1997, and since then it has won numerous national and regional awards for reporting and design. In 2000, the U.S. Small Business Administration named the magazine's editor and publisher, Leslie Light, the National Small Business Journalist of the Year.

Its signature issues – The Hawaii Business Top 250; the Black

Book; the Annual Commercial Office Guide; and, Hawaii's Wealthiest Landowners – are considered to be must-reads by business executives.

Hawaii Business is the oldest regional business magazine in the United States and Hawaii's only business magazine.

The Hawaii Hochi

"*The Hawaii Hochi* story is the story of two outstanding, unusual, dynamic, individuals," says former editor Arnold Hiura.

Fred Kinzaburo Makino, who founded the *Hawaii Hochi* in 1912, was born in Yokohama, Japan in 1877 to a British father and Japanese mother. "He was *hapa* and bilingual," says Hiura. "But he was bold and adventurous and got into a lot of trouble. So his parents sent him to Hawaii to live with an older brother."

Because he was bilingual, he found himself helping the Japanese immigrant community and became an activist. He quarreled with the owners of popular local Japanese newspapers because they took advertising from some of the companies Makino felt were oppressing immigrants. He believed they would not print the truth because of it.

In 1909, he learned that Portuguese and Puerto Rican plantation workers were paid $22 per month but Japanese workers were only paid $18. Makino and others led a strike that dragged on for four months. Five thousand field workers were evicted from plantation housing, and the strike organizers found themselves feeding and sheltering them until they were arrested. "The more times I am arrested, the firmer the Japanese will stand," exclaimed Makino. The strike caused minimum pay to increase to $22 a month, and living quarters improved.

In 1912, Makino founded his own paper, the *Hawaii Hochi.* "It was a paper people could trust, but it suffered serious financial consequences and almost went bankrupt several times," says Hiura.

Makino owned a Chinatown drug store and ran the paper out of the back. "People would

Fred Makino, founder of the Hawaii Hochi

come to him with their grievances, and he'd do what he could for them."

On one occasion, an immigrant property owner was deported without due process when a renter was found to be involved in an illegal activity. "Makino heard about it after the man's ship left," Hiura continued. "He rushed to court, got a stay, jumped on a skiff, and caught up with the boat at sea and got him off."

On another occasion, he fought the state's 1920 attempt to control the 144 Japanese language schools that were called "un-American." "He felt that Act 30 was unconstitutional," Hiura recalls. "He hired an attorney and won in the State Supreme Court. But the state appealed. Makino won in the Ninth U.S. Circuit Court of Appeals. Again, the state appealed, and it went all the way to the U.S. Supreme Court, where again, Makino prevailed. "The Japanese parent has the right to direct the education of his own child without unreasonable restrictions," the court ruled.

Makino called the ruling a "victory for Americanism and for the principles of constitutional liberty upon which the founders of our nation and our civilization depend."

"His standing up for the little guy earned him the respect and gratitude of the community," Hiura says. "The lean years passed, and the paper became a success."

During World War II, the *Hochi* changed its name to the *Hawaii Herald*. It reverted to its original name 10 years later, in 1952, and the *Herald* became the name of the English language paper that is now printed bi-monthly.

When Makino died in 1953, 1,500 people attended his funeral. The newspaper then floundered for several years until Konasuke Oishi, a successful newspaper magnate from Japan, bought the paper. Oishi had heard about how Makino had fought for the Japanese immigrants and language schools on yearly trips he made to the islands. He fell in love with the *Hawaii Hochi* and decided to save it.

"Oishi was a Renaissance man," Hiura recalls. "He was interested in science, art, business, everything. He acquired many newspapers in post-World War II Japan and consolidated them into the *Shizuoka Shimbun*. He also owned the major radio and television stations in Shizuoka.

The *Hawaii Hochi* is Hawaii's last daily Japanese newspaper, publishing six days a week in English and Japanese. It also publishes the *Hawaii Herald* and several tourist guides.

Busts of Makino and Oishi, who died in 1971, are in a garden courtyard in the Hawaii Hochi building in Kapalama.

According to managing editor Gwen Bataad Ishikawa, "Ho" means "to inform or report." "Chi" is "knowledge."

Hawaii Medical Service Association (HMSA)

The Great Depression in the 1930s caused many in Hawaii difficulty in obtaining medical care, even of the most basic type. Margaret Catton, the head nurse at Queen's Hospital, came to the Territorial Conference of Social Workers with a plan in 1935.

Catton proposed the creation of "a community association of participating members who, through regular monthly dues, would share their medical costs among themselves." Three dollars a month provided a maximum of $300 in medical coverage in a year.

HMSA's service to the people of Hawaii began on June 1, 1938. It was a non-profit mutual benefit society with a volunteer board. A rent-free office was provided on Alapai Street, and employees brought their own desks and chairs from home.

In the first year, 671 people, mostly teachers and social workers, enrolled in the program. Blue Shield formed in 1946, and HMSA joined and expanded to the neighbor islands. By 1948, 30,000 were members. Today, 600,000 people, over half the state's population, belong to HMSA.

—Researched by Vera Sunanto

Hawaii Sugar Planter's Association

The sugar industry in Hawaii, which started around 1850, began to get organized in 1882, forming the Planters' Labor and Supply Company. The trade association's task was to help growers find laborers, and form a buying *hui* for equipment, which was very expensive for small farmers.

The Planters' Labor and Supply Co. was located on the corner of Keeaumoku Street and Wilder Avenue where Makiki District Park now stands. In 1895, its name was changed to the Hawaii Sugar Planters Association (HSPA), and its job expanded to include sugar cane research. Members were assessed by the volume of sugar they produced.

"What was different about sugar production in Hawaii was the introduction of a business model to agriculture," says president Stephanie Whalen. "That's pretty common today, but this vertical integration of growers, refiners, and retailers started over 100 years ago in Hawaii. It was far ahead of its time."

Cane sugar is a commodity, identical in Cuba, the Philippines or Hawaii. It is a high volume, low margin business. Hawaii is 2,500 miles from the marketplace. Cooperation within the industry was considered to be a must.

From the 1920s through the 1990s, the HSPA focused on innovations and processes that would increase yields and decrease costs. Hundreds of mills on five islands were reduced to 12.

The HSPA formed the California and Hawaiian Sugar Refining Company (C&H) in 1905, located in Crockett, California. C&H was jointly owned by 33 sugar companies.

Central to sugar production in Hawaii was the need for water. Water was plentiful in mauka areas, but sugar production in the sunnier, leeward areas was 40% better. The solution was huge water engineering projects on all the islands.

The Waiahole Ditch collected Windward Oahu water and moved it to Central Oahu. The Hamakua Ditch built a tunnel through a mountain with the two crews meeting within inches in the middle. "Such projects were nothing new," Whalen continues. "The Romans built much bigger aqueducts 2,000 years ago, some of which still exist today."

The HSPA also engaged in massive forestation projects. "Growers saw a need to improve the forests and increase watershed. Before their projects, the Nuuanu Pali was as dry as Molokai," Whalen added. Forests cooled the air, causing clouds to condense and drop more rain.

Many of the island's botanical gardens were created to experiment with the right kinds of trees and plants to use. The Harold Lyon Arboretum was a nursery for these projects. The HSPA hired Dr. Lyon in 1918 and acquired 124 acres of Manoa land denuded by free-ranging cattle. Later known as the Lyon Arboretum, over 2,000 different tree species were grown there.

On Kauai, sugar baron George Norton Wilcox of Grove Farms is largely credited with launching the massive tree planting project that made Kauai the "Garden Isle" it is today.

Few know that the sugar industry in Hawaii did not use insecticides. "It used biological controls," continues Whalen. "Hawaii is the only sugar industry in the world that sought and found non-chemical ways of controlling pests. Tilapia, for instance, were brought in to control weeds growing in agricultural ditches."

The mongoose was introduced by some growers to control rats in sugar cane fields. In 1883, 72 mongoose from Jamaica were imported to the Hamakua Coast on the Big Island. They were also introduced on Maui and Oahu at about the same time. The ineffectiveness of the plan is now a legend in Hawaii.

A doctor at Queen's Hospital in the 1920s, Nils Larsen, approached the sugar growers with a proposal to improve worker health and productivity. His rural clinics were the first health care system for agricultural workers in the state. Nutritional training led to vegetable gardens around worker homes. Workers took less sick leave, and infant mortality rates fell. His programs went on to win national awards.

In many ways, the plantations provided services usually provided by municipal government. "They paid for and provided water, sewers, electricity, parks, ball fields, gyms, roads, lights, recreation, and cultural activities," Whalen continues. "You won't find an industry doing that anywhere else but Hawaii." Whalen believes municipal government was somewhat hobbled by industry's actions in these areas. "With the closing of all but two plantations (Gay & Robinson on Kauai and HC&S on Maui), government has had to take over these functions, and they really haven't gotten the hang of it yet."

In 1996, the HSPA name was changed again to the Hawaiian Agricultural Research Center (HARC) to help the state develop alternative crops to sugar. With a staff of 65 and a budget of $4.5 million, HARC is focused on creating the type of agriculture that will be viable into the next century.

Papayas, apple bananas ("perfect for children," Whalen believes) and flowers are getting staff attention as is seed development. Equally promising is bio-farming - the growing of drugs in plants rather than in factories. "It may be much cheaper," Whalen says. "Arthritis and herpes drugs are being tested now."

Hawaii Visitors and Convention Bureau

With six million tourists a year now, it is hard to imagine a time when few tourists visited the islands. Frommer's Tour Guide says that Hawaii tourism began in the 1860s with adventure travelers flocking to Kilauea Volcano, one of the world's prime attractions. Back then, they had to ride 29 miles on horseback or by wagon from Hilo to view Madam Pele's show.

In 1865, a grass version of Volcano House was built on the

Halemaumau Crater rim to shelter visitors. It was Hawaii's first tourist hotel.

When Hawaii became a territory in 1898, a mini tourist boom developed. The Moana Hotel opened in 1901, and the Alexander Young a year later. A bubonic plague outbreak, however, caused tourists to stop coming. Visitors may have wanted to see the islands, but not risk their lives.

In 1902, with the plague past, W. C. Weedon stepped forward with an idea. He offered to travel around the mainland and conduct Hawaii lecture tours and a "magic lantern" show for six months. A group of Honolulu businessmen paid him $100 per month.

Weedon sailed for San Francisco with photographs and the intention to communicate "a realistic and truthful representation of those remarkable people and beautiful lands of Hawaii." The plan was to persuade California visitors to go a little farther when they were out West and see Hawaii, too.

Mark Twain had preceded Weedon and spoke in glowing terms about the "the loveliest fleet of islands anchored in any ocean. No alien land in all the world has any deep, strong charm for me but that one; no other land could so longingly and beseechingly haunt me sleeping and waking."

Weedon drew packed houses on the West Coast. He wrote back to the merchants that "at every point I go, I find people ready and eager to learn more of Hawaii."

Governor Sanford Dole pushed a $15,000 allotment through the legislature in 1903 for what became the Hawaii Promotion Committee. The tourism office opened in the new Alexander Young Hotel, and soon advertisements were running in national magazines extolling the perpetual spring and romance of the islands. About 2,000 visitors came that year.

By 1919, the Hawaii Tourist Bureau, as it was then called, counted 8,000 visitors to the islands. Its $100,000 budget allowed for beautiful brochures, advertisements, and colorful community events, usually involving flowers and parades.

Matson opened the Royal Hawaiian Hotel in 1927 and launched the luxury line of White Ships to bring well-heeled visitors, their cars, and servants for months-long visits. Streamers, leis, music, and pomp welcomed each Matson liner at Aloha Tower.

Tourists were amused with personal tours, floral parades, wacky hapa-haole music, and shows spotlighting that naughty dance, the hula. The tourists loved it.

The Bureau took part in many promotional activities over the years, but the most enduring and successful was the radio program *Hawaii Calls*, launched in 1935 by Webley Edwards. It was broadcast from "beneath the banyan tree" at the Moana Hotel for nearly four decades to the mainland, Canada, and Australia every Saturday. The show was a huge hit and developed a lifelong desire in many listeners to visit the islands. Pan Am Clippers began flying the first visitors to Hawaii in 1936.

World War II brought an abrupt end to tourism in Hawaii. However, it did bring hundreds of thousands of service men and women, many of whom would later return. The Hawaii Visitors Bureau started in 1945 as the war was ending. A group of businessmen launched Aloha Week in 1947 to boost tourism in the otherwise slow fall season.

An important priority was to get the ocean liner Lurline back into passenger business after her wartime duty. It cost Matson $19 million, but in the spring of 1948, 150,000 people and an 80 vessel escort arranged by the HVB gathered to watch her steam into Honolulu Harbor and reclaim her title as "glamour girl of the Pacific." An 80 foot lei of orange crepe paper was draped across her bow.

Statehood in 1959 coincided with the arrival of jet airplanes,

The Hawaii Visitors Bureau worked hard to restore tourism after World War II. Spontaneous celebrations broke out in Waikiki and downtown on V.J. Day, August 6th, 1945.

and tourism took off, so to speak. Hawaiian entertainers and promotion experts circled the globe to spread the Islands of Aloha message. Color television came in the 1960s and brought *Hawaii Five-0* into millions of mainland homes. By 1970, tourism passed sugar and pineapple as the main driver of Hawaii's economy.

In July 1996, the HVB's name was officially changed to the Hawaii Visitors and Convention Bureau to reflect a new emphasis on business/meeting travel and a new responsibility for marketing the world class, state-of-the-art, Hawaii Convention Center.

"Over the years, the nature of tourism promotion has changed to keep pace with the rest of the world," says the HVCB web site. "The advertising programs that sold Hawaii with pretty girls and palm trees began to stress the Islands' diversity, its Hawaiian culture and history, and the wide range of sports, activities, shopping, and cuisine. We began to appeal to a wider base of travelers who wanted more of what Hawaii really is."

Hawaii today is one of the world's most desired destinations. Unsurpassed natural beauty combined with our world-famous spirit of aloha continue to be an unbeatable combination.

Hawaiian Airlines

In 1927, Charles Lindbergh was the first person to fly a single-engine plane from the United States to Europe. Stanley Kennedy, an assistant general manager at Inter-Island Steam Navigation Company, was inspired.

Kennedy approached the board of directors and convinced them that air travel was the wave of the future. They gave him the go ahead to start an airline. Inter-Island Airways began passenger service on January 30, 1929, and Stanley Kennedy became its general manager.

Inter-Island Airways was the first airline in Hawaii and the Pacific. The Pan Am Clipper did not begin passenger service between the west coast and the islands until 1936. At first, Inter-Island flew two eight-passenger Sikorsky S-38 amphibians from John Rogers field, a dirt strip on Lagoon Drive, to neighbor islands. In 1934, they started the first airmail service between islands.

Stanley Kennedy was inspired by Lindbergh's 1927 solo trans-Atlantic flight to start Hawaii's first airline.

In 1941, Inter-Island Airways became Hawaiian Airlines. Hawaiian Air has had several corporate logos through the years, but *Pualani,* meaning "flower of the sky," introduced in 1974, is the best known. The profile of island girl Leinaala Teruya Drummond (Miss Hawaii 1973) wearing a hibiscus in her hair was designed to promote Hawaii's exotic flora and its warm, friendly people.

Past slogans have included *Safety-Comfort-Speed* (1933), *Holder of the World's Safety Record* (1961), and *Hawaii's Flagship Airline* (1990). The current, *Wings of the Islands,* was coined in 1998.

"Today, Hawaiian carries more than five million passengers a year and flies to Las Vegas, Los Angeles, Ontario, Sacramento, San Diego, San Francisco, Phoenix, Portland, Seattle, Pago Pago, American Samoa, and Papeete, Tahiti," says Hattie Dixon, former senior director of advertising and promotion.

—Researched by Dolores Fung and Amy Ashizawa

Hawaiian Electric Company

King David Kalakaua's vision of lighting Hawaii's capital with electricity led to the formation of the Hawaiian Electric Company. Kalakaua was fascinated with technology, and arranged to meet Thomas Edison, the inventor of the incandescent lamp, in New York as part of a world tour in 1881.

Five years later, thousands came to Iolani Palace to see three electric lights in July, 1886. Then, to celebrate Kalakaua's birthday on November 16th, David Bowers Smith arranged for the king's residence to become the world's first royal palace to be illuminated by electricity. This was four years before the White House and before any building in California had electricity.

On March 23, 1888, electricity made its way through the streets of Honolulu. Soon after, a power plant was built in Nuuanu Valley where turbines were driven by the energy of flowing water. Princess Kaiulani, the king's niece, threw the switch that illuminated the town's streets for the first time.

The firm of E.O. Hall & Son installed and serviced the plants throughout Honolulu. In 1891, four men, Hall's son William, the manager of E.O. Hall & Son; Edwin Oscar White, the former manager of the Nuuanu plant; William V. Lockwood, and attorney Jonathan Austin formed the partnership, which was later incorporated as the Hawaiian Electric Company.

Over the years, the publicly held company expanded by serving Waikiki where the island's wealthier residents and luxurious hotels were located. In addition, the company extended by delivering electricity to U.S. military bases, the residents of Makiki, Kamehameha Schools, the University of Hawaii, and Waialae Ranch. In the process of expansion, Hawaiian Electric faced such challenges as establishing lines across the swamps to Waikiki and serving Kaneohe and Kailua, which required lines through Nuuanu Valley and over the Koolau Mountains.

Few recall that HECO once considered building a nuclear power plant in Kahe Valley.

Since 1983, the Hawaiian Electric Company has been a

King Kalakaua's fascination with technology led to Iolani Palace being electrified four years before the White House.

subsidiary of Hawaii Electric Industries, Inc. HEI is also the parent corporation of American Savings and HEI Power Corporation. Since 1968, the Maui Electric Company (MECO) has been a subdivision of HECO and serves Maui, Molokai, and Lanai.

In 1970, HECO acquired the Hilo Electric Light Company, today known as the Hawaii Electric Light Company (HELCO). This subdivision is responsible for the Big Island. As a result of the neighbor island subdivisions, all major Hawaiian Islands are dependent on HECO, except Kauai.

Ninety-five percent of the people in Hawaii are served by HECO. Nearly 2,000 people are employed throughout the islands.

—*Researched by Kathryn Acorda and Irena Deisinger*

Hawaiian Eye Center

John Corboy founded Hawaii's leading eye center in 1975. Where most medical offices are cold and impersonal, Dr. Corboy's vision was to provide the people of Hawaii with a personalized and compassionate approach to full service eye care. They view their patients as members of their *ohana* and strive to make each meeting as pleasant and enjoyable as a visit with a dear family member.

Known for treating their patients like celebrities, the Hawaiian Eye Center offers courtesy van transportation to their clinics and even overnight accommodations at Hale Maka, a ten-bed, wheel-chair-accessible facility for neighbor island surgery patients.

Their original office was just two tiny rooms in Wahiawa, but they have grown to three offices on Oahu, plus Hilo, Kahului, and Kaunakakai.

Now under the direction of Dr. Christopher Tortora, their state-of-the-art surgery and laser center, and impeccably trained doctors offers the most advanced procedures available. It is the best-equipped surgery center of its kind in Hawaii.

More people in Hawaii have turned to the Hawaiian Eye Center for cataract care than any other clinic in the state. Their "no-stitch, no-injection, patchless" 20-minute cataract surgery surprises most people with how easy, quick, and painless it all was.

Helena's Hawaiian Food

At 90 years of age, Helen Chock is still going strong. "This is our 61st year," Chock says. "Even though I'm 90, there's no reason to retire. This place keeps me healthy." Chock has slowed down a bit though. She's cut back to 14-hour days from 16.

Helen's parents had a general merchandise store on North King Street near Houghtailing. "My brother started a Hawaiian food restaurant next to the store but he was too young and got tired of it. My mom asked me to take over. I had been working at the Ford Island Laundry before that. No, I wasn't working *that* Sunday in 1941…"

Helen Chock has been training her grandson, Craig, to run Helena's Hawaiian Food. Behind them is their famous pipikaula spareribs.

"So we took over the restaurant in 1946, and my husband, Jong Chock, suggested we add an "a" to my name to make it sound more Hawaiian. The restaurant took about three years to catch on. We had a lot of the Kamehameha students come after school and football games for saimin or pipikaula, which were 25 cents back then."

"I used to make pipikaula from chuck steak, but it was a lot of work. We switched to U. S. Choice ribs which we marinate and then dry over the stove first, and that's what makes ours special."

Helena's Butterfish Collars are also very popular. "The cut is from behind the eyes to the gills. So many people tell me they'd never heard of them before and came just to try them. I was the first to make them, but now others carry the collars, and sometimes there's a shortage, and we can't get them at all!"

Helena's food is so popular, it is sometimes sent all over the world. "A group in Washington D.C. throws a luau every year, and we have sent lau lau, short ribs, poi, and lomi salmon to them for six years."

Helen got a call from the James Beard Foundation asking if she could come to New York for an award. The annual James Beard Awards are the Oscars of the food world. "I had never heard of them, so I asked my friends in the media if they were legitimate. They said it was very prestigious. My daughter took off work because, at 83 years old then, I wouldn't go to New York by myself."

Helena's was one of eight to win the James Beard Foundation's Regional Classics Restaurant Award. The criteria for winning is being "beloved in its region for quality food that reflects the history and character of its community." Hawaii is in the Pacific Northwest Region. Hawaii's only previous winners were Roy Yamaguchi, Alan Wong and Chef Mavro.

In 2002, Helena's moved to North School Street when the lease ran out on King Street. Grandson Craig, now 40, has been working with Helen and is being groomed to take over the place someday.

Hilo Hattie - The Store of Hawaii

Do you need a really large aloha shirt? If you wear 400 XL, you can find it at Hilo Hattie's, which displays the "World's Largest Aloha Shirt" at it's Nimitz store.

"Everything at Hilo Hattie is designed to exceed your expectations," says Carlton Kramer, marketing vice president. When you walk into their store, you are greeted with a shell lei. At Hilo Hattie, there is free fruit juice for the 2.5 million visitors who come by each year.

Jim Romig founded Hilo Hattie in 1963 under the name Kaluna Hawaii Sportswear in Kakaako. In 1965, it opened a manufacturing center where Ward Warehouse is today and changed their name to Hawaiian Wear Unlimited. With one van, the company brought tourists from Waikiki into the facility every day and be-

Hilo Hattie was one of Hawaii's more popular entertainers in the 1950s and 1960s.

came known as the "Home of the $3.95 Aloha Shirt."

Hilo Hattie was the stage name for a very popular entertainer in Hawaii from the 1930s through the 1970s. She was born Clarissa Haili on October 28, 1901, but everyone called her Clara. She began her career as a school teacher, but it was her singing and dancing that gave her a place in modern history. She popularized the comic hula style with such tunes as *Princess Pupule Has Plenty Papayas* and *When Hilo Hattie Does the Hula Hop.*

Clara passed away in 1979, and Hawaiian Wear Unlimited acquired the Hilo Hattie name. The company expanded to all the major islands and, in 1983, opened a new headquarters, an 80,000 square foot, $7 million showroom, manufacturing center and warehouse at 700 North Nimitz Highway. In the last five years, Hilo Hattie has opened stores in California, Nevada, Arizona and Florida. Hilohattie.com is Hawaii's busiest internet site with over 1 million sales a year.

Hilo Macaroni Factory

"The joke around here," said owner Hideo Ikeda, "was that we didn't make macaroni at the Hilo Macaroni Factory. The dozen or so people, including my father, Tatsunoke Ikeda, who founded the company in 1914, didn't know the difference between noodles and macaroni. We stopped making noodles in 1946!"

Hilo Macaroni Factory was famous for its Hilo Saloon Pilot and Hilo Creme Crackers. "The story is that the recipe for Saloon Pilot came from the cook of a German ship that was taken over during World War I," Ikeda continued. The recipe for Hard Tack, a firm biscuit with a long shelf life, used by sailors in place of bread, was passed to his father. "I don't know where the name Saloon Pilot name came from," said Ikeda who was just a boy when his father died.

Hilo Macaroni Factory also had a Japanese name - Hilo Seimen (noodle) Kabushiki Kaisha (stock company). "Shares cost $5 but some couldn't afford that, so two people bought one share. My dad and brother, Shiro, consolidated the stock ownership long ago. When my dad died in 1933, Shiro took over and ran the company for 60 years. I've been running the company since 1993, when he retired."

They also owned the T. Ikeda Factory, which made Maru Ichi ("Circle 1") Shoyu and Sun Brite Soda Works. "The original factory was on Kamehameha Avenue," Ikeda recalled, "and the 1946 tidal wave ruined our noodle making equipment. So we concentrated on our crackers and pastries. Even though we haven't made pasta in almost 60 years, 'macaroni' is still in our name!"

Advancing in years, and with no one interested in taking over the company, Ikeda closed the Hilo Macaroni Factory in 2003.

Hilton Hawaiian Village

In 1955, Henry Kaiser bought the eight-acre John Ena estate in Waikiki. He then added the six-acre parcel that was formerly the site of the Niumalu Hotel, built in 1928. The land cost him $2.5 million. He turned the property into the Hawaiian Village Hotel.

As a Matson employee, Bill Sewell remembers getting great price reductions at the Matson hotels. "However, when privacy was important, we would stay at the Niumalu. It was out of the mainstream. It had a salt-water swimming pool built into the shoreline so that the waves freshened the pool on a regular basis. Leading to the pool was a long line of maybe 20 individual cabins, which connected the pool to the main lobby, dining room, and hotel rooms. It was really neat."

"No wonder Henry Kaiser liked it, too," Sewell surmises. "The Buckminster Fuller inspired geodesic dome was all Kaiser Aluminum." The Hilton Dome was built in just 22 hours in 1957, and a concert was held there that night. Geodesic domes are stronger and require substantially less building materials. Kaiser flew to Hawaii on the day the dome was erected, wanting to see it go up. However, it was

Henry Kaiser built the Hawaiian Village Hotel in 1955 and went on to develop Hawaii Kai.

174

completed by the time he arrived. Needing more hotel rooms, it was replaced in 2001 by the Kalia Tower.

Kaiser's sons, who were running the various industries on the mainland, 'retired' their dad to Hawaii. Of course, at age 70, he still had a lot of creative energy, so he developed the hotel and KHVH radio and TV, which later became KITV. KHVH stood for Kaiser's Hawaiian Village Hotel.

Don the Beachcomber had talked to Kaiser about his idea of building a Polynesian village, but Kaiser did not back what became the International Marketplace. His Hawaiian Village Hotel was remarkably similar - a self-contained community, where the guests could find all the relaxation, shopping, and restaurants they needed.

Martin Denny developed the song *Quiet Village* at the Shell Bar at the Hawaiian Village in 1956 when it was a low-rise with 70 rooms. Denny noticed during one song that some bullfrogs in the pond next to him would croak. When the song was over, they would stop. Denny repeated the song later, and the frogs joined in again. Some of the guys in the band were inspired to make birdcalls.

The next day, a guest requested the song with the frogs and birdcalls. Denny was perplexed until he realized the guest thought it was part of the song. Later that night, Denny encouraged the band to make birdcalls, and he played a gourd with grooves that sounded like a frog. The song was a huge hit and was requested over and over. Denny guesses they played *Quiet Village* over 30 times that night.

Kaiser sold the Hawaiian Village Hotel in 1961 for $21.5 million to Hilton, and it became the Hilton Hawaiian Village. "Then Kaiser signed the largest lease ever with Bishop Estate for the 6,000 plus acres of land called Maunalua,"

The Niumalu Hotel, built in 1928, preceded the Hawaiian Village Hotel on the site.

Sewell continues. "He lined a smelly, rotten, trashy delta with rock walls, dredged and cleaned it, and renamed it the Marina at Hawaii Kai. I remember a little coffee shop there called 'The Pink Poodle' because Henry liked pink." DeSoto Brown recalls that Kaiser-owned heavy construction equipment was painted pink as well.

The Hilton Hawaiian Village today has 20 restaurants and lounges, more than 90 shops, a spa and full service salon, fitness center, florist, medical center, 24-hour business center, Bishop Museum Hawaiian Arts and Culture Center, church services, and children's programs.

Conrad Nicholson Hilton was born on Christmas day, 1887, in New Mexico. He passed away in 1979. On his gravestone are the words "Christmas is Forever." He bought his first hotel, the Mobley, in Cisco, Texas in 1919. The Hilton Hotel Corporation and Hilton International comprise over 2,500 hotels with over 350,000 rooms in 50 countries and all 50 states. They employ over 80,000 people.

KHVH (Kaiser's Hawaiian Village Hotel) radio broadcast from the hotel.

When Kaiser died in 1967, he left behind a legacy of 60 companies founded in 32 states and 30 countries. Revenues top $2.5 billion annually.

Honolulu Advertiser

The *Honolulu Advertiser* had its beginnings on July 2, 1856 as the *Pacific Commercial Advertiser*. Henry M. Whitney, son of the first company of missionaries to the Islands, published the then-weekly paper.

True to its name, the front page of the paper contained over 50 advertisements. The comings and goings of 300 ships were listed as was the wedding of a prominent member of the community - Alexander Liholiho (Kamehameha IV) to Emma Rooke.

When a daily competitor, the *Daily Bulletin,* started publishing in 1882, the *Advertiser* shifted to a daily edition as well. Sugar baron Claus Spreckels bought the paper in 1880 and Whitney left the Advertiser. Lorrin A. Thurston, who helped overthrow the monarchy, purchased the *Pacific Commercial Advertiser* in 1895 and was its publisher until his death 36 years later. In 1921, the paper's name changed to the *Honolulu Advertiser*

Thurston was one of the early owners of Hawaii's first radio station, KGU. Many old-timers remember when KGU's broadcast tower sat atop the Advertiser building on Kapiolani Blvd.

In 1931, Lorrin P. Thurston took the reins from his father, handing them off in 1961 to his nephew Thurston Twigg-Smith. In 1962,

Merchant Street in the 1870's shows the Pacific Commercial Advertiser building, center. At left is the Kamehameha V post office, which still stands today.

Star-Bulletin publisher Chinn Ho created the Hawaii Newspaper Agency to print, distribute, and handle advertising for both papers. Editorial and news gathering functions remained separate.

The Gannett Corp. purchased the *Star-Bulletin* in 1971. In 1993, they sold the *Star-Bulletin* and bought the *Advertiser* from Twigg-Smith's Persis Corp. Perhaps they saw morning papers as stronger then afternoon ones.

The *Star-Bulletin* was bought by David Black in 2001 and the joint operating agreement expired. Both papers are again true competitors. "Hawaii's Newspaper," the *Honolulu Advertiser* will be celebrating its 150th anniversary in 2006.

—Researched by Calvin Huang

Honolulu Magazine

The oldest continuously published magazine west of the Mississippi was originally named *Paradise of the Pacific*. Founded in 1888 under a Royal Charter from King Kalakaua, *Paradise of the Pacific* captured the essence of island culture with award winning writing and art.

Paradise of the Pacific was initially thought of as Hawaii's ambassador to the outside world. Part of its mission was to assure the U.S. that we were civilized here and worthy of consideration for statehood.

With that mission accomplished, the name was changed in 1966 to *Honolulu Magazine*. Its new focus was internal to the state – giving island readers insight into each other.

Honolulu Sake Brewery and Ice Company

The first sake brewery outside Japan was built by Tajiro Sumida and Tomokuni Iwanaga in 1908. Located in Pauoa Valley, it was called the Honolulu Japanese Sake Brewery Company. High import duties made Japanese rice wine very expensive, so Sumida and Iwanaga decided to make it here.

The Takara Masamune sake was very much appreciated by island Japanese. World War II halted sake production temporarily, and the company, then called the Honolulu Sake Brewery and Ice Company, turned to making shoyu and mirin. The Brewery closed in 1988.

Honolulu Star-Bulletin

In 1882, the *Daily Bulletin* began publishing. It listed ships, passengers, and cargo arriving in the harbor. In 1893, it was renamed the *Evening Bulletin*, and in the same year a new newspaper, the *Honolulu Star,* was launched.

In 1912, the papers merged, and the name became the *Honolulu Star-Bulletin*. Wallace Rider Farrington, who would later become territorial governor, was the publisher, and 28-year-old Riley Allen was editor. Allen, who would remain editor until 1960, was one of the "most extraordinary men" fellow journalist A.A. "Bud" Smyser knew. He had an "amazingly quick and sharp mind, stern in his rectitude yet always compassionate and with a great sense of humor."

On December 7, 1941, while bombs were falling only 9 miles away, Riley called his reporters, editors, and printers into action. Within hours, 250,000 copies were on the streets. Paperboys were mobbed on street corners for copies. **WAR! OAHU BOMBED BY JAPANESE PLANES** blared the headline.

At first, people got their news

Wallace Ryder Farrington became publisher of the Honolulu Star-Bulletin in 1912 and was later Governor from 1921 to 1929.

of the attack from radio. But authorities shut it down, and people hungry for news turned to the newspapers. The *Honolulu Advertiser* was stymied that day with a broken printing press, but the *Star-Bulletin* allowed it to use their press. **SABOTEURS LAND HERE** blared the *Advertiser* headline, incorrectly.

While other papers referred to the enemy as "Japs," Allen would not allow the term to be used in the *Star-Bulletin*. The *Star-Bulletin* saw itself as the newspaper of the common man and recognized the Asian ancestry of half of our residents.

The *Star-Bulletin* fought hard for statehood and was not shy about taking on the powerful elites in the state. Its 1998 *Broken Trust* articles about the Bishop Estate inspired a state investigation and eventual removal of all its trustees.

Editor Riley Allen would not allow the racial slur "Jap" to be used during WW II, and editorialized against internment.

In its 122nd year, the *Star-Bulletin*, under the new ownership of David Black, continues the tradition of reporting and fighting for the people of Hawaii.

Hotel Hana-Maui

The most remote resort in the islands opened in 1946 on a 20-acre property bought from the Hana Plantation. Paul Fagan was a successful San Francisco businessman, and the Kauiki Inn, as he first called it, had only six rooms.

The Kauiki Inn's name was later changed to the Hana Ranch Hotel, which some considered to be the first fine neighbor island resort.

The hotel says that Hana is "more than a place. Hana is a state of mind, a remote, protected corner of the world where past and present blend in a gentle union; where people still care for one another in a genuine, unaffected way, and where memories are born that will last forever."

Hudson's Bay Company

North America's oldest company, 333 year-old Hudson's Bay Company, once had a recruiting office in downtown Honolulu. They controlled the entire northwest fur trade, and according to the Hawaiian Journal of History, "virtually every fur-trading post west of the Rocky Mountains had a contingent of Hawaiians, repeatedly praised for their reliability, cheerful dispositions, and hard work."

There were so many Hawaiians working at Fort Vancouver that they had their own living quarters called "Kanaka Town." The Hudson's Bay Company was chartered in 1670 and is now Canada's largest department-store operator. They once owned over 10% of the earth's surface.

The Hungry Lion

The Hungry Lion restaurant, at Nuuanu and School streets, evolved from the dream of the former owner and founder, Roy Shimonishi. A fan of all sports, Shimonishi knew that he wanted to have a restaurant with a sports theme and a mascot. In 1982, he found an excellent location for the restaurant on Nuuanu Ave., and he knew that he wanted the name of the restaurant to incorporate the word "hungry," but he was still unsure of what type of mascot he should have to represent the restaurant.

Shimonishi considered all types of animals, including Hawaiian animals like the boar or the mynah bird, but nothing seemed to fit. Then one animal on his list stood out from all the others and made great sense to represent a restaurant. The lion. Lions have ferocious appetites, and the lion is the king of the animal kingdom. Both reasons made the lion the obvious choice to become the mascot for Shimonishi's restaurant, The Hungry Lion.

After that, Shimonishi decided to hire a full time "lion actor." "The lion is the best advertising vehicle the restaurant has ever used," Shimonishi said. He has tried advertising in newspapers and on the radio, but the lion has consistently been the best draw to his restaurant. When he is not out on the sidewalks, people start ask about the lion. When people see the lion, they think of the restaurant, and that is Mr. Shimonishi's goal - to keep the customers coming.

The restaurant is built around a Chinese banyan tree that was

Roy Shimonishi poses with his Hungry Lion.

planted around 1870 by Chun Afong, Hawaii's first Chinese millionaire. Chun had an estate on the property 140 years ago. He
planted Hawaii's first two Chinese banyans there, naming them
Yin and Yang. Chun Hoon later bought the property and erected a
supermarket that was there from 1935 until 1983.

The pictures of the many famous people who have dined at
The Hungry Lion adorn the restaurant's walls, from Tia Carrera to
Michael Jackson's agent (who signed the deal for Jackson to per-
form in Hawaii over lunch at The Hungry Lion), football players
Walter Payton, Jerry Rice, Dan Marino, and the entire Dallas Cow-
boys Team. Shimonishi decided to move on to other things in
2003 and sold the Hungry Lion. Today it's owned by Kazuyuki
Goto.

—Researched by Nicola Whistler

Hyatt Regency Resorts and Spas

Jay Pritzker, who bought the Los Angeles Airport Hotel, founded
the Hyatt Corporation in 1957. Pritzker wanted a different, ear-
catching name and decided to use the previous owner's, Hyatt
von Dehm's, first name.

In the late 1960s, a hotel under construction in Atlanta with an
indoor atrium ran out of money. Pritzker purchased and completed the hotel, and the atrium was a big hit. Now it's incorporated into all Hyatt Regencys and some of the Grand Hyatts.

They operate the Hyatt Regency Resorts & Spas on Kauai, Maui,
and Waikiki, and on every continent of the world except Antarc-
tica. The Hyatt Regency Waikiki, built by Chris Hemmeter in 1974,
replaced the smaller Waikiki Biltmore Hotel at Kalakaua and
Kanekapolei 30 years ago.

—Researched by Sharon Choong

Hygienic Store

The Kahuluu landmark with an odd name, the Hygienic Store, is
not named because of the products it sells. It got its name from
the Hygienic Dairy of Kahuluu, which used to exist on the Windward side. The current owner says the store has been there since
1905.

The Hygienic Store used to be a country market, selling local
produce grown in Waikane and Waiahole valleys. However, when
supermarkets opened on the Windward side, the Hygienic Store
shifted and became a convenience store.

Ideta

Ideta is a Japanese restaurant at Dillingham Boulevard and Kohou Street in Kalihi. "My father, Fred 'Windy' Shintaku, started the restaurant in 1969 with Takeshi Yokono and Yoshio Ideta," said Sharon Toma. "They chose 'Ideta' because it was the shortest of the three names."

Toma worked at the restaurant from the beginning. When the 25 year lease was up, none of the founders' kids wanted to continue except for her. "So, now I own the place outright," Toma explains.

Shintaku and Yokono were in the supermarket business before opening Ideta. In 1954, they opened a Big Way Supermarket in Waipahu and later owned several Piggly Wiggly stores in Hawaii.

The sushi at Ideta is of the highest quality and has a strong following among locals and Japanese nationals who have homes in Hawaii. "We don't advertise," Toma said. "But the word gets around. We're one of the few places in Hawaii that gets blue fin tuna."

"All my customers are dear to me," Toma continued. "They are my friends and family. The hours are long in a restaurant, but I really enjoy it. It's a very comfortable environment to be in."

Iida

Suisan Matsukichi Iida sold ceramic tea pots to a train company in Osaka, Japan before moving to Hawaii and opening a store in Chinatown in 1900. His idea was to provide goods from the old country to Japanese immigrants.

However, the Chinatown fire of 1900 forced him to move to Beretania Street, near Nuuanu. In 1920, son Koichi Iida took over the business. When Koichi was interned during World War II, they turned to Tsuyoshi Nishimoto, who had married into the family.

Nishimoto had a good mind for business and saw the opportunity to move into Ala Moana Center when it opened in 1959. Grandson Robert Iida, who started working at the store in 1947 then took over the family business that had been an island fixture for over 105 years.

"Iida's sold things you might not be able to find elsewhere in Hawaii," says HPU student Amy Ashizawa. "You could find Japanese tea cups, rice bowls, dishes, sake glasses, Japanese dolls, lanterns, charms (called *omamori*), Buddha statues, *Yukata* (Japanese kimonos), Japanese greeting cards, traditional Japanese wrapping paper, lucky cat dolls (*maneki neko*), Boy's Day carp flags, Ikebana vases, and much more."

Robert Iida says 70% to 80% of Iida's customers were local, and the rest were tourists. Iida's had a Japan office near the Shin-Osaka bullet train station in Osaka. Ninety percent of the store's merchandise was from Japan. Iida's never recovered from losing its original Ala Moana Center location and closed in 2005 after a spirited month-long "going-out-of-business" sale.

—Researched by Amy Ashizawa

Ilikai Hotel

The Ilikai Hotel was the brainchild of Honolulu entrepreneur Chinn Ho. Built in 1964, the hotel was built near his parents' rice field and duck ponds, which had existed there 80 to 100 years ago. Many thought it was too far from Waikiki to succeed.

Ilikai means the "surface of the sea." At the time it was built, it was the largest condominium in the world. Half the units were hotel rooms, and in 1964, you could have a room with a view of Manoa Valley for $12 a night.

The opening sequence of *Hawaii Five-O* showed Jack Lord as Steve McGarrett atop the Ilikai. *Magnum P.I.* and *Jake and the Fatman* were also filmed there. Famous guests include Presidents Lyndon Johnson and Gerald Ford, Elvis Presley, Lucille Ball, Otto Preminger, William Randolph Hearst, John Wayne, Mickey Mantle, Michael Jordan, Joe Montana, and countless others.

Chinn Ho became an entrepreneur at McKinley High School. When a group of his high school friends broke a window, Ho led the group in fundraising to fix it. After raising the money, another campus group asked them to help them with their fundraising. They discovered they were pretty good at it.

Ho worked for Bishop Bank, and later at a brokerage house. He founded Capital Investment Corporation in 1944 which invested in real estate, hotels, restaurants, and later publishing.

Chinn Ho was publisher of the *Honolulu Star Bulletin* and was the first Asian-American on the board of Theo. Davies. He also held high positions with the Hawaii Visitors Bureau and the Bishop Museum.

—Researched by Remy Cremers

I Love Country Café

Remember those stories from the 1980s of limousines pulling up to houses, and the driver running up to the door with an offer to buy? That is how Richard and Millie Chan got the money to open their restaurant. "We had bought our home for $400,000, and two months later, someone offered us $800,000," Richard recalls.

In the late 1980s, the Chans had a daughter. As she grew, they were pre-occupied with how to best feed her. "We discovered juice, grains, and fresh vegetables were healthiest," says Richard. "Walking around downtown at lunch time, I wondered if people downtown would eat that kind of healthy food too."

The Chans decided to open their own restaurant in 1987 on the Fort Street Mall near HPU. "It was a small, bright place and needed a good name to stand out," Richard recalls. "I liked the word 'country' in the name. For me, it said farm fresh, simple and healthy. We were thinking of Country Café when my five year old daughter, Elizabeth, suggested adding 'I Love' to it. And that's how I Love Country Café's name came about.

Millie and Richard Chan with manager Adela Visitacion, right, outside I Love Country Cafe.

"Millie had brought me a plate lunch from another place. It was a piece of fish, a lemon wedge, two scoops of white rice, and macaroni salad," Richard continues. "And I thought, this is all I get for eight dollars?

"So when we opened up our own place," Millie interjects, "we had brown rice or rice pilaf, and the entrée came with Asian vegetables, and a tossed salad. I thought we could offer more interesting, colorful, and tasty meals."

Body builders were quick to adopt the restaurant. "One even suggested what has become our most popular dish," Millie says. "He was a trainer and asked us to stir fry chicken and vegetables with no oil and serve it with brown rice."

The Chans now have three restaurants: Piikoi, Kahala Mall, and at the Pearl Harbor Navy Exchange.

—Researched by Rasel Taher

J. C. Penney

The first store that James Cash Penney opened was called "The Golden Rule Store," a dry goods and clothing store in Kemmerer, Wyoming in 1902. While most merchants operated their businesses under the motto *caveat emptor* – "let the buyer beware" - Penney wanted "to make money and build business through serving the community with fair dealing and honest value."

The Golden Rule Stores popularized money-back returns, standardized pricing, high quality merchandise, and friendly customer service that was not widely practiced 100 years ago.

In 1913, the Golden Rule Store name was phased out in favor of J. C. Penney. By the beginning of the 1920s, 197 J. C. Penney stores operated from coast to coast with total sales of nearly $43 million.

James Cash Penney lived to be 95, passing away in 1971. In 2001, there were over 700 J. C. Penney stores across the country including four in Hawaii. Sales topped $12 billion. However, in 2002, it was announced that more than 100 stores would close, including all in the islands.

Jack in the Box

Robert O. Peterson founded Topsy's Drive-in in San Diego in 1941. Drive-ins were immensely popular, and soon he had four locations and had changed the name to Oscar's.

In 1951, Peterson developed a drive-through restaurant (the nation's first) called Jack in the Box, which had been his favorite childhood toy. Located primarily in California, Texas, and Arizona, Jack in the Box restaurants featured a smiling clown named Jack who greeted motorists ordering through a two-way speaker encased inside Jack's head. It featured 18-cent hamburgers with a "secret sauce" of mustard, mayo, and ketchup.

Today, Jack in the Box tailors its menu primarily to adult tastes and features one of the most varied and high-quality menus in the fast-food industry. The company continues to explore new food trends, including ethnic and regional foods, snacks, and healthy offerings — all aimed at satisfying changing consumer demands.

Jack in the Box operates and franchises more than 1,600 restaurants in 15 states. They have 27 in Hawaii. Headquartered in San Diego, the company has annual sales of about $2 billion and has 42,000 employees.

Jack in the Box restaurants serve more than a half billion people each year. If the entire 6 billion Jack in the Box burgers made since 1951 were placed side by side, they would circle the earth 12 times.

—Researched by I-Jen Tsai

John Dominis

D. G. "Andy" Anderson opened John Dominis restaurant in 1979 and named it for his father, John Dominis Anderson. Many have carried the John Dominis name, and Anderson is probably honoring them, as well.

John Owen Dominis was the governor of Oahu from 1868 to 1891 and husband of Queen Liliuokalani. His father, John Dominis, was a sea captain who moved to Hawaii in 1837. He built a mansion on Beretania Street in 1846 that was later named Washington Place. He never returned from a voyage to Asia to purchase furniture.

"Everything about Washington Place reflects Queen Liliuokalani," says former First Lady Vicki Cayetano. "The governors who lived here were just caretakers. I'm always aware that this is the Queen's home, and when you walk through it, people should be honored to be in her presence."

The Anderson and Dominis families were close friends but not related. Andy's grandfather John C. Anderson was an elected official and best friend of John Owen Dominis. John C. Anderson named his son John Dominis Anderson after his friend.

John Owen Dominis was the Governor of Oahu and husband of Queen Liliuokalani

Andy Anderson attended but never graduated from Roosevelt High School. Out of high school, he opened Anderson Camera. Anderson spent 20 years as a state senator and representative and was Frank Fasi's managing director before Jeremy Harris. He ran for Governor in 2002 as a democrat. Former State Senator Whitney Anderson is his brother. Anderson also owns Michel's at the Colony Surf.

—Researched by Jane Ng

Jolly Roger Drive In

Art Salsbury opened the first Jolly Roger in the mountain community of Big Bear, California in 1947. It was a malt shop with ice cream and burgers and opened only in the summer. Around 1952, he moved it to Balboa Island, south of Los Angeles, where it thrived.

"Art liked Hawaii," said Biff Graper who worked for 34 years with the chain. "Jolly Roger restaurants soon opened in Waikiki and Kahala. He was a friend of John McIntosh who had started the Yum Yum Tree and Reuben's. When McIntosh wanted to sell, Art took over. Reuben's became the Spindrifter."

Upstairs in the Kalakaua Jolly Roger was a bar called the Crow's Nest. "We tried a lot of bands there," says Graper, "but none did all that well until we hired a couple of guys called the Blue Kangaroo. We offered them a percentage of the gross."

Mike Drager and Jay Cook (who was called "Toad") were a guitar and banjo folk duo with great voices and a good sense of humor. They played the Crow's Nest for 21 years and had a great following from all over the world. They retired in 1994 when Jolly Roger lost its lease. Mike Drager now lives in Ashland, Oregon while Jay Cook is still in Hawaii. Blue Kangaroo recently put out a CD of some of their music but warns that it is "politically incorrect by today's standards, and almost everything we did was off-color or insulting...or both."

"Kenny Kaneshiro, who also had Kenny's Restaurant, took a 49% interest in the two Jolly Roger Drive-Ins," says Graper. "He really built them up. There was, however, some confusion with the drive-ins and the Jolly Roger corporate name. We had 18 other restaurants, and they had different levels of pricing and quality, so the Jolly Roger corporate name was switched to Trans Pacific Restaurants."

With 20 restaurants in the islands, Trans Pacific was second only to the Spencecliff chain throughout the 1960s and 1970s, which had as many as 50 restaurants. In 1996, Trans Pacific Restaurants went into bankruptcy, and parts were sold, including Sizzler and Yum Yum Tree. Aloha Restaurants, a Southern California based chain currently owns two Jolly Roger Restaurants, one Dockside Grill, two Buster's Beach House and Longboard Bars, and six Monterey Bay Canners Restaurants, all in California, except for the one in Pearlridge.

KC Drive Inn

Banker George C. Knapp and realtor Elwood L. Christensen founded KC Drive Inn in 1929. "They started the first drive-in in Honolulu," Dayton Asato told us. "But, when the depression worsened, they couldn't make it. In 1934, they sold the restaurant to my grandfather, Jiro Asato. He had been a cook for them, and even though the price was only $100, he couldn't afford it. They accepted $10 a month until the debt was paid."

Out of gratitude, Jiro Asato kept the KC name, and when people started calling him KC, he had his name legally changed to KC Jiro Asato.

The original restaurant was in Waikiki at Ala Wai and Kalakaua, where the Landmark Building now stands. Open until 3 AM on weekdays and 5 AM. on weekends, KC Drive Inn and the Kau Kau Korner (located near where the Hard Rock Café now stands) were the only places open past midnight. "Because of that, we got all the Waikiki entertainers," recalls cashier Mildred Yoshida, who started with KC in 1939.

"Governor Farrington and his family used to come on weekends, but our most important VIP may have been Empress Michiko of Japan, before she married then Crown Prince Akihito. The first limousine I ever saw," Yoshida continued, "pulled in one day with Zsa Zsa Gabor inside.

"In those days, we had a surfboard-shaped tray that went from window to window in the back seat of the car. Those things were heavy," Yoshida recalls. "That was before plastic. The plates were china, and the cups were glass. We didn't have plastic until after the war.

"We worked ten-hour days," Yoshida continued. "We got paid fifty cents an hour, and patrons left five cent tips, which we divided weekly. The biggest tip I recall before the war was twenty-five cents."

KC Drive Inn at Ala Wai and Kalakaua was Hawaii's first in 1929.

188

Yoshida recalls being able to see the lights from the old stadium on Isenberg and King Streets. "When the lights would go off, we'd all say to each other, 'here they come!' And within a few minutes, the place would be packed."

Wilbert "Bozo" Tsuchiyama recalls smelling the teriyaki sauce from KC Drive Inn while driving in Waikiki. "My friends and I would be drawn irresistibly to that delicious aroma. KC had the best shakes in town. The Ono-Ono shake with peanut butter was great, but I liked pineapple and strawberry too." Besides the Ono Ono Shakes, KC is famous for its Waffle Hot Dogs, invented by Knapp and Christiansen in 1929.

KC opened a second location at the top of Kapahulu around 1983 before losing their Waikiki location. For a while, they operated restaurants at Holiday Mart, Manoa Marketplace, Moiliili, and two Mr. Waffle Dog locations in Kailua (now KV Drive Inn) and Waipahu.

The family also operated the Wisteria Restaurant on King Street, and at one time, had another in the Kaneohe Bowling Alley.

"Jiro's wife, Agnes Gusukuma's two sisters and brother all had restaurants," Dayton Asato continued. "Alice Gusukuma and husband Harry founded Like Like Drive Inn. Sister Norma Gusukuma married Sei Tamashiro, and they had Sei's Family Restaurant in Moiliili until retiring in 1990. And brother Jack Gusukuma ran the Central YMCA Coffee Shop."

"At one time, we had franchised Mr. Waffle Dog to a guy in Japan," said grandson Wendell Asato, "but someone embezzled money, and they closed."

Jiro Asato passed away in 1961. His children, James, Roy, Elsie, Mildred, and Helen took over the business.

Kaimuki High School Music teacher Darryl Loo remembers how friend Ben Char ate at KC Drive Inn and discovered he had forgotten his wallet at home. "The waitress said she would pay the bill, and he could pay her back whenever he could," Loo recalls. "He was so impressed he went home and returned immediately to pay his bill. That's the kind of people they were."

"Hard work, honesty, dedication, and a commitment to our customers is what made KC Drive Inn a success for over 76 years," Dayton Asato continued. "There's a pressure to uphold the legacy of my grandfather and his values."

KC Drive Inn served its last Waffle Hot Dogs in March 2005, three months after its sister restaurant, the Wisteria closed.

KFC

Colonel Harland D. Sanders (1890–1980) owned a restaurant in Corbin, Kentucky in 1939 where he perfected his fried chicken recipe (a blend of 11 herbs and spices). Sanders retired from the restaurant business in 1956. With his first Social Security check, $104, he started Kentucky Fried Chicken.

Nearly 50 years ago, Colonel Sanders invented what is now called "home meal replacement" — selling complete meals to harried, time-strapped families. He called it, "Sunday Dinner, Seven Days a Week."

Less than 20 years later, in 1964, he sold KFC to a group of investors including John Y. Brown Jr. and Jack Massey for $2 million. Sanders was then 73, and $2 million was a lot of money, but in 1986 Pepsi bought it for $840 million!

As America became more health conscious, Kentucky Fried Chicken wanted to move away from "fried" and shortened its name to KFC.

Today, KFC has about 10,000 restaurants worldwide with sales of $8.5 billion annually. It employs 275,000 people. KFC is part of Tricon Global Restaurants, Inc., which is the world's largest restaurant system with nearly 30,000 KFC, Taco Bell, and Pizza Hut restaurants in more than 100 countries and territories.

Colonel Harlan Sanders founded KFC in 1956 with his first Social Security check.

"It's an interesting business model," says Richard Manungas, Branch Manager of American Savings Bank at Kamehameha Center. "Many of their locations have three restaurants run by just one set of staff. It keeps costs down. And, you can go to one place and have three choices."

Colonel Sanders died at age 90 in 1980 and is buried in Louisville's Cave Hill cemetery.

KTA Super Stores

The Big Island's most popular supermarket chain had humble beginnings in 1916. Koichi Taniguchi was a bookkeeper. To keep his wife Taniyo, who was pregnant, occupied he bought a house in the Waiakea section of Hilo that had a dry goods business on the lower level.

The business, K. Taniguchi Store, did well, and they expanded to groceries. In 1939, they opened another store in downtown Hilo. The tidal wave of 1946 wiped out their little Waiakea store, but the store in downtown Hilo was relatively unscathed. "They shifted their operations to that store and recovered relatively quickly," said Andrew Chun, director of marketing.

Taniguchi opened a Kona store in 1959 and another in the Puainako Shopping Center in Hilo in 1966. Their Waimea store opened in 1990. In 1979, they were the first in the state to install checkout scanners.

The K. Taniguchi Store became KTA in the 1970s, but no one is sure exactly how the name was selected. The popular story is that shipments to another Hilo store, K. Tahara, were marked "KT" by the shippers. Those to K. Taniguchi were marked "KTA."

Today, KTA is the dominant grocery chain on the Big Island with five locations in Hilo. There is also a Waikoloa Village Market and a Circus Shop Us convenience store in Keauhou. Barry Taniguchi, grandson of Koichi, is president. They are the seventh largest employer in Hawaii County, with 775 employees.

Kamaka Hawaii

The first physician at Queen's Hospital, Dr. William Hillebrand, may have been indirectly responsible for the invention of the ukulele. He was the first to suggest bringing workers from the Portuguese Madeira Islands to Hawaii. Those first Portuguese settlers brought with them the *braguinha*, a small, four-stringed instrument that evolved in Hawaii into the ukulele.

Many credit Manuel Nunes, who arrived in the islands in 1879, as the man who invented the ukulele, which means "jumping flea" in Hawaiian. Craftsmen Augusto Dias, Jose do Espirito Santo, Joao Fernandes, and Joao Luiz Correa were also early ukulele manufacturers.

Manuel Nunes began making ukuleles in 1879. Samuel K. Kamaka Sr., an apprentice to Nunes, left to start his own ukulele business in 1916 out of his basement. He made a dozen ukuleles per week and sold them for $5 a piece. In five years, he was able to hire staff and move into bigger quarters.

There may have been as many as 15 competitors back then, but Kamaka created a design that proved to be very popular, a pineapple-shaped ukulele. The oval shaped instrument has a full, warm sound. Kamaka is the only one still around from those early days, and today, his sons Sam Jr. and Fred manage the 88 year old company. Even though they make 3,000 instruments a year, you might have to wait for one as there is a year's backlog.

Kamaka's wife, Gerry, encouraged the hiring of handicapped people 50 years ago, and today, two-thirds of the craftsmen are deaf or have muscular dystrophy. The deaf, they have found, often have a fine sense of touch, and are good at gauging the perfect thickness of wood that will produce the best tone.

Manuel Nunes' tombstone calls him the "inventor of the ukulele" and has a ukulele carved into the top.

Kamaka has made ukuleles for such popular entertainers as Genoa Keawe, Peter Moon, Israel Kamakawiwoole, Tiny Tim, Arthur Godfrey, and Laurel and Hardy.

Kamehameha Garment Company

It is unclear exactly who made the first aloha shirt around 1930. It may have been Ellery Chun who made a shirt from a bright, flowery piece of kimono fabric he had lying around his King-Smith Tailor Shop. No one knows for sure.

By the early 1930s, several tailors were making the shirts. Herbert Briner took note of the garments and had an idea. He bought a uniform manufacturer and converted it into Hawaii's first ready-to-wear garment company, christening it The Kamehameha Garment Company. It opened for business in 1936.

Named for Hawaii's legendary King Kamehameha I, the company experienced immediate success and established a reputation for high quality garments that captured the unique spirit and traditions of island living. Original Kamehameha "silky" aloha shirts are prized today by collectors of the genre, fetching hundreds, and even thousands of dollars.

The modern day renaissance of Hawaiian fashion has again brought the company to the attention of the trend-conscious fashion world. By reintroducing the prints and color stories that made the company preeminent in the industry so many years ago, Kamehameha is winning the allegiance of a whole new group of aloha shirt lovers. The styling is purely retro, virtually duplicating the old shirt designs that are now so prized by the collectors.

"In the sixty-odd years since Herb Briner founded the Hawaiian ready-to-wear industry, there have been many inferior send-ups of the Hawaiian shirt, many not even made in Hawaii," says company President Brad Walker. "Kamehameha alone continues the traditions and tailoring methods that made the Kamehameha aloha shirt a fashion statement so many years ago. With a nod to this history, in 1996, the members of the Hawaiian Fashion Association named Kamehameha Manufacturer of the Year in the Traditional Division."

In 2001, Forbes Magazine selected Kamehameha Garment Company's shirts as one of the "Fifty Best American Products".

Kapiolani Health

Two organizations joined together in 1976 to form Kapiolani Medical Center - Kapiolani Maternity Home and Kauikeolani Children's Home.

Kapiolani Maternity and Gynecological Hospital was founded in 1890 when Queen Kapiolani raised $8,000 to remodel a house at Makiki and Beretania Streets. At the time, women would spend two weeks at the home, delivering their baby, then learning how to care for it. The cost was only $1.75 a day.

Gov. Sanford Dole, above, and Dr. James Judd founded Kauikeolani Children's Hospital in 1909 to counteract Hawaii's 28% infant mortality rate.

Kauikeolani Children's Hospital was conceived by then Governor Sanford Ballard Dole and Dr. James Robert Judd in 1906. Governor Dole met Dr. Judd on the street and asked about the health of the community. Dr. Judd told him he had just found that the infant mortality rate in the islands was over 28% and that another 20% died between their first and fifth year. Dole was appalled and both pledged to form a group to take action on it.

Kauai resident Albert Wilcox contributed over $50,000 to build the hospital, and it named after his wife, Emma Kauikeolani. In 1909, the first hospital devoted to children in Hawaii, and one of the first such in the world, opened its doors on Kuakini Street where the Rehabilitation Hospital of the Pacific now stands.

In 1910, 354 patients were admitted, spending an average of 19 days at a cost of only $1.08 a day. The first president was Sanford B. Dole, who ran the hospital until his death in 1926.

Harold Garfield Dillingham, the son of Benjamin Franklin Dillingham, took over in 1926 and was president for three decades until 1958. A Rehabilitation Center was started at Children's Hospital in 1945 and grew into the Rehabilitation Hospital of the Pacific in 1975.

Honolulu Shriners Hospital was originally established as a ward of Kauikeolani Children's Hospital. It moved to the former Dowsett Mansion in Makiki in 1930.

In 1976, Kauikeolani Children's Hospital and Kapiolani Maternity Home merged and moved to their current Punahou Street location. Roger Drue is now president of Kapiolani Health.

Kapiolani Health, Straub, and Wilcox Health System merged in 2001 to form Hawaii Pacific Health making it the largest health care system in the state. Each of the three retained their individual names and identities.

Kemoo Farm

Percy Pawn founded Kemoo Farm in 1909 as a pig and dairy farm near Schofield Barracks in Wahiawa. Within 20 years, the farm added a milk depot, ice cream parlor, coffee shop, and market.

An elegant dining room overlooking Lake Wilson was built in the 1930s. Many formal dinners and banquets were held there, and "many generals stood in line during World War II to eat one of the famous sizzling steaks," said Dick Rodby, whose father Leo bought Kemoo Farm in 1935.

Rodby says there are many rumors as to how they got their name, which means "lizard or reptile." "Most likely it was the name of the housing area or an amusement camp for the people that worked the pineapple fields," Rodby said. "Unfortunately, the founder has passed

Kemoo Farm was founded in 1909 as a dairy and pig farm near Schofield Barracks.

away, and no one seems to know if it was a Kemoo Camp that gave its name to the farm."

In 1967, the bakers perfected their recipe for pineapple macadamia nut cakes. These Hawaiian Happy Cakes are a real treat if you have never tried them. Former President and Mrs. Reagan even posed for a picture with a Happy Cake in the White House.

—Researched By Neil Illane

Ken's Pancake House

Everyone in Hilo knows the only restaurant open 24-hours a day is Ken's Pancake House at 1730 Kamehameha Avenue. "Ken" is Ken Pruitt, who started the restaurant in 1971, after opening four in Northern California. "Ken comes over about twice a year," says General Manager Debbie Maiava.

"My husband Rick is the chef," continues Maiava. "He's a big, jovial guy with a moustache. A lot of people call him 'Ken,' and he doesn't correct them." Rick has an interesting past. He was born in a Polish concentration camp to a 14 year old girl and a Russian soldier. In 1947, she and Rick were able to get on a boat to Canada where they settled and later met the famed wrestler Neff Maiava. The wrestling circuit took him to Canada where he met Rick's mom. He married her, adopted Rick, and moved them to Laie. Neff is busy with his second career now, writing children's books. "The Rock" is a cousin of Rick's as well.

"Samoan 'Neff' was the first dark person I ever saw and he scared me," said Rick who was just five years old at the time. "He wore a *lava lava* and boar tusks in a necklace, but we got along right away."

Debbie's parents, Lei and Lindy Ching, bought the business from Ken in 1990. "My dad heard about the business being for sale on the golf course from a realtor. Co-owner Bonnie Twitchell wanted to sell it to someone who would keep the crew."

Lindy flew over and liked the place. He asked his daughter if she wanted to move to Hilo and run it. "I wasn't sure I would," said the former Windward Oahu resident. "But it has been the best move of my life. I love it here."

Her father, Lindbergh Ching was one of 16 kids and was born in 1927, the year that Charles Lindbergh flew solo across the Atlantic. Many Windward Oahu residents may remember Lindy's Foods convenience stores.

The Hilo restaurant was the idea of Mike Twitchel. He saw that the corner near the old entrance to Hilo Airport would be a good location for a restaurant. "Ken didn't think Hilo had a large enough population for a 24-hour place," Rick continued, "but we were smashed from the opening day. Unfortunately, Mike got an infection from a coral cut, became infirm, and died."

Would you believe that Ken's Pancake house is a romantic setting for marriage proposals? "We're open after the bars close," said Rick. "I guess a lot of people are inebriated, and their girlfriends are more beautiful than ever because a lot of proposals happen here. Years later, they come back with their kids!"

Ken's is also famous for Merril's Marvels fabulous desserts, named for baker Merril Kanna. They include papaya chiffon, coconut, sweet potato haupia pies, and German chocolate cake. They make their own Cajun spice, called Hilo Heat, and they roast macadamia nuts in it and call them Hot Nuts.

Kenny's Coffee House and Restaurant

Kenny Kaneshiro, John Fujieki Sr., and Herbert Sousa opened Kenny's Burger House in 1963 in Kamehameha Shopping Center. Kenny had been in the restaurant business for some time, having had three other places before.

The Burger House was a success, and two years later, they opened Kenny's Restaurant, serving local foods. General Manager Warren Matsunaga says the success of the restaurant is due to the staff, many of whom came from Spencecliff. "Several have been here 20 to 30 years. Yuri Takai has been here since 1965," says Matsunaga.

Kenny's Burger House closed in 2003 and McDonald's took over. Kenny's Restaurant is doing well and specializes in fresh fish, serving 12 to 18 different kinds a day. At Thanksgiving, Kenny's prepares 400 turkeys and all the trimmings for thankful customers.

Kenny's Restaurant had a Kaneohe location for a dozen years but closed it in the 1990s. Kenny Kaneshiro sold to John Fujieki of Star Markets and went on to manage the Jolly Roger restaurants.

Kincaid's Fish, Chop & Steak House

Kincaid's Fish, Chop & Steak House and Palomino Euro Bistro are two of several restaurants owned by Seattle based Restaurants Unlimited (RUI). Ryan's Grill and Cinnabon are also part of their group.

Rich Komen first opened The Red Baron, a steak and lobster house in Seattle, in 1969. The restaurant responded to a new trend in the restaurant business - fine food in a casual atmosphere.

Not too long after the opening of The Red Baron, Komen capitalized on another emerging restaurant concept: theme restaurants. "I started thinking about the possibilities of combining the casual steak and lobster menu with a strong theme restaurant," said Komen.

"Not just any theme, but something bold and authentic that would give the "guest" a total dining experience unlike anything they had known before." RUI applied its creative mind to this new idea and three new restaurants were born: The 17th century public house themed Clinkerdagger, Bickerstaff & Petts; and Horatio's, a restaurant with a nautical theme. The restaurants were a huge success. Horatio's at Ward Warehouse opened in 1976.

Long before "customer focus" became the rage, RUI banned the word "customer" from its vocabulary. What they came up with is still considered the central core of what RUI is today: the term "guest first." "We act guest first. We deliver high quality food every time at reasonable prices. We give great service and engage each guest. We hire the best and care about them, and we are clean."

During the nineties, guests became much more dining-savvy. They concerned themselves with specific ingredients, prided themselves on their knowledge of fine wines and beers, and refused to accept anything but the most professional service. RUI reacted to this trend with distinct restaurant concepts: Kincaid's Fish, Chop & Steak House, and the Palomino Euro Bistros.

Kincaid's was really an evolution of the original Red Baron classic fish and steak house. The first Kincaid's opened in Bloomington, Minnesota, followed soon thereafter in Burlingame, Oakland, and Redondo Beach, California, Honolulu, and Norfolk, Virginia. Kincaid's is a traditional, special occasion eatery whose trademark is a modern interpretation of the traditional steak, chop, and fish house.

Horatio's at Ward Warehouse became a Kincaid's in 1995. The Kincaid's name was chosen because it conveys a masculine, traditional, special, and strong American image.

In 1989, the first Palomino restaurant opened in Seattle. The Palomino concept centers around exhibition cooking in wood-fired rotisseries and ovens, with foods inspired by Italy and the Mediterranean. Palomino restaurants are dramatic in their decor utilizing curved millwork, marble surfaces, red finishes, and exotic "glass-art" light fixtures. Palomino elevates guests' moods and provides a sense of beauty and graciousness without a sense of formality.

Palomino Euro Bistro opened at Harbor Court in 1997. RUI felt the name expressed a bold, energetic, leading, independent, and graceful image. Rising rents led to its closure in 2007.

RUI also owns Ryan's Grill at Ward Center, and the name was picked because it portrayed an image that is sturdy, fun, approachable, joyful, playful, understandable, and down to earth. This is a place for anyone in any mood.

Today, Restaurants Unlimited operates 29 restaurants in 12 states and grosses over $150 million a year.

Horatio's was named for Horatio Nelson (1758-1805), Britain's greatest naval hero. Horatio's restaurant became Kincaid's in 1995.

K-Mart

In 1899, Sebastian Spering Kresge opened a variety store in downtown Detroit and sold everything for five and ten cents. The low prices appealed to shoppers. Kresge's success led to an expansion to 85 stores with annual sales of more than $10 million by 1912. Inflation during World War I forced Kresge stores to raise prices to 25 cents. However, the open displays and convenient locations continued to attract customers.

Company President Harry Cunningham opened the first K-Mart discount department store in 1962. Just four years later, sales in 162 K-Mart stores and 750 Kresge stores topped the $1 billion mark.

Ten more years of growth ensued, capped off by a record-setting occurrence in 1976: S. S. Kresge opened 271 K-Mart stores that year, becoming the first-ever retailer to open 17 million square feet of sales space in a single year.

K-Mart has been shifting to Big K-Marts, which means they have big assortments, big floor plans, and big changes that improved the shopping experience. K-Mart employs more than 200,000 people in more than 1,500 discount retailing centers across the U.S. This has not been bad for a chain that Sebastian Spering Kresge started as a nickel-and-dime store in downtown Detroit.

Kobayashi Travel

Perhaps better known for its subsidiary Polynesian Hospitality, Kobayashi Travel traces its roots to the Kobayashi Hotel, started over a century ago by Unosuke Kobayashi in 1892. Kobayashi had come from the Jigozen Village in Hiroshima, Japan. The hotel was located across from Aala Park. It was sold in 1982 and is presently operated as the Town Inn.

Kanae, Hichiro, and Tatsukichi Kobayashi started Kobayashi Travel Service in 1945. They have retail travel agencies in Hilo, Kaneohe, and Honolulu.

Kobayashi offers wholesale travel and tours through the Tour Shop and Aloha World, and provides motorcoach tours through Polynesian Hospitality, Paradise Discovered, and Discover Maui.

Koehnen's Interiors

If you want to see who ended up with the koa staircase that H. Hackfeld & Co. built for their flagship Hilo store in the 1890s, you can find it today at Koehnen's Interiors furniture store. "Some tourists have wandered in thinking we're a museum," says Karyl Franks, Hilo store manager and granddaughter of the founder. "All our display cases are *koa*, and the floor is *ohia*. I can see why they think that."

Koehnen's was founded on May 13, 1929. "It was a Friday the 13th," Franks remembers. "Friday the 13th has always been a lucky day for us. My husband proposed to me on that day 35 years ago!"

F. W. "Fritz" Köehnen came to Hilo to work as a bookkeeper for Hackfeld in 1908. In 1929, months before the start of the Great Depression, he bought out H. Hackfeld's jewelry business.

World War II brought Carl Rohner to the islands where he met and married Fritz's daughter, Helie. They added a furniture department to the business. It did well, and in 1957, they bought out the old Hackfeld building at 76 Kamehameha Avenue. In 1979, they closed the jewelry department and now sell furnishings exclusively.

Today, grandson Randy Rohner runs the Kona store, and granddaughter Karyl Franks runs the Hilo store. "Granddad was very trusting," Karyl recalls. "Every now and then, people tell us that in the old days he gave them several wedding rings to show their future bride on the plantation. They'd propose. Hopefully, she'd say 'yes.' Then she would make her selection and the other rings would be returned. No money would change hands until then."

However, business has not been a cakewalk for Koehnen's or for many other businesses in Hilo. They have been struck by two major tidal waves and flooded five times.

In 1946, when they were in their old location on the mauka side of Kamehameha Avenue, the tidal wave washed the buildings across the street into theirs. Two weeks before their 1957 grand opening in the Hackfeld building, a flood hit them. "Our dad put my brother and me on the mattresses that were floating in the basement, with wooden sticks to row with, and told us to collect anything that floated." Karyl recalls. "We still opened on time!"

"We got a call several hours before the 1960 tsunami from the chief of police. He said there was an earthquake in South America and that we should batten down the hatches in case a tsunami hit."

"The building has concrete walls 24 inches thick. The beams were railroad tracks, which must have been cheap and available when it was built. And we have a walk-in vault with 24-inch thick walls."

"We loaded our important papers into a truck and parked it at the police station. We hauled everything we could up to the second floor and boarded up all the windows."

"When the tidal wave hit at 1 AM, it pushed the front doors open and three feet of water came in. Dad and I rushed down and pushed the water out with brooms. When the sun came up, it looked like another planet. Nothing was recognizable. So much was destroyed around us."

"But it also brought out the best in people," Karyl continued. "Complete strangers came by in the days that followed and offered to help. All our mainland silverware suppliers replaced our water-damaged silver at no charge. We opened again in three weeks."

Koehnen's was flooded in December of 2000 when three feet of rain fell in 24 hours. The store's 9,000 square-foot basement was filled by the ten container deliveries they got each month. "This is a great location, right across the street from the ocean. But the basement is below sea level and flooding was expected."

Koehnen's water pumps didn't work when the electricity went off, like it did in 2000. They elevated things on 2-foot high shelves and only put things in the basement that could handle water. "Flood insurance is expensive and unaffordable."

"The next day we had a flood sale. People lined up an hour before opening and 2,300 items were sold in just a few hours. We just keep going. It was not the end of the world. We had a good cry, and life goes on."

Kuakini Medical Center

The story of Kuakini Medical Center begins with the California Gold Rush and the building of the Transcontinental Railroad. Thousands of Chinese came to the U.S. for the gold rush or to work on the railroad, and after it was completed in 1869, many Americans felt threatened by them. In response, Congress passed the Chinese Exclusion Act of 1882.

Hawaii's sugar growers had been employing Chinese workers and now faced a problem. The solution, they decided, was to bring in Japanese laborers. Between 1885 and 1920, 70,000 Japanese, mostly men without wives, moved to the islands.

To care for all the women-less men, the Japanese Benevolent Society (*Nihinjin Jizenkai*) was founded in 1892. They started the Japanese Charity Hospital in Kapalama in 1900 with doctors Sansaburo Kobayashi, Iga Mori, and Matsuji Misawa presiding. The hospital had 38 beds.

The hospital outgrew its first and even a second location, and the Society solicited funds for a larger hospital. Emperor Taisho of Japan and the Empress contributed to the building of a 70 bed facility at its current site on Kuakini Street. The four-acre site was large enough for current and even future needs. The name was shortened to Japanese Hospital.

The nurses and doctors spoke and kept records in Japanese. Doctors wore *yukata* and *geta*. Signs were in *kanji*. There were communal baths and teahouse parties.

The hospital grew, and by 1920, it was the second-largest civilian hospital in the country, according to the *Star-Bulletin*. In 1934, Emperor Showa of Japan contributed to the hospital's expansion to 100 beds.

World War II, however, changed everything. The large copper nameplate, with the words *Nihonjin Byoin* (The Japanese Hospital) was taken down, and everything Japanese was removed. Twenty-three civilian casualties were brought in on December 7, 1941 for treatment.

With the exception of Dr. Masaji Marumoto and Dr. Tsuneji Shinkawa, all Japanese Hospital administrators and *Jizenkai* leaders were interned shortly after the Pearl Harbor attack.

The U.S. Army took over the hospital in 1941. The name was changed to Kuakini Hospital and Home on August 1, 1942 because it was on Kuakini Street. Kuakini Street was named for John Adams Kuakini (1791-1844), the brother of Queen Kaahumanu and governor of the Big Island and acting governor of Oahu. Story has it that he and Chiefess Liliha were pledged

John Adams Kuakini was the brother of Queen Kaahumanu and governor of the Big Island.

to marry by their parents, but grew up hating each other. When they refused to marry each other, it created a great upset in the families. Liliha later married Governor Boki of Oahu. No matter how much they wanted to avoid each other, their streets now intersect in Nuuanu.

After the war, Kuakini Hospital returned to civilian control and its mission broadened to serving the medical needs of the entire community. On its 75th anniversary in 1975, the hospital was renamed Kuakini Medical Center. There were others, but Kuakini is the last surviving hospital established by Japanese immigrants in the United States. Today, in its second century of service, its 500 doctors treat over 6,000 patients a year.

—*Researched by Miho Mahler*

Kuhio Grill

When I was a college student at the University of Hawaii in 1974, we often went to a dingy, little bar with cheap beer and great *pupus* on South King Street. We'd buy drinks and tip the waitress well, and she would bring us plate after plate of *pupus*.

Waitresses at Kuhio Grill bought their own beef, chicken, shrimp, clams, seafood and vegetables. The cooks would cook it for them. Better tips brought better *pupus*, but we never knew what to expect. Waitresses were entrepreneurs. If they were smart, they could earn good money.

Some students were known to eat breakfast, lunch, and dinner at KG, as we called it. The Kuhio Grill was started by Mark Miyashiro in 1945.

Kyo-ya

A local *hui* started a Japanese restaurant on Kalakaua Avenue near Fort DeRussy in 1959, named Kyo-ya. *Kyo* was for the ancient capital of Japan, Kyoto, while *ya* meant "house or store."

After World War II, Kenji Osano bought used American cars in Hawaii and shipped them for resale in Japan. They sold like hotcakes, and he made a fortune. This was before the Japanese car industry got off the ground.

Osano was a visionary who could see where things were going and where opportunities were developing. With his money, he bought the Kyo-ya restaurant in Hawaii and the Fujiya Hotels in Japan, and his prosperity grew.

Osano saw the potential of Hawaii tourism and was one of the first Japanese investors to get into it. He purchased the old Matson hotels: The Princess Kaiulani and Moana hotels in 1963 for $19 million and the Sheraton Waikiki, Royal Hawaiian, and the Sheraton Maui hotels in 1974 for $105 million.

His acquisitions raised concerns at the time that Japanese investors were beginning to own too much of Hawaii's tourism industry.

Osano died a billionaire in 1986, leaving one of Hawaii's largest companies with interests in hotels, restaurants, insurance agencies, and retail stores. Kyo-ya is owned by Kokusai Kogyo Co. of Japan. The Honolulu restaurant closed in the middle of 2007. The company still owns the Sheraton Palace in San Francisco, the Grand Cypress Hotel in Orlando, Florida, and the Renaissance in Sydney, Australia.

L & L Hawaiian BBQ

"Plate lunches will be as popular as hamburgers on the west coast in ten years," Eddie Flores, Jr., owner of L & L Drive-Inn predicts. "We have 200 restaurants with more planned. And, there are at least fifty copycats. Every day, people come into our shops and take pictures. They are copying us because they know it works."

Kwock Yum Kam and Eddie Flores Jr. have turned their first L&L on Liliha Street into a fast-growing empire of more than 80 drive-ins in several states.

Flores bought L & L Drive-Inn as a gift for his mom, Margaret, in 1976. "She ran it, but didn't want to work at night," Flores said, "so, I brought in Kwock Yum Kam as a partner to run it in the evenings." Margaret left after five years, and Kam was in full charge. "Many don't know we were the first to offer a mini-plate," Flores says.

The L & L name came from the L & L Dairy, owned by Robert Lee, Sr. from 1952-1959. It was the third-largest dairy on Oahu. Robert Lee Jr. who now owns Pizza Bob's, recalls that when he was nine, "my dad pointed to the sign. The first L, he said, was for him, the second L was for me."

"The origin of the L & L name is actually more nebulous than that," says Bob Lee Jr. At first, it referred to my dad and his father, who died in Korea when my dad was eight. Later, L & L referred to my parents, Robert and Ida Lee."

Robert Lee, Sr. was a Korean immigrant. His first business was a restaurant downtown in 1940 called Molly's, son Bob Lee Jr.

Robert Lee Sr., left, founded the L&L Dairy in 1952. The L&L name stood for him and his father, and later he and his wife, Ida, right.

recalls. After the war, Lee bought farmland in Waimanalo and turned it into a dairy. "Dad had four L & L Milk Depots on Oahu, and one was on Liliha Street where the L & L Drive-Inn is today. They sold milk, juice, eggs, bread, ice cream and butter. The dairy had a slightly higher butterfat content than others on Oahu. The milk won

Bob Lee Jr. and his mother, Ida. As a boy, he recalls his father pointing to the L&L name. "The first L," he told him, "is for me, and the second L is for you."

many awards and had a cult following. People said it was tastier, and many would only buy our milk," said Lee.

Robert Lee Sr. sold the dairy and the milk depots in 1959 to the Hirayama brothers and they turned the Liliha Street depot into the L & L Dairy Liliha Fountain.

In 1976, Flores bought it from a subsequent owner, Mrs. Kitagawa who had changed the name to L & L Drive-Inn.

L & L Hawaiian Barbeque has an interesting business model. They find sites for their stores, sign leases, get loans, and then find a person to run it as a part owner. They might own 20-30% initially, and over time, they can own it completely.

L & L now has 50 restaurants in Hawaii, and 150 on the mainland. Its yearly revenues top $50 million. Flores wants to have over 1,000. Look out burgers, here comes L & L's plate lunches!

La Mariana Restaurant & Bar

One of Honolulu's best-kept secrets is the La Mariana Restaurant & Bar on Sand Island. "The ambiance is a delightful step back into old Hawaii," says Brad Walker whose Kamehameha Garment Company is nearby. "I feel I've gone back to a more relaxing time when I come here."

Charles Meminger of the *Honolulu Star-Bulletin* newspaper described it as a "lush hideaway decorated with rattan chairs, wooden tables, and nets with glass balls hanging from the walls and ceilings. It looks like it could have been the setting for an old *Hawaiian Eye* episode."

Owner Annette Nahinu built the marina in 1955 with her husband John Campbell, who has since passed away. "We get calls from Hollywood and New York all the time wanting to film or shoot pictures here," she says.

La Mariana is one of the last South Sea's style restaurants on Oahu. Many of the wicker chairs, tikis, koa tables, glass balls, and giant clam shells were bought from Don the Beachcomber's, Trader Vic's, or the Barefoot Bar auctions.

La Mariana means "little sea" in Italian," Annette tells us, "but, it was also my maiden name. So, that's a nice coincidence. Did you know this is the only woman-owned marina in the United States?" La Mariana Restaurant & Bar is located at 50 Sand Island Access Road.

Lex Brodie's Tire Company

"Are you still surfing," I asked 92-year-old Lex Brodie? "my eyesight isn't so good, and I stopped surfing at 90" Lex told me.

Extraordinary is a good word to describe Lex Brodie and his life. Lex was born Alexander Brodie in Kekaha, Kauai in 1914, and the third generation of five to be named Alexander Brodie, although none are juniors. Lex moved to Honolulu and was in the first graduating class at Roosevelt High School. He was a beach boy in Waikiki, selling canoe rides to such tourists as Bing Crosby and Jeanette McDonald. He learned to surf at age eleven in 1925.

"My first business was with Sam Kahanamoku. He'd offer tourists in front of the Royal Hawaiian and Moana Hotels three canoe rides for a dollar. I'd take them out. If one was a good looking young lady, I'd put her next to me in the canoe. We'd make conversation and often I'd be invited to dinner. After dinner, her parents would retire and we'd dance until midnight," Brodie recalls.

Lex Brodie with his Windward City Shopping Center Chevron station staff in 1961.

"She'd sign the chits. I did this for three years, from 1933-1935 and had a ball."

Brodie attended the University of Hawaii where he went out for football "because we got to go on the Mariposa to the mainland and play UCLA and Denver. I had never been to the mainland before."

After college, he went to work for Dole, then owned by Castle & Cooke. "We called it Hawaiian Pine back then," he added.

"After I left Dole, I heard that the Windward City Shopping Center was going to be built. I managed to get the Chevron Station there in 1958. We made money from the first day." Brodie specialized in tires, but lacked room to store them. "So, I warehoused them in my home garage. For some reason, people would stop by the house to buy tires, so we had to station an attendant there."

A little boy who couldn't say "thank you" led Lex to develop "thank you very much" as his slogan.

Brodie was the first to discount tires in Hawaii. "I bought tires for $6.95 and sold them for $6.95, if the customer gave us a used tire that could be recapped. We'd get $4 for that and that was our entire profit." Others in town sold tires for $12-14.

Brodie decided to move to town where most of the customers were. He wanted a space near his major competitors. Calling it National Tire of Hawaii, Lex opened on 1,700 square-feet at 701 Queen Street (where his gas area is today) in 1964.

"We advertised on KGMB for six months and got no results. Our account executive said, 'if you think you can do it better, why don't you try?' So I did. The results were instantaneous. It was like going from night to day. The store was jammed." Brodie wrote and made over 1,000 TV commercials.

On a trip to a mainland tire convention, Brodie came across a sign with a caveman making a wheel out of a rock. "I had been looking for a good logo and bought him for $25. It ran on two D cell batteries."

They called him "Little Joe," and put him in the TV commercials. The sound was often by his son, Sandy, banging a crescent wrench on concrete three times. Little Joe was popular, and Brodie had thousands of three-inch decals made with his image. "We asked all the drivers if we could put them on their rear bumper."

"One day a young boy asked if he could have one, and, of course I gave him one. He just stared back at me. 'What do you say?' I asked. His mom elbowed him, but the boy was silent. 'Say thank you,' she said. Silence. 'No,' I replied, 'say thank you *very* much.' "

Later, Brodie was reflecting on how courtesy seemed to be lacking in Honolulu, so he decided to thank his customers for watching his commercials. "That's what we're thanking you for, for watching the commercial."

"The commercials with Little Joe and 'thank you *very* much' were a hit. Everywhere I went, people would say 'there's the thank you man!' "

During a shipping strike in the 1970s, Lex realized he was running out of tires. Lex called Stan Kennedy at Hawaiian Airlines. "Can I rent an airplane to bring in tires?" Lex asked him. "He said he had a 707 in Los Angeles. Send it to Denver, I told him. I didn't even ask how much it would cost."

Lex then called the Gates Rubber Company. "Fill the plane up with 4,000 tires, I told them." We only ship by rail and truck was their reply. "The plane's going to be there in a few hours. You tell the pilot. They called me back in 5 minutes and said OK."

"We first flew to Hilo where we dropped off some tires for our Hilo store, then to Honolulu. It was a beautiful sight, watching the plane fly over the striker's picket line. We were the only store in town with tires after awhile. And, it only cost me $2 a tire to fly them in."

Brodie is well known for his high standards of customer service. His enclosed waiting room with a TV, magazines, and a phone was a first. He trained his sales people to only sell what customers needed. Never more. They were to ask, "how can I help you?" and to get the full story. Then, go over the car and show them their options.

"Many were told their tires were OK and to come back in 10,000 miles," Brodie said. "We'll send you a postcard reminder. Their jaws would just drop. 'You're not going to sell

Brodie with the original "Little Joe." It was 2 feet long and was bought at a mainland tire show for $25.

me anything?' they'd ask. Others didn't have money for a tire. We'd give them a used one at no charge. It got us great word of mouth."

Brodie sold his tire company in 1990, although they continue to use his name and commercials. In the same year, Brodie ran for the Board of Education and, even though he spent only $1,000, polled more votes than the governor.

Liberty House

The company that was "a tradition in Hawaii" for 150 years is now gone. Once the biggest of the Big Five, Liberty House was started by German sea captain Heinrich Hackfeld in 1849. Hackfeld first came to Hawaii with a ship's hold full of silk clothing, bird cages, crockery, dry goods, hardware, pens, pencils, window glass, and other household items. His wife, Marie, her 16 year-old brother, J.C. Pflueger, and a nephew, B.F. Ehlers, arrived with him.

He occupied a small store on Queen Street and called his store Hackfeld's Dry Goods. The public clamored for his wares. In 1850, he moved to a larger location on Fort Street. This store was so popular, it became known as "Hale Kilika" – the House of Silk. As business grew, the nephew took over management of the store while Hackfeld traveled the world for merchandise. The company took B. F. Ehler's name in 1862.

When sugar plantations came to Hawaii, Hackfeld became involved in financing sugar growers. From there, Hackfeld bought into eight plantations including the Lihue Sugar Plantation with Paul Isenberg, who founded the Dairyman's Association (later sold to Meadow Gold). In 1886, Hackfeld sold his interest in the company and returned to Germany.

During World War I in 1918, Germans were forced to sell their property and businesses, and the new board of directors thought a German name was a liability. Wanting to prove their patriotism, they chose the name "Liberty House" for the retail store and "American Factors" for their sugar operations.

American Factors (Amfac) became the largest company in the state and was the biggest of the Big Five. Liberty House was the only major department store in Hawaii for decades and, at one time, operated over 20 stores under the Liberty House, Penthouse, Collections, and Gear Up names.

Sheila Matsumoto Wakai, who worked from 1967 until 1989 as a buyer said Liberty House really had no competition until Ala

Moana Center opened. "Our motto was 'first, best, and only.' We wanted to be the first in the state to carry things. It was our attitude to find the hottest trends, the best products, and be the first to have it, exclusively if possible. Price was no object."

"It was fun being a buyer then," Wakai says. "We were the fat cats on the block. We had the best goods and the best selection. We were the leader. Consumers had fewer choices. Everyone who wanted quality came to Liberty House."

Staff adhered to a strict dress code in those days. "Women had to wear solid colors," Wakai continues. "No prints, plaids, or stripes. Skirts were of modest length. We had to wear nylons. If your hair wasn't short, it had to be worn in a bun or pony tail."

"We gave old world service back then," Wakai says. "Customers would often be greeted at the door by name. Sales people would telephone their customers to tell them a shipment had arrived. We would do anything to make the customer happy. Our strong relationship with customers put us and kept us on the map."

Liberty House opened a modest Kailua store in 1946.

Wakai recalls how the store went into a tizzy when Imelda Marcos, the wife of the Philippine dictator, came to town. "Imelda would come to the store with an entourage of a dozen security people and handmaidens. All the managers would be awaiting her in their departments. She'd walk through the store and point at things. 'Three dozen,' she'd say."

"Marcos would make her way through the floors, pointing and buying and then she would leave. She never tried things on and rarely touched them. She'd point and say how many she wanted. She behaved like royalty."

"I recall her buying sixty 34B white bras, to 'give to the poor,' she said. "Most of her purchases were commodities. She never bought jewelry. One year, when her first grandchild was born, she went straight to the children's department and bought everything – cribs, clothes, and toys. She cleared out the department."

"After her visit, it took us the rest of the day to assemble and total her order," Wakai continued. "It would all get packed and delivered, and her people would then pay. She never handled money herself."

By the mid-1980s, Liberty House found itself facing more competition from Sears, J. C. Penney, boutiques, and major discounters. The downturn in Hawaii's economy in the early 1990s caused sales to fall from about $400 million to $300 million, and the company did not reduce costs fast enough. It later sought protection in Chapter 11 bankruptcy. Federated Department Stores, owner of the Macy's retail chain, bought Liberty House for $200 million.

In November 2001, the Liberty House signs came down and Macy's signs went up. A tradition in Hawaii is no more.

—Researched by Hsiao-Hui Sheng

Like Like Drive Inn Restaurant

Like Like Drive Inn was the third restaurant started by James and Alice Nako. The first was the New Emma Café in 1932. The second was the Donald Duck Drive Inn in 1945, and the last was Like Like Drive Inn, started in 1953.

James Nako thought Like Like meant "gathering place," but several Hawaiian friends said it had no meaning. Miriam Likelike was the sister of King Kalakaua and Queen Liliuokalani and the mother of Princess Kaiulani.

Donald Duck Drive Inn was sold to Bea Miyasato in 1953 and she went to Disney and asked if she could use a picture of the illustrious duck. They said she could not use the likeness *or* the name. So she changed it "Bea's." Bea retired in 2001 after 48 years on Kapiolani Blvd.

"Like Like Drive-in is not named for the Highway or after Princess Miriam Likelike, who was the sister of Kalakaua and Liliuokalani and mother of Princess Kaiulani," said Dora Hayashi, who owns the restaurant now with her husband Roy.

"Dad used to hang out with

several friends after golf at Like Like Store which was near Likelike School in Palama, continues Hayashi. "He believed it meant "gathering place" and named the restaurant based on that. But after opening, we asked several Hawaiian friends and they told us that the words didn't mean anything. Dad kept the name anyway."

Very few restaurants on Oahu were open 24 hours a day, but Like Like Drive-in was from the beginning. "We treat our employees like family," Dora said. "We give and they give. One, Nancy Fujiwara, worked with us for 50 years. Manea Nakata is still here after 41 years."

The Hayashi's are related to several other businesses. Dora's sister, Agnes Asato's family, owns Wisteria and KC Drive Inn. Husband Roy's family owns the Pacific Beach Hotel.

"Mom told me, before she passed away, that the restaurant is your baby," Dora said. "Cherish it."

Liliha Bakery

Roy and Koo Takakuwa founded Liliha Bakery in 1950. The original location was at 1703 Liliha Street where the H-1 Freeway is today. When the freeway was built, the Bakery moved further up Liliha Street near where L&L Drive-Inn is today. In 1961, it moved to its current location on Kuakini Street but kept the Liliha name.

Everybody knows Liliha Bakery is famous for its Coco Puffs, but most people do not know they sell four to six thousand Coco

Liliha Bakery sells an average of 5,000 Coco Puffs a day.

Puffs every day. That is about the same number of Napples sold every day at 22 Napoleon's Bakery locations. Liliha Bakery has only one location.

Mari Peros, cashier at the bakery since 1971, once took Coco Puffs to Germany. "They were for my daughter and her family. I packed them very carefully, and they made it just fine. People buy them and take them all over the U.S."

The Coco Puff was not the first signature item at Liliha Bakery. "Our Chantilly Cake was first sold in the 1950s," says former manager Bill Takakuwa, "and it was a favorite with the locals." With a rich, buttercream frosting, the cake is similar to a German chocolate cake but without the nuts and coconut.

The Coco Puff was crafted by a Liliha baker in the 1960s as a shell of puff pastry with a chocolate pudding-like filling. But, it was a huge flop. About 1990, a new chief baker, Kame Ikemura reformulated the Coco Puff and added a dollop of chantilly frosting to the top. This time the Coco Puff was a success.

Liliha purchased the recipe from him when he retired in 1994 for a reported $15,000.

The bakery is open 24 hours a day except from Sunday night to Tuesday morning. The lunch counter serves about 20 customers at a time. The bakery grosses about $4 million a year and employs about 70.

Longs Drug Stores

Longs Drug Stores began in Piedmont, California in 1938 when brothers Joe and Tom Long opened the first Longs store and helped institute the idea of self-service in the retail drug industry. Low prices, excellent service, and a tradition of "treating others as we, ourselves would like to be treated" brought quick success to Joe and Tom's first store. They opened another store ten months later.

Joe (left) and Tom Long founded Longs Drug Stores in 1938 in Piedmont California. Here they are at the opening of the first Longs in Hawaii in 1954.

The first Longs in Hawaii, and the ninth in their chain, came in 1954 and was located on the corner of Hotel and Bishop Streets. Bishop Street had al-

The first Longs in Hawaii at Bishop and Hotel Streets. Longs is the only retailer to be successful on Bishop Street.

ways been known for hosting the corporate headquarters of many of Hawaii's giants. Fort Street was the main shopping street. No large retailer has ever been successful on Bishop Street, except Longs.

Pacific Business News founder George Mason remembers seeing lines around the block to get into Longs from his office across the street in the Alexander Young Building. "The Big Five had controlled prices, and Longs was one of the first discounters. They changed retailing in Hawaii, and we've never been the same since."

Longs Drug Stores is one of the top ten drug chains in the nation with over 460 stores in six western states: California, Colorado, Hawaii, Nevada, Oregon, and Washington. Sales in 2001 were $4 billion.

Today, President & CEO Warren Bryant and Chairman Bob Long carry on the business beliefs and traditions that Joe and Tom Long established with their first store. At Longs, caring and serving valued customers have been top priorities for over half a century. Longs Drug Stores remain successful because they are committed to providing customers with prompt and professional service. Longs employees must be willing to do "whatever it takes" to satisfy customer needs.

In Hawaii, there is no doubt we make Longs a part of our day.

—Researched by Oguz Ulucayli

Love's Bakery

Love's Biscuit & Bread Company was founded downtown on Nuuanu Avenue in 1851 by Robert Love, Sr., who had just come from Scotland. However, the family was to suffer several tragedies. Robert Love, Sr. died just seven years later. In 1883, his son Robert Love, Jr. passed away, and his wife, Fanny Love, took over the business.

Love's moved to Iwilei in 1924 then to 836 Kapahulu Avenue in

1942. They have been at 911 Middle Street since 1991. A highlight for many school students is a tour of Love's Bakery. Each year about 10,000 students take a field trip there and receive a wooden loaf of bread souvenir to take home.

The current owner of Love's bakery is the Japanese company Dai Ichiya. Love's Bakery is the largest bread distributor in Hawaii. The bakery employs 670 and has revenues of $31 million annually.

—Researched by Carol Lai

M's Coffee Tavern

Emma Millikin founded M's Coffee Tavern in the 1920s. It was located at 112 Merchant Street, where the Financial Plaza of the Pacific is today. It became the hangout for staff at the *Honolulu Star-Bulletin* next door, much the same as Columbia Inn would become 40 years later.

Millikin started with a small coffee house and added a restaurant later with arched doorways, red brick, and a wrought iron fence.

After World War II, Millikin sold the business to Ken Emerson and retired to Maui. She died in 1958.

Emerson added the Cheerio Room and M's Garden Buffet in the downtown YWCA and bought the Ranch House in Aina Haina, calling it M's Ranch House. Emerson later sold the business to Herbert Loui.

M's was famous for its coconut cream pies. They also had a men's table, with women prohibited, and a women's table, with men prohibited. Spencecliff later took over the Ranch House, and for many years, it was the most popular restaurant in East Honolulu.

McDonald's

Raymond Albert Kroc (1902-1984) was a distributor for a five-spindled milkshake maker called the Multimixer. In 1954, he visited Richard and Maurice "Mac" McDonald who had eight of his Multimixers in their restaurant in San Bernardino, California.

The McDonald brothers had a low priced, high volume, limited menu concept. They created a mechanized kitchen to sell hamburgers, cheeseburgers, French fries, milkshakes, coffee, and soft drinks. They opened in 1948.

Kroc was flabbergasted at the number of patrons the McDonald's had and how fast they were served. He suggested they allow him to franchise more McDonald's and they agreed.

Kroc's first McDonald's was in Des Plaines, Illinois in 1955. The first day's sales were $366. Burgers, fries, and shakes cost nineteen cents. It was a huge hit.

The Big Mac was the brainchild of Jim Delligatti, one of Ray Kroc's earliest franchisees. It was introduced in 1968. Bob Wian of Bob's Big Boy is credited with creating the double-decker hamburger in 1936. The Big Mac is probably McDonald's version of that.

McDonald's used to report how many billions of burgers they had sold but stopped after passing 100 billion. Since then, McDonald's has grown to over 28,000 stores with annual sales in excess of $40 billion.

Supermarket king Maurice Sullivan brought McDonald's to Hawaii in 1968. The first store was in Aina Haina, and now there are 68. The company's trademark "Golden Arches" are often built into the restaurant's architecture on the mainland, but Hawaii's outdoor sign regulations prohibit it.

McInerny

Hawaii's premier resort retailer began in the days of whaling ships when Patrick Michael McInerny, a ship's carpenter, opened a small store at the corner of Beretania and Maunakea Streets in 1857.

McInerny had twin sons who were well known and regarded in the community. Jim managed the men's and women's ready-to-wear store at Fort and Merchant Streets while brother Will managed the family shoe store at Fort and King Streets. Jim was head of the City's planning commission, and Will was a Territorial Senator.

With tourism's boom after World War II, McInerny expanded into Waikiki's resort market and grew to 18 stores. In 1989, McInerny merged with Andrade, a men's haberdashery that began after World War I, and Carol & Mary, an upscale woman's fashion store established in 1937 by Carol Singlehurst and Mary Afong. However, in 2002, they announced they would be closing in 2003 after 144 years in business.

McKinley Car Wash

On an average sunny day, 800 cars come to McKinley Car Wash on Kapiolani Boulevard, making it the state's busiest and, for that matter, one of the nation's busiest. Malia Zimmerman of Hawaii

Reporter.com said, "if there were a Hall of Fame for such things, McKinley Car Wash would be displayed as a national champion."

Yukio, Tsuneo, Sueo, and Hiroshi Yoshikawa opened a service station, McKinley Motor Services, in 1947, soon after the end of World War II. A manual car wash was opened in 1963. Eight employees served 250 customers a day, an astounding number that soon encouraged the brothers to close down the service station and install a conveyor-style car wash. "We were the third car wash in Honolulu," says manager Craig Yoshikawa, "but, the first two are gone."

"We get all kinds of people here," Craig continues. "One day, a staff person found a paper bag that a customer had left. He probably thought it was their lunch and almost threw it away. Something made him look inside and he found several thousand dollars! He turned it in to my uncle. A few hours later, a woman called and asked about the bag. We told her it had been turned in and she was very relieved." The slogan "We make you shine" took on a different meaning that day!

The car wash is named for McKinley High School across the street, which is named for President William McKinley, who supported the Annexation of Hawaii in 1898.

—Researched by Nelia Visitacion

Macy's

Rowland Hussey Macy left his Nantucket, Massachusetts home at 15 in 1837 aboard a whaler. He received a red star tattoo at sea, which store shoppers will recognize is now part of Macy's logo. Macy retired from whaling a few years later and opened a dry goods store. It was a failure. He then moved to California but failed to find gold in the Gold Rush. Over the next ten years, six other retail ventures he started failed.

In 1858, Macy opened a store in Manhattan on 14th near Union Square. The first day's sales amounted to $11.06. Macy established fixed, marked prices, then an innovation, and advertised heavily. He spent over $2,800 the first year, and revenues reached $85,000. After eight failures, Macy had found success.

Macy's has been on the forefront of innovation. The first woman to hold an executive position in retail, Margaret Getchell, led Macy's to post Civil War prosperity. The first in-store Santa Claus and elaborate, illuminated window displays were introduced in 1870.

Lazarus Straus and his sons took over the store upon Macy's death and moved it to its present location at Herald Square and 34th Street in 1902. Macy's expanded to 7th avenue in 1924, making it the world's largest store and a Mecca for shoppers.

A Macy's wine and food buyer, William Titon, invented the tea bag in 1912. In 1926, he introduced America to the baked potato, which quickly became a staple in our diet.

Macy's launched its Thanksgiving Day Parade in 1926. Employees dressed as cowboys, knights, sheiks, and clowns marched from 145th Street down to 34th Street, with bands, floats, and 25 live animals loaned from the Central Park Zoo. By 1927, Macy's replaced the animals with giant balloons made by Goodyear. Felix the Cat was one of the earliest.

In the first few years, the balloons were released and floated for days over the city. The lucky person who found one would win a prize. Flying ace Clarence Chamberlin lassoed a floating Jerry the Pig balloon above Brooklyn in 1931 and brought it back down to earth to the acclaim of the public below.

Macy's continued to innovate, and in 1934, introduced clothing in standard sizes and in a variety of styles and colors. In the 1970s, Macy's moved from cheap goods for the masses to upscale and designer merchandise. Federated Department Stores merged with Macy's in 1994, forming the largest department store chain in the country with over 200 stores. In 2001, Macy's bought out Liberty House, Hawaii's largest retailer.

Makiki Christian Church

A Japanese castle in Honolulu? The Makiki Christian Church is a replica of one, namely the Kochi Castle. One of the founders, Reverend Takie Okumura, grew up in Kochi Prefecture, Japan, near the Kochi Castle. As a boy, Okumura had played around the castle, which had been built in 1603.

Okumura came to Hawaii and organized the Makiki Christian Church in 1904 at Kinau and Pensacola Streets. The congregation outgrew its first location and moved to its current site on Pensacola Street across from McKinley High School in 1932. Okumura suggested a replica of the Kochi Castle. When some resisted such a design, Okumura reminded them that the Old Testament says that "God is my fortress."

—Researched by Amy Ashizawa

The Makiki Christian Church on Pensacola Street is inspired by the Kochi Castle, built in Japan in 1603.

Manago Hotel

The Manago Hotel was founded in Kona in 1917 by Kinzo and Osame Manago. The original hotel had two cots and futons. Today, it has 64 full rooms and a new three-story wing overlooking Kealakekua Bay and the City of Refuge.

The inn has a low-key style that makes it a favorite with island folks. The rooms are simple but spotless. Prices are unbeatable at $38 for a single room.

Harold and Nancy Manago took over and managed the business for 42 years. Today, the hotel continues to operate under the third generation management of Dwight and Cheryl Manago.

Over the last 30 years, more and more tourists from the mainland and foreign countries have discovered Manago. "At the same time, we're lucky the same local working people keep coming. It's a good mix where we don't just cater to one or the other," Dwight says.

Maple Garden Restaurant

Robert Hsu grew up in Taiwan where there were a lot of maple trees. "We used to put the leaves in books to keep them," Hsu says.

The night before he left Taiwan, an uncle took him out to dinner to a restaurant named Maple Garden. Soon after arriving in Hawaii, he opened his restaurant in 1970 on Isenberg Street across from the old stadium, and named it Maple Garden after his beloved maple trees and his last meal in Taiwan.

Years later, the owner of the Maple Garden in Taiwan came to Hawaii and ate at Hsu's Moiliili Maple Garden Restaurant. Pictures of the two owners were taken in front of the restaurant. Later, Hsu learned that the Taiwan restaurant owner put the picture up in his place and jokingly told customers that it was a picture of his Honolulu branch.

The food continues to be excellent, and the service friendly. The murals by John Young on the walls are stunning. Be sure to pet Hsu's dog, Coco, before you leave.

Matson Navigation

Captain William Matson (1849-1917) did not have a single day of formal education in his life. He left his native Sweden when he was only 10 as a deck hand on a ship. Yet, it was this man, perhaps more than any other, who was most responsible for starting Hawaii's modern tourism industry in the early 1900s.

In 1882, Matson purchased the three-masted schooner Emma Claudina and set sail from San Francisco to Hilo carrying 300 tons of food, plantation supplies, and general merchandise. That voyage launched a company that has been involved in such diversified interests as oil exploration, hotels, tourism, and even briefly, the airline business.

In 1887, he bought a larger boat to transport sugar and pineapple and named it the Lurline. He bought the *Falls of Clyde*, now moored at the Hawaii Maritime Center, a few years later.

Matson observed that Europe had first class ships taking visitors to first class hotels and thought Hawaii could do the same. He understood shipping, but he needed luxury hotels.

The old Royal Hawaiian Hotel downtown had closed in

Capt. William Matson built luxury ships to bring wealthy tourists to his Waikiki Hotels.

1917. Matson bought the name to put on the luxury hotel he planned to build in Waikiki. The new Royal opened in 1927. Soon thereafter, the Moana was purchased.

Matson built four White Ships to bring passengers to his hotels and Hawaii. "The Lurline was the flagship of the fleet," says former Chief Purser Bill Sewell, who sailed with Matson Lines on all their White Ships in the 1950s. "The highest-ranking officer in each category, such as skipper or engineer, crewed the Lurline."

"The Lurline was launched in 1932," Sewell said, "as was the Matsonia. These two ships sailed from the west coast to Hawaii. About the same time, the Monterey and the Mariposa were launched, and they sailed from the west coast to Tahiti, New Zealand, Australia, Fiji, Samoa, and Hawaii. All four ships carried about 720 passengers, and all were painted white. The White Ships were famous for their spaciousness, speed, capacity, accommodations, cuisine, service, and Hawaiian hospitality. Art work used on their menus is still cherished today."

The Lurline was called the "Glamour Girl of the Pacific."

"As for the name Lurline, that originated as the name of a yacht owned by Claus Spreckels that Captain Matson used to sail aboard," says Matson representative Jeff Hull. "He liked the name very much and named one of his early sailing ships Lurline. He later gave the name to his daughter - who later christened the second Lurline (in 1908 - not the famed Lurline built in 1932)." Six Matson ships have carried the Lurline name.

Sewell has many wonderful recollections of his days aboard the Matson ships. "In 1952, the Kefauver Crime Commission made it illegal for American flagged ships to have slot machines on board. Soon thereafter, as the Lurline approached the Golden Gate, we emptied all the coins from the dozen or so slot machines we had on board, took them to the aft end of the ship where a priest was waiting (this was 3 AM), to give 'last rites' to each machine as we tossed them overboard. A few hours later, we sailed under the bridge and into American waters, cleansed of all those nasty slot machines."

Once jets planes came in, Matson lost a great deal of traffic and eventually gave up passenger ships. In 1970, Matson sold its passenger vessels and concentrated on its Pacific Coast-Hawaii freight service.

When Captain Matson died in 1917 at age 67, the Matson fleet was comprised of 14 of the largest, fastest, and most modern ships in the Pacific passenger freight service. During World War I and II, Matson vessels became troopships and military cargo carriers. During World War II, they made 119 voyages, covered one and a half million miles and carried 736,000 troops. "After the war," Sewell recalls, "our beloved government paid Matson enough money to rebuild one ship only - the other three had to temporarily mothballed."

In 1925, the company established Matson Terminals, a wholly owned subsidiary, to perform stevedoring and terminal services for its fleet. Matson's freight containerization program, which began in 1958, greatly increased productivity and speed. It revolutionized Pacific cargo shipment.

Two new Matson hotels were built in Waikiki in the 1950s, the Surfrider in 1952 and the Princess Kaiulani in 1955. The surfrider they were honoring was Olympian Duke Kahanamoku, who was one of the first guests at the P.K. and the first to try the pool.

In 1959, Matson divested itself of all non-shipping assets, including the Matson hotels, which were sold to the Sheraton Corporation.

Alexander & Baldwin (A&B) owns Matson today. They, C. Brewer, Castle & Cooke, and Amfac shipped their sugar on Matson ships and were its largest customers. They invested heavily in Matson, and A&B took full control in 1969. Because of that move, A&B is the biggest of the Big Five today.

Several of the streets on Wilhelmina Rise are named for the Matson ships: Lurline, Mariposa, Monterey, and Malolo. Matsonia is named for Captain Matson. Wilhelmina Tenney, whose father was president of Castle & Cooke, gave her name to the Rise.

—Researched by Madeleine Wadelius

Matsumoto Shave Ice

Mamoru and Helen Matsumoto founded Matsumoto Shave Ice in Haleiwa over 50 years ago. Mamoru came to Hawaii from

Helen and Mamoru Matsumoto opened for business in 1951.

Hiroshima to work at a sugar plantation. He eventually became a salesman for the Sakai Store, which is now the Haleiwa IGA.

In 1951, they opened their own grocery store, M. Matsumoto Store (previous Tanaka Store) in Haleiwa. At first, Mamoru peddled his wares on a bicycle until he was able to afford a panel truck. He went from camp to camp, taking orders, and delivering the goods while Helen manned the store and did some sewing.

With the birth of their three children, Glenn, Janice, and Stanley, they felt a need to expand their business. A cool refreshment was offered to the carloads of tourists and locals coming to the North Shore – shave ice.

Up to 1,000 people come to the store each day to buy that special frozen treat, dripping with homemade syrup. Half of them are tourists. Celebrities such as Konishiki and Tom Hanks have been customers. Son Stanley has now taken the helm of the business and replaced groceries with T-shirts, snacks, and souvenirs.

Maui Divers

In 1958, Maui Divers was a Lahaina dive shop taking tourists on underwater tours. On one such expedition in deep waters off the Molokai Channel, divers discovered Hawaiian black coral, one of the ocean's rare treasures. It is now the official state gemstone.

Coincidentally, berthed next to Maui Divers at the time of the discovery was a boat that had a broken mast. Cliff Slater, pilot of the ship, had been sailing around the world and was temporarily stuck on Maui.

Slater suggested the company make jewelry from the black coral. Crude carvings became more intricate and beautiful over the years.

In 1962, Maui Divers moved to Oahu to sell its jewelry. Four years later, another major discovery, pink coral, was found, and in 1974, gold coral was discovered.

Maui Divers is more than a jewelry store. They are Hawaii's largest jewelry manufacturer and the only coral jewelry manufacturer. Maui Divers also has the only design center in the islands. The 350,000 people that visit Maui Divers on Liona Street each year tour the facilities and watch coral jewelry being made.

The design center is a destination in itself. The first stop is a theatre. Maui Divers has eight, with two holding 50 people and the others holding ten. An eight-minute video shows the history of coral jewelry and the steps in its manufacture. The video can be shown in eight languages - Spanish, French, Italian, German, Japanese, Mandarin, Korean, and English – with the push of a button.

Guides then take visitors on a tour of the design center, where staff work on the pieces behind Plexiglas. By the time the tour is over, visitors arrive at the main jewelry floor with a deep appreciation for coral jewelry and Maui Divers' artisanship.

Since most visitors have never heard of them before coming to Hawaii, Maui Divers feels trust is an important issue. How do they get customers to trust them? "It starts with trusting our own staff," says Slater. "While most jewelry manufacturers pat down staff upon leaving and do not allow purses or even pockets in smocks, Maui Divers does not. We trust our staff, and that trust is the starting point for visitors to trust us. We are honest and open with employees. We'll answer all their questions. We have no secrets."

That trust pays off. The average designer has been with Maui Divers for more than 20 years. "And our staff is our largest stockholder," Slater adds.

Maui Divers also has an unusual guarantee. It is a lifetime guarantee: not for the owner, but for the jewelry. They do not even require a receipt. "Customers are astonished, but we see it as a sensible business practice." Maui Divers has over 15 stores statewide.

—Researched by Jackie Chu and Marcela Solera

Meadow Gold Dairies

The name "Meadow Gold" was the winning entry in a 1901 employee contest to name Continental Creamery's new butter. Now, after many mergers and acquisitions, Meadow Gold is the company name and part of Dallas-based Suiza Foods, the nation's largest dairy processor.

It all started in 1897 when several dairy farms on Oahu joined together to form the Dairyman's Association. The original farm was located where the Waialae Country Club and Kahala Mandarin Hotel stand today, but moved in 1957 to the North Shore, and is now in Waimanalo.

The company was the first to introduce many milk products available in Hawaii including yogurt, cottage cheese, sour cream, and reduced fat milk.

The logo of Meadow Gold includes a man on a horse carriage delivering milk. The man is Mr. John Nevis. Several generations of the Nevis family have worked for Meadow Gold, a total of 365 employment years.

Richard Vogell, President from 1965 to 1971, was one of the people responsible for the start of Aloha Fridays. He was one of the first to allow his drivers to wear aloha shirts on Fridays.

—Researched by Maria Heljegård

Ming's

Wook Moon founded Ming's in 1939 as an art and antiquities gallery at 808 Fort Street. Ming's means "a room that one can enter and acquire cultural knowledge," says sister Sylvia Moon Gomberg, who worked with the store from the beginning. "Ming's did not refer to the Ming Dynasty as some think," Gomberg says.

World War II cut Moon off from his suppliers in China, so he switched to creating his own jewelry. "My brother was an artist," Gomberg continues. "He created his own unique lines. It was all done by him. He hired many local artisans and taught them how to make his designs. Many later started their own businesses."

Many family members worked in the stores, including son, musician Peter Moon. "Ming's was an officers' hangout during the War," Gomberg recalls. "So many of them were in Hawaii, and they wanted something to send back to their girlfriends that was typically Hawaiian. Back then, we carried flowers of Hawaii that were carved in gold and silver, and they were very popular."

Ming's unique creations caught on, and he opened many stores on Oahu and one in Hilo. Frank Sinatra, Perry Como, James Stewart, and Jacqueline Kennedy were customers. "We met a lot of lovely people," Gomberg recalls. "Visitors and *kamaaina* loved his decorative arts and jewelry."

Soon thereafter, he opened stores in New York, Florida, Georgia, Texas, and California. Those stores started closing in 1980 as Moon approached retirement. Ming's closed in October of 1999, but for months before, long-time customers crowded his store to buy their last pieces from one of Hawaii's greatest artisans.

Moanalua Gardens

Once three times its present size, Moanalua Gardens was laid out by Samuel Mills Damon II sometime after 1884. Moanalua Gardens Foundation consultant Lorin Gill traces ownership of the 7,000 acres that became the Damon Estate to the ancient *ahupuaa* (land division), which extended from the Koolaus to Keehi Lagoon. Moanalua was a center for religious practices for ancient Hawaiians for hundreds of years.

Lot Kamehameha V built a summer cottage there around 1853. Great luaus were held in Moanalua, and the king encouraged the dancing of hula which had been banned by missionaries. When he died, Lot left Moanalua to Princess Ruth Keelikolani, a half sister who had been born there. She built a home at Moanalua and held huge parties with chanting and hula.

Princess Ruth left Moanalua to her cousin Bernice Pauahi Bishop, the last of the Royal Kamehameha line. Although Pauahi grew up in her parents' home downtown, she was born at Moanalua.

In the last month of her life in 1883, suffering from breast cancer and heavily sedated with

Bernice Pauahi Bishop left Moanalua to Samuel Damon II in 1883.

morphine, Bernice Pauahi Bishop willed Moanalua to Samuel Damon, who was a family friend and business partner of her husband's. "She left land to many, but only for their lifetime. It all reverted back to the Bishop Estate upon their death, except for Moanalua," says Gill, who wonders if it was an oversight caused by the drugs.

Damon built a magnificent estate on the property and even had Dillingham connect a rail spur so guests could arrive in luxury for his lavish parties.

A Chinese Hall was built in China, disassembled, shipped to Hawaii, and reassembled near a pond close to where Servco is today. A two-story Japanese Tea Garden, mauka of the highway, was built. An artesian well was dug and operated into the 1950s, close to where the Verizon building is now.

Damon constructed several houses on the property, one near where Fort Shafter is today, another above Tripler, and one below.

The one above Tripler was a summer house, Maile Hehei, (which means maile twined) and some of the lumber came from a ship that had run aground in Keehi Lagoon. Two Cook pine trees on Moanalua Ridge that mark the spot are easily seen from below. Grand-daughter Gertrude Damon said she could see two-thirds of Oahu from there.

Moanalua Gardens in 1905 was three times its present size. Damon Estate leased the land below the freeway in 1960 and moved several of the buildings mauka.

The first golf course in Hawaii, or for that matter, west of the Rocky Mountains was built by Damon in 1898. Today, that course is the Moanalua Golf Course.

The H-1 freeway has altered the original landscape of Moanalua. King Street used to extend past Middle Street and joined Moanalua Road at the Gardens. The land mauka of the highway was set aside for public enjoyment by Damon's will. The land makai, two-thirds of the estate, was for private family use. In 1960, the estate decided to develop the land makai of the highway, and many of the structures were moved to the mauka property.

The Prince Lot Hula Festival, begun in 1978, continues the tradition that Lot encouraged 150 years ago. The Moanalua Gardens Foundation offers tours, hikes, educational programs, books, and videos, as well as the Hula Festival.

Molokai Ranch

Hawaii's second largest ranch, with 54,000 acres on the west end of Molokai, was originally owned by Prince Lot, who would become King Kamehameha V in 1863. The King was fond of the Ranch and visited often. After he died in 1872, the Ranch passed to Princess Ruth and then to Bernice Pauahi Bishop.

Molokai Ranch was purchased by a group of Honolulu business leaders in 1898, and one of them, Charles M. Cooke, bought out the others. Cooke raised cattle and planted pineapple, which was its primary industry for 50 years. The Cooke family sold the ranch to a New Zealand company in 1986 as pineapple was phased out.

The ranch has been rebuilt and now boasts comfortable visitor accommodations and an array of recreational activities, making it a unique adventure resort.

Mountain Apple Company

Jon de Mello lived in a house in Tantalus. Falling Mountain apples from a tree hit his roof, inspiring the naming of his company, recalls ex-wife and singer Melinda Carroll.

The Mountain Apple Company traces it roots to Aloha Records, founded in 1947 by Jon's father, Jack. The elder de Mello had played with both John Philip Sousa and Igor Stravinsky. Aloha Records evolved into the Music of Polynesia label.

Jack de Mello's first record, *Coconut Willie* warped in transit on Matson. All had to be trashed.

Jon grew up in the studio and traveled with his father to recording sessions in London and Los Angeles.

Today, the Mountain Apple Company represents dozens of artists such as the Brothers Cazimero, Cecilio and Kapono, Don Ho, The Beamer Brothers, Kealii Reichel, Robi Kahakalau, and Na Leo Pilimehana.

Israel Kamakawiwoole's 2001 CD, *Alone in Iz World*, is the first Hawaiian album to sell over 1,000,000 copies.

Musashiya

A small fabric and dry goods store in Ala Moana Center, is how most of us remember Musashiya, which closed in 2001. However, 75 years ago, Musa-shiya the Shirt Maker was known and loved around the world.

It all started in 1896 on the makai side of King Street near River Street where Chotaru Miyamoto opened his tiny shop near the Fish Market. He had come from the district of Musashi in Japan. He added "ya," meaning "store" to the end.

An error would change his life dramatically. In his own words, which is what endeared Miyamoto to the world, is how he became famous:

A twist of fate transformed Chotaru Miyamoto into world-famous Musashiya the Shirtmaker in 1920.

Kinely Observe Owel

This bird enjoying wide fame as wise kind we do not resume to dispute, but claiming also wise brains is not wholly owel.

Human person who Christmas shopping earlier have also more wisdom than brained bird who get fame by keep mouth shut.

Musa-Shiya
The Shirtmaker

(Also dry goods sell)

Proclaim special week Christmas shopping sale for less prices Dec. 5 all week early A. M. to 10 P. M. including Sat. Dec 10.

Ginghams, flannels, voiles, shirtings, pongee, hosery, longjerry, etc., etc.

HOW YOU LIKE THAT! I'LL SAY SO

HOW TO FINDING SHOP: Come along makai side King Street passing famous Fish Market, pausing before step on River. Sign speak Musa-shiya place.

Miyamoto's ads in broken English and pidgin were clipped by locals and sent to their friends all over the world.

"One time too much English shirting. All right, but how can selling make brains tired for thinking, but no can. One *haole* man speak advertise."

Miyamoto was told a shipment had arrived from England for

Musa-Shiya
The Shirtmaker
(Also Shoten Dry Goods To Sell)

Onnounce
Oh Happy Springtime

Here arrive Springs on gentle foot but hardly can tell from winter going which have gentle movement in Hawaii also. But feeling differents inside. Feeling very glad for do something but not work. Feeling kinely feeling for sweetheart also Funny kine wether.

Here are necessary consequence

Easter Shirt

Make as say so on any cloth very nice also name Musa-shiya Honolulu inside.

Cloth For Easter Kimono
(But make no can do because too busy just now)

How Finding Shop: Pass away from Fish Market on King St. going for River until not arriving River. Musa just between. Easy finding because reading sign say so. All right.

him and was astonished to see it was four years' supply, much more than he could even get into his store. What to do? He and his son, Koichiro, who would later take over the store, went to George Mellon, an advertising man, who thought his broken English and pidgin would be funny and touching.

Mellon crafted a unique ad campaign that turned Miyamoto into "Musa-Shiya The Shirtmaker" and turned his small Chinatown shop into a world-famous landmark.

Bishop Museum Archivist DeSoto Brown wonders if Miyamoto really talked like that or if Mellon created the whole thing.

The first ad ran in May of 1920 in the *Star-Bulletin*. From *How Musa-shiya The Shirtmaker Broke into Print*, Miyamoto describes what happened next. "Result are delightfully. Surprise deplores conscience because business. When day for burst open arriving, many persons are but shop no holding one time. Business doing like hot cake and cash machine choke for money. All right!"

Local residents found the *Star-Bulletin* ads hilarious and sent them to friends outside Hawaii. Soon the ads were reprinted around the world in various newspapers and magazines. Wealthy tourists beat a path to Miyamoto's Chinatown store and his silk shirts, pajamas, robes, and kimonos became highly desired. Those who could not visit flooded the store with mail orders.

Miyamoto reprinted his ads in a small booklet because "everybody say very nice advertisement, and asking one copy keeping personally, which have not got, so order make some more on piece paper from house of printing."

The advertising campaign won awards. The Pacific Advertising Clubs Association bestowed a trophy for the "most constructive and effective display of advertising for a specialty shop for three years in a row, 1925-1927. Stanford University used them as a textbook in advertising classes.

The younger Miyamoto sold the business in 1933 to the Fujii Family and opened a shirt making business in Waikiki. He retired in 1968, and died 18 years later at age 90. Joyce Masuda bought the business in 1978 from George and Mary Fujii. The River Street and Kaneohe stores closed when their leases were up, and Musashiya was left with only its Ala Moana Store. Masuda closed that store in 2001.

Natsunoya Tea House

Many Hawaii residents have heard that a spy from the Japanese Consulate in Honolulu watched ship movements in Pearl Harbor and sent coded messages to Tokyo in the months before World

War II. What is largely unknown is that he did it from Natsunoya Tea House in Alewa Heights.

"A customer named Yoshikawa used to come here during the day for tea or beer," recalls current owner Lawrence Fujiwara Jr. "When he was tired, my grandmother let him sleep in an upstairs room where we had a telescope. Unbeknownst to us, he was using it to watch the ship movements at Pearl Harbor."

Natsunoya, which means "Summer House," is the last remaining full-time tea house in the islands. "My grandfather, Shuuji Fujiwara, had a small tea house in Alewa Heights in 1921, named Shinchoro. He had to build his own road and put in his own telephone poles."

Shuuji Fujiwara went to Japan to visit his dying father before World War II and was stuck there during the war. As an American citizen, he was treated poorly. Natsunoya was used by the Red Cross during the war.

In 1958, his son Lawrence Fujiwara Sr., took over and changed the name to Natsunoya. Natsunoya can host five events at a time. Their large banquet room can hold 300; two cottages can hold 30 each, and there are two *tatami* rooms that can hold 12-60.

Dignitaries of all sorts have visited Natsunoya. "John Wayne shot a scene from one of his movies here. Actors and singers from Japan regularly come. Konishiki and many of the *sumotori* ate us out of tea house and home. The Pittsburgh Steelers came when they had won the Superbowl. Local politicians, military leaders, and many others have all been here."

Lawrence Fujiwara Jr. has run Natsunoya since 1996 when his dad passed away. "It's a tough job," says the father of four. "I have to work until the job is done."

Neiman Marcus

Herbert Marcus, his sister Carrie Marcus Neiman, and her husband Al Neiman opened the first Neiman Marcus store in Dallas in 1907 "It shall be the store's policy to be a leader at all times," they advertised. "With this aim always in view, exclusive lines of high-class garments have been secured, lines which have never been offered to buyers in Texas."

Herbert Marcus laid out the company's principles: "It is never a good sale for Neiman Marcus, unless it's a good buy for the customer. And "We want to sell satisfaction, not just merchandise."

According to Stanley Marcus, "quality is remembered long after the price is forgotten." Richard Marcus added, "Care for your customers and they will come back. Care for your merchandise and it won't."

—Researched by Johan Hedin

New England Financial

There are only a handful of companies that have been in Hawaii for over 150 years. C. Brewer, Theo. H. Davies, Castle & Cooke, and Love's Bakery were here in 1852 as was the New England Mutual Life Insurance Company, the very first insurance company in Hawaii.

New England Financial was founded in Boston, Massachusetts in 1835, and Honolulu was its first branch office in 1852. "That's why we are designated as Agency #2," said John Yanagihara, Hawaii Manager.

The first Hawaii insurance policy written was for Dr. Gerrit P. Judd for $9,000. The well-known medical missionary was a minister and advisor to King Kamehameha III. Gerrit P. Judd, his son

Albert Frances Judd, and Joseph Atherton were the first three agents for the company. By 1864, Castle & Cooke took over as the Honolulu agent. Gerrit P. Judd's grandson, Lawrence P. Judd, would later become Governor. King Kalakaua was a policyholder in 1874.

The first insurance company in Hawaii was started by Garrit P. Judd in 1852. He poses here with Alexander Liholiho, center, and Prince Lot, right, who became Kamehameha IV and V.

Other well-known residents that worked for New England Financial included Sanford B. Dole, Henry Baldwin, James Castle, James Dickey, Charles M. Cooke, William O. Smith, and B.F. Dillingham.

Yanigihara points out that insurance, as an industry, is over 300 years old. "It began with Lloyds of London in 1687. Ship owners and wealthy individuals used to meet at Edward Lloyd's 17th century coffee house near the Tower of London. The idea was to form a group of people that would provide money to cover the cost of a shipping accident. A 'premium' was paid by the person requiring the insurance. Insurance spread the risk and minimized the chance that a lost ship would be a catastrophe."

Insurance worked for shippers, and it spread to other uses, chiefly life, health, home, and car insurance. Hardly anyone in Hawaii today wants to live without it.

Nordstrom

Sixteen year old John W. Nordstrom left his native Sweden in 1887 and arrived in New York with just five dollars in his pocket. He labored in California and Washington mines and logging camps to make ends meet. He taught himself to read with the help of newspapers. In 1897, he read that gold had been discovered in the Alaskan Klondike and he made immediate plans to go there and try his luck.

Despite difficult terrain, an over-supply of eager workers, and grueling hard work, John earned $13,000 in two years (about $260,000 in today's dollars) and returned to Seattle.

In 1901, he and a friend from Alaska named Carl Wallin invested Nordstrom's gold rush stake in a small Seattle shoe store named Wallin & Nordstrom. Their commitment to "offer the customer the best possible service, selection, quality, and value" led to prosperity and growth.

By 1960, their downtown Seattle store was the largest shoe store in the country, and they had eight stores in Washington and Oregon. In 1963, Nordstrom became a general merchandise department store, and today, they are one of the nation's leading fashion specialty retailers, employing 43,000 in 106 stores in 23 states with sales of $5 billion annually.

Four generations later, Nordstrom is still known and emulated worldwide for its excellent customer service. The "Nordstrom experience" is synonymous with exceptional customer care. A 1998 Consumer Reports Magazine nationwide survey ranked them number one in overall quality, service, and value.

Nordstrom has been in Hawaii for over 35 years, operating the shoe stores at Liberty House. A full scale department store is tentatively set to join Nordstrom Rack and Nordstrom Shoes in Ward Center in 2005.

Outrigger Canoe Club

What is now the Outrigger Canoe Club was founded in 1908 in the heart of Waikiki by Alexander Hume Ford who resurrected the forgotten sport of surfing. The original club was located on a lagoon that flowed between the Moana and Royal Hawaiian Hotels until the Ala Wai Canal was built.

Ford was concerned that residences and hotels were crowding out surfers in Waikiki and that the sport was dying. He decreed that "the property should be used only for the purpose of preserving surfing on boards and in outrigger canoes."

The original clubhouse was two grass houses. In 1910, a bigger clubhouse was built, and the club evolved beyond surfing to a sports and social club. Women were allowed to join in 1938, and a dining room and cocktail lounge were added.

The Outrigger Canoe Club in 1908 sat on a lagoon between the Royal Hawaiian and Moana Hotels.

Lex Brodie joined the club in 1931 and recalls that dues were just $25 a year. "Alexander Hume Ford was a friendly fellow. He got me started in my first business, offering rides to tourists in a canoe he owned." Sam Kahanamoku and Lex split the work and money with Ford.

When the lease was up in 1964, the club moved to its present site, the former estate of James B. Castle, near the end of the streetcar line at the foot of Diamond Head. Today, Outrigger Canoe Club is best known for its winning canoe paddling and volleyball teams.

Outrigger Enterprises

Roy Kelley was born in Redlands, California, in 1905. He studied architecture and graduated at the top of his class at the University of Southern California.

Kelley and his wife of four months, Estelle, came to Hawaii in 1929 and worked as an architect for C. W. Dickey, who was responsible for designing many of Honolulu's landmark buildings including the main building of the old Halekulani Hotel and the Waikiki Theater on Kalakaua Avenue.

Kelley foresaw the post-war wave of middle class visitors to Hawaii and saw a niche for himself. While most hotels were expensive and catered to the wealthy, Kelley targeted the middle class. As an architect, he could build hotel rooms for half the price of others and keep his rates low.

His first was the 33-room Islander Hotel, which opened in 1947, where the Waikiki Twin Theatres were. Room rates were an affordable $7.50 a night.

In the 1950s, he built the Edgewater Hotel, the Reef Hotel, and the Reef Tower. The Outrigger Canoe Club used to occupy a beautiful beachfront property between the Moana and Royal Hawaiian Hotels. When their lease expired in 1963, they moved to their current location at the foot of Diamond Head.

Sheraton Hotels wanted the property, but an impasse developed during negotiations with the Queen Emma Foundation that owned the property. Sheraton objected to a $10,000 a month increase in lease rent after ten years they believed had been inserted into the proposed lease at the last minute. The Foundation said it had been there all along.

During a lunch break, Roy Kelley walked into the room and learned about the impasse. He offered to meet the terms. When the Sheraton people returned from lunch, they were told that the property was no longer available. Kelley borrowed the Outrigger name for his growing hotel chain.

Kelley built the Outrigger Waikiki Hotel on the former canoe club site in 1967. The Outrigger East, Outrigger West, and Coral Reef hotels went up soon after on parcels that were part of the deal with the Queen Emma Foundation.

Roy Kelley was a frugal man. He maintained a desk inside the lobby of the Edgewater hotel for many years and could often be seen helping tourists with their bags. He also was not adverse to answering the phones or running to the supply room for toilet paper. "I don't want any upstairs office and secretary keeping me away from people," Kelley said. Kelley was also a generous man who went out of his way to help friends and employees in need.

During the next two decades, Outrigger expanded to over a dozen hotels in Waikiki. By 1984, Outrigger Hotels had over 7,000 rooms, making it the largest chain in the state. Roy and Estelle's

Roy and Estelle Kelly founded the Outrigger Hotel chain in 1947.

son, Dr. Richard Kelley, took over and expanded Outrigger to the neighbor islands and internationally to the Republic of the Marshall Islands, Guam, Fiji, and Australia. Dr. Kelley has since retired to Chairman of the Board, and son-in-law David Carey has taken the helm as president and CEO.

While Roy operated out of a cigar box with cash and a mental record of all his financial transactions, Richard brought in computers and reorganized all the myriad Kelley entities and partners into one Outrigger Hotels Hawaii.

Recently, Outrigger has created a new class of hotels called OHANA. "Outrigger has traditionally been a two to three star chain of hotels," says advertising executive Tim Deegan, "but there's a huge market for four and five star properties. Outrigger decided to upgrade the Outrigger brand and create OHANA Hotels to serve the two to three star market."

Today, Outrigger employs 3,000 people who take care of 15,000 guests a night and has revenues of $400 million a year.

Roy Kelley passed away in 1997 and Estelle a year later, both at the age of 91. They are gone, but their legacy remains. They revolutionized tourism and ushered in an era of affordable travel for the common man.

—*Researched by Sujin Park, Glen Peterson and Stephanus Suryaatmadja*

Pacific Business News

For a short time, *Pacific Business News* was the only daily newspaper in Honolulu. How could that be? In 1963, the *Honolulu Advertiser* and the *Star-Bulletin* were closed for two weeks due to a strike. The weekly *Pacific Business News* shifted to printing a daily paper during that time to provide the public with the news it needed. With the strike settled, PBN went back to its regular weekly format.

George Mason founded *Pacific Business News* in 1963 soon after statehood. "George saw that Hawaii's economy was not going to be driven by large businesses like many mainland states," says Editor Gina Mangieri. "Hawaii was ruled by the Big Five back then, so it was pretty revolutionary on his part to see that most of the new jobs would come from small businesses."

"PBN was designed to give a voice to the small business community and to provide in-depth reporting of issues concerning the business community."

Pacific Business News has grown beyond its weekly paper format and has found new ways to get its information to the community. "We do four live radio reports a day on Hawaii Public Radio," says Mangieri. "And we post 20 new stories a day on our web site. At 3 PM, they are e-mailed to approximately 4,000 subscribers.

For 40 years, George Mason has pointed the way forward for business and government in Hawaii. In a 2001 editorial in PBN, Mason said "it costs more to do business in Hawaii than any place in the world. We have, to put it bluntly, almost priced ourselves out of any market. And we are on the verge of doing that in the visitor industry."

"We have allowed government to become highly centralized, extremely bureaucratic and totally unionized. No other state is in such total control of government employee unions. No other state has a single Department of Education with more bureaucrats than teachers. No other state has so

George Mason founded Pacific Business News in 1963.

strongly avoided almost any form of privatization of public services."

"As long as our costs of doing business, and our cost of living are 35 percent to 40 percent higher than any other state, we will continue to lose our best and brightest — and our retirees. But, mostly, we will lose the tourists."

Mason urges major changes in how we do business in Hawaii, but says what we really need is "a new climate among legislators."

A compilation of Mason's insights can be found his book, *Mason on Management – 25 Years of the Best Editorials in Pacific Business News.*

Pacific Club

The oldest club west of the Rockies, called The Mess, was founded by 13 British men between the ages of 21 and 32 in 1851. It was a place for "promoting friendship and the mutual exchange of opinions among its members and for providing a place for the reception of strangers, travelers, and residents of the Kingdom."

Princess Victoria Kaiulani was born in the Queen Emma Street home that now houses the Pacific Club.

Some of the travelers and residents entertained at the club included Mark Twain, Robert Louis Stevenson, the Duke of Edinburgh, and Alexander Joy Cartwright, who standardized the rules of baseball.

The Mess started out on Maunakea Street and moved several times before buying Archibald Cleghorn's former home on Queen Emma Street in 1926 for $150,000.

Archibald Cleghorn had been president of the club from 1865 until 1910. His wife Miriam Likelike and he had a daughter born in the home, Princess Victoria Kaiulani.

While the club had been referred to as the British Club since its inception, it was not formally called that until 1867. At annexation in 1898, the club officially changed its name to the Pacific Club.

Parker Ranch

The Parker Ranch had its beginnings in 1809 when 19-year-old John Palmer Parker, a sailor from Massachusetts arrived in the islands. He jumped ship and hid until it departed.

John Parker came to the attention of King Kamehameha I who noticed Parker and gave him the privilege of being the first man allowed to take charge of the thousands of cattle that roamed Hawaii's remote plains and valleys. These cattle were the legacy of British Captain George Vancouver who presented Kamehameha with five head just 21 years earlier.

Due mostly to Parker's efforts, salt beef eventually replaced the increasingly scarce sandalwood as the island's chief export. As the need for beef increased, so did John's fortune and influence.

In 1816, he married Kipikane, the daughter of a high-ranking chief, who took the Christian name Rachel. Rachel and John had a daughter and two sons, and the Parker dynasty began.

As the Parker family fortune grew, the highlands of Waimea became a bustling center of trade. There were good times and bad times, and in 1887, events led to a search for a good, strong manager. Alfred Welling Carter, a respected Honolulu businessman and judge, took over Parker Ranch and guided its growth with a steady hand for nearly half a century.

Richard Palmer Smart, John Parker's great, great grandson, was the last of the family to live on the ranch. A Broadway and cabaret performer, Smart's show-business history is memorialized in the Broadway Room in one of the historic homes. When he died in 1992, Smart left the ranch in a trust to benefit several organizations in the Waimea Community including Parker School, Hawaii Preparatory Academy, North Hawaii Community Hospital, Lucy Henriques Medical Center, and Hawaii Community Foundation

Today, Parker Ranch is the largest private ranch under single ownership in the United States and the home of Hawaii's paniolo. Paniolo are tough, hard-riding cowboys that for six generations have taken care of the 50,000 cattle that range over the ranch's 225,000 acres. The Ranch produces 10 million pounds of USDA choice beef a year.

The Parker Ranch Visitor Center and Museum and the Parker Ranch Historic Homes are open daily for wagon rides, museum tours, shopping, and dining.

Patti's Chinese Kitchen

"My dad, Calvin Chun, wanted to open a Chinese Kitchen and decided to use one of his four daughter's names," Patti Louie says. "The oldest was Charlene, but he didn't think Charlene's Chinese Kitchen would work, so he went down the list of daughters. My name was next and it sounded good, so he used it. He ended up putting all our names on his restaurants."

After Patti's, which opened in 1967, came Lyn's Delicatessen, Cathy's at Holiday Mart, and Charlene's downtown. Lyn now lives in San Francisco. Cathy is a local make-up artist, and Charlene lives in Los Angeles.

Chun owned or was a partner in several other businesses, including Bella Italia, Asian Palate, the Oceania Floating Chinese Restaurant, and Paradise Sportswear.

Patti Loui, center, with her husband James, left, and father Calvin Chun.

"Many people are surprised there is a Patti and that I'm still around. Dad opened Patti's when I was 16, and I was flattered to have a place named for me. But, I worked at Cathy's. I didn't want to work with James, my boyfriend and now husband, *and* my dad."

Patti recalls the long customer lines back in their original location, 50 feet Diamond Head of the present food court. "We had double lines open all day, plus a separate manapua line. It was crazy. And yes, we did have Elizabeth Taylor, as is widely rumored, stand in line, and many other celebrities, too."

Patti, who now runs the restaurant with her husband, James Louie, has maintained the high standards set by her father. "Color and freshness are very important to him. He's a very down to earth man. He told me others always know something I don't know, and that I could learn something from everyone." Calvin Chun is 89 and mom, Thelma, still works occasionally."

—Researched by Rasel Taher

Pearl City Tavern

A landmark for over 50 years, and once the Leeward area's swankiest place to dine, the Pearl City Tavern began in 1939 when only 800 people lived in Pearl City. It started as Mae's Drive-in a block away and moved to the corner of Kamehameha Highway and Lehua Avenue. Military personnel crowded into Pearl City Tavern during the war years, and the place developed a reputation as a gambling den.

The Tavern was famous for its Monkey Bar, which began as a misnomer. Owners Irene and George Fukuoka had several different animals, including a gorilla. Patrons began referring to the bar as the Monkey Bar, and after the gorilla died, they put actual spider monkeys in a glass enclosure behind the bar. The question patrons would ask was: "who was watching who – the monkeys or the people?"

Pearl City Tavern was one of the first places to bring in live Maine lobsters, which was a huge draw. George's brother Jerry was the head chef, and he was highly regarded. His bread, sandwiches, soups, and steaks were outstanding. They served American, Japanese, and Chinese dishes.

Keiki Kani Music Studio owner Camilla Corpuz Yamamoto remembers a roof-top garden where the owner had a bonsai and orchid collection. "We'd climb a winding staircase and find ourselves in this beautiful, romantic setting on the roof."

Fukuoka died in 1970, and the new owners were never able to provide the magic that had made the Tavern a success. It closed in 1993. The monkeys were sent to live with a veterinarian on the Big Island. Termite damage made the building irreparable, and it was torn down. Pearl City Cutter Dodge now sells cars on the property.

The Good Luck rock at the Pearl Country Club.

Pearl Country Club

Joe Pao built the Pearl City Golf Course in 1967 and named it the Francis I'i Brown Golf Course. The Tokai Land Company bought the course in 1972 and changed its name to the Pearl Country Club. In 1976, Soichiro Honda, founder of the Honda Motor Company in Japan, bought the course.

"This is the only business he owned in the islands," said assistant General Manager Lois Parker. "He was a real nice gentleman, and he liked to golf. His intention was to provide a great golf course for the local population, not to make money. It was his way of giving back. And today, 85 percent of our golfers are locals."

Soichiro died in 1991, and his wife Sachi and family now own the Pearl Country Club. The company's full name is Honda Kaihatsu Kogyo Kabushiki Kaisha.

As you drive into the club, off Kaonohi Street, you will notice a large stone on the right. "When we were designing the course, this huge boulder was right in the middle of a fairway," said Parker. "Workers tried but couldn't move it. When they came to work the next day, it had moved. It really spooked the workers. Now it's our good luck rock. It has a new home, under a tree."

Geologists say the rock is a basalt volcanic rock two million years old. The *kahuna* that blessed it says it is a male rock that is very happy in its present location because it is in love with a leguminosae tree nearby.

Pegge Hopper Gallery

Pegge Hopper gets her inspiration watching TV. "Or, other times, it just comes," says Hopper, whose art revolves around women at leisure. "I see an image, and it sparks something."

"My art is not political or controversial. It has women of strength and beauty, lacking self-consciousness."

One might think Pegge uses models for her art, but she has none. "Except for hands and feet. I use my own hands and feet," Hopper says.

"Japanese magazines come and want to do a story about me," Hopper continues. "They all want to take a picture of me in front of one of my paintings. Months later, tourists come into the store, and they want to buy the picture I was standing in front of. So I've learned to stand in front of my most expensive works."

Pegge Hopper Gallery on Nuuanu Avenue near Beretania opened in 1983. Her magnificent art has price tags reaching $30,000.

Pizza Bob's

Robert Lee Jr. started the Pizza Shop in Haleiwa in 1974. "There was too much confusion with Pizza Hut, so when we moved to our present location, we changed the name to Pizza Bob's."

"We had search lights for the grand opening and gave away free pizza," Lee continued. "We hired the Makaha Sons, and they never showed up. But 700 customers did. It was crammed three deep in the aisles."

What makes their pizza so special? "It's the sauce," Lee says. "It has 26 different spices and herbs. I worked on it for 89 straight days, tinkering with the combinations until I perfected it."

Bob Lee and his father are the L&L in L&L Drive-Inn. The father operated L&L Dairy in the 1950s. Before that, he owned Molly's downtown, serving steaks to sailors during World War II. "Molly Williams was dad's favorite waitress. She was a bright, hard-working, part-Hawaiian woman who taught my dad how to run a restaurant."

"He bought a soda fountain on Hotel Street and sold drinks for a nickel, sandwiches for 20 cents, and ice cream sundaes for 35 cents. He didn't make any money," Lee continued, "so he switched to steaks for $1.75. He only had 14 tables, and there was often a line down the street. He made $2,000 a day, but upset Wo Fat because the line sometimes blocked their entrance."

Bob Lee Jr. opened his second restaurant in Haleiwa in 1978 – The Wizard of Eggs. "It was next to Pizza Bob's and was busy until 11 AM, and then it was quiet. In 1981, we decided to change the name and concept to Rosie's Cantina."

Marty Robbins' song *El Paso* inspired the name. "Out in the West Texas town of El Paso, I fell in love with a Mexican girl. Nighttime would find me in Rose's Cantina. Music would play and Felina would whirl."

"The song says Rose's Cantina," Lee continues. "We changed it to Rosie's."

A year later, Lee opened Steamers. Lee also opened Pizza Bob's and Rosie's Diner at Restaurant Row, but "they kept raising the rent, so we left." Lee started the Haleiwa Beach Grill and Howzits Sports Bar, but sold them.

Pleasant Holidays

Few locals appreciate the magnitude of Pleasant Holidays' impact on Hawaii. Since its founding in 1959, Pleasant Holidays has brought over five million tourists to Hawaii and over $4 billion in revenue to the state.

"I just can't believe that more than four decades have passed since we opened our small retail travel agency in Point Pleasant, NJ," says co-founder Ed Hogan, who attributes his success to consistently offering the best possible travel values.

Ed and Lynn Hogan opened Pleasant Travel Service in Point Pleasant, New Jersey but moved to California in 1962 to focus more on Hawaii. In 1974, they began purchasing hotels in the islands, including the Kahana Beach Resort Condominium Hotel, the Royal Lahaina Resort on Maui, the Royal Kona Resort, and the Kauai Coconut Beach Resort.

Today, Pleasant Holidays focuses on Hawaii, Mexico, Tahiti, Australia, and New Zealand. Each year, they bring in over 400,000 visitors to the state.

The Hogans have won numerous awards and accolades, including Ed being named "Mr. Tourism Hawaii" by the Hawaii State Legislature. Following the terrorist attacks of September 11, Pleasant Holidays created a "Keep 'em Flying" marketing campaign to encourage their valued customers to continue traveling and raised $500,000 to benefit New York firefighter and rescue worker's widows and orphans.

The Queen's Medical Center

From Captain James Cook's arrival in Hawaii in 1778 until 1850, diseases like smallpox and measles devastated the native population, whose numbers fell from about 300,000 to less than 60,000.

The legislature passed a law to build the first hospital in the islands, but there were no funds. King Kamehameha IV and Queen Emma, both in their twenties, personally solicited funds and exceeded their $8,000 goal with $13,350.

In 1859, The Queen's Hospital opened on Fort Street with 18 beds. A year later, the hospital bought the dusty and barren area named Manamana (which means to branch out, or much spiritual power in Hawaiian) for $2,000. It erected a facility with 124 beds. In its early days, patients stayed for long periods in the hospital. In 1875, the average patient stayed for 73 days.

The first physician at Queen's, Dr. William Hillebrand, had a huge impact on Hawaii aside from his work at the hospital. His home became Foster Gardens. It was his suggestion that Portuguese workers from the Madeira Islands be invited to come to Hawaii to work the plantations. Those first immigrants invented

The Queen's Hospital in 1904. In its early days, the average patient stayed for 73 days.

the ukulele soon after arriving in the islands.

Dr. Hillebrand, who was also a botanist, and Queen Emma took on the task of beautifying the hospital grounds. They brought in rare, exceptional trees and exotic plants. A new variety of shower tree was created with cross pollination in the 1930s that became known as Queen's Hospital White. It has yellow blossoms that become white at maturity and can now be found all over Oahu.

In 1967, The Queen's Hospital was renamed The Queen's Medical Center to reflect the broader scope that includes medical research and education. Currently, The Queen's Medical Center admits 19,000 patients a year

William Hillebrand was the first physician at The Queen's Hospital in 1859 when it opened on Fort Street.

and serves 200,000 outpatients. It has over 550 beds, 1,000 doctors and 3,500 employees.

If you look closely at Queen's logo, you can see that it's made from two intertwined E's, derived from the royal cipher. They're Queen Emma's Royal E's. Atop it is her crown. Beneath is a banner which reads The Queen's Medical Center and the year 1859.

—Researched by Hui Chin Chua

Red Dirt Shirt Company

Many of the companies in Hawaii survived great adversity: fires, tsunami's, or the depression. Bob Hedin's Tropical Shirts survived Hurricane Iniki, which swept through Kauai on Sept. 11, 1992. His factory was badly damaged, and his T-shirts were dirt-stained.

Hedin experimented with the red dirt and found that it produced a uniquely-colored dye. Hedin liked it and decided to coat his entire shirt inventory with dirt. These later came to be known as Red Dirt Shirts.

By 1993, Hedin's Red Dirt Shirts were a hit among residents and visitors alike. He and his wife, Margo, christened their company Paradise Sportswear. Today, Paradise Sportswear is a $3 million business with 60 employees and more than 150 wholesale accounts. There are eight stores in Hawaii and one in the red-dirt area of Utah.

Reyns

Reyn McCollough came to Hawaii for a vacation in 1959 and saw Ala Moana under construction. He thought it would be a good location for a store, but all spots were taken. He left his number and returned to Catalina Island off the coast of California where his men's apparel business was originally located.

Fortunately, Ala Moana developed a vacancy, and Reyn's moved to Hawaii to take it. Their original slogan was "The Brooks Brothers of the Pacific."

Ruth Spooner, who owned Spooner of Waikiki, was well known for her surf trunks. Reyn's bought out Ruth Spooner in 1962, and Reyn Spooner was born.

Reyn did not like the brightness of the 1960s aloha shirts, most of which were made from leftover muu muu fabric. He liked the sun-faded look of the surfer's shirts and tried to recreate it. The result was the reverse print concept. Coinciding with the beginning of Aloha Friday in 1966, it was a huge hit and is still popular 30 years later.

Reyn McCullough passed away in 1984, and his children and family continued on. Reyn's has 11 stores on four islands and is headquartered in Kamuela because Reyn liked the Big Island and the flowers that grow there.

—Researched by Yuki Moromizato

The Ritz

Nenichi Kamuri sold appliances in the 1920s, calling his company Standard Sales. Tom Hanrahan joined forces with him and they opened their first shop on Union Street downtown in 1938.

"A lot of our sales were to the military," says daughter Rose Kamuri, "but when World War II began, the military wouldn't let dad on base because he wasn't a U.S. citizen."

Undaunted, the company decided to switch gears and sell ready-to-wear clothing. "Hanrahan suggested we needed a better name, and came up with The Ritz.

The name came from The Ritz Hotel which Cesar Ritz opened in Paris in 1898. Ritz provided guests with superb accommodations, sublime cuisine, and grand entertainment. The name came to represent the pinnacle of luxury. Irving Berlin wrote the song *Puttin' On The Ritz* in 1928 for the movie of the same name.

Robert's Hawaii

It is hard to imagine, but 60 years ago, Hawaii's largest tour and transportation company had humble beginnings as a taxi company in Hanapepe, Kauai.

Robert Iwamoto Sr. built his business around U.S. servicemen stationed on Kauai during World War II. He started with two cabs and hired his uncles and aunts as drivers. When he was filming *Blue Hawaii*, Elvis Presley was a passenger.

Son Robert Iwamoto Jr. joined the company when he was only 15 years old. He would often awake at 3 AM to wash the cars and work until 10 PM as a dispatcher and mechanic. Their hard work

paid off, and they expanded from cars to buses and limousines. In the 1960s, Iwamoto created room and car packages for the tourists that arrived on Kauai without hotel reservations.

Foreseeing the rapid growth in tourism, Iwamoto relocated the business to Oahu in 1964.

Robert's first rabbit mocked the Greyhound Dog.

By 1967, Robert's Ilima Tours and Robert's Rent A Car operated on four islands. In 1981, they purchased the catamaran Alii Kai, taking hundreds of tourists on cruises off Waikiki every day.

Other businesses include Robert's Overnighters, the Magic of Polynesia show, and Rainbow Trolley. Robert's transports thousands of youngsters to school each day. Robert's Hawaii is the largest transportation company in the state with over 1,000 buses. All told, their two dozen enterprises employ over 2,000 and gross over $100 million annually.

Their chief competitor through the 1970s was Greyhound, which used greyhound dog logos on the sides of their buses. Iwamoto Jr. recalls a childhood trip to the dog races in Mexico where he saw that the greyhounds chased a mechanical rabbit around the track. They never caught the rabbit, Iwamoto observed.

That observation led him to choose the rabbit as his logo in the 1970s. When Greyhound decided to pull out of the Hawaii market a few years later,

When Greyhound left Hawaii, the Rabbit waved goodbye.

Robert's sported a waving bunny, bidding farewell to their defeated competitor.

—Researched by Mandy Y.C. Liew

Royal Hawaiian Hotel

When visiting dignitaries came to the islands in the 1870s, the only places for them to stay were personal homes, boarding houses, and rooms above saloons. King Kamehameha V decided to encourage the building of a three-story hotel on the parcel of land bordered by Richards, Hotel, Alakea, and Beretania Streets. The hotel property was where the Hemmeter Building, now called One Capital District, stands today.

Originally named the Hawaiian Hotel, it opened in 1871 with 12 cottages in a beautiful tropical setting. It became the Royal Hawaiian Hotel soon after King Kalakaua ascended the throne in 1874. Some think it became Royal because the king spent a lot of time there.

Another possibility is that it got its name from the Royal Hawaiian Theatre, 100 feet Ewa on Alakea and Hotel where the courthouse is now. The Royal Hawaiian Theatre opened in 1848, closed in 1879, and was demolished in 1881 according to theatre historian Lowell Angell. Both hotel and theatre were open at the same time.

King Kalakaua was fascinated with technology. On a trip to the mainland, he visited Thomas Edison, and his interest led to Iolani Palace being wired for electricity. The Palace and the Royal Hawaiian Hotel were electrified four years before the White House.

Soon after the turn of the century, better, more luxurious hotels were built, most notably the Moana, Waikiki Seaside, and the Alexander Young. The Royal Hawaiian Hotel declined and closed in 1917, and the YMCA took over the building. It was demolished, rebuilt and became the Armed Forces YMCA.

Captain William Matson, who founded the Matson Navigation Company, saw the possibility of building luxury ships to bring people to Hawaii. Luxury hotels needed to be built for them

The original Royal Hawaiian Hotel was built on Richards Street in 1871.

to stay in.

Matson manager William Roth teamed up with Ed Tenney, who headed Castle & Cooke, and they secured fifteen acres on the beach where King Kamehameha I and Queen Kaahumanu previously had a summer palace.

The New York architectural firm of Warren and Wetmore chose a Spanish-Moorish style that was very popular in the 1920s, partially due to the popularity of Rudolph Valentino movies.

Former KGU GM Jim Carroll passed along a story that a house next door on the beach and was pink. Matson liked the look and matched the color for his hotel.

Bill Sewell, who had been Chief Purser on Matson's White Ships in the 1950s, recalls hearing that the Royal was painted pink because "the architect liked the color and considered it a cool color for the tropics." Unfortunately no one knows for sure

On February 1, 1927, The Pink Palace of the Pacific opened with a gala dinner for 1,200 of Oahu's elite.

The Royal Hawaiian, prior to all the current encroachment, was a stunningly beautiful oasis in the middle of a gigantic garden. "The times I stayed at the Royal," Sewell continued, "it was quiet, well protected, and one had the feeling of being in the middle of a well kept jungle. The grounds stretched to Kalakaua Avenue and to Lewers Street. The low rise, unobtrusive Outrigger Canoe Club was next door. There was also a parking lot and a few stores between it and the Moana Hotel."

Since 1927, The Royal Hawaiian has been a symbol of ocean-front luxury on Waikiki Beach and the favorite resort for royalty and sophisticated travelers alike. The famous pink facade, vaulted Spanish arch- ways, 525 rooms and suites, offer a unique

The "Pink Palace of the Pacific" opened in 1927 in Waikiki.

ambience found only at the Royal.

Captain Matson commissioned a luxurious ship to carry passengers to Hawaii. The *Malolo*, built in Philadelphia, carried 650 passengers. Many of them even brought their own cars and servants.

Bill Sewell says, "*Malolo* is a flying fish, and Matson thought the name would be a good omen. However, on launching, it hit a scow and they had to cut off a few feet at the propeller end of the ship. This caused the ship to roll (side to side) more than anticipated, and so the locals called the ship the 'Roll-olo.'"

DeSoto Brown, whose father, Zadoc, sailed on the Malolo many times as a child when the ship was new, recalls his father calling it the "Ma-rollo."

A golf course was built for hotel guests some distance away in Kahala. Greens fees were $2.50 on weekends at opening. The Golf Course later became the Waialae Country Club's golf course.

During World War II, the Navy took over The Royal Hawaiian and used it for R&R. The hotel staff sealed the wine cellar with concrete, making it look like the wall of the underground tunnel it was part of. After the war, they returned to see if the Navy had found it, and lo and behold, it was still hidden. For four years, the Navy never discovered the secret cache of fine wine.

By the mid-1950s, more than half of all Hawaii tourists stayed in Matson's Moana, Royal Hawaiian, Surfrider, and Princess

Matson's Malolo sailing into Honolulu Harbor in 1927.

Kaiulani hotels. In 1959, the hotels were sold to Sheraton for $17.6 million. Sheraton sold the hotel to Kyo-ya in 1963 but still manages it. Today it is called the Sheraton Royal Hawaiian Hotel.

Roy's

What began in 1988 with a restaurant in Hawaii Kai has blossomed to six in Hawaii, four in Japan, and 21 on the mainland. Chef Roy Yamaguchi is largely credited with founding Hawaiian-Fusion Cuisine.

"We set out to explore new directions," says Yamaguchi, "blending freely the European techniques in which I was trained with familiar ingredients of Asia and the Pacific. While highly personal, it is a style of cooking that is easily transplanted with the use of the freshest ingredients of any locale, wrought with the same sense of fun and freedom found in our original restaurants in Hawaii."

In 1999, Yamaguchi partnered with Outback Steakhouses, in a 50-50 cash deal with them contributing their expertise in restaurant management and Yamaguchi controlling the menu.

Roy's New York was closed for four months in the aftermath of September 11th. The Marriott World Financial Center, where it is located, served as the temporary Red Cross headquarters.

St. Francis Healthcare System

The story of St. Francis Healthcare begins with Father Damien and the sisters who came from Syracuse, N.Y. to help him.

In the 1860s, leprosy was rampant in the Hawaiian Islands. When Father Damien De Veuster of the Sacred Hearts Fathers heard that there was no religious leader at the colony on Molokai for those with leprosy, he volunteered and, in 1873, started his mission there. He needed help caring for the people and asked Bishop Maigret in Honolulu to find him some assistants, but none of the sisters in Honolulu would go. In 1883, he sent Father Leonor on a search mission that took him across the entire United States. Although he approached 50 religious communities, none of them was willing to join him.

Finally, he arrived at Syracuse, New York and met the Sisters of the Third Order of St. Francis where he had a conversation with the superior of the order, Mother

Father Damien as a young priest. Drawing by Edward Clifford.

Marianne Cope.

Mother Marianne convened a meeting of the sisters and novices and told them of the need in Hawaii for nurses. It was a dangerous mission, she told them, but immediately 35 of the sisters volunteered to go. Mother Marianne chose six sisters, and they soon departed for the three-month trip by train and then steamer for Hawaii in 1883.

They started their work on Oahu. In November 1888, together with two other sisters, Mother Marianne left for Molokai because Father Damien was dying from leprosy. On April 15, 1889, he passed away. Mother Marianne remained responsible for the

Kalaupapa settlement for the next 27 years, seeing the settlement through a hurricane and an epidemic of the black plague, until she passed away in 1918.

She was buried at the settlement on Molokai until 2005 when her body was exhumed, as required by the church, and moved to Syracuse, New York. In 2005, Venerable Mother Marianne be-

Mother Marianne Cope stands in the center of this 1899 photograph at Kalapaupa with sisters Eilers and Burns, left, and Gomes and McCormick, right.

came Blessed Mother Marianne and closer to sainthood.

Robert Louis Stevenson visited Kalaupapa a month after Damien's death. He was so taken by her faith and strength that he wrote a poem about "Mother Marianne" and the sisters.

> To see the infinite pity of this place,
> The mangled limb, the devastated face,
> The innocent sufferers smiling at the rod,
> A fool were tempted to deny his God.
>
> He sees and shrinks, but if he looks again
> Lo, beauty springing from the breast of pain
> He marks the sisters on the painful shores,
> And even a fool is silent and adores.

During those 27 years, and thereafter, no sister caught leprosy because they practiced safe hygiene techniques that Father Damien had no knowledge of, without medical training.

Besides her work at Kalaupapa, Mother Marianne Cope was also instrumental in a number of other good works: She was influential in starting Malulani Hospital, Maui in 1884, St. Anthony School in Wailuku, Maui in 1885, St. Joseph School in Hilo in 1900, and Hilo Hospital in 1915.

With the inspiration of their flourishing establishment on Molokai, the Sisters of Saint Francis followed up on their dream of a general hospital to care for the needy sick on Oahu. They raised the then-staggering sum of $24,000 and opened St. Francis Hospital in Palama in 1927.

In the beginning, it was a 70-bed hospital. Sister M. Flaviana Engel was St. Francis Hospital's first CEO and was the first of eight female CEOs to lead the hospital up to the present.

Following her were Sister M. Eugenia Bopp, Sister M. Bernadette Wunsch, Mother M. Jolenta Wilson, (these "M's" honor Mary, the mother of Jesus), Sister Maureen Keleher, Sister Aileen Griffin, Sister Beatrice Tom, the first local sister to head the hospital, and Sister Agnelle Ching, the current CEO.

No other company in Hawaii has been run by eight successive female CEOs.

St. Francis has dealt with union conflicts in unusual ways. "Sister Maureen would begin bargaining sessions in the 1960s with the words 'let's start with a prayer,'" Sister Be recalls. "It would be hard for the union leader, Art Rutledge, to maintain an adversarial relationship with someone he prayed with moments earlier. Sister Maureen also sent out coffee to the nurses walking picket lines."

The St. Francis Healthcare System was created in 1984. Today, the Healthcare System consists of St. Francis Community Health Services, St. Francis Healthcare Foundation, St. Francis Healthcare Enterprises, St. Francis Residential Care Community, and St. Francis-Our Lady of Kea'au.

In 2007, the two medical centers were sold to the Cardio-vascular Hospitals of America (CHA). The Vatican had to approve the sale. The Medical Centers transitioned to Hawaii Medical Center East and Hawaii Medical Center West.

St. Francis Community Health Services

Mother Marianne brought six nuns from Syracuse, New York to help Father Damien on Molokai. Painting by Peggy Chun.

offers home care, hospice, rehabilitation services, mobile van services, health centers for senior citizens, and managed care programs.

St. Francis was the first to offer kidney dialysis services in 1965 and the first to offer kidney transplants in 1969. The renal dialysis services were sold to Liberty Dialysis-Hawaii in 2006.

They opened the first hospice in Hawaii in 1978 and performed the first heart, liver, pancreas, lung, and bone marrow transplants in the islands.

In the spirit of doing what was best for the islands, St. Francis gave up pediatrics and gynecology so that Kapiolani Hospital could focus on them, survive, and grow.

St. Francis Medical Center is named for St. Francis of Assisi, who was born in 1182 and died in 1226. "His father was a wealthy cloth merchant and named him for France, where he had just visited on business," said CEO Sister Agnelle Ching.

"He was a very popular, handsome man with a great voice. But he was captured and taken prisoner during a

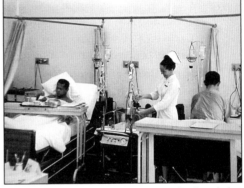

Many firsts happened at St. Francis. The first dialysis services in Hawaii, shown here, were in 1965.

war and came to the realization that there was more to life than war and materialism. After the war, he decided that being poor freed him. He lived simply, with only one robe and a pair of sandals. He shifted to knowing his heart instead of knowledge.

"He believed in preaching through action, not words, which is maybe why the order has so many projects," Sister Agnelle continued. "There is a story of St. Francis meeting a person with leprosy on the road. He gave him a coin and kissed him. This may have moved the Order in Syracuse to come to Hawaii."

Interestingly, the name of the Third Franciscan Order of Syracuse, New York was chosen by Pope Pius IX. Bishop John Newman of Philadelphia had suggested to the Pope that the Order be Dominicans (teachers). The Pope said they were more like Franciscans (care givers). Therefore the Pope, in naming the order in Syracuse, NY, indirectly named St. Francis Hospital in Hawaii.

The Franciscan Sisters live according to the values promulgated by St. Francis: peacemaking, simplicity, charity and joy.

Today, their organization includes two hospitals in Syracuse and Utica, New York; two adult day centers, one in Hawaii and one in Syracuse; a long-term care rehabilitation facility in Auburn, NY; the St. Francis School in Manoa; the Gingerbread School in Syracuse; a spiritual life center in Skaneateles, NY; Francis House - a home for the dying; Alverna Heights - farmland dedicated to ecology; collaborative ministries in Syracuse with the Franciscan friars in a food pantry, shopping mall ministry; and Franciscorps, a clinic for the poor.

Eight female CEO's have headed St. Francis Hospital since 1927. Sister Beatrice Tom became the seventh CEO in 1990.

A joint venture with Queens, Kuakini and Kapiolani Hospitals led to United Laundry, headed by former first lady Vicky Cayetano. "To save money," Sister Be said, "we all got together and put our laundry machines in one building."

In the early 1960s, Kenneth Kingrey, a professor of art at the University of Hawaii, designed the hospital's corporate symbol. The logo represents the hands of St. Francis and Christ.

—Researched By Irena Deisinger

Sam Choy's

It is not his 350 pounds that makes Sam Choy the huge success that he is. "Hawaii's Culinary Ambassador" owes his success to the huge portions of delicious food he serves up daily at his nine restaurants.

Choy, who believes you should never trust a skinny chef, is the author of five top-selling cookbooks and has been nominated four times for the James Beard Best Pacific Regional Chef award.

Sam grew up in Laie and learned to cook in his father's restaurant, the Hukilau Café. Parents, Clairemoana and Hung Sam Choy, sent their son to Kapiolani Community College. After brief stints at several hotels, he opened his first restaurant in 1981 on the Big Island. Today, Choy has four restaurants in Tokyo, three in Hawaii, and one in Guam and San Diego. You can watch his Sunday cooking show, *Sam Choy's Kitchen*, on KHNL.

Sam Sato's

Some of the best manju and dry mein in the islands can be found at Sam Sato's in Wailuku. Sato leased a little plantation store in Camp 3, Spreckelsville on Maui in 1933. It was a little grocery store, and the previous tenants also made manju, a Japanese bean cake.

His mother Mite Sato went to Japan to perfect the manju recipe, using lima beans as the filling. She, along with Sam and his sisters, operated the little store.

In 1935, Sam married Gladys Watanabe who had worked at a bakery. She brought expertise in making turnovers and other pastries.

Four daughters were born and raised in that first location. "Then in 1964, the plantation decided to close up Camp 3, and we all had to move out," said daughter Lynne Sato Toma. "My parents then leased another old plantation store in Puunene which had been run by the Hamada family who used to make and sell their own saimin noodles."

The Satos decided to continue making the saimin but bought their noodles instead from the Iwamoto Natto Factory. "A Chinese man, whom my dad had hired and was known to us only as 'Chief Cook,' introduced 'dry noodles,' seasoned and mixed with fresh bean sprouts and char siu. Today, we serve it with broth and call it dry mein."

"In 1981, we found another old building, this time in Happy Valley, Wailuku," Toma continued. "We bought the place, and my husband Charles and I incorporated the business and took over. My husband was a school counselor at that time, and after a year or so, had to quit his position to help me with the business. My mother, who was the very backbone of the business, passed away in 1990. My dad, the founder and idea man, the boss of the business, passed away in 1997."

"In 1993, we moved into a new building in the Millyard, Wailuku, our present location. We have tried very hard to maintain the quality and standards that my parents had, and are ever grateful to them."

Sears

Picture America in the late 1880s. There were only 38 states and a population of 58 million. Only a dozen cities had 200,000 or more residents. Amidst these rustic times, Richard Sears began the R.W.

Sears Watch Company in Minneapolis in 1886 and moved a year later to Chicago. In 1887, Alvah C. Roebuck answered Sears' classified ad for a watchmaker.

Thus began the association of two young men, both still in their twenties, that was to make their names famous. In 1893 the corporate name of the firm became Sears, Roebuck and Co.

Sears, Roebuck and Co. and other mail-order companies prospered by buying in volume and offering an affordable alternative to high-priced rural general stores.

By 1895, their Sears, Roebuck Catalog topped 500 pages and offered shoes, clothing, stoves, furniture, china, musical instruments, saddles, firearms, bicycles, baby carriages, and jewelry. Sales were so good that Sears built a 40-acre, $5 million mail-order plant and office building on Chicago's West Side. When it opened in 1906, the mail-order plant, with more than three million square feet of floor space, was the largest business building in the world.

The Sears catalog is fondly remembered by many old-timers for having a special place in the family outhouse, and not just for reading material.

However, America was changing. With cars and modern roads,

When Sears agreed to be the anchor tenant, downtown retailers felt comfortable taking a gamble on the new Ala Moana Center, seen here under construction in 1955.

Sears' rural customers were no longer limited to shopping by catalog. Sears, which did very little business in cities, decided to test the retail waters in Chicago. It was a surprising success. By the end of 1933, Sears had 400 stores in operation. During one 12-month period in the late 1920s, stores opened on the average of one every other business day. In 1931, Sears' retail sales topped mail-order sales for the first time.

Sears developed several "independent" brands during this time - Craftsman, Kenmore, and DieHard. Allstate Insurance Co. was launched as a wholly owned subsidiary in 1931. Its name was taken from Sears' line of Allstate automobile tires.

When Sears needed new headquarters, it built the 110-story Sears Tower, the world's tallest building at 1,454 feet when it was opened in 1973.

Before Ala Moana Center was built, most shopping was downtown. Dillingham first proposed building the center in the late 1940s but few retailers would consider moving to what had been outlying swamp land. When Sears committed to be the anchor tenant for Phase I, it pushed smaller stores into making the move, and the rest is history. Little shopping is done downtown nowadays.

Today, Sears has over 2,000 stores and does over $40 billion in annual sales.

Sheraton Moana Surfrider

A century has come and gone since the Moana opened its doors on March 11, 1901. The Moana was the first luxury hotel in Waikiki. Each room had a bath and telephone, and the room rate was $1.50 a day (about $25 today).

Walter C. Peacock built the Moana for $150,000 (more than $2.5 million in today's dollars). Unfortunately, the hotel did not

Moana means the "broad expanse of the sea."

do well in its first few years, and Peacock was forced to sell to Alexander Young in 1907. In 1918, the two wings and two additional floors were added.

Architect Oliver G. Traphagen designed the hotel in the Beaux Arts style. The Louvre in Paris and the Vienna Opera House were also built in this style.

"Meet You Beneath the Banyan Tree" has been the hotel's slogan as well as a place to rendezvous. Peacock planted the Indian banyan in 1895. Today it is 75 feet tall and 150 feet wide.

Webley Edwards launched a Hawaiian music program called *Hawaii Calls* from beneath the banyan tree of the Moana Hotel in 1935. *Hawaii Calls* highlighted Hawaii's musical entertainers to 600 radio stations and millions of listeners on the mainland. It made a number of songs world famous including *Sweet Leilani, Beyond the Reef, The Hawaiian Wedding Song,* and *Lovely Hula Hands.*

For several decades, the Royal Hawaiian Hotel, left, and the Moana Hotel, right, had Waikiki largely to themselves.

Moana means the "broad expanse of the sea." At one time, it was owned by the Territorial Hotel Company, which owned the Royal Hawaiian Hotel, making the two the first family of hotels in the islands.

Bill Sewell recalls that the Moana had 40 cottages located directly across Kalakaua Avenue where the Princess Kaiulani is now. "When I first went there as a Matson trainee, they put me up at the Moana bungalows. There were lots of trees and foliage, and I thought I was in heaven to stay there for two weeks. We left our wallets and valuables on the desk and went swimming - never a problem. Lyle Guslander was manager, and he always treated trainees well."

The Moana Hotel did not have any termites until about l970, Sewell recalls hearing. "Seems that when it was built, all the lumber was dumped off the ships into the ocean where it soaked up salt water, and termites hate salt water. But eventually, the timber dried completely, and the termites found them."

The Surfrider, named after surfing legend Duke Kahanamoku,

was built in 1952 as part of the Moana. It is now called the Sheraton Moana Surfrider. Kenji Osano, owner of Kyo-ya bought the Moana, Royal Hawaiian, Princess Kaiulani, Sheraton-Waikiki, and Sheraton-Maui in the early 1970s. The Moana is the oldest surviving hotel in Waikiki.

Shirokiya

Which company in Hawaii is the oldest? Shirokiya can make that claim. Its roots go all the way back to 1662 in the town of Nihonbashi, Edo (now Tokyo) when Hikotaro Omura opened a notions and draper's shop. Hawaii's oldest home-grown company, C. Brewer and Company, in contrast, did not get started until 164 years later, in 1826.

Shirokiya literally means "white tree store," referring to the White Birch.

Soon after Commander William Perry opened Japan to western trade in 1854, Shirokiya was designated by the Japanese government as the store to trade with the west. In 1886, Shirokiya was the first store in Japan to sell western clothing.

The Tokyu group was originally known as the Meguro-Kamata Railway Company. It was formed in 1922 and now spans four hundred companies. Tokyu Department stores were established  in 1934 and bought Shirokiya in 1958. A year later, the first store outside Japan opened in Hawaii. Junzo Sakahura, Japan's most-famous architect, designed the Ala Moana store. Rocks from Japanese riverbeds were brought to Hawaii for its rock gardens.

The Tokyu Group, one of Japan's largest companies, sold Shirokiya in 2001 to its Hawaii managers for $1. Shirokiya employs 180 and has revenues of about $35 million. Three hundred years after it opened, locals still find Shirokiya the best place in Hawaii to find Japanese food and merchandise.

—Research by Ahmed Malkawi

Singha Thai Cuisine

In 1972, Chai Chaowasaree opened Singha Thai Cuisine in Bangkok, Thailand. In 1988, he moved to Hawaii and opened his restaurant on Ala Moana Boulevard, across from the Wailana Coffee House and Fort DeRussy.

The restaurant was named after one of Thailand's famous beers, Singha Beer. The owner reasoned that if the beer was popular with Americans the name might make his restaurant popular too. In Thai, Singha means "power and prosperity."

The current slogans are: "Experience Thailand in Hawaii" and "Home of the Royal Thai Dancers." The Royal Thai Dancers perform age-old dances, telling stories with their hands and eyes. They let customers know why Thailand is the land of a thousand smiles.

At one time, this beautiful art form was performed only in front of the Royal Family in Thailand. Their costumes are crafted of Thai silk and are decorated with pure gold and silver.

Singha Thai Cuisine has won numerous awards, accolades. and glowing reviews. In 1999, Chai's Island Bistro opened at the Aloha Tower Marketplace with Hawaii regional cuisine and local entertainment.

—Researched by Chutima Tivattanasuk

Sizzler

A well-known aphorism in sales is to sell the sizzle, not the steak. "Sizzler steaks were originally served sizzling on a hot aluminum plate that rested on a wood plank," says Hawaii owner Gary Sallee. "Don't touch the platter, we'd tell people."

Del and Helen Johnson and J.W. Thomason founded Sizzler in Culver City, California in 1957. Gary's parents, Frank and Betty opened the first in Hawaii in 1964 on Nimitz Highway and at one time had 12 Sizzlers.

The original concept was self service to keep costs down. There was a choice of two steaks that came with potatoes, cheese toast, and a salad.

Long-time employee Harry Parks says that a lot of firsts for Sizzler started in Hawaii. "We were the first to serve breakfast in the chain, stay open 24 hours, serve rice, cole slaw, and fresh fish. Hawaii was the pioneer."

"We had to convince them to let us sell rice instead of potatoes," continues Sallee. "My father got a university professor to show that people in Hawaii consumed 55 pounds of rice a year, compared to five on the mainland. The Sizzler policy was that no deviation was allowed in their menu, except for Hawaii."

In 1972, Sizzler offered steak and lobster tail for $4.49. "It was a big hit," Parks recalls. "We probably sold 400-500 platters a day for years."

Small Business Hawaii

Tire dealer Lex Brodie started a small business organization, Lex Brodie's Small Business Association in 1974 as a result of a dispute with the Department of Labor. "An employee of mine decided he wanted to fish instead of work," Brodie recalls. "He quit and filed for unemployment benefits. He said he figured out how he could be paid to fish."

"Another employee left for a different job and collected unemployment benefits from me. I fought it and lost!"

"Lex appealed the decision and lost again," says current SBH Executive Director Sam Slom. "He appealed and eventually won a decision in state court. Lex instantly became the hero of thousands of small employers who had been victimized by the same unfair law."

"Later, there was a strike at Hawaiian Telephone (now Verizon), and the workers applied for unemployment benefits," Brodie recalls. "Unemployment insurance is a tax employers pay, and workers can collect benefits if, through no fault of their own, they lose their job. It's for people who are laid off or fired, but not for workers who quit or strike," Brodie continued. "But the telephone company workers applied for benefits and the Department of Labor approved it."

Brodie thought it was wrong for the government to subsidize strikers. "I went before a judge, and he issued a stay. This is a legal prohibition, but the Department of Labor ignored it." Brodie went back to court and the Department of Labor was found in contempt.

The then head of the Department of Labor, Mario Ramil, was later appointed to the State Supreme Court by Governor Benjamin Cayetano.

"We got a lot of publicity for these efforts," says Brodie, "and the Small Business Association of Hawaii (SBAH) was the result. Over 3,000 people joined." It was incorporated as a 501 (c) (6) tax exempt organization in 1976.

SBH Exec. Director Sam Slom, center, presents the Small Business Person of the Year Award to Bill and Joyce Edwards of the SystemCenter.

Lex Brodie's Small Business Association of Hawaii began in his Kakaako tire shop. Former Bank of Hawaii economist and small business owner, Sam Slom was hired in 1983 to help

Brodie organize and expand the association statewide.

Slom renamed the organization Small Business Hawaii (SBH), and has remained its executive director ever since. He moved the organization to its first office (the former Cooke Street Building in Kakaako, now the Imperial Plaza condominium) and added member benefits, action programs, the state's first business website, legislative action and a professional staff, pioneering health, and wellness coverage for very small businesses along the way.

Small Business Hawaii exists today to provide effective advocacy for the growing numbers of small businesses in the state. It is the only completely private, independent, statewide small business association operated entirely by business owners for business owners. Its influence in business issues such as taxation, mandated benefits, health care, privatization, and educational partnerships, has crossed America and gone international.

In 1993, SBH moved its corporate offices to Hawaii Kai in East Honolulu but still maintains close contact with the downtown business district and State Capitol. SBH operates as any small business, and its business-owner-members take an active leadership role in the community, working to make positive economic changes.

SBH members, through its independent, non-partisan political action affiliate PAYCHECKS HAWAII (founded in 1984 by Brodie and Slom), were directly involved in recent election campaigns. Their activism culminated in 2002 in the historic election of Linda Lingle as Hawaii's first woman and the first Republican Governor in 40 years.

SBH pioneered many group benefits, has been an active and effective small business advocate at the State Capitol and City Hall, and assisted in passage of positive business climate reform legislation. SBH has a strong member referral directory, monthly newsletter, monthly networking meetings, annual conferences, business trade shows and expos. SBH also publishes award-winning books and provides advisory and consulting services to businesses.

Spencecliff

The most popular and successful restaurant chain in the islands from 1939 through the 1970s was Spencecliff, which owned over 50 family places.

Spencer and Clifton Weaver were the sons of one of the nation's leading architects. Fullerton Weaver designed the Waldorf-Astoria, the Hotel Pierre in New York City, and the Breakers in Palm Beach. The boys' mother was Emily Stokes, a great beauty who won the U.S. Open in mixed doubles tennis one year.

The boys fell in love with Hawaii on a trip with their father around the world. They moved here and found jobs as cafeteria workers at Pearl Harbor in the late 1930s.

In 1939, they opened Swanky Franky's Hot Dog Stand on Ena Road. Swanky Franky's Drive-inn opened a few months later where Singha Thai Cuisine is now. After service in World War II, they formed the Spencecliff Corporation. "Spencecliff" is a composite of Spencer and Clifton's names, but most do not know it was also the name of their family's summer home in East Hampton, Long Island, New York.

The "Hula Cop," Sterling Mossman, packed Queen's Surf six nights a week.

The Sky Room, which opened in 1948, was atop the airport terminal at John Rogers Field, a great location with constant traffic. "It was a fancy place with great steaks," recalls Miyuki Hruby, who started with Spencecliff in 1944.

Next, they purchased M's Ranch House (and dropped M's) and then Fisherman's Wharf in Kewalo Basin. One of their most famous acquisitions, in 1949, was the Waikiki beach home of millionaire Christian Holmes, heir to the Fleischmann's Yeast fortune. They turned it into Queen's Surf. Such luminaries as President Roosevelt, General Douglas MacArthur, Admiral Nimitz, and Amelia Earhart had been houseguests at the estate.

The Barefoot Bar, upstairs at the Queen's Surf, was one of the most popular places in town. "You couldn't get in unless you knew someone," Hruby recalls. "There was always a big line."

Kula Mossman remembers being in the backup band for his late father, Sterling Mossman, the Hula Cop. "Dad loved entertaining," Mossman recalls. "But being a cop paid the bills. Few remember that he was president of the HGEA. He was also a very generous man. He helped many get their careers going, including Don Ho, Danny Kaleikini, and this big guy who parked cars at Queen's Surf named Zulu."

Don Ho, who started his career at his mother's bar, Honey's in Kaneohe, began to sit in at the Barefoot Bar when Sterling Mossman took breaks. Local audiences followed Ho, and tourists began to take notice, too.

Sterling Mossman played at the Barefoot Bar from 1952 until 1969 when the city closed it so the beach could be expanded. "The last show, in December 1969 was huge," Kula recalls. "The place was packed with local and Hollywood celebrities. Dad was a very funny guy. I laughed at the same jokes every night, even though I knew the punch line. It was the *way* he told it."

"Sterling Mossman *was* the Barefoot Bar," Hruby says. "Mossman was a cop by day and an entertainer at night. He sang, danced the hula, and was a comedian. He was a very versatile man."

Spencecliff also owned the Hob Nob in the old Alexander Young Hotel. "It was famous for its Lemon Crunch and Dream Cakes, but we never made any money there," Hruby recalls.

They also purchased the lease on the site of the Kau Kau Korner in 1960, much to the dismay of owner Sunny Sundstrom, who had run the place since 1935. They turned it into Coco's. "Spence liked short, catchy names. I don't think there was a Coco," Hruby maintains. "It was probably short for coconut."

Bill Kelly lent his name to Kelly's Coffee Shop on Nimitz Highway. "He was the manager and Spence liked him. Spence thought it was a good-luck kind of a name," Hruby says. It took Spencecliff five years to negotiate the lease with the Damon Estate. Originally called Kelly's Drive-in Diner when it opened in 1951, it was the eighth restaurant Spencecliff opened. A few years later, they opened a bowling alley on the site. Kelly's served 125 bowls of saimin a day, and Spencecliff served a total of 3 million meals that year.

"Spence was a Yale grad and the brains of the operation." Hruby says. "He was fiery and flamboyant. Cliff was the younger brother by six years. Everybody loved him. He was a kind man, but Spence was 99% of the business. We were the most popular chain in town because Spence knew what the public wanted and could change at any time to meet their needs."

While on a trip to Tahiti, Spence met his future wife Turere, a native dancer at the hotel where he stayed. To show his love for her, he opened a Tahitian themed restaurant, the Tahitian Lanai in 1956 with outdoor tables and grass huts for private parties. They were famous for their Eggs Benedict and banana muffins. The waitresses wore *pareos* and bathing suits. Many drinks were served in a coconut.

Spencecliff owned over 50 restaurants, including such landmarks as Coco's, Kelly's, Tahitian Lanai, Ranch House, Trader Vic's, Popo's, Fisherman's Wharf, Yacht Harbor Towers, Queen's Surf, and the South Seas.

They owned the Hotel Tahiti and Tahiti Village, the Pioneer Inn and Lahaina Broiler on Maui and also had the Snowflake Bakery on Kapahulu, which became Holsum Bakery. They ran cafeterias for the military and Airline Catering, which served 190,000 in-flight meals in 1959. Total meals served that year topped 5 million, and revenues topped $20,000,000.

Coco's, on the corner of Kalakaua and Kapiolani.

Spencecliff was renowned for taking care of its employees, many of whom served over 20 years. For instance, each employee received a birthday cake on the day *before* his or her birthday. Then they got their birthday off with pay. This was no small feat, given that they had 1,400 employees!

In 1986, Nittaku Corporation bought Spencecliff for $6 million, but losses forced them to close restaurants until only Fisherman's Wharf remains today.

—*Researched by Ilima Guerrero*

Star Markets

Star Markets had its humble beginnings in 1927 as the Kakaako Meat Market, founded by Tsunejiro and Mika Fujieki. Sons John, Richard, and George expanded it into a general grocery store. By the time World War II was over, the business had grown to four stores.

In 1954, John Fujieki Sr. came up with a new concept, Star Markets, which he opened in Moiliili. Star bought out the last Piggly Wiggly stores in Hawaii to add to their chain.

Fujieki named it Star Markets because he thought it was an easy name to remember. Stars shine bright, and everyone sees them each night. They figured a star would help bring the best to what they were doing.

Fujieki was a friend of Kenny Kaneshiro, and in the 1950s decided to purchase Kenny's Restaurant, located in the Kamehameha Shopping Center. Kenny went on to manage some of the Jolly Roger restaurants. Star Markets now has six stores on Oahu, three on Maui, and one on Kauai.

Starbucks

Coffee houses go back 450 years to Constantinople, where the first on record opened in what was then the Ottoman Empire in 1554. The first Starbucks Coffee shop opened in Seattle's Pike Place Market in 1971. The original store was a modest place, a narrow storefront with a solo violinist at the entrance.

Partner Gordon Bowker wanted to call the shop *Pequod*, the name of the ship in *Moby Dick*. Artist Terry Heckler wanted something distinctive and tied to the Pacific Northwest. A search of turn-of-the-century mining camps uncovered the name *Starbo*. In a brainstorming session, it evolved into *Starbucks*, who was the first mate on the *Pequod* in *Moby Dick*. The name evoked the romance of the high seas and the seafaring tradition of the early coffee traders.

Starbucks has an interesting logo of a longhaired woman wearing a crown. The inspiration was a fifteenth century woodcut depicting a siren, a mythical creature with two tails that sat high on a cliff near the water and sang to passing ships.

In 1983, Director of Retail Operations Howard Schulz traveled to Italy and saw how popular coffee bars were. He left Starbucks and founded his own place, *Il Giornale*, offering brewed coffee and espresso beverages made from Starbucks coffee beans.

Schulz then bought out the original Starbucks owners for $3.8 million and in two years had seventeen stores in Seattle, Vancouver, and Chicago. By 1992, Starbucks had 165 stores and expanded to Oregon, California, and Colorado.

In 1996, Starbucks International opened stores in Hawaii, Japan, and Singapore. The local owners are Coffee Partners Hawaii, who manage 33 Starbucks in Hawaii as well as Jamba Juice. There are over 6,000 Starbucks across the globe today.

—*Researched by Susan Goh*

Straub Clinic and Hospital

Dr. George F. Straub formed The Clinic in 1921 with four other prominent physicians: Guy Milnor (OB/GYN), Arthur Jackson (internist), Howard Clarke (eye, ear, nose and throat), and Eric Fennel (pathologist).

The Clinic started off at 401 S. Beretania Street (one block from Iolani Palace). It grew steadily and became one of Honolulu's largest group practices. It needed new facilities in the 1930s and moved to its current site on King Street and Ward Avenue in 1933.

Dr. George Straub, co-founder of "The Clinic" in 1921.

Dr. George Straub retired in 1933 and pursued hobbies such as making violins and other stringed instruments. In 1952, The Clinic was renamed Straub Clinic, and in 1973, it was changed to Straub Clinic and Hospital.

Since the 1980s, Straub has expanded to satellite health care centers (Hawaii Kai, Kapahulu, Kaneohe, Kapolei, Mililani, Pali Momi, downtown, Lanai, and Kailua-Kona). They also operate Doctors on Call at several hotels on Oahu.

They have 200 doctors, over 600 medical staff, and 1,200 other staff. Straub is considered by many to be the best in Hawaii in the treatment of heart attacks, angioplasty, by-pass surgery, stroke, respiratory treatment, orthopedics, and sports medicine.

Many Hawaii medical firsts occurred at Straub: The first arthoscopic knee surgery, the first minimally invasive heart surgery, and deep brain stimulation. They even invented a new procedure for vascular surgery that is now used worldwide. Straub, Wilcox, and Kapiolani Health merged in 2001 to form Hawaii Pacific Health.

—*Researched by Tina Chen*

"The Clinic" was on Beretania Street one block from Iolani Palace.

Strawberry Connection

"Executive chefs in Hawaii couldn't get decent strawberries back in 1984," says Becky Choy, "and John Stoudt and I were cocky and young and thought we could find sources for them. But we kept our main jobs."

Starting as local chefs' connection for strawberries, they soon expanded to asparagus and other hard to find gourmet items. Soon own-

Becky Choy and John Stoudt founded the Strawberry Connection in 1984.

ers Stoudt and Choy were opening a store in lower Kalihi with three huge, walk-in refrigerators. Heavy coats were provided for patrons.

Tiki's Executive Chef Fred DeAngelo called Strawberry Connection first when he was looking for unusual ingredients. "If they didn't have it, they could get it. They were resourceful and honest, which is very important to me. They were not just a great store. They are great people."

"Food TV has demystified cooking for many people," says Choy. "They see things being prepared on TV and realize they could do it too. And we are their resource for hard to find, high-quality items."

In 2001, Strawberry Connection moved to Dole Cannery next to Signature Theatres. However, a poor economy forced them to close in the Spring of 2003.

Suisan Company, Ltd.

One of the largest businesses on the Big Island, Suisan began over 95 years ago in 1907 as a hui of Japanese fishermen in Waiakea. Originally it was named Suisan Kabushiki Kaisha ("Sui" means "water" and "san" means "products." "Kabushiki" refers to a publicly traded corporation and "kaisha" means "a business entity.")

Suisan went from fresh fish to become the largest distributor of frozen foods on the Big Island. They also expanded into produce and real estate.

Suisan currently has over 1 million cubic feet of freezers and cold storage rooms. Their revenues are in excess of $40 million, and they have 140 employees.

Like most of the businesses in the Waiakea section of Hilo, Suisan was hard hit by the tsunamis of 1946 and 1960. After the 1960 tsunami, they moved to a location behind the airport.

Liliuokalani Park stands now where so many of the Waiakea businesses once were.

The president of Suisan is Rex Matsuno, the son of one of the company's founders, Kamizo Matsuno. In the last 10 years, Suisan has expanded to become a worldwide food distributor.

Swiss Inn

Martin Wyss left the Kahala Hilton, where he had been executive chef for 18 years, to start the Swiss Inn in 1982. Martin ran the kitchen while his wife Jeanne and her sister Sharon ran the dining room.

The Niu Valley restaurant won national awards and a loyal local following for its delicious Swiss food. In 2001, the Wyss's sold the restaurant and the name was changed to Swiss Haus. Martin now sells 600 bottles a month of his famous salad dressing at R. Field Food and Wine Co., Fujioka Wine Merchants, and a few Longs Drug Stores.

In 2001, Wyss was presented with a Lifetime Achievement Award at the Hawaii Chef de Cuisine chapter and the National Association of Catering Executives. Wyss was honored for his 18 years at Swiss Inn, and almost as many at the Kahala Hilton, and for mentoring many local chefs over the years.

Tamashiro Market

If you are driving Ewa on North King Street, you are sure to pass one of Kalihi's most recognizable landmarks - Tamashiro Market. With a giant red crab hanging from the roof, the store is hard to miss. If you love seafood, hey, you already know about this place! It is a favorite of locals and visitors alike.

What you may not know is that Chogen Tamashiro founded his

Tamashiro Market was wiped out by the 1946 Hilo tsunami and moved to Honolulu.

store on the Big Island, but the 1946 Hilo tsunami wiped out the family business. Seafood was not the original focus of the business, which provided pork, and feed to serve the agricultural community.

Undeterred by the natural disaster, Tamashiro moved his business to Oahu. In 1954, Chogen's son Walter took over the business and shifted the focus to seafood. Walter passed away in 2002, and his son Cyrus runs the business with other family members. Chogen's wife, Iris Yoshiko, passed away at age 99 in 2004. Many old-timers fondly remember Iris for her friendliness.

Larry Ng grew up in Palama and shopped at Tamashiro when it first opened up in 1947. "It was a grocery store then," recalls Ng, who was in the 5th grade at the time. "It had meat, fish, and canned goods, but what interested me was the comic books and ice cream. It was two scoops for a nickel. Iris was a nice, beautiful lady."

Tamashiro market was one of the earliest importers of live crab and lobster and one of the first commercial preparers of poke in the islands.

Telecheck

Few know that the idea for the service that guaranteed checks started in Hawaii at a Boy Scout leaders' meeting. "Several of the leaders were businessmen," said business man Bob Baer. "One day they had a conversation about bounced checks, and they found out that some had come from the same customers.

One volunteered to keep a file in his office for the others to check. "They would call on the telephone to verify a check," Baer continued. "It grew into a local business. They called me in Milwaukee and asked me to come help the business grow."

"The idea was ahead of its time. Remember, before credit cards, checks were more commonly used, and a risk for businesses to accept. Telecheck, for a small fee, would guarantee the check if the writer had a clean record with them. If not, the customer would have to settle it before another check was approved."

"In 1963, I expanded the company nationally. In ten years, we had 85 franchises and had expanded to Australia, New Zealand, Hong Kong, and South America."

Today, Telecheck is headquartered in Houston, Texas, and Bob's son Jeff Baer is Chairman of the Board. Telecheck is the world's leading provider of paper and electronic check services helping more than 270,000 retail, financial institution, grocery, and other industry clients. In 2002, Telecheck authorized over 3.2 billion transactions worth more than $160 billion dollars.

Teshima's Restaurant

At 100 years of age, Mary Teshima can still be found serving customers at her restaurant almost every day. Four of her five children, five of her 12 grandchildren, and five of her 24 great-grand-children work in the restaurant (during school breaks).

Mary's story starts with her father, Goichi Hanato, leaving Japan in the 1890s for Hawaii to search for work. He arrived in Kona and worked at a dairy and a hotel. He started a farm and a tofu manufacturing plant. In 1915, he opened T. Hanato Store. Shizuko "Mary" Hanato was born in 1907 and grew up in the store.

In 1927, Shizuko married Harry Teshima. Shizuko's father did not want his daughter to work on the farm because she was small. He decided, instead, to build a small store for her, and Teshima's General Merchandise store opened in 1929.

In 1940, Shizuko opened Teshima's restaurant and in 1941 opened Elsie's Bar. The bar was named for her sister-in-law, whom Shizuko raised as her own child. All three businesses were in the same building. Shizuko did alterations (sewing shirts for 75 cents), dry cleaning, flower arrangements, tea ceremonies, homemade ice cream and saimin.

During World War II, soldiers had trouble pronouncing her name, and called her Mary. Mary became a mother to many of them. She would put them up and write to their mothers because letters were being censored by the military.

In 1953, Mary opened the first night club in Kona called Kalakikai, which means "heavenly ocean" in Hawaiian. When the nightclub would close at 2 AM, patrons would head over to Teshima's Restaurant for an early breakfast. Mary kept the nightclub for two years before selling it.

Mary moved her restaurant and bar into a new building in 1957 and closed down her general store. In 1960, a chef from Japan came to work for Mary. He worked at the restaurant for 10 years. Three other chefs have come from Japan since then. From these chefs, Teshima's was able to offer authentic Japanese cooking. Mary's specialty is shrimp tempura.

"Mary is the oldest living restaurant owner in Kona," says Martha Kaneao, who worked at Teshima's when she was a young girl. "She's very friendly. Stop in when you're in Kona and visit her."

—Researched by Stacy Tritt

Theo. H. Davies & Co.

"The story of Hawaii's Theo. H. Davies & Company reads like a good historical novel," says writer Bill Woods in a company brochure. "It's a tale of high adventure set in a momentous period of world history. It's the story of three generations of descendants who, for more than a century, guided the business through storms of international intrigue, revolution, world wars, changing economies, personal triumphs and tragedies, and the rush of history that transformed a remote island kingdom into an important player in the coming Pacific Century."

Theophilus Harris Davies was born to the son of a poor clergyman in England in 1824. At age 23, he sailed to the remote Sandwich Islands, as they were then called. He had a five-year contract to work for Janion, Green & Company, a Liverpool trading company that had a small presence in Hawaii beginning in 1845.

It took Davies six months to reach our shores. At the time, Honolulu was a bustling port serving the whaling industry. It was a time of rapid change in Honolulu. Whaling was coming to an end, and sugar was beginning to take hold.

Sugar was well suited to Hawaii's tropical climate, and the industry got a boost when King Kamehameha III overturned centuries of native tradition and allowed private ownership of land. By 1860, there were 32 sugar plantations in Hawaii with about 500 tons harvested a year. Davies pushed his employer into the sugar business.

When the U.S. Civil War broke out, the north was cut off from southern plantations, and sugar prices soared. Hawaii growers raced to meet that demand, and there were soon 50 plantations producing 9,000 tons a year. However, Davies' contract was up, and he returned to Liverpool.

Within a few years, however, he was made a partner and was sent back to head the Honolulu office just as the Civil War was ending and sugar prices were plunging. Many growers went out of business. Davies saw it as an opportunity to expand. He bought out distressed plantations, particularly on the Hamakua coast of Hawaii, and related businesses. He bought a major interest in Honolulu Iron Works, which made field equipment for the sugar plantations.

He traveled back to England and returned in 1870 with a bride. He left his original partners behind and became Theo. H. Davies & Company.

The local labor market could not support the need for field workers, so the industry turned to China, Japan, the Azores, Madeira, Korea, and finally the Philippines. Hawaii's modern multicultural society is a direct result of the sugar industry.

Theo and Mary Ellen "Nellie" Davies had a son, Theophilus Clive Davies in 1871. He was the first of seven children and was brought up to take the helm of the company one day. Theo. H. Davies retired to England, in the 1880s, leaving the operation to his son Clive and Francis Swanzy. He passed away in 1888 at age 64.

By 1900, there were 70 plantations in Hawaii producing 100,000 tons a year. Theo. H. Davies & Co. held interests in at least a dozen of those plantations.

When Swanzy died of a heart attack during World War I, Clive returned from England to take the operational reins of the company. He moved on Swanzy's plans to open an operation in the Philippines and to build an office downtown. The four story building on Bishop, Merchant, and Queen was the largest in Hawaii at the time and the most expensive. It stood for 50 years before being replaced by the current Davies Pacific Center.

The time from the great depression through World War II and into the 1970s were difficult for Theo. H. Davies & Company as they struggled to deal with the decline in sugar and other economic issues.

In 1973, Hong Kong-based Jardine Matheson bought Theo. H. Davies in a stock swap. Jardine Matheson was and remains one of Hong Kong's famous trading houses or "Hongs," and was founded in 1832 by Scots William Jardine and James Matheson. They were the first to challenge the East India Company's tea monopoly, but opium trade was a large component in their fortune. They later moved into banking, insurance, textiles, sugar, brewing, silk trading, and real estate. Jardine Matheson introduced steamships to China and built the country's first railway.

David Heenan, representing the new owner took over as CEO and moved the company out of the sugar business. The company added Jaguar, Landrover, and Porsche to its existing Hawaii Mercedes-Benz franchise, naming it TheoDavies Euromotors.

Heavy equipment sales were consolidated into Pacific Machinery and maritime services into TheoDavies Marine. The company acquired the Hawaii, Guam, and Saipan franchises for Pizza Hut and the Hawaii franchise for Taco Bell. In 2004, Jardine Matheson sold much of their Hawaii assets. After 158 years and many changes, it remains to be seen what lies ahead for the famous name of Theo H. Davies & Co.

—Researched by Gloria Liu and Grace Nguchu

Tiffany & Company

The world's premier jeweler, Tiffany & Company has four stores in the islands – Ala Moana, Waikiki, Wailea Shops, and Whaler's Village on Maui.

Charles Lewis Tiffany and his schoolmate John Young opened their New York store in 1837. Tiffany became well known for carrying one-of-a-kind objects that charmed and fascinated the wealthy of New York. However, when the store obtained some of the French crown jewels in 1887, Tiffany's fame spread far and wide.

Charles' son Louis Comfort Tiffany was born in 1848, and his work as a jewelry and glass designer took Tiffany and Co. to new heights. He was the first American artist to achieve international stature. His work has been honored by museums and treasured by collectors around the world. How expensive are Tiffany lamps today? A Pink Lotus lamp sold for a record $2.8 million at a Christie's auction in 1997.

Times Supermarket

In April 29, 1949, brothers Wallace Takeshi Teruya and Albert Takeo Teruya opened their first Times Supermarket store in McCully. However, the story starts long before that.

Wallace and Albert left a Big Island sugar plantation in 1929 and came to Honolulu to work in a restaurant. They worked 14-hour days washing dishes and waiting on tables. Albert learned to cook while working with the chefs.

Hard work is very essential for success, they discovered. Five years later, they bought a small drugstore's lunchroom for $600. They named it T & W lunchroom. "T" stood for Takeo and "W" for Wallace. On June 14, 1939 Wallace and Takeo along with Kame Uyehera opened the 24-hour Times Grill. The restaurant occupied the site that Columbia Inn later took over on Kapiolani Boulevard.

In 1947, they sold The Times Grill and opened Times Supermarket. The McCully store was a small neighborhood store catering to the local population living in the vicinity. Three basic ingredients that contributed to the success of Times Supermarket were high quality merchandise, competitive prices, and excellent customer service. Their customer service included the then-innovative concept of air-conditioned stores.

Albert and Wallace believed that "each customer is an individual and deserves individual attention to his or her needs and wants."

The personal welfare of their employees have also been a leading concern. Albert has often said, "We owe our success in business to the excellent and loyal co-operation of all our employees."

In 1956, a store dedicated to the memory of Herman Takeyoshi Teruya, the younger brother of Albert and Wallace who lost his life while serving with the 100th Battalion during World War II, opened on Waialae. The Kailua and Kaneohe stores were opened in 1958 while the Waipahu branch and Niu Valley opened in 1964.

In the 1970s, Times opened stores in Aiea, Temple Valley, Liliha, Waimalu, and in Honolulu on Beretania. They now have 12 supermarkets.

Times Supermarket has constantly worked hard to provide the best possible produce, good quality meat, and groceries at the best possible prices in a clean and friendly environment. The success of Times Supermarket can be attributed to the hard work and persistence of Albert and Wallace and their sprit of growing as a family.

—Researched by Faisal Abdulla

Tori Richard

No, Tori Richard is not a person. It is two people, two of Mortimer Feldman's children, Victoria and Richard Feldman. Feldman was a clothing manufacturer in Chicago after World War II. He came to visit an old war buddy in Hawaii in 1955 and decided to "retire" here, says son Josh Feldman, of his then-35 year old father. A year later, in 1956, he founded Tori Richard.

"Most people assume we're an aloha shirt company," Josh says. "However, most of our business is printed sportswear. Only 20% of our business is in Hawaii. Seventy percent is on the mainland, and 10% is Asian."

When they began, Tori Richard created women's wear. In the late 1960s, they started designing men's wear as well. "Today, we also make uniforms and have licenses to make goods for Harley Davidson and several others," Josh says.

At one time, Tori Richard operated 15 Holiday Shops in Waikiki. Today, their sportswear is carried in 3,500 stores in Hawaii and around the world. Such luminaries as Steve Case, Kevin Costner, Tim Allen, Jay Leno, and Sammy Hagar wear their shirts. Mortimer Feldman, who turned 82 in 2003, still comes in to work every day.

Trader Vic's

Victor J. Bergeron opened Hinky Dink's pub, a small bar and restaurant in Oakland, California in 1932. He renamed it Trader Vic's in 1934. Bergeron was a world traveler and thought that South Pacific-style bars, tropical cocktails, and exotic foods would be a big hit, and he was right.

His Hawaii branch opened in December 1940. Four months later, he sold his interest in it to co-owner Granville Abbott. Trader Vic's had a Polynesian, thatched hut building on the corner of Ward and King Street, where TGIF and the Honolulu Club are today.

Trader Vics occupied the corner of Ward and King Streets where TGIF is today.

In 1967, Spencecliff bought the local franchise. Bergeron's grandchildren run the international company today and have branches in Atlanta, Beverly Hills, Chicago, Bahrain, Egypt, England, Germany, Japan, Lebanon, Oman, Spain, Singapore, Taiwan, Thailand, and the United Arab Emerites.

Tripler Army Medical Center

Tripler came into being in 1907 on North King Street in Kalihi as the Fort Shafter Hospital. It replaced an earlier Army facility at King and Sheridan Streets that had been built to handle casualties from the Spanish–American War in the Philippines.

In 1920, the Fort Shafter Hospital was renamed in honor of Brigadier General Charles Stuart Tripler, who had been Medical Director of the Army of the Potomac during the Civil War.

Doctors and nurses rushed to Tripler General Hospital on Dec. 7, 1941, with many working for 72 hours straight to treat the wounded from Pearl Harbor. Their hard work saved all but 13 of the 344 battle casualties they treated.

World War II casualties overwhelmed the 450-bed hospital at Fort Shafter and facilities were leased at Farrington High School, Kamehameha School for Girls, Kuakini Hospital, and the Kaneohe Territorial Hospital, increasing their beds to almost 2,000.

During World War II, 1,800 patients from all branches of the armed forces were cared for daily. The first casualties were victims of the attack on Pearl Harbor and other Oahu installations. Later patients came by hospital ship and airplane from fighting in the battlegrounds of the Pacific.

Tripler credits Kamehameha Schools as the "first of provisional hospitals started by the U.S. Army anywhere in the world after the onset of hostilities. Kamehameha provided sorely needed beds immediately after Pearl Harbor. Students, faculty and school authorities cooperated in giving up the beautiful buildings located on Kapalama Heights, and which commanded a magnificent view of Honolulu that few will be able to forget. Not just the view, but the cool mountain air will be missed by many."

The Fort Shafter Hospital in 1913 on No. King St. In 1920, it was renamed Tripler General Hospital.

Despite the increased capacity, a new facility was needed and ground was broken in 1944 on Moanalua Ridge. In 1948, it was complete and ready to be occupied. At 7:50 AM on August 9, "a large convoy of ambulances, their lights ablaze, roared from the motor pool of new Tripler General Hospital down the winding road to old Tripler to begin the evacuation of medical patients," states their web site.

"Operating with clock-like precision, the patients were loaded and by 8:30 AM they are streaming into the Receiving Office at the new Tripler. At 9:30 AM, the last patient from old Tripler arrived and was carried to his bed, completing the move of 102 patients in less than 90 minutes."

One of the unique features found in the new Tripler General Hospital was the hospital's own radio station, KTGH. KTGH was part of the famed *Bedside Network* of the Armed Forces Radio Service that provided programs for military and naval personnel in hospitals throughout the mainland United States and Hawaii.

A pool and theatre were added in 1950, and 80 monkey pod trees were planted on the grounds in 1961 for shade and landscaping.

Over the years, Tripler Army Medical Center has treated soldiers from World War I, World War II, Korea, Vietnam, and Desert Storm. Returning POWs from Vietnam and Korea were examined at Tripler.

Gemini 8 astronauts Neil Armstrong and David Scott stopped at Tripler. Seventeen Vietnamese orphans of Operation Baby Lift were hospitalized at Tripler on their way to the mainland and new homes.

Five Costa Rican fishermen who had been adrift in the Pacific for five months in a 30 foot boat before being rescued were examined at Tripler – all, surprisingly in good health. Of course, thousands of babies a year have made their first appearance at Tripler maternity wards.

Charles Stuart Tripler was the medical director of the Union Army in the Civil War.

Tripler has even treated animals needing medical care including Papale, a Pacific bottle nose porpoise; Empress, the Honolulu Zoo's 9,000 pound elephant; and Goliath, the ailing 45 year-old, 500 pound Zoo alligator who had gotten into a fight with another alligator.

Tripler has also had its share of the unusual and bizarre. It kept the body of a retired Army major who died in 1978 for more than a year until a dispute was settled between the two women who claimed to be his wife. Tripler had a three-week-long robbery spree in 1983 with 15 thefts. Quick-acting security personnel apprehended the purse-snatcher who was finally caught in the act.

Rumors abound about Tripler. One is that it was built backwards. "The rumor," says Michelle Rowan of Tripler's Public Affairs Office, "is that while Tripler was being built, the main archi-

Tripler was painted "rose coral" to mask Hawaii's red dirt, which was expected to be blown on it by tradewinds.

tect was called back to the Mainland because of an ill relative. When he returned, he saw that they had reversed the plans and it was too late to fix it."

"This is not true," Rowan says. "Tripler was built the way it was planned. If you look at it from above, you can see that the outer wings kind of resemble airplane wings. Since there wasn't air conditioning back then, it was built this way to take advantage of the winds that sweep down from the mountains behind it to help keep the hospital cool."

The other persistent rumor is that the pink color was a mistake; the wrong paint was ordered or delivered. But in a 1995 interview with the Channel 2 News, retired Colonel Robert B. Wood, who was with the Army Corps of Engineers when Tripler was built, set the record straight.

"The architect came into my office one day and said 'it's time we selected the color for the hospital.' I looked out the window of my office at the red dirt on Moanalua Ridge and said 'You've got to get it as close to that color as you can because that's the color it will be when you're through.'"

"At that time, there wasn't any landscaping on the entire ridge, and the winds would blow the red dirt of Moanalua on the hospital, making it pinkish or a terra-cotta color." Actually, Tripler is not pink. Its color is officially called rose coral.

During a typical day at Tripler, 157 hospital beds are occupied; 2,188 people visit clinics; 115 come for treatment in the emergency room; 30 surgeries are performed; and 8 babies are born.

Verizon - now Hawaiian Telcom

The first telephones in Hawaii connected Maui shopkeeper C. H. Dickey's home and business. They were installed in 1878, just two years after Alexander Graham Bell invented them.

Two years later, in 1880, Hawaiian Bell Telephone went into service in Honolulu. In 1883, a competing service, Mutual Telephone Company opened shop on Oahu making it necessary for some to have phones with both services.

By 1894, Mutual bought out Hawaiian Bell. Back in those days, an operator would answer your call and connect you to your party. A year later, the first phone book came out with 1,400 subscribers listed. Oahu's first phone numbers contained only three digits.

An undersea telegraph cable was laid in 1902 landing near the present site of the War Memorial Natatorium. Automatic switching and dial telephones came to Honolulu in 1910, but many mourned the passing of "Central," as the operators would answer. "The telephone has lost its soul!" the Honolulu Advertiser cried. "The girls are gone!"

Calling around the island was not toll free back then. Tolls were charged between Honolulu and "country" areas such as Waipahu and Kaneohe. It was not until 1960 that tolls were dropped on each island. The Big Island became the largest toll-free calling area in the United States.

Smaller telephone companies existed on neighboring islands, but Mutual began acquiring them in 1913. In 1935, the islands were connected by ultra-high frequency radio, and it was possible to call any other phone in the islands.

World War II brought rationing of phone service with subscribers encouraged to share four-party lines. Calls were censored, and sand bags and armed guards were posted at company buildings. Operators were issued gas masks in case of attack.

In 1954, Mutual changed its name to the Hawaiian Telephone Company to better reflect its image. Over 100,000 telephones made up its network.

An undersea cable, costing $42 million from the mainland to Hawaii was laid in 1954. It came ashore at Hanauma Bay, where a channel for the cable was blasted out of the coral in the right side of the Bay. President Ballard Atherton placed the first call at a special ceremony in the Throne Room at Iolani Palace.

More cable connecting Hawaii, Japan, Canada, Australia, and New Zealand was laid in the 1960s, and in 1966, the first "Lani Bird" Satellite was launched. The satellite brought Hawaii's first live television broadcast from the mainland: Michigan State versus Notre Dame football.

In 1967, Hawaiian Telephone merged with General Telephone and Electronics (GTE). Push button phones connected the 350,000 phones in the state by 1968.

The company built a new 17 story headquarters on Bishop Street in 1971, a site it has occupied since 1919 with smaller buildings, fronting Alakea Street.

Direct Distance Dialing, meaning that anyone in Hawaii could be called directly by anyone outside of the state and vice versa, was inaugurated in 1973. All numbers had to be converted to seven digits for that to happen.

The Verizon name comes from the Latin "veritas," which means truth and also connotes certainty and reliability, and "horizon," which signifies the endless possibilities ahead, says Data Technician Brandon Onishi.

Verizon Hawaii was bought by the Carlyle Group in May, 2005 and renamed Hawaiian Telcom. It employs 2,600 in Hawaii and generates $680 million in revenues. It serves 660,000 customers on all islands, and its statewide infrastructure is worth $2 billion.

—Researched by Sisi Maw and Hung-Ming Tseng

Victoria Ward

Victoria Ward and her husband, Curtis Perry Ward, once owned an estate comprising over 100 acres in central Honolulu. At its greatest extent, these lands stretched all the way from Thomas Square to the shore.

Victoria was born in Nuuanu in 1846, the daughter of English shipbuilder James Robinson and his wife, Rebecca Previer, a woman

of Hawaiian ancestry whose chief lineage had roots from the Big Island and Maui.

C.P. Ward, Victoria's future husband, was born and reared in Kentucky, and arrived in Honolulu in 1853. A vocal defender of his southern homeland during the Civil War, C.P. Ward is remembered for his business acumen and staunch family loyalty. In the years before his marriage to Victoria in 1865, Ward established a thriving delivery (using horses) business that serviced bustling Honolulu Harbor.

Victoria Ward lived on 100 acres where the Blaisdell Center is today with her husband, Curtis, and seven daughters.

For many years, Curtis and Victoria made their home near Honolulu Harbor on property presently occupied by the Davies Pacific Center. Seven daughters were born during these years.

The Wards built their final home, "Old Plantation," on property now occupied by the Neil Blaisdell Center. Completed in 1882, this stately, southern-

"Old Plantation" was built in 1882.

style home featured an artesian well, vegetable and flower gardens, a large pond stocked with fish, and an extensive pasturage for horses and cattle. When it was built, it was considered to be on the outskirts of Honolulu. Curtis died later that year, and Victoria carried on with the help of her daughters.

Once considered the outskirts of town, the Ward Estate, "Old Plantation" was filled with trees and streams.

Self-sufficient as a working farm, Old Plantation was surrounded by a vast coconut grove. A few of these palms, all well over one hundred years old, remain on the Concert Hall property. Old Plantation became one of the showplaces of Honolulu and remained substantially unchanged for nearly 80 years.

The City bought and tore down the estate in 1958. They built the Honolulu International Center, now called the Neal Blaisdell Center, named for the well-loved former mayor (1955-1968) of Honolulu.

Victoria Ward Ltd. was left with 65 acres of land along Ala Moana Blvd. Ward Warehouse was built in 1975 and Ward Center in 1982. Victoria Ward Centers today has 140 shops and restaurants. Ala Moana Center owner, General Growth Properties of Chicago, bought Victoria Ward Center in 2002 for $250 million.

Volcano House

The oldest hotel still in operation in Hawaii, Volcano House, opened for business as the Crater Hotel in 1866. The first tourists to the islands were visiting a wonder of the world - an active volcano. They sailed to Hilo and then walked, rode horses, or took a stage coach 29 miles to Kilauea.

The hotel grew out of a series of grass huts and shacks that travelers built to pass the night. *Kahunas* and others came to make offerings to Pele for hundreds of years. High Chiefess Kapiolani, a convert to Christianity, journeyed to Kilauea in 1824 and built a grass shack on the crater rim to challenge the superstitious faith in the goddess.

William Ellis and four other missionaries traveled there in 1823 and built a hut. Captain Lord Byron, returning the bodies of King Lunalilo and Queen Kamamalu, who had died while on a trip to

England, went to Hilo. He named the bay Byron's Bay and journeyed to Kilauea with a group of about 40.

A scientific expedition went to Kilauea in 1838 and found 26 volcanic cones, with eight of them active. An 1840 expedition hired 300 young men in Hilo to build a wooden house and observatory.

All this activity encouraged Julius Richardson and George Jones to start the first hotel there in 1866, a year after the U.S. Civil War ended. The *Commercial Advertiser* remarked that 400 had visited the volcano in 1865, and with comfortable lodging at the Crater Hotel, 1,000 could be expected to visit.

Mark Twain was one of those to visit that year, and he commented that he was "surprised to find a good hotel at such an outlandish spot." Twain wrote articles for U.S. newspapers extolling the beauty of the volcano and the comfort of the new hotel.

In 1877, a new building was erected, and the Volcano House name was first applied. Still standing today, it houses the Old Volcano House Museum. A fire was lit in the massive fireplace that year and it burns to this day, uninterrupted. Even when a fire burned down the hotel in 1940, embers were taken from the fireplace and kept burning until the new hotel opened.

Ripley's *Believe it or Not* reported that "the Park Rangers transported several scoops full of the glowing coals to the Volcano House Museum, which, from 1877 to 1891, served as the Volcano House, until the larger building was erected."

Visitors have recorded their thoughts and impressions of Kilauea in books left at the hotel for that purpose. Now extending to over

Hawaii's oldest hotel, then called the Crater Hotel, was built at Kilauea in 1866.

a dozen volumes, the books contain the observations of thousands of visitors, statesmen, and scientists. The tradition, which continues to this day, was begun by Benjamin Pitman Sr. who built the first grass hut for Kilauea visitors in 1846.

Waikiki Lau Yee Chai

"Best Restaurant Any Country in World," P.Y. Chong called his little bit of heaven. Chong emigrated from Canton, China in 1917 and opened Lau Yee Chai in 1929 with 14 tables. Initially in the Ala Moana area then known as Squattersville, Chong soon moved to Kuhio Avenue where the Ambassador Hotel is today.

Patrons found his food to be delicious, and soon he was expanding. The restaurant could seat 1,400 and contained a rock garden with waterfalls and caverns.

Chong was usually at the entrance with one of his young sons, "General" Clyde Hock Hin Chong, bowing in unison as guests arrived. "Me P.Y. Chong," he would say to them. Many have misunderstood, thinking "Me" was his name, but he meant "I am."

Pang Yat Chong was the founder of Lau Yee Chai in 1929.

When Lau Yee Chai closed in 1965 to move to its present location on Kalakaua Avenue, General Manager Patricia Chang threw three nights of farewell banquets. Nine course meals were fed to 3,600 as a way of saying thank you for the previous 36 great years.

The fifth floor ceiling of the Waikiki Shopping Plaza had to be built higher than on other floors to accommodate a beautiful, 17-foot high, 44-foot wide mural brought from the old location.

"Shangri-La" was painted in 1946 by famed artist, Pick Kai Ho. It portrays a fisherman who's lost in the storm and finds himself in Shangri-La, where no one ages or is in poor health.

Waikiki Lau Yee Chai was on Kuhio Avenue until 1965.

"Lau Yee Chai" means "Food so good the Gods will come back to eat again."

—*Researched by David Chang*

Wailana Coffee House

Do you remember when the Wailana Coffee House was the Kapiolani Drive Inn? That would take you back before 1969 when founder Francis Tom tore down his drive-in and built a 24 story condominium in its place.

Tom started the Kapiolani Drive Inn as the food concessionaire at the Zoo in Kapiolani Park in the mid-1940s. In 1948, a fence was put up that effectively cut off the drive-in from its customers. Tom bought an acre of land along the dirt road that was then Ala Moana Boulevard. Before the Hilton Hawaiian Village and the Ilikai, this was considered by many to be "out in the country."

The Kapiolani Drive Inn soon opened there, but Tom's wife, Mary, had her doubts. "I counted cars one evening, and only a few went by! We were scared. But eventually word got around, and people found us."

KDI, as it was popularly called, rode a wave of popularity for "meals on wheels." Fourteen car hops would wait on customers in the 125 cars that could squeeze onto his lot. Some days as many as 3,000 hamburgers were served. KDI was open 24 hours a day and became known for its huge neon animated hula girl sign.

KDI was the "in spot" in the late 1950s, and on some Friday and Saturday nights, particularly after proms and sporting events, cars had to wait for a space to open up. "Dad dragged us kids down to work," says son Kenton Tom, "when he'd run sales and specials - things like 19-cent hamburgers or five burgers for $1. The place was packed then."

"KDI had a huge menu," says Mary. "Our orange freeze was very popular as were floats, malts, banana splits, peach melba, and sundaes.

"Drive-ins declined somewhat in the 1960s," Kenton continued. "Dad decided a classier place might be better. He hooked up with Bruce Stark, and they developed the property with the new restaurant beneath the condominiums. The Wailana name was Stark's idea." Wailana means "floating on water." Their logo is a lily, which floats peacefully in water.

"The area has changed tremendously since we moved here," Mary Tom says. "The road was paved. The Ilikai and Hawaiian Village were built. Waikiki expanded to include us. Now it's a great location. We're busy 24 hours a day."

"Broasted chicken is still a specialty," says Kenton, "as it was in the KDI days. "The meat loaf, French toast with guava jelly, and Eggs Benedict are also big sellers."

For about a year, there were two Kapiolani Drive Inns - the food establishment and Hawaii's first outdoor Drive In theatre less than one mile away. Originally called just the Drive In when it was built in 1949, it was re-named Kapiolani Drive-in when the Kam Drive In was built in 1962. The Kapiolani Drive In closed later that year.

"We'd get calls all the time for the theatre," recalls long-time employee Tony Cabral, who started working there in 1954. "It was confusing. Maybe that's why we came to be known as KDI."

"Mr. Tom was a very good employer to work for," Cabral continues. "He was very understanding, and he loved his business."

Waioli Tea Room

Five acres in Manoa that had once belonged to King Kamehameha III were donated to the Salvation Army in 1905 to be used as a home for orphaned and needy children. George N. Wilcox of Kauai

was the primary benefactor. Waioli, which means "happy" or "singing waters," was the name of the old Wilcox Mission house on the island of Kauai.

In 1922, the Waioli Tea Room was built so that the children could learn "cooking, baking and the arts of gracious living." Since then, society has replaced orphanages with foster homes, and

The Waioli Tea Room was a training center for the Salvation Army orphanage when it opened in 1922.

the Tea Room is now run by a private company.

A grass shack once belonging to Robert Louis Stevenson was moved from Princess Kaiulani's Waikiki home in 1927 to the Tea Room grounds. The shack, now reconstructed with the original materials, was a place where Stevenson, who visited Hawaii between 1889 and 1893, and the teenage Kaiulani spent many hours together.

Waltah Clarke Hawaiian Shops

After attending USC, Walter Clarke came to Hawaii in 1938 and became general manager of Don the Beachcomber restaurant. He wrote a society column from Waikiki for the Los Angeles Times,

Chicago Tribune, San Francisco Chronicle, and Seattle Post Intelligencer.

Walter hung out with the beach boys, who pronounced his name "Waltah." Waltah and Gretchen Clarke started their resortwear chain in 1952 in Palm Springs, California. The enthusiasm for aloha wear spread very quickly as mainlanders flocked to their stores for clothes from the islands. At one time, they had 31 stores in Florida, California, Arizona, Texas, Nevada, and Hawaii.

Clarke produced the 1963 record album *Duke Kahanamoku: A Beachboy Party with Waltah Clarke*. Such beach boys as Fat Boy, Splash Lyons, Chick Daniels, and Squeeze Kalana performed with Clarke as emcee.

The Willows

Known for its fabulous curries and mile-high pies served in a Polynesian thatched roof setting, the Willows occupies the site of the former Kapaakea Springs, once owned by Queen Kamamalu. Hawaiian royalty, including her brothers Kamehameha IV and V picnicked and feasted in the area in the mid-1800s.

Henry and Emma McGuire Hausten built a house on the site in the late 1920s, and the street is named for them. Daughter Kathleen and her husband, musical legend Al Kealoha Perry, converted the family home into a lush garden restaurant with strolling musicians, and opened on July 4, 1944. They named it after the Willow trees that populated the area.

At one time, Moiliili had dozens of artesian springs. Island youth would swim in them and crawl through the caverns. Henry Hausten had stocked the pond on his property with koi, and when the restaurant was built, patrons found the pond and fish delightful.

Gradually the springs in the area were covered until, the only place they surfaced was at the Willows. Construction work around Date and University punctured the spring and the pond at the Willows emptied. When the restaurant was rebuilt some years later, concrete was poured to cover the springs, then dirty with construction debris and breeding mosquitoes.

Former Halekulani general manager Randy Lee Jr. bought the Willows in 1980 and quickly became one of the most gracious and best-loved hosts in town. Under his tutelage, the Willows won international acclaim. His poi luncheons combined great Hawaiian food with top-notch Hawaiian entertainment.

Wo Fat

The oldest restaurant in Honolulu, Wo Fat was opened in 1882 by Wat Ging. One source says it was named in honor of Ting Wo, a Shang Dynasty prince. "I was told the name means 'peace, prosperity and harmony,'" Ted Wong, owner from 1973-1978 said.

"My dad, Henry Awa Wong, had a liquor store across the street from Wo Fat in the 1930s after prohibition. He supplied liquor to the restaurant, and they fell behind in their payments. Instead of collecting, he ended up with a controlling interest in the place."

Wong says 150 shareholders owned Wo Fat in his dad's time. "Awa," as he was called, was the unofficial mayor of Chinatown for forty years. "My father was a very political guy. He had a board of directors with 40-50 prominent people on it."

People wanted to be on the board because of the director's parties he threw every four months. "He served them fabulous dinners, spending maybe $50 a person, and this was in the 1940s and 1950s." They were also paid $100 a meeting and received a case of whiskey at Christmas. "Dad figured if each one hosted one party a year at Wo Fat, he would make money. Some had several."

"Our chief competitor was Waikiki Lau Yee Chai," Wong

The oldest surviving restaurant in Honolulu, Wo Fat, opened in 1882.

continued. "But we had an advantage over them. The taxi drivers could make a better fare bringing Waikiki tourists to Chinatown. So they recommended us."

Awa Wong was the first Chinese director of a *haole* bank and was a vice president of Liberty Bank. He helped start the Narcissus Festival. Ted Wong took over the business in 1973 when his dad died.

Hawaii Five-O borrowed the Wo Fat name for Steve McGarrett's arch villain. Actor Khigh Dhiegh, who interestingly wasn't Asian, played Wo Fat. He was born Kenneth Dickerson in New Jersey in 1910.

In a 1980 episode, McGarrett captured him. Did he then let Danno (James McArthur) book him? "I've waited a long time for this, Wo Fat," McGarrett said. "Now I'm going to have the unique pleasure of booking you myself." Danno looked on silently.

Alan Wong's

Celebrity chef Alan Wong has an interesting background. He was born in Tokyo to a Hawaiian-Chinese father and Japanese mother and grew up with Pacific cuisine. His family moved to Hawaii when Wong was five and he graduated from Leilehua High School.

Wong started his culinary career as a busboy at the Waikiki Beachcomber Hotel. Money was his motivation, but sous chef Wally Nakamura took him under his wing. Wong was inspired with food preparation and decided to enroll at Kapiolani Community College's culinary program. He graduated at the top of his class.

Wong moved to the Greenbrier Resort in West Virginia and then to one of New York's top restaurants – Lutéce. Returning home to Hawaii in 1985, Wong worked at the Moana and Mauna Lani, until a dinner guest at the home of a friend, Zippy's co-founder Francis Higa, offered to back the chef if he wanted to open his own place.

In 1995, Alan Wong's opened on King Street in a building owned by Higa. Since then, Wong has garnered Restaurant of the Year awards for 1996, 1997 and 1999 by *Honolulu Magazine*, a James Beard Foundation Best Chef award and many others.

Wyland Galleries

USA Today calls Wyland a "marine Michaelangelo." On his way to paint 100 Whaling Walls, Wyland is, without a doubt, the most influential marine artist in the world. "If people see the beauty in nature," Wyland believes, "they will work to preserve it before it's too late."

In, 1992 Wyland completed painting the largest mural in the world at the Long Beach Arena. Entitled "Planet Ocean," it was completed in only six weeks and required 7,000 gallons of paint.

Featuring marine life indigenous to Southern California, the finished mural included a pod of Grey Whales, Orca Whales, Blue Whales, Pilot Whales, Pacific Bottlenose Dolphins, California Sea Lions, Sharks, and a variety of other fish. The mural is over ten stories high and 1,225 feet in diameter (almost 3 acres).

The Whaling Walls evolved out of the difficulty Wyland was having painting the great whales on small canvases. He needed larger canvases so he looked at the sides of buildings to capture the true size and majesty of these huge marine mammals.

Wyland's interest in the oceans was inspired by Jacques

Cousteau in the early 1970s and the efforts of Greenpeace. "I started diving into libraries to learn more about cetaceans and began drawing and painting them on many canvases. I soon realized if I really wanted to learn about these animals and share their beauty with the public, I would have to paint them life-size in their natural environment."

In 1981, he completed his first Whaling Wall, a tribute to the California gray whale. "I decided after I finished the first mural that I would complete 100 walls throughout the world by the year 2011 to raise public awareness not only for the great whales, but for all life in the sea."

Wyland opened his first Studio Gallery in 1978 in Laguna Beach, California. At that time the starving artist was the only employee. "I used to personally deliver each and every painting if collectors had a good bottle of wine," states the artist.

The gallery was a success and soon Wyland and his younger brother Bill opened the first Wyland Galleries in Hawaii on the North Shore of Oahu.

In a few short the years, the brothers had opened 14 fine art galleries on Oahu, Maui, Kauai, and the Big Island. Today, Wyland Galleries are located throughout the United States and feature original oil paintings, watercolors, sculpture, limited edition prints, and other collectibles by Wyland and many other artists.

Does Wyland have a first name? Well, he used to. However, he dropped "Robert" some years ago. Today it is just Wyland.

Y. Hata

The list of Hawaii businesses that started in Hilo is impressive. The largest food distributor in the state today, Y. Hata, had its humble beginning as a mom and pop wholesale products operation in Hilo. Yoichi and Naeko Hata began the business out of their "warehouse garage" in 1903.

In 1939, Minoru, the eldest of Yoichi's 10 children, moved to Honolulu to open a branch there. However, the outbreak of World War II was a setback. Yoichi was interned on the mainland. Daughter Yukiko took over management in Hilo. After World War II, sons Susumu, Akira and Frank, the current chairman of the board of directors, returned from military duty and university studies to join the company.

Y. Hata's success has been through diversification. After the war, the company acquired Ligget & Meyer's tobacco line, the Schlitz/ Primo beer franchise, P & P Grocery Stores, and formed Japan Foods Hawaii, which was a joint venture with Kikkoman USA.

The company further diversified into public warehousing and foodservice distribution under the name Diversified Distributor, Inc. They have secured major accounts with the Department of Education's Federal Commodity Program, Nabisco, Quaker Oats, Hunt Wesson, and the Burger King and SAGA Foods contracts.

Laurence Vogel joined the company as CEO in 1998. The company soon landed the military's Prime Vendor Contract for Hawaii, servicing all military foodservice operations. In 2000, Y. Hata purchased MidCity Restaurant Equipment and Supplies and expanded its market share to include durable kitchen and catering goods. In 2001, Hans Weiler Foods was acquired, giving Y. Hata a major presence in the baking supply field. In 2003, it created Island Epicure to service the gourmet foods market.

As Y. Hata celebrates its 100th year, it is the leading foodservice, equipment and supply wholesaling and distribution service in the state, serving hotels, restaurants, schools, prisons, military foodservice operations, and national accounts. Not bad for a company that started in a Hilo garage!

Young Brothers

In the year 1900, four brothers named William, Edgar, Herbert, and John Young started offering shark hunting and "bum boating" services (taking orders from sailing ships for fresh supplies when they were close to Diamond Head and having the goods ready to load when the vessels arrived in the harbor). They invested $86 to purchase the "Billy," a four-horsepower boat, with which they started the Young Brothers partnership.

The Young brothers came originally from San Diego, California and had the first glass-bottom boat service at Catalina Island two years before moving to Hawaii.

John A. Young, called "Captain Jack," and his three brothers began to transport cargo to Molokai on regularly scheduled trips. Soon, however, three of the brothers left the company to pursue other activities, and Captain Jack found a business partner in Walter Dillingham, who bought Young Brothers entirely in 1913.

In 1929, the pineapple industry was growing. Pineapples were grown on Lanai, Molokai, and Kauai and canned in Honolulu.

This led to the first common carrier service offered in 1935 between the ports of Honolulu and Molokai.

Dillingham ordered high-powered diesel towboats among which the Mikimiki is the most famous. Built in 1929, this pineapple tug became the prototype for hundreds of military ships serving in the Pacific. Young Brothers contributed to America's defense during World War II by providing equipment and personnel.

After World War II, Young Brothers continued to grow. In the year 1947, service was expanded to the islands of Hawaii, Maui, and Kauai. Service to and from Lanai had been offered since 1991.

Due to capital needs, the company became part of the Dillingham Corporation in 1961. Hawaiian Electric Industries (HEI) bought Young Brothers in 1986. Its subsidiaries today offer liner services to Alaska and Puerto Rico and provide tug and barge services on the West Coast.

The Young Brothers slogan "Lifeline of the Hawaiian Islands" expresses the supply of important necessities to the neighbor islands. The company's ultimate aim has always been to offer a fast, dependable, economical inter-island freight cargo service.

Yum Yum Tree

John Reuben McIntosh opened his first restaurant, the Snack Shop, in Corona Del Mar California in 1948. He opened several before a friend who worked for Matson suggested starting one on Kalakaua Avenue in Waikiki.

"John was one of the greatest innovators in business that I've ever met," says former partner James L. Gray. "John suggested we open a steak house in Newport Beach California based on Buzz's Steak and Lobster in Waikiki. He liked the simple menu and casual style. The restaurant was called Reuben's, his middle name, and opened in 1960. It was a big hit and soon we had three in California, one in Kahala Mall, Kona and Kauai."

The inspiration for the Yum Yum Tree was Vi's Pies in California.

"We were building a sandwich shop in Kahala Mall," Gray continues "when John bought Vi's Pies in California. Halfway through construction, we shifted the concept to pies, and the Yum Yum Tree was born."

Neither John nor James recall exactly where the Yum Yum Tree name came from. "It could have come from the 1963 Jack Lemmon movie, *Under the Yum Yum Tree*, but I'm unsure," John says. "A manager suggested the name."

The Yum Yum Tree did well, but the small kitchen hampered things. Gino Boero, who worked with them for over two decades, recalls not having enough room for the pies when they came out of the oven. "We'd stack them on boxes, shelves, and anywhere we could find a place."

"We used to have a Pie of the Month," recalls Biff Graper who worked for 34 years with the chain. At district manager meetings, we'd taste six different pies and vote for the one we liked best. It was a weight-gaining experience."

McIntosh also founded the Coco's chain on the mainland, naming it after Los Cocos bar in La Paz, Mexico. "Spence Weaver had a Coco's here, so we couldn't use that name in Hawaii," McIntosh recalls. There are over 300 Coco's around the world today.

McIntosh sold the six Yum Yum Trees in 1987 to Trans/Pacific Restaurants, which at one time operated 28 restaurants in Hawaii, including the Jolly Roger, Monterey Bay Canners, and Sizzler. The last Yum Yum Tree, at Ward Center, closed in 2005.

Zippy's

Zippy's was founded in 1966, three years after the zip code came out in 1963, and conveyed a fast food message. Brothers Francis and Charles Higa started the popular chain of fast food restaurants with a single store on the then two-way King Street in McCully. They considered naming it Zip Drive In, before settling on Zippy's. Saimin was 50 cents, and French fries were 25 cents.

"Francis was a visionary and ambitious," says Nick Kaars, who was a graphic designer for the company. "He was the CEO and marketing director. He developed products and oversaw the expansion. He saw himself as a risk-taker. Charlie was in charge of kitchen operations, supplies, and managing food costs." Charlie's Bar at their King Street and Maunakea Street restaurants is named for Charley Higa. "The were looking for a name for a bar and I said, "how about Charley's?" Karrs continued.

"There are a lot of plate lunch places with just one location. What separates Zippy's from them is desire and ambition," Kaars believes. "Zippy's does a whole bunch of things right. Instead of malls that close at 9:00 PM, Zippy's bought mostly freestanding buildings so that they could stay open 24 hours. They do more business per store than McDonalds because of those hours."

"They always have plenty of parking. They do sit down and take out. Unlike others, they do regular TV advertising. Through proper portioning, they keep costs under control. They keep their stores clean and the food is good. Francis believed that 'you got to spend money to make money,' says Kaars.

"They decided to open a bakery and wanted it to be a hit right off," Kaars continued. "They decided to make it look like a mainland company had opened in Hawaii to establish instant credibility. The best pastries are French and Belgium, and when we were considering names, someone in my firm put Napoleon's on the list."

Glenn Crane a former drama teacher at the University of Hawaii plays Napoleon. "We auditioned maybe 50 people. They all had to say the same line – 'No one is flakier than Napoleon's!' Glenn just stood out from the rest. He had a good voice and the comical quality we wanted. He's since retired to Indiana, but we brought him back to shoot more commercials around 1990."

Zippy's has its signature dish, chili, and Napoleon's needed one too, the brothers thought. The solution was the Napple.

All 23 Zippy's are on Oahu although there used to be one in Kapaa, Kauai. It lasted four years. Part of the problem might have been their large menu. "It was hard to franchise or manage and keep costs under control when you have a 100 item menu," Kaars continued. "They have a central kitchen on Oahu but how would you get these things to Kauai and still have them be fresh?"

Similarly, Zippy's has shied

The name Napoleon's Bakery was chosen because the French make the best pastries.

away from Waikiki. "Tourists don't understand the concept of plate lunches. They did try Waikiki once, but it didn't last. Prostitutes used the bathrooms for tricks."

In 2003, Zippy's announced the planned opening of its first Maui store, set for Kahului, Maui.

The Higa's have also helped a young chef start a popular restaurant. They have formed a partnership, and the chef has moved into a building they own on King Street. That chef is Alan Wong.

—*Researched by Norhidayah Abdul Rahman*

The origins of the plate lunch

The origins of the plate lunch are somewhat obscure, but Arnold Hiura, who investigated it as editor of the *Hawaii Herald*, says it started on the plantation. "Plantation workers ate out in the fields and needed a big lunch that would not spoil," Hiura says. "They carried two-tiered tins with rice on the bottom and meat and vegetables on top." The meat was likely smoked or salted like sausage or salt cod. Pickled vegetables, like kim chee, would make up the salad.

Macaroni salad had to wait for refrigeration to earn its place on the plate. Actually, the origins of macaroni salad are easier to trace. It was first popularized around 1900 at Delmonico's restaurant in New York and quickly became a craze. Many Hawaii hotel chefs were trained in New York and brought it with them when they came here.

The plate lunch moved off the plantation and to the harbor in the late 1920s or early 1930s. Hiura says food vendors started serving hungry harbor stevedores and dock workers plates with rice, stew or meat, and macaroni salad for 25 to 50 cents.

Star-Bulletin reporter Cynthia Oi calls macaroni salad "one of the plate lunch's holy trinity, the 'show' horse in a trifecta. No self-respecting plate lunch is without it."

Why it has stayed so popular in Hawaii, while other locales have forgotten it remains a mystery. Some speculate it's the low cost, or contrast to warm rice and meat, but whatever the reason, there's no doubt it's earned a place at our table. Hawaii consumes over 1 million pounds of it a year.

Do you know of a great story we overlooked? E-mail us at CompaniesWeKeep@Yahoo.com

Behind the Scenes at Hawaii Radio and TV Stations

LESS THAN TWO YEARS AFTER THE FIRST commercial radio station came to the United States in 1920, KGU was on the air in Honolulu. Hawaii has had a rich history in broadcasting perhaps because so many zany characters have been attracted to the profession.

Bob Sevey was "Hawaii's Walter Cronkite." It was Paul Udell, now at KITV, who came up with the "Shaka Sign-off" at KHON.

Hal Lewis, who adopted the name J. Akuhead Pupule, was once the mostly highly-paid DJ in the country. Ron Jacobs left KGU and K-POI to turn Los Angeles radio station KHJ into "Boss Radio," the top Rock & Roll station in the country.

"All Hawaiian, all the time" KCCN has never been owned by Hawaiians. It did not make a dime in its first year, and founders Carle, Cloward, and Neville (the C, C, and N) were forced to sell.

Most station call letters have hidden meanings that readers will find listed at the end of this chapter. KHVH, for example, was an acronym for "Kaiser's Hawaiian Village Hotel." The SS's in KSSK stands for "Super Station." KGMB does *not* stand for Greater Mormon Broadcasting as has been rumored for years.

Here are some of the behind-the-scenes stories from key players in the industry.

KCCN

While most local stations played some Hawaiian music, KCCN was the first to play "all Hawaiian, all the time." Launched on Halloween,  October 31, 1966, at 1420 on the AM dial, KCCN has had a lasting impact on Hawaiian music. If it wasn't for KCCN, we may not have the strong local music industry we have today.

"KCCN played Hawaiian music when no one else did," says station General Manager Mike Kelly. "KCCN enabled groups to perform and record. No other place in the world supports its own music industry like Hawaii does.

"Locally recorded music does $20 to $30 million a year in business," Kelly continued. "That doesn't happen anywhere else but here. Twenty percent of music store sales are locally recorded products. Hawaiian music is our country music. It's our indigenous music."

KCCN's Diamond Head Broadcasting was founded by Perry W. Carle, who was President; Dr. Ralph B. Cloward, Vice President; and Jerry Neville, Secretary-treasurer. The C, C, and N in KCCN come from their initials.

Carle had been a sales manager at KAIM. "Perry Carle was the main guy responsible for KCCN," said Jim Sattler, son-in-law of Dr. Cloward. "It was his life-long dream to have his own radio station."

Dr. Cloward, who died in 2000 at age 92, was a specialist in treating spinal cord injuries and was chief of neurosurgery at Queen's and later St. Francis Hospital.

"Jerry Neville was the Hawaii representative of United Press International," says nephew Harry Soria, Jr.

Perry Carle saw Dr. Cloward as the financial backer of the station. "He sold Cloward on the idea of an inexpensive, automated station using the latest technology," Sattler continued. "He appealed to his ego, putting his initial in the station name. Cloward contributed $50,000 and signed a personal guarantee with Hawaii National Bank for a line of credit of another $50,000."

Perry erected a transmission tower and a small concrete block building off Nimitz and Waiakamilo. A year later, the bank called and wanted their money. "My father-in-law was not really a business person," says lawyer Sattler. "He asked me to look into it.

"Outside the station, I found a station wagon with "KCCN – All Hawaiian All the Time – Mobile unit #7" painted on the side. Did they have a fleet?" Sattler wondered. "Perry told me it was the only one and that he wanted people to think they had a fleet."

The car was not even owned by the station. The auto dealer had traded it for advertising. "In a year, KCCN had not had a single cash sale. Everything was 'contra,' traded for advertising. They also had no immediate prospects," Sattler said. He recommended finding a buyer for the station. "We found a bunch of guys who had owned the International House of Pancakes and sold the station to them. They took on the $50,000 loan, but Dr. Cloward never recouped his investment. Perry Carle was terminated, but they kept the name and format."

KCCN used to broadcast from the banyan tree in the International Marketplace. "We were the only station in the world to broadcast from a tree," Kelly added. "One day, Victor Opiopio was climbing up the tree to go to work and he fell. Lucky Luck, who was on the air, christened him with a nickname that stuck – Krash Kealoha."

"KCCN drove record sales of what had been fairly unknown Hawaiian musicians," says Harry Soria, Jr. "That, in turn, increased the demand for live performances and lounge shows."

Today, KCCN FM100, KINE 105.1, along with KRTR, KXME, KGMZ, and 83 mainland stations are all owned by Cox Radio in Atlanta. KCCN 1420 AM was sold in 2002 and became a sports-talk station called KKEA.

What happens behind the scenes at radio stations? "Things have changed a lot in the 18 years I've been here," Kelly says. "The program director used to decide what to play. We'd get feedback on whether people liked it from their calls to the station."

"Now, everything is researched first. We hire companies to test songs before we play them. We now know which songs are popular with which demographics."

"Also, the station is now run by computers. It's a little more sophisticated than in 1966. We have 4,000 songs on our hard drive. The system, including hardware and software cost about $150,000. It's a 60 gigabyte hard drive, which seemed like a lot then, but now it's common."

The system runs the station from midnight until 5 AM and on some weekends. Using a system called Voice Tracking, a DJ can record his shift in 30 minutes. The computer will mix songs, commercials, and their voice in a seamless presentation.

KGMB - KSSK

The first radio station on the air in Hawaii was KGU. Racing to be the first, KGU beat out KDYX by 15 minutes. However, KDYX had Governor Farrington, while only a few "hello's" came from KGU. KDYX shut down in 1924 but came back  on the air in 1927 as KGMB. Broadcasts came from the Royal Hawaiian Hotel.

Honolulu's first TV news anchor, Wayne Collins

Rumors abound that the GMB stands for Greater Mormon Broadcasting. Many long-time residents remember the Mormon Tabernacle Choir singing at the sign-on and sign-off of KGMB TV. However, the GMB was actually George M. Bowls, the chief engineer at the radio station in the mid-1930s.

The Japanese fleet used KGMB's signal to help find the islands. Webley Edwards was the popular broadcaster of

KGMB the day that the Japanese bombed Pearl Harbor and went on the roof of the building to report the attack. Before being shut down by military censors, Edwards announced, "This is not a maneuver. This is the Real McCoy. The Japanese are attacking Pearl Harbor."

Television came to Hawaii in 1952. The first words broadcast on TV in Hawaii, "Hello, everybody" came from Carl Hebenstreit, more affectionately known as Kini Popo. The date, according to *Firsts and Almost Firsts in Hawaii* by Robert Schmitt, was December 1, 1952. The 25-minute show carried live interviews until 5:30 PM when a Gene Autry western movie was shown.

KONA-TV (which became KHON) had been broadcasting the islands' first test pattern from November 17, 1952. Their programming did not start until December 16, two weeks after KGMB.

"The first TV news anchor in Honolulu was Wayne Collins on KGMB-TV," says former newsman Bob Sevey. "He was an absolutely amazing performer. He had a voice that God must have envied, a photographic memory, and a total grasp of the news. In the beginning, he used no script at all. He went into a little booth about a half-hour

The Perry and Price Show celebrated its 20th anniversary in 2003.

before the newscast and memorized it — not the word-for-word scripts but the facts of the stories. Then he went on camera and delivered the news flawlessly with perfect eye contact.

"The fact that he had no script made the sponsor, Pan Am, nervous, so he began to take a sheaf of blank paper to the anchor desk and made check marks on the paper as though he were checking off items in a script. Collins was hands-down the best news anchor I have ever seen, network or local, and one of the brightest individuals I have ever met.

"He eventually left the business, served the state as Director of Land and Natural Resources under Governor Quinn. Wayne retired some years ago to Pennsylvania.

Cec Heftel bought KGMB in the early 1960s and turned the call letters of the radio station to K-59 and later to KSSK.

Michael W. Perry has been with KSSK radio since 1978. There was a big deal made when "Uncle Mikey," as he was called, moved from KKUA radio to then KGMB radio (now KSSK) in 1978. He became the afternoon drive DJ on KGMB, opposite Aku's morning show.

"I was 30, and he was 72," Perry says. "I was the kid. We had zero in common, but we got along. Hal Lewis, or Aku as he was known, had been the top guy in radio locally for 20 years. And he was a prankster. He was most famous for his Second Annual Easter Parade on April 1st down Kalakaua Avenue. More than 7,000 people went down with beach chairs and coolers to watch a parade that never happened. We could never get away with that today!

"Another famous Aku prank was doing a live remote from the nude beach on the North Shore. Aku would check in with a reporter out there periodically who conveyed everything he saw. This went on for three days before they admitted it was all being done in the studio.

Hal "Aku" Lewis was the top morning DJ through the 1960s and 1970s.

"People often relied on the radio to know what time it was. Aku, on more than one occasion told people it was an hour earlier than it really was," Perry recalls. "Thousands of people were late to work that day!"

Lewis enjoyed making his listeners angry. One story is that a listener was so incensed she called him an aku head and Lewis supposedly adopted the name, calling himself J. Akuhead Pupule. Others say Lewis just made up the name.

Then PR guy Buck Buchwach (later an editor of the *Honolulu Advertiser*) helped Aku with many of his stunts, including an April Fools' Free Money Giveaway and a fake Statehood announcement.

Radio historian Mel Ah Ching recalls that Cec Heftel owned KGMB radio and KPUA radio in Hilo. "The *Coconut Wireless* at the time was the network of these two stations. Aku's news was broadcast in Hilo during the 1960s and 70s on Mynah Bird's morning show when he was with that station."

"KGMB radio became K59 when Cec Heftel sold the TV station, and we had to change the radio call letters. K59 was chosen because we were at 590 on the AM dial. A while later, we came up with KSSK," Perry continues. "The SS stood for Super Station."

Hawaii's Walter Cronkite – Bob Sevey.

Perry recalls that the RCA console in the studio has serial number 0005 on it. "It was very old and had to be one of the first they made."

When Aku died in 1983, Larry Price and Michael W. Perry took over the morning show. Price had been in public relations with the station. "It was Cec and Earl McDaniel's idea to pair us," Perry recalls. "They had considered his possible death and we were their Plan B."

"We liked each other from the first day. We have a similar sense of humor. We think the other is funny." The Perry & Price Morning Show has been a ratings leader for KSSK for over 20 years now.

"The show at the Hanohano Room came about because Larry and I were bored with Saturday morning radio. There's nothing happening on Saturday mornings. It is like sensory deprivation. We decided to get out of the studio and deal with a live audience. I thought a restaurant or shopping center would do. The producers came up with the Hanohano Room at the Sheraton Waikiki Hotel.

"At first, we were concerned that the people who came wouldn't sit still while we were playing commercials and songs. They'd be bored, we thought. But they are happy to sit there and chat with people at their table.

"We've had every celebrity, singer, actor, sports star, and astronaut as guests. We've done this 45 times a year for 17 years. It's a blur. I can't even remember who was on last week!"

Maybe you have heard stories that the Dole Cannery, where KSSK is located, is haunted. KSSK receptionist Auntie Ulu James claims it is true. "Once, five of us got in the elevator to go down. It stopped at the ground level but the doors wouldn't open. Then it went back up, and down, and up...the doors wouldn't open. We went up and down nine times before the doors finally opened, and we all ran out!

"They don't really bother people," Ulu says, referring to the four ghosts that roam the halls. "One we call the Janitor. There's the Mailman, a tutu lady in a muu muu, and a little Japanese boy.

"The area was used as a makeshift morgue after the 1900 Chinatown fire. After Pearl Harbor was attacked, the Honolulu morgue couldn't hold all the bodies. Dole had the biggest refrigerators in the state, and they were temporarily used. Maybe that's where they came from," Ulu thinks.

The Hawaiian Moving Company

What is so moving about the Hawaiian Moving Company? "In its first year, it was a disco dance show," says producer Randy Brandt. Thus began the longest running weekly local TV show in the country, The Hawaiian Moving Company.

It all started in 1979 when disco was king. KKUA DJ Kamasami Kong premiered a new television show on Monday nights at 6:30 PM. The local audience was invited to "move" around the night club scene while learning a few "moves" to use on the dance floor. The name Hawaiian Moving Company was a double entendre.

After a year and a half and 62 episodes, it fizzled out. Hawaiian Host then came to KGMB looking for a show to sponsor. The Hawaiian Moving Company was taken off the shelf and turned into a Hawaiian magazine show. Michael W. Perry was brought in as host, and the rest is history.

Michael W. Perry "on location" for a Hawaiian Moving Company story on an Oahu nudist camp.

Michael W. Perry ushered the show out of the fading disco lights and into the mainstream of magazine format television.

"On the very first shoot," Michael W. Perry muses, "we covered a new TV show that was filming in Waimanalo. It starred John Hillerman and some new guy with a moustache who drove a red sports car. Nobody knew Tom Selleck back then, and I was no exception!"

In 1984, Hawaiian Host Chocolates picked up sole sponsorship of The Hawaiian Moving Company. From that point on, it was at the top of the ratings for Hawaii's local TV shows. As a multiple Emmy and Iris award winner, the Hawaiian Moving Company has produced nearly 2000 segments highlighting outstanding people, places, and things from all over Hawaii and all over the world. Audiences have been taken from Niihau to Hana, Russia to Switzerland, Australia to Hong Kong, but always with a Hawaiian perspective.

Perry believes the Hawaiian Moving Company was revolutionary. "In the days before cable, there was nothing that focused on local artists and musicians. We exposed such performers as Rap Reiplinger, Cecilio & Kapono, Frank DeLima, and many others," says a proud Perry.

On each show, host Michael W. Perry takes the audience on an interesting look at life in the islands through the interesting folks he tracks down. The show tries to uncover unusual segments that will entertain everyone. It is not unusual for viewers to scuba dive with sharks, meet the world's most prolific Barbie Doll collector, and discover a man who risks his life to get incredible molten lava photos, all in a half-hour episode.

"We began a tradition that first year called 'abusing the host.' They put me up in F-15's and hoped I'd turn green," Perry recalls. "They made me meditate at a Buddhist temple. The priest would whack you with a stick if you didn't do it right. I figured they'd give me a 'tourist whack.' I soon discovered there is no 'tourist whack.'"

Michael W. Perry hosts the most successful local, prime time show in the country.

"I'm a quiet kind of guy," Perry says. "I like to read. I wouldn't do most of these things if they weren't part of the job. Tandem skydiving, F-15's, snakes, bats - I'd never do that stuff in a million years. So this is good for me.

"Quite a few of the show's ideas originate with me. Randy has contacts with the hotels and events. I get a lot of calls from people whose uncle has a one-legged dog that skydives, or a surfing cat."

What behind the scenes details would the public find interesting about the Moving Company? "The earliest shows were shot on two inch video tape," Perry says. "We can't even find a machine to play them anymore."

"We tried to have a Hawaiian Moving Company radio show in 1982 on KGMB radio. It was part of my afternoon show, but it didn't work."

"Local folks may not know that the Moving Company is syndicated in Japan, Korea, and Singapore on cable. We shoot new ins and outs and de-localize it," Brandt says. "It gets dubbed in Chinese."

From June through August, The Hawaiian Moving Company re-packages the best segments of the prior season. "The summer is kind of a best-of-year thing," Brandt continues. The *Best of the Hawaiian Moving Company* videos have been the top selling, locally produced video for two years in a row.

The Hawaiian Moving Company is the most successful local prime time show in the country. It has dominated the airwaves for two decades, and it may continue to do so long into the future.

KGU

On May 11, 1922, the "Voice of Hawaii," radio station KGU went on the air. It beat out KDYX (which became KGMB and is now KSSK) by a scant 15 minutes. "Hello, hello," said the announcer at 10:57 AM, then *Ave Maria* was played by the renowned violinist, Kathleen Parlow. KDYX went on the air with an "aloha" at 11:12 AM. There were 25 radio receivers on Oahu at the time.

The next day, the *Honolulu Advertiser* reported the beginning of radio broadcasting in Hawaii. On the evening of Friday, May 11, 1922, "the first successful radio broadcasting concert given by any newspaper in Hawaii was broadcast from the powerful radio station on the roof of the Advertiser building between 7:30 and 9 PM last night."

Marion Mulrony, a friend of Alexander Graham Bell, got the first license for a radio station in Hawaii. The 33-year old partnered with the Thurstons of the *Honolulu Advertiser* to launch KGU. In the early days, call letters were assigned by the Department of Commerce and had no meaning.

Three letter calls were assigned until 1922 when they ran out. Four letter calls then began to be issued. In the late 1920s, stations began requesting call letters that had meaning to them.

Although it was powered by only 500 watts, KGU was often heard by listeners on the mainland because the airwaves were empty. A KGU Listeners Club developed there.

Actually, Hawaii could often receive mainland broadcasts. When the first ratings were compiled in 1940, three stations shared the honors. This was a bit surprising since there were only two stations on Oahu – KGU and KGMB. The third station was WLW in Ohio, which operated with 500,000 watts.

Radio was quite primitive by today's standards. It often signed on and off several times during the day. If it had no sponsor, KGU would often just go off the air.

KGU was first in many ways. It was the first to carry news of D-Day in Hawaii and the death of President Franklin Roosevelt.

Harry B. Soria, Sr. was the first disc jockey in Hawaii before the term was coined in the 1930s. "He had a show called *Going to Town with Harry Soria*," says son Harry Soria Jr. "He was the first to have his name on a show here."

Despite being Hawaii's first radio personality, Soria needed to keep his day job at Von Hamm-Young. Radio paid him only 50 cents an hour.

The term "disc jockey" was coined in a 1941 *Variety* magazine article and referred to someone who skillfully maneuvered records live on the radio. "Paul Wilcox, Leslie Wilcox's dad was the first to have that term applied to him in Hawaii," Harry Soria Jr., says.

KGU and KGMB were the only stations on Oahu until after World War II. Within a few months of the war's end, KHON, KPOA and KULA came on the air using surplus military radio equipment bought for pennies on the dollar.

The radio market is very competitive, and stations often change formats. Today, KGU is a Christian station. It is part of the Salem Media of Hawaii Group, along with AM 650 KHNR and 95.5 FM "The Fish" Christian Music Broadcasting.

KHNL

In 1962, David Watumull of Watumull Broadcasting Company launched KTRG Channel 13. KTRG's studio was located on Kalakaua Avenue, and its transmitter was atop the Hilton Hawaiian Village. Broadcasting began on July 4, 1962 with primarily English programs and one or two Japanese presentations. Programs included *High School Bowl, You Bet Your Life, Dragnet, Riverboat,* and a locally-produced nightly news.

Richard Eaton, President of Friendly Broadcasting of Ohio and United Broadcasting of Maryland, bought KTRG in 1966 and moved the station to 150-B Puuhale Road where it is today.

A year later, KTRG changed its name to KIKU, which means "chrysanthemum" in Japanese. Eaton unveiled the new name with a marked increase in Japanese broadcasting. Japanese programming was scheduled from 5-10 PM, with English presentations running from 1-5 PM and from 10-11 PM.

KIKU was sold in 1979 to Mid-Pacific Television Associates.

Japanese programming was pared down and moved to late evening. KIKU switched to a "kid vid" format, scoring success with *The Children's Hour* and *Professor Fun.*

In 1984, the call letters were changed once more to reflect the reduction of Japanese programs to KHNL. "HNL" is the Honolulu airport designation," said General Manager John Fink. "It's on six million people's luggage tags each year. That's great advertising for us."

Maybe that was a good thing for they have used that theme for Maui as well on KOGG ("OGG" is the Maui Airport designation).

The broadcast of the WAC Baseball Tournament in May 1984 and subsequent NCAA Regionals in Arizona marked the beginning of KHNL's close relationship with the University of Hawaii's Athletic Program.

In 1986, KHNL became associated with the fledgling Fox Broadcasting Network and picked up syndicated programs like *Arsenio Hall, The Joan Rivers Show, The Tracey Ullman Show,* and *Married with Children.*

KHNL began operating KFVE-TV (K5) in 1993. All University of Hawaii sports programming moved from KHNL to K5, "The Home Team." In January 1996, KHNL and KHON switched affiliations to NBC and FOX, respectively. K5 became home of the WB network, and KHNL referred to itself as "News 8."

KHON

Like many of our TV stations, KHON started as a radio station. KHON, "Radio Honolulu" went on the air in 1946. Six years later, it competed with KGMB to be the first to air television signals.

Viewers who tuned in to Channel 11 on the night of December 16, 1952 were treated to President Dwight D. Eisenhower's arrival in Honolulu en route home from his historic trip to Korea.

Using the call letters KONA, the TV station had run test patterns since November 17, 1952. KGMB offered the island its first television program on December 1st.

Some of the best shows in the 1950s at KONA-TV were the *Texaco Star Theater, The Red Skelton Show, The Milton Berle Show* and *Bonanza.*

KONA-TV was bought in 1953 by the Honolulu Advertiser, which also owned radio station KGU. They moved the station from Channel 11 to Channel 2 a few years later. After 43 years at their cramped Auahi Street studio, KHON moved to its new $20 million facility at 88 Piikoi Street. Once a lagoon until filled in 50 years ago, the site formerly housed Records Hawaii, Stone Free Waterbeds, and many other businesses at 404 Piikoi. Some considered the number four to be unlucky, so the address was changed.

Few know that KITV morning newsman Paul Udell created KHON's signature Shaka Signoff. Udell, who co-anchored the KHON News with Barbara Tanabe before Joe Moore, recalls a new general manager wanted to use film clips of people waving at the end of his newscast, like they had done on the mainland.

"Why don't we use the shaka?" Udell suggested. "We tried to get our camera people to film islanders waving the shaka, but they never got to it. One day, I dragged a cameraman out on the streets, and I held a sign that said 'give us a shaka.' People did and we ran it at the end of the news. It was instantly popular."

Former news director Jim McCoy called it a uniquely Hawaiian way to end the news. "No matter how bad the news is, after sports and weather, we'll leave you with a smile."

Joe Moore was a sportscaster in the 1970s at KGMB before joining KHON.

"It drives the cameramen from other stations crazy, though," McCoy acknowledged. "People give them the shaka, thinking it's our channel. But, they can't use it. It's our signature."

"The Shaka is occasionally not used at the end of the news when it's been a particularly bad day, like 9/11 or when a gunman shot those Xerox employees," McCoy pointed out.

KITV

KITV went on the air April 16, 1954 under the call letters KULA-TV on Channel 4. The building at 1290 Ala Moana Blvd. also housed KULA radio. In 1954, the other two TV stations in Honolulu were KGMB-TV (CBS) on Channel 9 and KONA-TV (later KHON) on Channel 11, affiliated with NBC.

In 1957, Henry J. Kaiser bought KULA-TV and changed the call letters to KHVH-TV. KHVH stood for Kaiser's Hawaiian Village Hotel. "He brought in a brilliant broadcaster named Dick Block to run the station, and it quickly ran the competition into the ground," said former news anchor Bob Sevey.

"Until that time, KGMB-TV had dominated the ratings. Block

initiated the first early evening (6 o'clock) newscast in Honolulu. He also developed a dynamite kids show called *Captain Honolulu* based on a non-existent hero whose sidekick, named Sgt. Sacto, hosted the show. KHVH-TV became king of the hill," Sevey recalled.

Sevey joined KHVH in 1961 as a news anchor and eventually became news director. In 1965, the station was sold by Kaiser to a partnership headed by Bob Berger from Casper, Wyoming. "Berger was a guy with a strong, if somewhat controversial, personality. He was also an innovative broadcaster," said Sevey. "Among other things, he brought in the first live satellite event — a Notre Dame football game in 1965."

Sevey left KHVH in late 1965 and was hired by Cec Heftel, who bought KGMB in July of 1966. Several years later, Berger sold KHVH and the call letters were changed to KITV. "ITV" was an acronym for "Island Television." For a short time, Roy Disney Jr., Walt's nephew owned KITV.

"As far as I know, Kaiser bought KULA because Channel 4 had better studio facilities, was on a better frequency and had better

coverage than Channel 13. It was also affiliated with ABC. Remember, there was no cable in those days. Reception was through rooftop or rabbit ear antennas, and it was spotty because of the terrain of mountains and valleys on Oahu."

"KGMB-TV had superior coverage because they had satellite stations on Maui and the Big Island," Sevey continued. "Much of Windward Oahu got its only TV from Channel 3, the KGMB-TV satellite on Haleakala. Kaiser later put a KHVH-TV satellite on Haleakala (Channel 12) and eventually all the Honolulu stations had neighbor island satellites.

Bob Sevey joined KITV in 1961 when it was KHVH-TV.

"The call letters KULA went with the radio station which Kaiser did not buy. He had his own KHVH radio which he moved into 1290 Ala Moana along with the TV station.

"Disney may have changed the Channel 4 call letters to KITV because he thought KHVH was too closely identified with Kaiser and the Hawaiian Village Hotel," Sevey speculated.

Did Sevey remember any interesting anecdotes from the early days of broadcasting? "Oh my," was his response. "You're asking me to dredge up things that happened more than 40 years ago.

The spirit is willing, but the memory is suspect.

"I do recall that we had a Japanese department at KULA-TV headed by a gentleman named Harold Sakoda. They put on a weekly variety show that ran for at least an hour, maybe two. Most of the performers spoke only Japanese, but we had no Japanese-speaking director on staff. Our Assistant General Manager, Art Sprinkle (KITV News anchor Gary Sprinkle's father), directed the show. It was not scripted. Art had only a format sheet written in Japan-ized English.

"More often than not, what happened in the studio bore little or no relationship to what was on the format sheet. It was a director's nightmare. Art knew only one word of Japanese, the word for 'Stop!' When things got out of hand, he would pop a slide onto the screen, kill all the studio mikes and shout that word, usually followed by 'Goddammit!!' into the intercom. That would bring the proceedings to a halt.

"Sprinkle would explain to Mr. Sakoda that it was quite necessary to follow the format. Mr. Sakoda would put the people in the proper places, and the show would continue. That process often took several minutes during which the TV audience was treated to a video of a slide and audio of Japanese music. No one seemed to mind.

"Then there was the strike at KULA-TV," Sevey recalled, "the first ever by the IBEW against a Honolulu TV station. All the technicians and cameramen walked out. The management staff was able to keep things on a reasonably even keel during the day of routine programming on film or kinescope (before videotape was invented).

"The six o'clock news, however, was another kettle of fish. There were salesmen pushing and trying to focus the cameras, promotion people were editing news film, the floor director was a copy writer, the sports guy was on the audio board, and on camera was me.

"I led to the first piece of news film, and instead, a commercial came up. I led to the second piece, and the fourth piece appeared. For a solid half-hour, absolutely nothing went according to the script. Everything was screwed up. It soon became funny, and I decided I had to play it that way. Somehow, we finished the half-hour."

In the hours and days that followed, the station got thousands of phone calls and hundreds of pieces of mail. "Ninety-nine percent of them said they loved the newscast, thought it was the best, and certainly the funniest one they'd ever seen. Most were quite disappointed when we got our act together and figured out how to do it right, in spite of the strike.

"One of my favorite memories of the Kaiser/KHVH period concerned the late, lovable and extremely talented Lucky Luck," Sevey continued. "Most people thought Lucky was a local boy. Actually, he was Robert Melvin Luck from St. Louis, Missouri. He went to the Pacific as a Marine officer during the latter days of World War II. Stationed in Samoa, he discovered that he had an affinity for Pacific and Asian languages and a mastery of every possible pidgin dialect.

Robert "Lucky" Luck

"After the war, he moved to Hawaii and embarked on a career as a driver for Primo Beer. Somehow he wound up on the radio and, along with J. Akuhead Pupule, became a dominant morning disc jockey.

"At the time of this incident, Lucky was also the morning DJ on KHVH radio from 5:30 to 9:00 AM and the star of a KHVH-TV show called *Lucky's Luau*. Lucky was a gregarious guy who loved two things: talking story with people and drinking beer. He spent a lot of time at the Palm Tree Inn in Waikiki. There were mornings when Lucky was suffering the symptoms of Primo flu and was unavailable for duty, so the station hired the late Sam Sanford as his regular on-call replacement. Sometimes they'd both show up after spending most of the night together, and the resulting shows were classics of hilarious and often outrageous radio."

One afternoon shortly before 5:30 PM, Sevey was in the front office when Lucky came through the front door, greeted everyone, and headed back in the direction of the radio studios - twelve hours late. "I followed him," Sevey said. "At precisely 5:30, Lucky punched off the automated Hawaiian music that the station played during the day, started his theme song, opened the mike, and said, 'Good morning everybody, this is old Lucky Luck with you for the start of another beautiful day in Paradise.' He introduced a record and prepared to do his 3-1/2 hour show.

"I went into master control, faded down the song Lucky was playing and turned on the automation. Then I went into the studio, patted Lucky on the back and said, 'Great show, Lucky.' He grinned and said, 'Thank you, Bobby,' got up and walked out, probably headed back to the Palm Tree Inn.'"

KKUA

"Kokua" Radio was a Top 40 Station at 690 AM in Honolulu from 1967 to about 1989. The call letters were dropped when the owners turned it into KQMQ AM. KHPR now uses the KKUA call letters for their Maui relay station at 90.7 FM.

Jim Peters, Ron King, Steve Nicolet, Lan Roberts, Lou Richards, Ron Jacobs, and Michael W. Perry were some of KKUA's better known DJs. It was Jacobs who spearheaded the 3 KKUA-Habilitat *Homegrown* albums.

Long-time listeners may remember that, back then, Michael W. Perry was called Uncle Mikey.

"Uncle Mikey started with *Uncle Mikey's Storytime* when I was in college," Perry recalled. "I worked at WILS AM 1320 in Lansing, Michigan and created 90-second, stupid, modern fairy tales. I did all the voices and it somehow passed for creativity in radio.

"I brought Uncle Mikey when I was hired by KKUA in 1973. To everyone's surprise, especially mine, it became a big hit, so I kept it up for two or three years sporadically. Meanwhile, I was introduced as Uncle Mikey at every school, luau, prom, or speaking engagement that I attended, and it stuck.

"I started the Uncle Mikey Telephone Song in 1974 with those early push-button phones that actually had 7 pure notes. It was an attempt to create a unique audio ID for radio and it worked very well. We later based the Uncle Mikey jingles on the tune and kids would play it for requests on the radio. Tiny Tadani was one of the early touch-tone phone-playing experts.

"I even composed what, to

Uncle Mikey's Storytime began in Lansing, Michigan, as 90-second, stupid, modern fairy tales, says Michael W. Perry.

my knowledge, is the only pop song based completely on 7 notes ('Uncle Mikey, play my song, on the radio...'). Island Band did the music track (one of Hawaii's earliest exposures to a reggae beat) and Billy Kaui of Country Comfort did the vocals.

"Although it was one of the most technically perfect accomplishments of my life," Perry concluded, "it was an underwhelming musical success and had a short life."

K-POI

K-POI was originally KHON radio, which went on the air shortly after World War II. After a change of call letters and a shift to Hawaii's first all-rock format in 1959, the station became the top radio station in Hawaii. K-POI was Hawaii's most outrageous station. Its DJ's were called the "Poi Boys."

The Poi Boys were Ron Jacobs, Tom Moffatt, Tom Rounds, Bob Lowrey, Sam Sanford, and Donn Tyler. Ron Jacobs likened their antics to "Circus Radio."

They held "thons" and stunts that generated lots of newspaper publicity. "The first and greatest was when Tom Rounds, our news director, stayed awake in a funky department store window for 8- 1/2 days thus breaking the Guinness Book record," said Ron Jacobs.

He also recalled that "K-POI jocks hung from cars suspended from cranes, broadcast underwater from a glamorous Waikiki pool, and competed in Drum-A-Thons, Pool-A-Thons, Insult-A-Thons, donkey basketball games, and endless stuff that caught the fancy of the kids turning on to Elvis, Frankie, Ricky, and Fabian."

"For their second anniversary in 1961," Harry Soria, Jr., said "a 345-pound cake was baked. It measured 16-feet by 5-feet with the Poi Boys depicted in frosting. It fed 5,000 fans."

The Hidden Meanings of Hawaii Radio and TV Station Call Letters

MANY OF THE CALL LETTERS OF LOCAL RADIO AND TV STATIONS were chosen because they conveyed an island flavor or held some special meaning for owners or listeners. Here are some of those stations and the hidden meanings of their call letters:

KAHU – "Guardian or servant" in Hawaiian. Buddy Gordon bought 1060 AM in Hilo and changed the call letters to KHBC, which had been Hilo's first radio station.

The KAHU call letters once belonged to a Waipahu radio station (940 AM) that played country music. In the mid-1970s, they started an FM station at 92.3 on the dial - KULA "The Space Station," which played top 40 music for some time. The FM was later acquired by Heftel Broadcasting and eventually became KSSK FM.

KAIM – "Kaimuki." (95.5 FM and 870 AM) The first 4 letters of the "Kaimuki Bowl" sign were visible from the station. KAIM today is no longer in Kaimuki, and their transmitters are on Molokai. KAIM is owned by Salem Media, which also owns KGU and KHNR.

KAOI – "The best." (95.1 FM) KAOI was a cool rock station from 1977 to August 2000. It now plays Adult Contemporary. KAOI was the first FM station on a neighbor island (Maui).

KAPA – Cloth made from tree bark. The Big Island's only all Hawaiian radio at 100.3 FM in Hilo and 99.1 in Kona.

KBIG – "Big Island." This was the first FM station on the Big Island in 1980. It broadcasts at 106.1 FM in Hilo and 97.9 FM in Kona.

KCCN – Initials of founders Perry W. Carle, Dr. Ralph B. Cloward, and Jerry Neville. The original station at 1420 AM was recently sold and is now KKEA. KCCN FM 100.3 remains.

KDNN – "K'den – OK, then" FM 98.5, this was formerly KHVH FM and KKLV FM.

KDUK – "The Duke" - KPOI FM 97.5 spent a few years with those call letters as a disco station in the late 1970s.

KFVE – "Five." KHNL's sister station, "The Home Team," carries University of Hawaii games and the WB Network.

KGMB – GMB is George M. Bowls (possibly spelled Bowles), 1930s radio station chief engineer, and does not stand for Greater Mormon Broadcasting as has been rumored for decades.

KGU – Hawaii's only current three letter designation, KGU was assigned by the Department of Commerce in 1922 and was the first station on the air in Hawaii. It beat out KDYX, owned by the Star Bulletin, by 15 minutes. KDYX became KGMB radio and is now KSSK.

KHBC – Hilo Broadcasting Company. KHBC signed on at 1370 AM in 1936. It became KPUA (AM 670).

KHBZ – "Hawaii Business." 990 AM.

KHLO – "Hilo." Hilo's first AM station went on the air in 1955 at 850 AM. It is now a TV transmitter relay station for KHNL Honolulu. (Channel 2 - Hilo)

KHNL – "Honolulu." HNL is Honolulu Airport's three letter designation. It calls itself "News 8," since most people receive it over cable and not over the air, where it is Ch. 13.

KHON – "Honolulu." Ch. 2, KHON TV was originally KONA TV. KHON radio called itself "Radio Honolulu" when it went on the air in 1946. It later became K-POI.

KHNR – "Hawaii News Radio." AM 650.

KHPR – "Hawaii Public Radio." 88.1 FM.

KHVH – "Kaiser's Hawaiian Village Hotel." It once broadcast at Channel 13, then 6. It became KITV in the 1960s. The radio station still broadcasts at AM 830. It switched from music to news in 1964.

KIKI – Originally 830 AM, with 250 watts, KIKI was short for "Waikiki," which means spouting water. The founder dropped the "Wai" and used "KIKI." It is now I-94, but was once called Disco 94. Duke Kahanamoku wanted to buy it in 1954 and turn it into a Hawaiian music station but never did.

KIKU – "Chrysanthemum" in Japanese. Now at UHF Channel 20 or Oceanic Cable 9.

KINE – "Thing." FM 105.1.

KIPA – KIPA means "to entertain" in Hawaiian. 620 AM, 100.3 FM Hilo. Melvin The Mynah Bird ruled the roost in the mornings here for 22 years

KITV – "Island Television," TV channel 4.

KJMD – "JM" stands for "Jam." Maui. "Da Jam 98.3" was formerly KMVI-FM.

KJPN – "Japan." 1370 AM.

KKOA – "Koa," as in the wood. Koa can also mean "brave or fearless." 107.7 FM in Hilo.

KKON – "Kona." AM 790 on the Big Island.

KKUA – "Kokua" (help) radio. Jeff Coelho left KPOI and founded KKUA in 1973. "It was a popular phrase back then – 'I need your kokua,'" Coelho recalled. KKUA was at 690 AM in Honolulu from 1967 to about 1989. The station played country music until 1969, and then changed to top 40. The call letters were dropped when owners made it KQMQ AM. The call letters are now used by KHPR for their Maui relay station, KKUA 90.7 FM.

KLEI – "Flower wreath for the head or neck." KLEI was the call letters for a radio station in Kailua at 1130 AM. Founded by restaurateur Fred Livingston, it was the Big Island's first all-Hawaiian station. It is now a Kailua-Kona TV transmitter relay for KXPO 66 Honolulu (Pax TV).

KLHI – "Lahaina," Maui. 101.1 FM.

KLHT – "Light." 1040 AM. Calvary Chapel station goes by the moniker "K-Lite."

KLUA - Kailua-Kona. 93.9 FM in Kona and 95.9 FM in Hilo.

KMVI – "Maui Valley Isle." AM 550 and FM 98.3.

KNDI – "Candy" radio. 1270 AM. Started as an all girls rock and roll station to compete with KPOI, AM 1380, in the early 1960s.

KNUI - "Nui" means "very" or "important." Maui radio, 99.9 FM, 900 AM. KNUI AM plays Hawaiian music. The FM plays an urban contemporary music format - The Vibe 99.9.

KNWB – "New Wave Broadcasting." Hilo 97.1 FM

KOGG - Maui Airport's 3 letter code is OGG. It honors aviation legend Capt. Bertram J. Hogg, a Lihue native who flew for 41 years, mostly for Hawaiian Airlines. KOGG TV Channel 15 is a relay station for KHNL 13 Honolulu.

KONA – This was the former name of KHON TV. There is a KONA radio station on the mainland that now uses these call letters.

KORL – "Coral" – Originally 650 AM, it is now 99.5 FM - Soft Rock and Island Music. Ted Sax and Tom "Dynamite" Dancer worked here when it was Top 40. KHNR took over their AM frequency in the late 1980s.

KPIG – "The Pig." FM 93.9, now I-94 FM. Robert Abbett, the "Rabbett," Austin Vali, and a few other East Coast DJ's were brought to Hawaii to form this station in 1979. The original focus was disco.

KPOA – "Pacific Ocean Area." This Maui station is at 93.5 FM, but originally signed on in 1946 on Oahu. Many of the crates with classified information sent to the military here during the war were simply marked "POA" in black stenciled letters. The station began with used military radio equipment that came in boxes marked "POA."

K-POI - "Hawaiian Super Glue." Formerly 1380 AM and 97.5 FM ("The Rock You Live On"), K-POI is now The Big Kahuna 105.9 FM. Ron Jacobs suggested separating the K and the POI with a dash for emphasis. K-POI had been KHON radio at one point.

KPUA – Pua means "flower" in Hawaiian. AM 670 Hilo.

KPXO – TV 66. PAX is from Bud Paxson Communications. PAX also means "peace."

KQNG – AM 570, FM 93.5 Kauai. Founder John Weiser was an old movie buff and particularly liked King Kong, which was shot on Kauai. KONG was not available, so they took KQNG in 1985, putting a banana across the Q. The station also has a 60-foot inflatable gorilla.

KRTR – "Crater" 96.5 FM. It is part of the Cox Radio Hawaii group.

KSHK – "Shaka Radio." 103.3 FM, Kauai.

KSRF – Kauai 95.9 FM refers to "surf."

KSSK – The SS stands for "Super Station" (590 AM and 92.3 FM). KSSK started in 1922 as KDYX and missed being the first on the radio airwaves to KGU by only 15 minutes. KDYX changed its call letters in 1927 to KGMB.

"When Cec Heftel sold the TV station to Lee Enterprises of Davenport, Iowa, the radio station call letters had to be changed," says Doug Carlson, who worked with Heftel. "Heftel considered K-TEL for a while before settling on K59 for their 590 AM position." A few months later, it became KSSK. Ron Jacobs points out that lower frequency stations require higher towers but produce a better sound.

KTGH – "Tripler General Hospital." It was part of the "Bedside Network" of the Armed Forces Radio Service that provided programs for military and naval personnel in hospitals throughout the United States. It signed on in 1948 when Tripler moved to its current site atop Moanalua Ridge.

KTOH – "Kauai - Territory Of Hawaii," 99.9 FM, Lihue. KTOH was started by the Office of War Information during World War II at 1490 AM.

KTUH – "The University of Hawaii," (90.3 FM). From 1966-1969, the call letters were KUOH for "University of Hawaii." KTUH plays alternative music and is a training ground for its student DJs.

KUAI – "Kauai," 720 AM. A radio station in Eleele, on Kauai's west side.

KULA – 1460 AM. Harry Soria, Sr. named this station, which means "highest" in Hawaiian. It was used in the 1920s meaning "first." Johnny Almeida recorded a *Kula Hula* in the 1950s. "Kula Loaa" means "source of profit." KULA-TV went on the air in 1954, and later became KITV.

KUMU – "Kumu" can mean "teacher" in Hawaiian but station General Manager Jeff Coelho said founder John Weiser named it for the kumu fish. 1500 AM, 94.7 FM.

KVOK – "Voice of Kamehameha." Hawaii's first FM station was from Kamehameha Schools at 88.1 with 10 watts in 1953. Nowadays, that would be enough strength to reach Kamehameha Shopping Center, but back then, it could be heard as far as Schofield Barracks due to uncluttered airwaves.

KWHI – "Hawaii." 92.7 FM in Hilo.

KXME – "Extreme." 104.3 FM

KZOO – Polynesian Broadcasting, AM 1210. "Zoo" was chosen because it is a magical, fun place for children. Founded in 1963, it is the oldest and largest Japanese radio station operating outside of Japan. Hawaii programs are aired live in Japan and vice versa.

Kamehameha graduates took turns staying on Jarvis, Howland and Baker Islands in the 1930s to help the U.S. claim them. An airstrip was built for Amelia Earhart, who never arrived.

Kamehameha School boys wash and then dry their feet after recess in this 1890s picture.

Making the Grade at Hawaii's Schools and Universities

WHAT ARE SCHOOLS DOING IN A BOOK ABOUT companies? Many of our schools *are* companies. Punahou, for instance, was Hawaii's first corporation.

In the course of researching this book, we discovered that there were many fascinating stories about Hawaii's schools, of which the public had little knowledge.

Few know that School Street was named for Royal School, which had been the Chiefs' Children's School, founded in 1839. The school moved from the palace grounds in 1850 to its present site. The H-1 freeway cut the school off from School Street in the 1950s.

Iolani started in Lahaina in 1867 as Luaehu School. Saint Louis School was originally Ahuimanu College in Kaneohe (1846). It moved to the banks of Nuuanu Stream in 1883, and College Walk is named for it. Saint Louis is named for Louis IX of France, who led two crusades.

Kamehameha Schools had a program for senior girls from 1925 until 1962. A baby was lent to the school each year for them to learn child raising skills, in a cottage on Kalihi Street.

McKinley was once Honolulu High School. It began in 1865 as the Fort Street English Day School. Leeward students who wished to attend public high school 100 years ago took the train to McKinley in town.

The Academy of Arts Learning Center across from Thomas Square housed three schools at different times: The University of Hawaii started off there as the College of Agriculture and Mechanic Arts in 1907; McKinley High School was there before moving to its present site in 1923; and finally, Linekona (Lincoln) Elementary School moved in.

Here are some of those stories.

Schools in this section

Damien Memorial High School
Hawaii Pacific University
Iolani School
Kamehameha Schools
Kumon Math and Reading Centers
Lahainaluna School
Leilehua High School
Linekona Elementary
McKinley High School
Mid-Pacific Institute
Punahou School
Royal School
St. Andrew's Priory School
Saint Louis School
University of Hawaii
Waipahu High School
Waldorf School
A Timeline of Schools and Universities

Damien Memorial High School

Soon after the end of World War II, the Catholic Diocese of Honolulu saw the need for a second Catholic school on Oahu. Enrollment at Saint Louis was increasing and the Diocese decided to build another school to accommodate the growing student population.

While Saint Louis honored King Louis IX of France, who had led two crusades, Honolulu Bishop James J. Sweeney looked closer to home for inspiration. He found it in Father Damien de Veuster and decided that naming the new school in his memory would be a fitting tribute to a great man. It would also provide a strong Christian role model for young men to emulate.

The Houghtailing family in Kalihi-Palama had offered their family estate to the Diocese for a nominal price. George Washington Houghtailing, Jr. had opened the Horse Saloon on Hotel Street in the 1850s. Four of his 12 children, Olivia, Sophie, Emmeline, and Eliza passed the time making exquisite quilts.

One interesting anecdote concerned family grave sites on the property. All were relocated to cemeteries except one that could not be found. Houghtailing's wife, Eliza, had her grave hidden so that she would always be "home." School President Brother Gregory O'Donnell believes it is still somewhere on campus.

The Congregation of Christian Brothers, students, and parents volunteered to turn the land, which included four acres of taro patches and a good deal of uneven swampland into a school campus. A considerable portion of construction expertise, equipment, and materials were donated.

Damien was the 50th high school in the 50th state when it opened three years after Statehood in 1962. Tuition for the 180 boys who first enrolled was then $250 a year. Today, 450 students attend Damien.

Hawaii Pacific University

From small beginnings, Hawaii Pacific University has grown to become the leading private university in the state. Founded in 1965, HPU now has 9,000 students from over 110 countries.

HPU started as Hawaii Pacific College on Nuuanu Avenue. In 1966, it merged with Honolulu Christian College. In 1968, HPU moved downtown, and in 1992, it merged with Hawaii Loa College. "Hawaii Loa was the name of the legendary explorer who discovered the islands," says HPU professor Ken Schooland. The first class of 11 students graduated in 1972.

HPU celebtated its 40th anniversary in 2005. President Chatt Wright says that Hawaii is an easy sell. "People are excited about Hawaii. It's a beautiful place. All we have to do is tell them about the exotic, exciting, dynamic, learning center that HPU is. We're successful at attracting students from all over the world."

An interesting aside is the importance of the date September 17th to HPU and Chatt Wright. "HPU was incorporated on September 17, 1965. I joined HPU on September 17, 1972, and I was named President on September 17, 1976," Wright says. Three September 17th's is an interesting coincidence, but there's one more. Chatt Wright was born on September 17th!

Like many businesses, HPU had its share of adversity. "We were essentially bankrupt several times in the early days," Wright continues. "There were never enough financial resources. In my first year, I worried about making payroll twice a month. On one occasion, half the faculty – in those days there were ten professors – marched into my office and demanded I allocate

Chatt Wright has been HPU president since 1976.

$40,000 for library upgrades immediately. I couldn't tell them we didn't even have the cash to pay their salaries in five days unless the bank lent us some money.

"We created our sports teams in the early days to give HPU a more collegial feeling. We needed school colors so Jim Hochberg and I looked out the window of my office and saw green and blue. We made them our colors. We needed a team name too, and student Peter Burns (nephew of Governor John Burns) suggested the Sea Warriors.

"In 1972, Chaminade had about 4,000 students, and we had 200," Wright recalls. "Our goal was to pass them. There was a lack of acceptance of us in the early days. When we passed them around 1988, we felt we were finally established and accepted. We declared we were a university and no longer a college."

HPU's famous series of commercials were designed to reduce the resistance, some in the community had, to bringing in large numbers of students from Asia. "We had just created our global vision of bringing students from all over the world to HPU," Wright says, "and we wanted to let the community know that they would make a contribution to the state."

The commercials showed young men and women naming their country or community: "Kaimuki ... Waipahu ... Hilo ... Singapore ...

Author, Bob Sigall, center, and one of his classes at Hawaii Pacific University. Students from several classes researched many of the companies in this book.

Kailua … Japan … Waianae … Sweden … Maui." The students were bright, smiling, and attractive. It was obvious to viewers that they fit in with each other and the community.

Wright says HPU's intention is to provide twice the educational quality of the University of Hawaii. "We're more expensive than UH but our average class size is only 24. That allows a greater interaction between students and teachers. Only faculty teach at HPU whereas the UH often uses teaching assistants."

When the Miss Universe Pageant was held in Honolulu a few years ago, they asked UH for 72 translators. "They couldn't do it, and the organizers called us," Wright recalls. "We were able to recruit them in a couple of hours."

HPU is one of the most diverse schools in the world. "Students come from every state and from over 110 countries. All these people enrich the state intellectually. They bring different perspectives, values, and insights to the conversation," Wright believes.

—Researched by Adriana Camara

Iolani School

Iolani School was founded in Lahaina, Maui in 1863 by the Diocese of Honolulu. King Kamehameha IV and Queen Emma had invited the Church of England to come to Hawaii and start schools to liberate people from "gross superstitions and witchcraft." Anglican priest Father William R. Scott opened a school for boys in Lahaina called Luaehu School. *Luaehu* means "many and colorful."

A sister school for girls, St. Andrew's Priory School, opened four years later in 1867. In 1870, Father George Mason succeeded Scott and moved Iolani to several locations before settling into Clive Davies' former home at Nuuanu Avenue and Judd Street in 1927.

In the same year, Queen Emma bestowed on the school the name *Iolani* or "royal or heavenly hawk." Emma's husband, Alexander Liholiho Iolani, had died in 1864 at the young age of 29. The first Iolani Palace

Kamehameha IV, Alexander Liholiho Iolani, founded Iolani School with his wife, Queen Emma.

was also named for him. The name also honors Kamehameha II (Liholiho Iolani), and some say Iolani refers to the Supreme Being.

Iolani School moved in 1953 to its present Ala Wai site. The school has gradually built a multi-million dollar facility. From a small mission school for young men, founded during the reign of King Kamehameha IV, Iolani has grown into one of the largest coeducational independent schools in the nation with more than 1,700 students.

Iolani School moved from Lahaina to the corner of Nuuanu Ave. and Judd St. in 1870.

Kamehameha Schools

The royal students of the Chiefs' Children's School were taught to serve the community, and none has had as much impact as Bernice Pauahi, daughter of Maui High Chiefs Abner and Konia Paki.

The last of the royal Kamehameha line, Pauahi owned or inherited more than 300,000 acres, one-ninth of the land in Hawaii. It was valued at only $474,000 at the time of her death in 1884. Childless and with a wealthy husband, Pauahi left her estate to educate the children of Hawaii.

Charles Reed Bishop had a substantial influence in the development of the school. Much of the initial funding was his. He picked the first trustees and served as one himself.

At Kamehameha Schools' grand opening in 1887, King Kalakaua and Queen Kapiolani led a delegation of *alii*, legislators, and businessmen to the dusty plain of Palama on the outskirts of Honolulu. Four teachers and 37 students hosted the royal fete. King Kalakaua urged the students to uphold the name of Kamehameha and told them that happiness in life came from

Bernice Pauahi Bishop left 300,000 acres to the education of the children of Hawaii.

"doing any work well."

The School for Boys was located on the grounds of what is now Farrington High School and the Bishop Museum. It was comprised of a few wooden buildings until 1891 when Charles Bishop built, at his own expense, a large lava block classroom building. The Kamehameha School for Girls opened seven years later, on King Street, makai of the Boys' School, where the Kamehameha Homes are today.

The first inter-class Song Contest was held in 1920 at the School for Boys. It was held outdoors, and the stage was lit with car headlights. In 1940, KGMB began airing the contest on the radio.

In 1931, a bigger campus was desired. Only 300 could be accommodated in Palama. Locations in Kahala and Manoa were considered, but Kapalama Heights was chosen for its "remoteness from the outside world," which was considered "advantageous for study." Thirteen hundred students could be accommodated with room for expansion. The site was designed by the famous San Francisco firm of C.W. Dickey and Bertram Goodhue of New York.

Frank Midkiff, who became president of Kamehameha in 1923, instituted a unique, practical program for girls in child-rearing. A baby was lent to the school each year, and the senior girl boarders took turns caring for it. The first child, in 1925, was six month old Lillian Kimakea from the Salvation Army Home.

A house, called Keopuolani Senior Cottage, was built on Kalihi Street where Kalakaua Intermediate is today, and the students lived there for six to 12 weeks. They took turns cooking, cleaning, and taking care of the baby. This remarkable program, totally unthinkable today, continued until 1962.

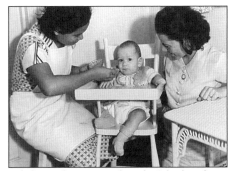

A special assignment came to Kamehameha Schools in 1935. The U.S. Government wanted to declare three Pacific equatorial islands U.S. territory, but had to have them occupied for three years to do so.

A baby was lent to Kamehameha Schools each year from 1925 until 1962 for the senior girls to learn child rearing. Pictured here is baby Kinney Rankin.

Kamehameha graduates volunteered for the secret mission, not knowing what they were getting into until they were out at sea. "Three boys from Kamehameha and the military personnel were left on each island for three month periods with no contact with the outside world," says school archivist Janet Zisk. "When they were picked up, the military guys were going out of their minds with boredom. The Kamehameha boys had a great time."

Jarvis, Howland, and Baker Islands were eventually declared U.S. Territory, however, there were consequences. Two of the Kamehameha boys were killed when the Japanese attacked the island on December 8, 1941. They were buried at Schofield Barracks until 2003 when they were moved to the Hawaii State Veterans Cemetery in Kaneohe.

During World War II, the military occupied much of Kamehameha Schools and used it for a hospital, mostly for noncombatant medical needs. Over a dozen babies were born on campus during that period. Students served as nurses and orderlies.

The first FM radio broadcast in the state came from Kamehameha Schools in 1953. KVOK (Voice of Kamehameha) was found at 88.1 on the FM dial. With a powerful 10 watts, it could be heard as far away as Schofield Barracks, due to uncluttered airwaves back then.

Kamehameha has emphasized development of the whole individual, more than any other school in the state. Besides the typical school studies, Kamehameha students were taught practical job and homemaking skills, such as tailoring, dressmaking, cooking, agriculture, printing, electronics, bookbinding, nursing, and welding. They studied etiquette, ethics, religion, music, Hawaiian language and culture. In the 1920s, Kamehameha operated a 300- acre farm and dairy in Hahaione Valley.

From the dusty plains of Kalihi to the cool campus of Kapalama Heights, Kamehameha has grown from a *poor boy's school* to the wealthiest, richest learning experience in the

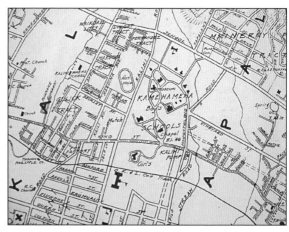

Farrington High School occupies the former Kamehameha Schools site on King and Kalihi Streets in this 1918 map.

state. Despite recent travails with trustees, Kamehameha has stayed focused on its vision of providing the best education for Hawaiian children in the state.

Imua Kamehameha.

Kumon Math and Reading Centers

The Kumon Method of learning was developed in Japan in 1954 by Toru Kumon, a high school math teacher whose son was struggling with second grade arithmetic. Kumon created a series of worksheets for his son to complete after school. Through daily practice and a commitment to mastering each concept, his son was able to solve differential equations and integral calculus problems by the time he was in the sixth grade.

Kumon Centers are independently owned and operated by the instructors. The first Kumon Center in North America was opened in New York in 1974. Currently, there are more than 1,300 franchised Kumon Centers in the U.S. and Canada, and over 2.5 million students are enrolled worldwide.

Lahainaluna School

Lahainaluna is the oldest school west of the Rockies. Established in 1831 as a seminary for young men, its purpose was to train teachers. In 1831, there were only nine other high schools in the United States.

Situated two miles mauka of the town at an elevation of 600 feet, *Lahainaluna* means above Lahaina. Lahainaluna sits on the largest campus in the state: more than 600 acres. There are two dormitories for boarding students, 33 teachers, and 600 students. A farm grows 20 different types of fruits and vegetables, raises cattle, chickens, and pigs.

The first newspaper in Hawaii and the first west of the Rocky Mountains was published at Lahainaluna in 1834 as *Ka Lama Hawaii* (Hawaiian Luminary). The print shop was Hale Pa`i, and it still remains on campus as the only original building.

In 1923, Lahainaluna became part of the territorial school sys-

The oldest school in the islands is Lahainaluna School, founded in 1831.

tem, and for the first time, girls were admitted.

Lahainaluna has some unique traditions. Twice a year, before graduation on Memorial Day and before the football season, the giant "L" on Mt. Ball (Puu Pa`u Pa`u) is limed by the boarding students. On graduation night, flaming torches light cans of kerosene around the "L"- a sight that can be seen from miles away and never forgotten.

Lahainaluna has the only school song in the state that is written and sung in Hawaiian. It resembles a traditional Hawaiian chant. The senior class also writes and sings a class song each year at graduation.

Among the first students at the school was David Malo (1793-1853) who published the book *Hawaiian Antiquities*. He served as superintendent of Hawaii's schools from 1841 to 1845. When he died in 1853, his body was entombed on Puu Pa`u Pa`u, and students clean his grave site twice a year.

Leilehua High School

Leilehua High School was once on the grounds of Schofield Barracks. Begun in 1924 as a branch of McKinley High, it was originally named Schofield High and Grammar School.

The school was built near what had been King Kalakaua's hunting grounds. In 1926, the name was changed to Schofield and Leilehua High Schools for the abundant Lehua trees in the area. The school colors, green and gold, represent the green of the pineapple fields and the gold of its fruit.

When World War II broke out, Schofield and Leilehua High Schools moved to three separate areas in Wahiawa. The present site was built in 1949.

Schofield Barracks was founded in 1908 and named for Lt. General John M. Schofield, who first saw the possibility of establishing a naval base at Pearl Harbor in 1872. An echo of its Schofield history remains today. Leilehua and the Army have the same mascot – the mule.

Linekona School

Linekona is the Hawaiian word for Lincoln. At the turn of the last century, the Fort Street School divided into Kaiulani Elementary and Honolulu High School. The high school outgrew several locations and moved to the former Thomas Maertens' mansion across from Thomas Square.

When McKinley High School moved to its new King Street location, Lincoln (Linekona) Elementary School began. The University of Hawaii was founded at the rear of the building in 1908 and was called, at the time, the College of Agriculture and Mechanic Arts. It moved to Manoa in 1912.

From 1957 until 1973, Linekona was a school for children with learning disabilities and for classes in English as a second language. Since 1986, the Academy of Arts has had a lease to use the site as an education center.

Few sites in Hawaii can claim to having housed an elementary school, high school, and a college.

McKinley High School

McKinley High School was founded during the U.S. Civil War in 1865. It was originally known as the Fort Street English

McKinley High School began in 1865 as the Fort Street English Day School.

Day School and was established by Reverend Maurice B. Beckwith. Classes were held in the basement of the Fort Street Church. It was the only public school in Hawaii at the time and its initial enrollment was just 40 students.

The Board of Education assumed the responsibility for the school in 1869 and moved it to a new stone building off the corner of Fort and School Streets. Beckwith continued to conduct classes and acted as principal until his retirement in 1879.

The student body population suddenly rose from 78 boys and 38 girls to a total of 249 after students from St. Alban's College enrolled in the school. The cost of education was just 50 cents a week, a bargain compared to the five dollars a month other schools charged.

The school moved in 1895 into Princess Ruth's palace, where Central Middle School is today, and was renamed Honolulu High School.

Marion M. Scott, who would later be called "the Father of McKinley High School," became head of Fort Street School in 1881. Principal Scott brought with him new discipline and proven teaching methods. Fort Street School had become the government school of the kingdom by 1888. The work of the primary division rivaled the best in the United States.

In 1895, the student body had outgrown the site, and the school moved to the palace of Princess Ruth Keelikolani, Central Intermediate School's present location. Princess Ruth, in choosing a design for a palace had unknowingly selected plans for a schoolhouse. Because of this, the Board of Education purchased it for $30,000 and used it as a school. The school was renamed Honolulu High School.

Enrollment continued to grow, and in 1901, the former palace could no longer handle Honolulu High School's student body. The Board of Education decided to build a new campus on Victoria Street at Thomas Square. At the same time, news of President William McKinley's death arrived. When the building was finished in 1907, Honolulu High School was renamed McKinley High School. The school honors the late president for his influence in the annexation of the Hawaiian Islands to the United States.

In 1907, Honolulu High School moved to Victoria Street across from Thomas Square and was re-named McKinley High School for the president who supported the Annexation of Hawaii.

Dillingham's railroad made it possible for young people outside of Honolulu to get to McKinley, and enrollment climbed every decade.

By 1913, enrollments had jammed the school beyond capacity, and plans were made to build a new campus on McKinley High School's present King Street location. Construction started in 1922. In 1923, the new campus of President William McKinley High School was unveiled.

When World War II broke out, everything changed in the islands. McKinley students responded enthusiastically and quickly. Many young men volunteered at the nearest recruiting station. The school openly welcomed students from Saint Louis School, which was being used as an Army hospital.

Mid-Pacific Institute

The beginnings of Mid-Pacific Institute can be traced to 1864 when the U.S. Civil War was raging. Originally called Kawaihao Seminary, it began in the private home of Dr. and Mrs. Luther Gulick. Gulick was the son of missionaries who arrived in 1828. The school was originally for Hawaiian girls, and funding the first year was $100.

Among the many early supporters of the Ragged School, as it was affectionately called, were William R. Castle and Mother Rice, wife of William Harrison Rice, an early missionary.

In 1908, Kawaihao Seminary joined with Mills Institute to form Mid-Pacific Institute. Mills Institute had begun in the home of Mr. and Mrs. Francis Williams Damon on Chaplain Lane, off Fort Street, in 1892.

Francis Damon was the son of the Reverend Samuel C. Damon and Julia Mills Damon. Mills Institute was originally a school for Chinese boys because Damon believed they could play an important role in international understanding between Asia and the west. Those that could afford to, paid for their education. The poor, however, were not turned away.

In 1908, these two schools joined forces and located to the present 32-acre site in Manoa. The site was chosen because of an artesian spring on the property, and its accessibility to public transportation, the trolley.

Two smaller schools also joined – The Okamura School and the Korean School for Girls. Dr. Syngman Rhee, the president in exile of the Republic of Korea, lived in Honolulu at one time and was the Chairman of the Board for the Korean School for Girls.

On December 7, 1941, when all schools were temporarily closed, Mid-Pacific Institute housed evacuees from Hickam Field. Punahou was taken over by the Army Corps of Engineers. Kamehameha, Saint Louis, and Farrington became hospitals. Most of the other schools became barracks and military offices.

The Hawaiian Pineapple Company housed 500 of their neighbor island female workers at Mid-Pac during the summers of 1944 and 1945.

Punahou School

New England Congregational missionaries founded Punahou School in 1841. The name Punahou was derived from the land area known as Ka Punahou. It was given to the Reverend Hiram

Bingham, pastor of Kawaihao Church, by Oahu Governor Boki and his wife Liliha at the urging of Queen Kaahumanu.

The original land area stretched from where Central Union Church now stands, back to where Oahu and University Avenues intersect, encompassing 224 acres. *Ka Punahou* means "the new spring," referring to an artesian spring in the center of the campus where a famous lily pond exists. King Kamehameha the Great reportedly swam in the pond.

Queen Kaahumanu urged Liliha to donate the parcel of land known at Ka Punahou to the missionaries for a school.

Early missionary children were often sent back to New England for education, causing great family pain. A school in Hawaii was essential. The first school the missionaries founded on Oahu, though, was the Chiefs' Children's School (now Royal School) in 1839. Punahou came two years later.

The Reverend Daniel Dole (father of Sanford Dole) was the first teacher and school president. In the first year, 34 children enrolled at a cost of $36 per school year. Dole Street was named for Daniel Dole.

Several names adorned the school in its 163-year history, including Ka Punahou (1849), Punahou School and Oahu College (1853), and Oahu College (1857). In 1934, the name was changed for the last time to Punahou School. The school colors, buff and blue, were adopted to reflect the colors of the sand and sea.

In 1941, Punahou celebrated its centennial, but events would challenge the school's very existence. Within 24 hours of the bombing of Pearl Harbor, the Army Corps of Engineers occupied the school, and classes had to be moved to private homes and the University of Hawaii.

Punahou School in 1860. Punahou means the "new spring."

A rumor that still goes around to this day is that the Army was sent to occupy the University of Hawaii as a base. They came to Punahou and thought it *was* the University and occupied it for the duration of the war, refusing to admit they had made a mistake. The rumor, however, is untrue. The Army had planned months earlier to use the school in case war broke out. The trustees leased Punahou to the Army for $10,000 a month. The University charged Punahou $2,500 a month in rent.

Punahou School is famous for its night-blooming cereus hedge, a cactus that covers the walls on Punahou St. and Wilder Ave. Mrs. Bingham originally planted them in 1836. Its extraordinary blossoms come out for one night only in late summer.

Today Punahou has 3,700 students, making it the largest independent college preparatory school in the U.S. Tuition now exceeds $13,700 a year. Four hundred students graduate each year, and 99 percent go on to college.

Hiram Bingham III, grandson of Punahou's founder, discovered Machu Picchu in 1911.

Hiram Bingham III, grandson of the school's founder, became an explorer and is famous for discovering Machu Picchu, an ancient Inca city high in the mountains of Peru. He is also the inspiration for the movie character Indiana Jones.

Royal School

In 1837, the *alii* of the Kingdom of Hawaii asked the Sandwich Isles Mission to create a school for their children, thus beginning the Hawaiian Chiefs' Children's School, now known as Royal School.

Amos Starr Cooke (1810-1871) and his wife Juliette Montague Cooke (1812-1896) were the founders and teachers of the school, which opened in 1839. Their mission was to instill the virtues of honor, fair play, and the habits of industry.

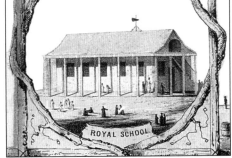

The famous students included David Kalakaua, Lydia Liliuokalani, William Lunalilo, Bernice Pauahi, Victoria Kamamalu, Lot Kapuaiwa

School Street is named for Royal School, founded in 1839 as the Chiefs' Children's School.

Amos and Juliet Montague Cooke's students were all the kings and queens from Kamehameha IV on, as well as Bernice Pauahi.

(Kamehameha V), Alexander Liholiho (Kamehameha IV), and his future wife, Emma Rooke.

The royal students lived in the Cooke's home, which was mauka of Iolani Palace and Hotel Street, near Richards, about where Iolani Barracks is today. In addition, the Cookes had six children, and all the students brought servants or *kahu* to care for them.

It is interesting to note that the missionaries created this school for Hawaii's royalty before establishing a school for their own children. Punahou was founded in 1841, two years later.

"Mrs. Cooke was the mother and presiding genius of Royal School," said Martha Chamberlain. "All 16 children, varying in age from two to 13 years, she had to love, control, and train, besides raising a family of her own. Her affection for every one was deep and sincere. They invariably called her 'mother' and none could tell the unwritten history of how much they acknowledged their love and indebtedness to her."

Besides their studies, the students had the opportunity to meet with visiting dignitaries and the leaders of the community. They made trips to the heiau on the slope of Diamond Head, then known as Diamond Point. They rode horses on the new Pali Road, which opened in 1845, and visited the new home of Captain Dominis (now Washington Place). They took the King's best schooner to Molokai, Maui, and the Big Island.

One of the major dramas at the school was the romance of Bernice Pauahi and Charles Reed Bishop. Pauahi's mother and father (Konia and Abner Paki), and her Hawaiian friends wanted her to marry Prince Lot, who became Kamehameha V. She met with Lot and told him that she would marry him but would be unhappy for she did not love him, nor did he love her. Lot then released her from their childhood promise. Lot never married.

Bishop was the Collector General of Customs and called on Bernice nearly every evening. He was "in every way worthy of her heart and hand," said Juliette Cooke.

Despite her parent's opposition, Bernice Pauahi married Charles Bishop on June 4, 1850 in the parlor at Royal School. Paki and Konia refused to attend. The ceremony was small. Only six people attended.

Cooke descendent, Anna Derby Blackwell remembers Robert Midkiff pointing out that "missionary children were raised to do good, and did so, to the extent that the only major charitable foundations in Hawaii that were not founded by missionary descendants were McInerny, Watumull, and lately Weinberg. All the rest have at least one, and sometimes several, missionary ancestors.

"Midkiff's other point was that the royal pupils at the Chiefs' Children's School were all taught to be charitable. The results are: The Lunalilo Home (for the *kapuna*); Queen Liliuokalani Trust (for children and families); Kapiolani Hospital, started by King Kalakaua and Queen Kapiolani; The Queen's Hospital, begun by Kamehameha IV and Queen Emma; and the grandmother of them all, Bishop Estate/Kamehameha Schools, for the children of Hawaii," Blackwell points out.

After 11 years, the Cookes retired from the school. The school then moved to its present site in 1851, on the slopes of Puowaina (Punchbowl), and the enrollment was opened to the community. It had been affectionately called the Royal School since its beginning, but the name was formally changed in 1846. School Street is named for Royal School.

Amos Cooke went into business with Samuel Castle. Castle & Cooke became one of the Big Five, and was heavily involved in sugar cane and many other businesses.

St. Andrew's Priory School

St. Andrew's Priory School was founded in 1867, by Queen Emma of Hawaii and Mother Sellon of the Anglican Church of England as a school for girls. Queen Emma picked the name St. Andrew because her husband, King Kamehameha IV had died on his feast day, November 30, 1864, at age 29, mourning the death of his son, Albert, a year earlier. A priory is a convent or monastery.

Queen Emma picked the school's name because her husband, Alexander Liholiho, Kamehameha IV, died on the Feast Day of St. Andrew at the age of 29.

St. Andrew

Queen Emma was concerned about the educational needs of the young women of Hawaii. Her mission of establishing a girls' school in Honolulu took her to England and the Archbishop of Canterbury. Under his authority, the Sisters of the Church of England returned with Queen Emma to begin their work.

St. Andrew's Priory School for Girls first opened its doors on Ascension Day in 1867. The Episcopal Church of the United States took jurisdiction of the Priory School in 1902.

The companion school for boys was Iolani School, founded initially in Lahaina four years earlier in 1863. According to alumnus Fran Wakashige, St. Andrew's Priory and Iolani would support each other. "When Iolani needed a homecoming queen and court or cheerleaders, St. Andrew's would provide them. When we needed boys for a dance, we'd call them. Actually we also called Saint Louis, Kamehameha, and Mid-Pac."

It was at one of those dances that she met sophomore Roy Wakashige, from Mid-Pac, whom she later married.

Saint Andrew was the first of Jesus' twelve apostles and the brother of Simon (later the apostle Peter). Andrew was a Galilean fisherman and a disciple of John the Baptist. After Jesus' death, he preached Christianity among the Scythians of Central Asia, thus becoming the patron saint of Russia. He was also the patron saint of Greece, and fishermen.

Prince Albert Leopapa was the last child born to Hawaii's royalty. He was named for England's Queen Victoria's husband, Albert.

Andrew was crucified in Greece around 64 AD on an X-shaped cross, the form of which became known as Saint Andrew's Cross. In the 8th century, relics of Andrew were taken to Saint Andrews in Scotland, so he became the patron saint of that country as well. A white Saint Andrew's cross on a blue field is the national flag of Scotland. His cross can also be found on Hawaii's flag along with the crosses of St. George and St. Patrick.

Saint Louis School

In 1846, missionary priests of the Sacred Hearts founded Ahuimanu College just north of Kaneohe for the education of Hawaiian boys. *Ahuimanu* means "a gathering of birds."

In 1881, with the shift of population to Honolulu, the Catholic Bishop Louis Maigret invited the Roman Catholic Society of Mary, from Dayton, Ohio to come to Hawaii. In 1883, the Marianists arrived to administer the school in its new location at Kamekela on the Ewa bank of Nuuanu Stream and Beretania Street. The path entering the school was named College Walk.

According to the late Brother Edward Gomez, formerly the vice-president of the Marianist Center of Hawaii, the school's name was changed to Saint Louis College to honor Bishop Maigret, whose patron saint was Saint Louis (King Louis IX of France).

King Louis IX was born in 1214 and ascended the French throne at age 12. Louis IX led two crusades and brought the Crown of Thorns of Christ from the Eastern Emperor in Constantinople and enshrined it in the Sainte Chapelle in Paris. The King died during the second crusade at the age of 56 in Tunis. The city of Saint Louis, Missouri is also named for him.

Bishop Louis Maigret's patron saint was St. Louis (King Louis IX of France) who died leading two crusades.

In 1923, the school bought 204 acres of Kalaepohaku (the "rock pile") in Kaimuki (the "red ground oven") from the Bishop Estate for $65,000. A few years later, 80 acres were sold to a contractor/realtor who developed Saint Louis Heights. The $100,000 he paid was used to retire the debt on the new school buildings.

Many of the streets in the lower part of St. Louis Heights bear the names of priests or brothers who were original teachers or

Saint Louis School began as Ahuimanu College near Temple Valley in 1846.

administrators at the school: Gulston, Bertram, Robert, Maigret, Libert, Herman, and Frank. Also, Kanalui Street is the Hawaiian word for Saint Louis while Kaminaka Drive is the Hawaiian word for Chaminade.

Originally, Dole Street was to be the entrance to Saint Louis College. The city took too long

Saint Louis College moved to the banks of Nuuanu Stream, between Beretania and Kukui Streets in 1883.

to extend the street, so the school decided to move the entrance to Waialae Avenue, which necessitated the building of a bridge across Palolo Stream. Classes began in September 1928.

In commemoration of the original College Walk, the entrance to the present Waialae Avenue campus was officially named College Walk in 1931. Today, few remember or refer to it by its designated name.

In 1950, the school responded to the desire for a Catholic college in Hawaii, and the decision was made to eliminate the elementary grades of Saint Louis College. In 1955, Saint Louis Junior College opened, and grades 9-12 became Saint Louis High School.

In 1957, the two-year college became a four year co-educational college. The name changed to Chaminade College of Honolulu. In 1977, the college expanded its academic programs and became Chaminade University of Honolulu.

In 1979, Saint Louis added a middle school (seventh and eighth grades) and changed its name in 1986 from Saint Louis High School to Saint Louis School.

Chaminade University is named for Father William Joseph Chaminade (1769 – 1850), a priest who lived and worked during the French Revolution. He founded the Society of Mary,

Saint Louis College under construction in Kaimuki in 1928. A bridge over Waialae Stream had to be built when the city failed to extend Dole Street, the planned entrance, in time.

whose philosophy and educational pedagogy guides Saint Louis School and Chaminade University.

Saint Louis School has about 800 students while Chaminade has 900 day students and about 2,000 part-time and evening students. Among its alumnae, Saint Louis counts former Governor John Burns, Honolulu Mayor Neil Blaisdell, First Hawaiian Bank CEO Walter Dods, Judge David Ezra, and a multitude of other community leaders.

University of Hawaii

At the time of Annexation, all states and territories except Hawaii and Alaska had colleges. Many at the time felt Hawaii was exotic and remote, but, without a college, it would not be taken seriously.

Over 190 schools existed in the islands at the time, but families had to send their children to the mainland for college.

The Morrill Act of 1890 offered territories about $500,000 annually (in today's dollars) for colleges of "agriculture and mechanic arts."

The 1901 legislature took up the issue and proposed building the new college on the Big Island in Mountain View. Two years later, Lahainaluna was considered. A committee appointed by Governor Carter focused on Honolulu because of its many scientists, engineers and research facilities.

With five students and 12 staff, the College of Agriculture and Mechanic Arts of the Territory of Hawaii opened in 1908 at a temporary site on Young Street near Thomas Square.

The college moved into the 15 room Maerten's House next to McKinley High School, where the Academy of Arts Learning Center is today. McKinley moved to its present campus in 1923.

The college's name was shortened in 1911 to what everyone was calling it - the College of Hawaii. Four seniors made up the first graduating class in 1912, held on the steps of Hawaii Hall at the new campus in Manoa.

In 1948, the University of Hawaii centered around the Quadrangle, next to University Avenue, left.

In 1919, William Kwai Fong Yap successfully petitioned the legislature to broaden the college's mission beyond agriculture and mechanics, and it became the University of Hawaii in 1920.

From the beginning the University prohibited racial discrimination, unlike many private schools. A 1922 survey showed half the enrollment was of Asian ancestry, a third was Caucasian, and one tenth was part Hawaiian.

The original campus is referred to as "the quadrangle." The quad is bounded by Hawaii Hall, Gartley Hall, George Hall, Dean Hall, and Crawford Hall. All were built between 1922 and 1938 in a Neo-Georgian style.

The Territorial Normal School, founded in 1895 to train teachers, merged with the University in 1933 during the depression. The Varney Circle fountain was paid for by the Normal School's class of 1929 to honor long-time history teacher Ada Susan Varney.

A minor rebellion was launched on a particularly humid day in 1946 when four teachers refused to wear the standard coat and tie and donned aloha shirts instead. President Sinclair tried to discourage the undignified attire, but that only caused more faculty to join the insurrection. Aloha shirts, worn mainly by tourists up until that time, became standard dress on the campus.

U.S. Senator Lyndon Johnson suggested the creation of a Center for Cultural and Technical Interchange between East and West in 1959. Johnson was the keynote speaker in 1961 at its groundbreaking ceremonies.

World class architect I. M. Pei designed several of the buildings in the complex, including Jefferson Hall, the Kennedy Theatre, Hale Manoa and Hale Kuahine, both residential dormitories.

Today, the University of Hawaii system includes ten campuses: UH Manoa, UH Hilo, UH West Oahu, and seven community colleges: Kapiolani, Honolulu, Windward, and Leeward on Oahu; Kauai, Maui, and Hawaii on the neighbor islands.

Waipahu High School

Waipahu was the first school on the Leeward side. It was founded in 1938 and served students from Aiea, Pearl City, Waipahu, Ewa, Nanakuli, and Waianae. The high school was initially located on the present site of Waipahu Elementary School. In 1969, the school moved to its present site to accommodate a larger student body.

High school students from Leeward Oahu originally had to take the OR&L train to McKinley, a long commute. They were able to transfer to Waipahu when it opened in 1938.

The school mascot, the Marauder, was named for a U.S. B-26 airplane that crashed on the school campus. The mascot was meant to rally support for our armed forces. Today, though, the Marauder has evolved and refers to a pirate.

Waldorf School

Waldorf School opened in Honolulu in 1961. It was then known as Mohala Pua School. Waldorf is part of a worldwide movement that began in Germany in 1919. The Waldorf Astoria Cigarette Company's owner, Emil Molt, asked Rudolf Steiner to design a school that would prepare individuals to create a peaceful and just society.

Dr. Steiner, born in Austria in 1861, was a leading figure in Europe on a variety of topics, including philosophy, religion, history, science, agriculture, and art.

Steiner saw an opportunity to design a system of education that would both meet the needs of the individual and be a model for education. In the autumn of 1919, the first Waldorf school opened in Stuttgart, Germany, with 12 teachers and 175 pupils. Most of the students were the children of Molt's employees.

It is a school in which art, music, and handcrafts are just as important as reading, writing, and arithmetic. Each day includes activities for the hands and heart, as well as the head. The teacher and class remain together for the first eight years. The Waldorf School's explicit purpose is to create free, independent, creative, moral, and happy human beings.

Today, there are over 130 Waldorf schools across the U.S. with over 10,000 students. The Waldorf school system has more than 700 schools across the globe.

Marjorie Spock, author and sister of Dr. Benjamin Spock, said that a "Waldorf education enables young people to be in love with the world as the world should be loved."

A Timeline of Hawaii's Schools and Universities

THE FIRST SCHOOLS WERE ESTABLISHED OVER 170 YEARS AGO in Hawaii. Here's a timeline of some of the more well-known schools in the state, with founding dates and original names.

Year Est. Current Name (Original Names)

1831	Lahainaluna High School (Lahainaluna Seminary)
1833	Oahu Charity School
1836	Hilo Boarding School for Hawaiian Boys
1839	Royal School (Chiefs' Children's School)
1841	Punahou School (Oahu College)
1846	Saint Louis School (Ahuimanu College)
1848	St. Anthony Schools (Maui)
1863	Iolani School (Luaehu School), Heald College (in California)
1864	Mid-Pacific Institute (Kawaihao Seminary and Mills Institute)
1865	McKinley High School (Fort Street English Day School, Honolulu High School)
1867	St. Andrew's Priory School
1869	St. Joseph School (Hilo)
1881	Wilcox Elementary School (Kauai)
1882	Waimea High School (Kauai)
1883	Kapaa High School (Kapaa English School)
1887	Kamehameha School for Boys, Kahuku School
1895	Territorial Normal School
1896	Maemae School
1902	Moiliili Language School
1904	Kalaheo School (Kauai)
1905	Hilo High School (Hilo Union School)
1907	University of Hawaii (College of Agriculture and Mechanic Arts), Pearl City School (Lehua Elementary)
1909	Sacred Hearts Academy, Hawaii Military Academy
1913	Kauai High School
1914	Waialua High (Mokuleia School, Andrew E. Cox School)

1918	Hanahauoli School
1920	Hawaiian Mission Academy
1924	Saint Francis School, Leilehua High School
1925	Lanakila School
1927	Maryknoll School
1928	Kauai Community College (Kalaheo Vocational School), Waialae Elementary School
1930	St. Patrick School
1931	St. Theresa School
1932	Roosevelt High School
1936	Farrington High School, Cathedral School
1937	Epiphany School
1938	Waipahu High School
1939	Baldwin High School
1941	Kaimuki High School
1946	Star of the Sea School
1948	Our Redeemer Lutheran School
1949	Hawaii Baptist Academy, Hawaii Preparatory Academy, Holy Nativity School, Hongwanji Mission School, Hawaii Business College
1951	Castle High School
1952	Hanalani School
1954	Kailua High School
1955	Brigham Young University Hawaii (Church College of Hawaii)
1956	St. Mark Lutheran School, Holy Family Catholic Academy, Holy Trinity School
1957	Chaminade University (St. Louis Junior College), Radford High School
1961	Aiea High School, Le Jardin Windward Oahu Academy, Honolulu Waldorf School, Academy of the Pacific (Honolulu Junior Academy)
1962	James Campbell High School, La Pietra–Hawaii School for Girls, Damien Memorial High School
1964	Seabury Hall, St. Elizabeth School
1965	Hawaii Pacific University, St. John Vianney School
1969	ASSETS School
1975	Kaiser High School
1986	Hoala School
1988	Lutheran High School of Hawaii

Miriam Likelike, left, looks very much like her young daughter, Princess Victoria Kaiulani in this photo, taken about 1887.

Games, Lists and Fun Stuff

YOU'VE READ THEIR STORIES, and you've walked their aisles and heard about them for years. But how well do you really know these companies and organizations? Here are some quizzes and lists to test your knowledge. Answers are on page 390.

Quizzes

How Well do you know Hawaii Companies?
How Well do you know Hawaii Retailers?
How Well do you know Hawaii Restaurants
 and Drive-Ins? Part 1 and 2
How Well Do You Know Fast Food?
How Well Do You Know Hawaii Schools?
How Well do you know Hawaii Punahou School?
How Well do you Know Hawaii Radio and
 TV Stations?
How Well Do You Know Hawaii's Royalty?
What Was There Before?
What Does Their Name Mean?
Formerly Known as . . .
How Well Do You Know Hawaii Slogans?

Lists

Businesses and Organizations Associated with Royalty
Hawaii companies you might not expect to have branches
 or franchises outside the state
Signature Dish – Specialty of the House
Hawaii Company Slogans
Upcoming Anniversaries
Gone but Not Forgotten

Answers to the quizzes start on page 390.

How Well Do You Know Hawaii Companies?

IF YOU'VE BEEN IN HAWAII A LONG TIME, YOU MIGHT KNOW which companies fit these clues. Answers are on page 390.

1   Robert's Hawaii's rabbit is waving goodbye to a former competitor, which has left the state. Who is the rabbit waving to?

2   This company was indirectly named by the Pope. It was founded by Catholic nuns who came to work with Father Damien on Molokai and has been headed by seven female CEOs in its 70-year history.

3   His innovation was canning, but his second cousin urged him not to use the family name because it was associated with politics and religion. Instead, he used HAPCO. It was only after his death that Castle & Cooke, the new owners, used his family name as the brand name.

4   This company was founded by the Dairyman's Association in 1897. The company name came from a 1901 employee contest to name their butter.

5   A nurse at Queen's founded this organization in 1938. Dues were $3 a month and entitled members to $300 a year in services.

6   The hotel's name means the "surface of the sea." It was built near Chinn Ho's family's duck and rice pond. Ho's company, Capital Investment, got its start at McKinley High School in the 1920s to pay for a broken window.

7   The name literally means "white tree store," and it was founded in 1662 in Edo, Japan as a drapery and notions store.

8   He sold his company only to find out he also had sold his name. Now, he does business as "Uncle Noname" and "Uncle Wally."

9   Its logo has two intertwined "E's" with a crown atop. It opened on Fort Street in 1864 with 18 beds. The legislature had no money, so royalty raised the $13,000 needed to get started.

10   Which hotel, now in Waikiki, once stood at Hotel and Richards Streets in the 1870s? It was Hawaii's first grand hotel.

11   Ricky named this company after himself and his friend "Crazy Arab."

12   This airline was originally named Trans Pacific Airways, or TPA. People affectionately referred to it as "The People's Airline."

13   This company, owned by the Fukunaga family, was once called Waialua Garage, a two-car service station in Waialua.

14   This company, in the entertainment business, was named for the fruit that fell on the roof of the founder's home in Tantalus.

15   Martin Denny and his band played at the Hilton Hawaiian Village's Shell Bar in 1956. During one song, some bullfrogs in the pond next to them would croak. When the song was over, they would stop. Denny repeated the song later, and the frogs joined in again. Some of the guys in the band were inspired to make birdcalls. The song they created that night sold several million copies. What was its name?

16   This company got its start with a 50-room hotel on Seaside Avenue in 1947 where the Waikiki Twin Theatres once stood. The name came from the club that once resided on the beach between the Moana and the Royal Hawaiian Hotels.

17   The Hawaiian name means "diamond" but the hotel is now owned by the Japanese. Robert Louis Stevenson used to hang out under the hau tree there. Its slogan is the "best hidden secret in Waikiki."

How Well do you Know Hawaii Retailers?

YOUR FIRST SHOES, YOUR FAVORITE ALOHA SHIRT or muu muu, the furniture in your home and almost every thing you own was purchased at a local retail store. You've walked their aisles since you were a small kid, but how well do you really know Hawaii retailers? Answers are on page 390.

1   This store chain stumbled into having locations close to each other accidentally. They opened one store nearby another that was soon to close. But while both were open, they noticed sales did not drop at the one that was closing and sales at the new store started matching sales at the older one. Sidney Kosasa wanted a name that was easy to remember.

2   Brothers Joe and Tom opened their first discount store in California in 1938. When they came to Hawaii in 1954, there were lines around the block. Their 400 plus stores on the mainland dwarf their 32 in Hawaii.

3   Heinrich Hackfeld opened a business on Fort Street in 1848 that grew into Hawaii's largest sugar producer and largest retailer. They were forced to sell the company when World War I broke out, and the retail side's name was changed to this.

4   Wook Moon founded this company in 1939 as an art and antiquities store on Fort Street. The company name does not come from a person or a dynasty but means "a room that one can enter and acquire cultural knowledge." World War II cut the store off from its suppliers, and it switched to designing its own unique jewelry. They once had many stores, but all were closed by 1999.

5   C.K. Ai founded this company 104 years ago. It burned down in its first 6 months and again 20 years later. To bring supplies to Hawaii, they built their own ship, the fastest five-masted schooner in the Pacific.

6   Retail guru Glenn Kaya brought this company to Hawaii in 1958. You had to be a member to come into the store. They leased out space to businesses that ran its various departments. ABC Stores, Wong's Drapery, C.S. Wo, Mid-Pacific Lumber, Kim Chow and Hauoli were all tenants of this company, which closed in 1993.

7   Most of us remember this company as a fabric and dry goods store in Ala Moana Center, but 75 years ago, the store was known and loved around the world as Hawaii's best shirt maker. Chotaru Miyamoto ran advertisements using pidgin and broken English that locals found cute and touching. They mailed them to friends all over the world where they were reprinted in newspapers and magazines, and wealthy visitors beat a path to his door. What was their name?

8   This company started as a Lahaina dive shop, but when they discovered Hawaiian Black Coral, they moved into retailing. Now they are the largest coral jewelry manufacturer in the state.

9   "The Brooks Brothers of the Pacific" opened at Ala Moana Center as one of its first tenants. They are best known for developing the reverse print aloha shirt.

10   The founder of this store struck it rich in the Alaskan Gold Rush and saved enough money to start a shoe store in Seattle in 1901. By 1960, it was the largest shoe store in the world, but now it has expanded into clothing and general merchandise.

11   Shopping on Oahu used to be in the downtown area. When Lowell Dillingham proposed building a 100-acre City of Tomorrow retail mall at Ala Moana, downtown businesses were reluctant to move, until this store made a commitment. It began as a watch company in Chicago in 1886.

12   This company takes its name from the wooden room that housed a ship's electronic equipment. Their original customers in 1920 were ship's engineers, but now they sell electronic gadgets to everyone.

13   This fashion giant, owned by the Gap, used to be called the Gap Warehouse.

14   Zenpan was too small to work the sugar fields so he was assigned to the job of taking care of field worker needs and he later founded "the big store in the little lane."

15   This store is named for a mystical, northern Arizona town with beautiful red mountains.

16   This man's store got started in 1939 and his specialty was tailoring military uniforms to fit well and look sharp. He later opened a Mens wear and Big and Tall store.

17   This retailer on several islands carries the name of a well-known Hawaiian entertainer from the 1950s who did the *Hula Hop*. You can see the largest Aloha Shirt in the world at their Honolulu store.

18   Can you remember the name of the super market on School Street and Nuuanu Avenue? It opened in 1935 and closed in 1983.

19   Mr. Yoshioka opend this appliance store in Kaimuki in 1923, but later specialized in music.

20   Sol Price founded discount warehouse membership shopping in 1976 in San Diego. They "stack it high and sell it cheap." What's their name today?

21   This Haleiwa store is world famous for making a frozen treat. Get it with azuki beans and ice cream.

22   This man legally dropped his first name, Robert. He's known world-wide as a "Marine Michaelangelo."

23   This 5-10-25 Cent store had architects on staff to design its 300 beautiful buildings across the country. Its first store in Hawaii was in Hilo in 1932. Their Fort Street store is now the First Hawaiian Tower.

How Well do you Know Hawaii Restaurants and Drive-Ins?

Part 1

YOUR PARENTS TOOK YOU THERE WHEN YOU WERE YOUNG. You and your friends hung out there as teenagers. But how well do you really know Hawaii restaurants, drive-ins, and food establishments? Answers are on page 391.

1 This leeward Oahu restaurant with a Pennsylvania Dutch theme has 20 sister restaurants in Japan. They are famous for their pies.

2 This was the first drive-in in town, founded in 1929 by banker George Knapp and realtor Elwood Christensen. The original location was on Ala Wai and Kalakaua, where the Landmark Building now stands.

3 Brothers Frank and Tosh Kaneshiro planned to open this restaurant on December 8, 1941, but the attack on Pearl Harbor delayed the opening. They were famous for being at the Top of the Boulevard. Tosh was a famous LA Dodger baseball fan. Their name came from a country famous for its coffee.

4 This restaurateur pioneered the South Seas village style bar and restaurant. He is credited with creating the Mai Tai, Zombie, Scorpion, and the International Marketplace.

5 This restaurant, which opened in 1939, was well known for its Monkey Bar. Serving Japanese, Chinese, and American food, it was the leading restaurant in leeward Oahu for many years.

6 Founder P.Y. Chong called his place the "Best Restaurant Any Country in World." For many years, Wo Fat was his main competitor. His restaurant grew from 14 tables in 1929, to seating 1,400 with waterfalls, rock gardens, and caverns.

7　All that's left of Tony and Peaches Guerrero's three restaurants (Hilo, Waikiki, and where the Ala Moana Hotel is today) is their famous salad dressing. Can you name it?

8　Thahn Quoc Lam started this sandwich place in 1984 and now has more than 20 franchises. The name means "Paris" in Vietnamese.

9　This Waimalu restaurant's name comes from an old English story about a young Spanish princess who came to England to marry a prince and tie the royal houses of England and Spain together. She was called *La Infanta de Castille*, which meant "the infant girl from Castille," a province of Spain. However, people in England could not understand this phrase and misunderstood it as this.

10　Zippy's owner Francis Higa has helped a young chef start a popular restaurant. They formed a partnership and the chef moved into a building Francis owned on King Street. The chef was born in Japan, but went to Leilehua High. Name him.

11　This Hilo restaurant is home of the Loco Moco and serves more than 15 different varieties. Founder Richard Miyashiro named it for his World War II army battalion.

12　This chain once had 50 restaurants, including the Ranch House, Tahitian Lanai, Queen's Surf, Coco's, and Kelly's. All that remains today is Fisherman's Wharf.

13　This is one of the last South Sea's style restaurants on Oahu. The owner bought the wicker chairs, tikis, koa tables, glass balls, and giant clam shells from Don the Beachcomber's, Trader Vic's, or the Barefoot Bar auctions. In Italian, the name means "little sea."

14　This now-gone sister restaurant to Patti's Chinese Kitchen at Ala Moana Center was famous for its pastrami sandwich. Calvin Chun owned both and named them for his daughters.

How Well do you Know Hawaii Restaurants and Drive-Ins?

Part 2

SINCE YOU WERE YOUNG, YOU'VE EATEN THERE. You and your friends hung out there as teenagers. But how well do you know Hawaii restaurants, drive-ins, and food establishments? Answers are on page 391

1   Restaurateur Francis Tom tore down his Kapiolani Drive Inn and built this coffee shop in 1968. The name means "floating on water" and their logo is a lily.

2   Frank Sinatra's touring chef founded this Italian restaurant in Waikiki after Frank stopped performing.

3   This neighborhood restaurant and bakery is famous for its Coco Puffs and sells an average of 5,000 of them daily.

4   The Japanese consulate spy who kept an eye on ship movements in Pearl Harbor prior to World War II watched from this tea house in Kapalama Heights.

5   This restaurant took the name of a Las Vegas hotel because they liked its giant sign.

6   This Waialae Avenue restaurant has the name that farmers in Aina Haina and Niu Valley used to refer to Kaimuki, the end of Honolulu many decades ago.

7   The Salvation Army operates this Manoa restaurant that used to be a home and training facility for orphaned and needy children. The name means "happy" or "singing waters."

8   This mainland-based company wanted to have a different flavor for each day of the month. The original name was Snowbird. When it opened in Hawaii near the University, there were hour-long waits to be served.

9   This Japan-based restaurant is named for a famous Italian fairy tale. Fifteen million bottles of their salad dressing are sold each year.

10   This restaurant began as a four-table Japanese restaurant on New York's west side in 1964. They are the most successful Japanese restaurant in the U.S., having prepared over 100 million meals. Their recipe for success was blending exotic Japanese dishes with a dazzling chef performance. The name means "red flower."

11   A sign-maker misunderstood Yoshio Hori's name and painted his North Kohala bakery's sign incorrectly. What did he paint on the sign?

12   Perhaps the oldest restaurant in Honolulu, it opened in 1882. When tourists asked cab drivers to take them to the best Chinese restaurant in town, they took them here, partially because the fare was larger. A Hawaii Five-0 character used the name.

13   Known for its fabulous curries and mile-high pies served in a Polynesian thatched roof setting, this restaurant occupies the site of the former Kapaakea Springs, once owned by Queen Kamamalu. Henry Hauston later had a home there.

14   Marian Harada named this restaurant for her sister. It was once the finest place for dining and entertainment in central Oahu. The concrete parking slab in their parking lot is all that remains of their roller skating rink, which preceded the restaurant in 1938.

15   In 1942, this restaurant offered fine French food in Wahiawa. They moved in 1959 to the Colony Surf in Waikiki.

How Well Do You Know Fast Food?

IN NEED OF A QUICK SNACK? THESE PLACES HOPE to fill the bill. Can you guess which companies fit these clues? Answers are on page 392.

1   Brothers Maurice and Dick were whipping up something good in San Bernardino, California. Ray Kroc, who sold them milk shake machines, expanded their business worldwide.

2   The founder of this company, a real southern gentleman, started it with his first Social Security check in 1956. Today, they have 10,400 restaurants worldwide.

3   This company began as Topsy's in San Diego, in 1941. Robert Peterson renamed it for his favorite childhood toy. They had the nation's first drive thru, and a "secret sauce."

4   A major innovation at the post office in 1963 inspired a local company to pick this "fast" name.

5   The Raffel Brothers, Forrest and Leroy, decided to develop a franchise operation based on something other than hamburgers. Their first restaurant opened in Ohio, in 1964. Today, they have more than 3,000 restaurants worldwide.

6   Glen started Taco Tia, then El Tacos before launching this chain in Downey, California, in 1962. Run for the border.

7   This company invented the double-decker hamburger in Glendale, California, in 1937. His burger and restaurant were named for a jolly, chubby youngster who loved to eat them.

8   "Grandpa" McCullough invented soft-serve ice cream in 1938 in Illinois. His company has 5,600 branches, with 8 in Hawaii.

9   Roy Allen invented a new soda in 1919 and, with Frank Wright, opened the nation's first drive-in, in Sacramento, serving it in frosty mugs. It's even better with ice cream.

How Well Do You Know Hawaii Schools?

WHICH HAWAII SCHOOL FITS THESE CLUES? Answers are on page 392.

1   This is the oldest school in Hawaii, built in 1831 as a seminary for young men. It is the ninth oldest school in the U.S. The neighbor island institution prides itself with being the "Oldest School West of the Rockies."

2   This school's name means "the new spring," for the source of water that bubbles to the surface and creates a lily pond.

3   This school occupies the former Dillingham estate, modeled after an Italian villa.

4   Queen Emma called on the Church of England to create St. Andrew's Priory School for Girls in 1867. The companion school for boys was originally called Luaehu School and was located in Lahaina. What is its current name?

5   The missionaries founded the Chiefs' Children's School on Oahu in 1839, two years before they founded Punahou. School Street got its name from it. What name does the school go by today?

6   Name the school that gave College Walk, near Chinatown, its name. The school moved from the area to its present site in the 1920s. It was named for a man who led two crusades.

7   This school is the most international school in the U.S., with students from all 50 states and more than 100 countries.

8   This school was originally known as the Fort Street English Day School, established in 1865 by Reverend Maurice B. Beckwith. In 1895, the school moved to the palace of Princess Ruth Keelikolani, Central Intermediate School's present

location and was renamed Honolulu High School. The name was changed in 1907 to honor a statesman for his influence in the annexation of the Hawaiian Islands to the United States.

9   This school in east Honolulu focuses on educating the whole person and uses an arts-based system developed by Rudolph Steiner 80 years ago at a Company in Stuttgart, Germany. They have 325 students, pre-school through 12th grade.

10   Name the school that had a baby lent to it each year, from 1925 until 1962 for the senior girls to practice child-rearing skills. They did so in a cottage on Kalihi Street.

11   This university was named for a priest who lived and worked during the French Revolution and founded the Society of Mary.

12   What do Punahou's school colors, buff and blue refer to?

13   The College of Agriculture and Mechanic Arts, founded in 1907 at Thomas Square, would grow to become what school?

14   This was the first high School in the Leeward area. It got its mascot from the name of a plane that crashed on the campus.

15   The private elementary school's name means "joyous work." It was founded in Makiki in 1918 and has many interesting traditions, including one in which students lay a stepping stone on campus.

16   This second catholic school on Oahu occupies the former Houghtailing estate in Kalihi.

17   This school was originally going to be called Waialae High School. Founded in 1958, it served all of east Honolulu.

18   A minor faculty rebellion struck the University of Hawaii in 1946. What was the issue that had faculty and the administration feuding?

How Well Do You Know Punahou School?

1 Which queen prevailed on chiefess Liliha to donate the tract of land called Ka Punahou to the missionaries for Punahou School?

2 What does the name *Punahou* mean?

3 A spring forms which famous school landmark in the middle of the campus?

4 Which missionary, a pastor at Kawaihao Church, founded Punahou school?

5 The grandson of Punahou's founder is famous for discovering which ancient Inca fortress in Peru?

6 What do Punahou's school colors, Buf 'n Blu, refer to?

7 From 1857 until 1934, Punahou went by this name.

8 Punahou female athletes earn a "P." The male athletes earn a different letter. Which letter do male athletes earn?

9 Dole Street is named for this man, the first teacher and president of the school.

10 Two years before founding Punahou in 1841, the missionaries founded this school for the children of *alii*

11 Mrs. Bingham planted a cactus hedge in 1836 that now covers the walls along Punahou and Dole Streets. Its extraordinary blossoms come out for one night only in late summer. What is the name of the plant?

12 Which organization occupied Punahou during World War II?

Answers are on page 393

How Well do you Know Hawaii Radio and TV Stations?

MOST OF US SPEND SEVERAL HOURS A WEEK WATCHING and listening, but how well do we really know Hawaii's 50 plus radio and TV stations? Answers are on page 393.

1 Before it was called KSSK and K59, at 590 on the AM dial, the call letters were this.

2 "All Hawaiian, All the Time" was this station's moniker. It once broadcast from the banyan tree at the International Marketplace.

3 This station had a crew of young men, including Tom Moffatt, Dave Donnelly, and Ron Jacobs that pulled pranks and "thons" designed to gain publicity for the first all rock and roll station in the islands. It was originally KHON radio. What call letters does it have today?

4 This KGMB newscaster was widely considered to be Hawaii's Walter Cronkite.

5 This morning DJ was famous for his Second Annual Easter Parade on April 1, down Kalakaua Avenue. More than 7,000 people took beach chairs and coolers to watch a parade that never happened. An irate listener may have given him his nickname. Name it and his real name.

6 Who anchored the KHON 2 News before Joe Moore?

7 What does KHVH stand for? Would it help to know that Henry Kaiser originally owned it?

8 Kamasami Kong was the first host of this Monday night TV show that moved from disco to disco each week. It was not a hit until it changed hosts, nights, and formats.

9   This radio station, the "Voice of Hawaii," was the first on the air in 1922. It's the only station in Hawaii with a three-letter call.

10   This TV station's call letters mean chrysanthemum in Japanese.

11   A famous Hawaiian radio broadcast came from "Beneath the Banyan Tree" at the Moana Hotel for nearly four decades to the mainland, Canada, and Australia every Saturday. Name the show hosted by Webley Edwards.

12   Cec Heftel owned KGMB radio and KPUA radio in Hilo. What did he call the network of these 2 stations?

13   This Kauai radio station's call letters were inspired by a big ape, whose film was partly shot on the Garden Isle.

14   When Michael W. Perry was at KKUA radio, he produced fractured fairy tales and did all the voices. Which nickname did he use for this?

15   Which radio station had an all-girl DJ lineup in the 1970s? It's rock and roll format competed with K-POI.

16   This is the largest and oldest Japanese language radio station outside of Japan.

17   DJ Mel Medeiros ruled the roost at KIPA on the Big Island for over 20 years. What is his nickname?

18   KKUA and Habilitat put out three albums in the 1970s with this name.

19   Robert Melvin Luck was a top morning DJ in Honolulu. He also had a luau TV show. What was his nickname?

20   When Bob Sevey was the anchor on KGMB TV, he had a young sportscaster who left for another station's news room where he's now anchor. Name him.

How Well Do You Know Hawaii's Royalty?

HAWAII'S ROYALTY PLAYED A SUBSTANTIAL ROLE IN the founding of businesses, organizations, hospitals, and schools. You know their names, but do you know what they did? Answers are on page 394.

1 This Waikiki hotel had an earlier incarnation downtown. Kings Kamehameha V and Kalakaua helped get it built.

2 Kings William Lunalilo, Lot Kamehameha, Alexander Liholiho, David Kalakaua, Queens Emma, Victoria Kamamalu, Liliuokalani, and Bernice Pauahi were some of the original students at this school.

3 She was the last of the royal Kamehameha line but refused to marry Prince Lot, preferring a banker instead. Even though she died in 1884 of breast cancer, her impact on Hawaii is greater today than ever.

4 At 400 pounds, this princess was considered the ugliest woman in the kingdom, but carried candy in her pockets to give to children. When she died, her home became a school.

5 This princess was born in her father's, Archibald Cleghorn's home on Emma Street. The home is now the Pacific Club. She was groomed to be queen but died after catching a cold.

6 This king left money to care for elderly Hawaiians. The original building is where Roosevelt High School is today.

7 Queen Emma founded St. Andrew's Priory and this sister school, in 1863, which was named Luaehu School on Maui.

8 Lydia Liliuokalani grew up with Bernice Pauahi and her parents, Abner and Konia Paki in Haleakala, their downtown home where Bishop and King Streets are today. She married John Owen Dominis and moved to this famous house.

What Was There Before?

HERE ARE 21 BUILDINGS, SITES, OR BUSINESSES that currently occupy their premises. Can you recall what was there before? Answers are on page 394.

1 Bishop Museum _____

2 Don Quijote (Honolulu) _____

3 Tamarind Park/Pauahi Tower _____

4 Neil Blaisdell Center _____

5 Sports Authority (Ward) _____

6 TGI Friday's (Ward)_____

7 Zippy's (Kahala) _____

8 Academy of Arts Learning Center (Victoria St) _____

9 Hard Rock Café _____

10 Ala Moana Hotel _____

11 City Mill (Waialae) _____

12 K-Mart (Nimitz) _____

13 First Hawaiian Bank (Moiliili) _____

14 McDonald's (Haleiwa) _____

15 Hawaii Prince Hotel Waikiki _____

16 3660 on the Rise _____

17 Wasabi Bistro (Kapahulu) _____

18 First Hawaiian Tower (Fort Street) _____

19 Hawaii Convention Center _____

20 Central Middle School_____

What Does Their Name Mean?

Can you match the company or school with the meaning of its name?

Company	Meaning
1. Shirokiya	A. Gangster
2. Fook Yuen Seafood Restaurant	B. Fish impression
	C. Butterfly
3. Genki Sushi	D. Beautiful or fragrant garden
4. Ba-Le	
5. Tesoro	E. Kisses
6. Halekulani Hotel	F. Singing waters
7. Suehiro	G. Outlying land
8. Pohai Nani	H. White tree store
9. Hanahauoli School	I. Royal Hawk
10. Moana Hotel	J. Broad expanse of the sea
11. Mariposa	K. Joyous work
12. Gyutaku	L. Surrounded by beauty
13. Iolani School	M. Further expansion in the future
14. Buca di Beppo	
15. Kua Aina Sandwich Shop	N. Joe's basement
	O. Happy or fine
16. Waioli Tea Room	P. Treasure
17. Baci Bistro	Q. Paris
18. Cholo	R. House befitting heaven

Answers: 1-H; 2-D; 3-O; 4-Q; 5-P; 6-R; 7-M; 8-L; 9-K; 10-J; 11-C; 12-B; 13-I; 14-N; 15-G; 16-F; 17-E; 18-A

Formerly known as

Below is a list of previous company and school names. **Can you recall the current or last name?** Answers are on page 396.

1   Hawaiian Pineapple Co. _____
2   Horatio's _____
3   Kahala Hilton _____
4   Inter-Island Airways _____
5   Waialua Garage _____
6   Mister K Stores _____
7   H. Hackfeld and Company _____
8   Kapiolani Drive-inn _____
9   Trans-Pacific Airways _____
10   Bullwinkle's _____
11   KGMB radio _____
12   Oahu Railway & Land Co. _____
13   Japanese Hospital _____
14   Kuilima Hotel _____
15   Dairyman's Association _____
16   Bishop and Company _____
17   The British Club _____
18   Olympic Grill _____
19   GTE Hawaiian Tel _____
20   Crater Hotel _____

Schools

21   Oahu College _____
22   Chiefs' Children's School _____
23   Ahuimanu College _____
24   Luaehu School _____
25   Honolulu High School _____
26   College of Agriculture and Mechanic Arts _____
27   Saint Louis Junior College _____
28   Church College of Hawaii _____

How Well Do You Know Hawaii Slogans?

WHICH HAWAII COMPANIES USED THE FOLLOWING SLOGANS?
Answers are on page 395.

1   Wings of the islands _____

2   Thank you *very* much _____

3   One of the good things about Hawaii _____

4   Look at all the things we are _____

5   All Hawaiian, all the time _____

6   And away we go _____

7   The pulse of paradise _____

8   We'll make a believer out of you _____

9   The power of yes _____

10 We make you shine _____

11 If you're not buying your diamonds from _____ ,
    you are paying too much.

12 Two distinctive campuses – one great university _____

13 Giving you the power _____

14 Entertaining Hawaii since 1917 _____

15 Hawaii's newspaper _____

16 Hawaii's center _____

17 Hawaii's radio station _____

18 Hawaii's bank _____

19 Pink Palace of the Pacific _____

20 Creative Italian and Chinese cuisine _____

21 Doing our best for you _____

22 Meet you beneath the banyan tree _____

23 An oasis in the heart of Honolulu_____

24 Walk in, hula out _____

25 You're going to find it at _____

Hawaii Company Slogans

HERE ARE SOME OF THE BETTER-KNOWN SLOGANS of Hawaii companies, some current and some past.

Company	Slogan
ABC Stores	The store with aloha.
Ala Moana Center	Hawaii's center.
Aloha Airlines	Expect more.
Aloha Power Equipment	We sell the best & service the rest.
Altres	Making business simple.
Arakawa's	The big store in the little lane; if you don't know what you're looking for, you'll find it at Arakawa's.
Aston Hotels & Resorts	Pleasantly exceeding your expectations.
Bank of Hawaii	Hawaii's bank.
Big Island Candies	Hawaii's finest handmade chocolates & cookies.
Bill Green's Kahala Shell	My mother always said, "a clean car runs better."
Central Pacific Bank	Fiercely loyal banking.
Charley's Taxi	The way to go.
Ciao Mein	Creative Italian & Chinese cuisine.
City Bank	It's worth it to switch.
City Mill	Your superhardware store.
Columbia Inn	Our taste is right on the money.
Consolidated Theatres	Entertaining Hawaii since 1917.
Consumer Tire Warehouse	Go Now Hawaii, Why Pay More?
Crazy Shirts	Hawaii's favorite since 1964.
Creative Holidays	And away we go.
Finance Factors	A family you can depend on.
First Hawaiian Bank	The power of yes.
Foodland	Doing our best for you.

GTE Hawaiian Tel .... Beyond the call.

Halekulani Hotel .... On the beach at Waikiki.

Hawaii Pacific University ..... Two distinctive campuses –
one great university.

HPM Building Supply .... Hawaii's single source for all.
your building needs!

Hawaiian Airlines .... Wings of the islands.

HECO .... Giving you the power.

Helen's Haven .... A unique facial salon.

Hilo Hattie .... Life Is a Luau.

Honolulu Advertiser .... Hawaii's newspaper.

Honolulu Magazine .... The magazine Hawaii lives by.

Honolulu Star-Bulletin .... The pulse of paradise.

House of Adler .... If you are not buying your
diamonds from the House of
Adler, you *are* paying too much.

Hy's Steak House .... Waikiki's award-winning fine
dining restaurant.

I Love Country Café............. Homemade just the way
mom made it.

Island Insurance.................. Always there to help.

KC Drive-Inn .... Home of the waffle dog.

KCCN .... All Hawaiian all the time.

KGMB .... One of the good things about Hawaii.

KGU .... The voice of Hawaii.

KHNL .... Live, local, late breaking.

KHON .... Hawaii's news channel.

KITV .... Island television.

KSSK .... Hawaii's radio.

Kapiolani Health .... Keeping you healthy for life.

Kilgo's .... You're going to find it at Kilgo's.

King Kamehameha's
Kona Beach Hotel .... Rich in the history and hospitality
of the Big Island of Hawaii.

Kona Village Resort .... Hawaii as it was meant to be.

Kuakini Medical Center .... Caring is our tradition.

Lex Brodie's Tires .... Thank you *very* much.

Liberty House .... A tradition in Hawaii.

Lion Coffee .... Hawaii's gourmet coffee.

Longs .... Make Longs a part of your day.

McKinley Car Wash .... We make you shine.

Meadow Gold .... Hawaii's dairy since 1897.

Mauna Loa Macadamia Nuts All the goodness of Hawaii.

Moana Hotel .... Meet you beneath the banyan tree.

Oceanic Cable .... Look at all the things we are.

Pagoda Hotel .... An oasis in the heart of Honolulu.

Pfleuger Honda .... Serves you right here in town.

Pleasant Hawaiian Holidays . Escape to paradise.

Prudential Locations .... Where Hawaii feels at home.

The Queens Medical Center . Hawaii's health care leader.

Reyn's .... The Brooks Brothers of the Pacific.

Robert's Hawaii .... Hawaii's leader in tours
and transportation.

Royal Hawaiian Hotel .... The pink palace of the Pacific.

Royal Hawaiian Movers .... Where in the world are you going?

Saint Francis Healthcare ...... Caring for a healthy community.

Servco Pacific .... A commitment to service excellence.

Shirokiya .... In pursuit of a total lifestyle.

Signature Theatres .... State of the Art Cinemas.

Singha Thai Cuisine .... Experience Thailand in Hawaii.

Slumber World .... Good nights start here.

Star Markets .... A five-star experience.

Taro Brand .... Hawaii's largest poi producer.

Top of Waikiki .... Hawaii's only revolving restaurant.

Waltah Clarke's .... Walk in, hula out.

Windward Honda .... We'll make a believer out of you.

Young Brothers .... Lifeline of the Hawaiian islands.

Zippy's .... Good fun for everyone.

Signature Dish - Specialty of the House

MANY OF HAWAII'S RESTAURANTS ARE FAMOUS for a particular item. Most are still around. Some are long gone, but not forgotten. Here's a list of some favorites that were nominated by the dining public.

Oahu

Aiea Manapua	Pizza manapua
Alan Wong's	Ginger crusted onaga
Ba-le	Pho
Barbecue Inn	Pork chops
Big City Diner	Kim chee fried rice
da Big Kahuna	Garlic cheese balls
Boots and Kimo	Macadamia pancakes
Char Hung Sut	Manapua, mai Tai soo
Chez Michel's	French onion soup
Chicken Alice's	Spicy fried chicken
China House	Dim sum
Compadres	Fajitas
Crouching Lion Inn	Slavonic steak
Columbia Inn	Oxtail soup
Deb's Ribs and Soul Food	BBQ ribs
Diêm	Pho
Doug's Gee...a Deli	Pastrami sandwich
Elena's	Adobo fried rice
Golden Dragon	Curried lobster with fried haupia
Gordon Biersch	Garlic fries
Grace's Inn	Chicken katsu
Gulick Delicatessen	Butterfish
Halekulani Hau Tree Terrace	Popovers
Hale Vietnam	Pho
Haiku Gardens	Prime rib
Hau Tree Lanai	Chicken papaya
Helena's Hawaiian Food	Pipikaula short ribs, butterfish collars
Hifume	Shrimp tempura

Hoku's	Seafood tower
House of Hong	Deep fried lup cheong
Indigo	Ginger creme brulee, Lobster potstickers
Irifune	Garlic ahi, breaded tofu, ahi boat
Jon's	Curry
Kapiolani Coffee Shop	Oxtail soup, 35¢ hot dogs
Keo's	Evil Jungle prince
Kelly's Coffee Shop	Buttermilk pancakes
Lyn's Delicatessen	Pastrami sandwich
Marujyu Market	Lau lau
McCully Chop Sui	Kau yuk
Mitsu-Ken	Garlic chicken
The Olive Tree	Souvlaki
Original Pancake House	Apple pancakes
Paramount Cafe	Fried rice
Queen's Surf	Surf wagon dinners
Royal Kitchen	Baked manapua
Roy's	Pan seared ahi katsu
Ruger Market	Poke, boiled peanuts
Ryan's	Cajun chicken fettuccini, pea salad
Sam Choy's	Fried poke
Sanoya	Gyoza
7-Eleven	Big Gulp
Sheraton Waikiki	(Original) lemon chicken
Shiro's Saimin Haven	Won tun min
Side Street Inn	Pork chops
Stuart Anderson's	Prime Rib
Tahitian Lanai	Eggs Benedict, banana muffins
Tanioka's	Sushi
TGI Fridays	Loaded potato skins
The Third Floor	Naan bread
Tony Roma's	B-B-Q ribs, onion ring loaf
Waimalu Chop Suey	Gau gee
Windy's	Teri burger
Yen King	Hot and sour soup
Yama's	Lau lau
Young's Fish Market	Lau lau
Zippy's	Chili

Salads

Buzz's Steak House	Salad bar
Ciro's	Salad bar
Kenny's Coffee Shop	Chinese chicken salad
La Mancha	French salad dressing
Matteo's	Caesar salad
Pacific Grill	Popcorn salad
Planet Hollywood	Caesar salad
The Shack	Chinese chicken salad
Sunset Grill	Gorgonzola salad
Swiss Inn	Vinaigrette salad dressing

Sweets

Alexander Young Bakery	Lemon crunch cake, brownies, palm leaves
Ani's Bakeshop	Sweetbread
Anna Miller's	Strawberry pie
Aotani's	Chocolate, vanilla, cherry cokes
B&S	Shave ice
Bea's Bakery	Custard pumpkin pie
The Bistro	Cheesecake
Buck's	Sweet bread
Café Laufer	Chocolate banana Oreo cake
Dave's Ice Cream	Green tea ice cream
Dee Lite Bakery	Rainbow chiffon cakes, custard pie
Duke's	Hula pie
Dutch Girl Bakery	Ensemadas
Flamingo Restaurant	Double-crusted banana pie
Hy's Steak House	Banana's Foster
Kakaako Kitchen	Bread pudding
Kamehameha Bakery	Haupia doughnuts, malasadas
Kapiolani Bakery	Dobash cake
Kemoo Farms	Hawaiian Happy Cakes
Kilani Bakery	Brownies, banana pie
King's Bakery	Sweet bread
Kincaid's	Burnt cream
Kimuraya Bakery	Cake doughnuts
Leonard's Bakery	Malasadas
Liliha Bakery	Coco puffs
M's Coffee Tavern	Coconut cream pie

Makiki Bake Shop .... Biscuits
Matsumoto's .... Shave Ice
Mililani Restaurant .... Shoyu Chicken
Mitsuba Delicatessen .... Sweet Potato Crumbles
Napoleon's Bakery .... Napples
Nori's .... Chocolate Mochi
The Nosh .... N.Y. Cheesecake
9th Avenue Bakery .... Buttercup, Potato Rolls
Sunnyside .... Chocolate Cream Pie
Ted's Bakery .... Chocolate Haupia Pie
Top of Waikiki.................... Red Velvet Cake
Tropilicious .... Haupialani Sorbet
Violet's Grill...................... Double Crusted Banana Pie
The Willows....................... Sky High Coconut Pie
Yama's .... Sweet Potato Haupia Pie

Drive Ins

Alex Drive In...................... Watermelon Freeze
Andy's Drive In .... Mustard-mayonnaise Spread
Byron's Drive-Inn .... Broasted Chicken, Shrimp Burger
Chunky's Drive-In .... Corned Beef Hash Plate
KC Drive Inn .... Ono Ono Shake, Waffle Dog
Rainbow Drive-In .... Mushroom Chicken, Slush Float,
Teri Beef

Big Island

Amano Fish Cake .... Tempura
Atebara............................. Potato Chips
Big Island Candies.............. Chocolate Dipped Shortbread
Cookies
Café 100............................ Loco Moco
Hilo Lunch Shop .... Fried Chicken
Hilo Macaroni Co. .... Saloon Pilot Crackers
Hirano Store....................... Chili
Holy's Bakery..................... Apple Pie
Ken's Pancake House .... Hot Nuts
Kona Bakery .... An Pan
Manago Hotel .... Pork Chops
Mrs. Barry's Cookies........... Chocolate Dipped Shortbread
Cookies
Teshima's Restaurant .... Shrimp Tempura
Two Ladies Kitchen .... Strawberry Mochi

Maui

Avalon .... Appetizer platter
Azeka's Ribs .... Ribs
Homemade Bakery .... Manju
Komoda Bakery .... Cream puffs, double crusted
                                   azuki pie
Kitchen Kooked .... Potato chips
Mama's Fishhouse .... Papaya seed dressing
Sam Sato's .... Dried mein
Shishido Manju Shop .... Manju
Tasaka's Guri Guri .... Goodie goodie
Tasty Crust .... Hotcakes

Kauai

A Pacific Cafe .... Wok-charred mahi mahi
Bull Shed .... Prime rib
Casa d'Amici .... Grilled eggplant
Duke's .... Caesar salad
Green Garden .... Lilikoi chiffon pie
Hamura Saimin .... Saimin
Hanamaulu Restaurant
  & Tea House .... Fried chicken
King & I .... Eggplant with tofu
Kintaro .... Hanalei roll
Robert's Bakery .... Macadamia nut cookies
Tip Top Bakery .... Pineapple/coconut jam,
                                   Macadamia nut cookies
Wong's Chinese Restaurant .. Lilikoi chiffon pie

Molokai

Kanemitsu Bakery .... Molokai bread

Businesses and Organizations Associated with Hawaiian Royalty

Hawaii's kings and queens played a significant role in encouraging, supporting or founding some of the most important companies and organizations in Hawaii today. Here are some of those organizations.

King Kamehameha I - Parker Ranch
Kamehameha the Great asked John Parker to take charge of the thousands of cattle that roamed the Big Island's remote plains and valleys. The cattle were descendants of 5 head given by British Captain George Vancouver in 1778. The result was Parker Ranch, which began in 1809.

Queen Kaahumanu - Punahou School
Queen Kaahumanu, the favorite wife of Kamehameha I, urged Chiefess Liliha to donate the land called Ka Punahou to the missionaries for a school. Liliha was resistant but Kaahumanu was persuasive. Punahou opened in 1841.

King Kamehameha III - Honolulu Police Department, the Royal Hawaiian Band, The City of Honolulu, Royal School, and DOE
Kauikeaouli, King Kamehameha III reigned from 1825 to 1854. He founded the Honolulu Police Dept. in 1834, and the Royal Hawaiian Band In 1836. Kamehameha III declared Honolulu a city in 1850. He helped start Royal School, and established the statewide public school system that grew into our Dept. of Education.

King Kamehameha IV and Queen Emma - The Queen's Medical Center, Iolani School and St. Andrew's Priory
The King and Queen personally raised $13,350 to open an 18-bed hospital on Fort Street in 1859 at a time when thousands of Hawaiians were dying from diseases they had no resistance to. It moved a year later to its present site.

Queen Emma and Alexander Liholiho Iolani asked the Anglican Church of England to help establish two schools in Hawaii. The school for boys began in Lahaina in 1863 and became Iolani School. The girl's school, St. Andrew's Priory School, opened four years later in 1867.

Kamehameha V – Royal Hawaiian Hotel, Molokai Ranch
Prince Lot, Kamehameha V was embarrassed by the visit of Alfred Ernest Albert, the Duke of Edinburgh, who came to Hawaii on a state visit in 1869. There was no place fitting for him to stay, except for private residences. Lot encouraged the building of a grand hotel, across from the Iolani Palace grounds at Hotel and Richards Streets. The Royal Hawaiian Hotel was the finest hotel in the pacific when it opened in 1872. Lot also founded the Molokai Ranch.

King Lunalilo - Lunalilo Home
The estate of King William Lunalilo called for the founding of the Lunalilo Home, an institution devoted to providing shelter and support for Hawaiian elderly. In Hawaii Kai for the last 75 years, the first site was in Makiki, where Roosevelt High School is today.

King David Kalakaua and Queen Kapiolani - Kapiolani Health, and the Hawaiian Electric Company.
King Kalakaua (reigned from 1874 – 1891) was fascinated by technology. He met with Thomas Edison on a world tour, and encouraged scientists to electrify Iolani Palace. The Palace and the neighboring Royal Hawaiian Hotel had electricity 4 years before the White House and before any building in California. Out of this venture grew the Hawaiian Electric Company.

Queen Kapiolani raised $8,000 to start Kapiolani Maternity Home in 1890. The Home merged with Kauikeolani Children's Hosptial in 1976 to become Kapiolani Hospital.

Queen Liliuokalani - The Queen Liliuokalani Children's Center and the Hawaii Girl Scouts
Queen Lydia Kamakaeha Liliuokalani created a trust to help orphaned Hawaiian children - the Queen Liliuokalani Children's Center. She also helped the Girl Scouts get started in Hawaii in 1917.

Princess Bernice Pauahi Bishop - Bishop Estate/Kamehameha Schools

Pauahi was heiress to most of the Kamehameha lands, totaling close to nine percent of the area of the Hawaiian Islands. Her will established the Kamehameha Schools to educate the young people of Hawaii. The boy's school opened in 1887 and the girl's school in 1894.

Very few of the companies and organizations that existed 100 to 150 years ago in Hawaii are still with us. That our kings and queens established so many surviving, powerful organizations is a tribute to their wisdom and foresight.

Our royalty would be proud to see that the organizations they helped found are making a bigger difference today than ever before.

Hawaii companies you might not expect to have branches or franchises outside the state

ABC Stores – Guam and Las Vegas
Altres – California, Nevada, Utah
Anna Miller's – has 20 franchises in Japan
Ba-Le – opening soon in Nagoya, Japan
Bonded Materials – Guam, Saipan, Phoenix, Las Vegas
C.S. Wo - California
Cinnamon Girl – Las Vegas
Commercial Data Systems - Seven mainland states
Crazy Shirts – Florida, California, Louisiana, Nevada
Finance Factors – Guam
Fun Factory – Eight mainland states
Following Sea – Formerly in California
Hawaiian Brian's Billiards – Anchorage, Alaska
Hilo Hattie – Las Vegas, California, Florida, Arizona
KC Drive Inn – had 6 franchises in Japan at one time
Kua Aina Sandwich Shop – Eight branches in Japan
L&L Hawaiian Barbecue - 100 plus in California, Arizona,
        Nevada, Washington, and Connecticut.
Magoo's Pizza – 20 franchises in the Philippines,
        one in Dubai
Maui Divers – Orange County, Las Vegas, Orlando
Mings Jewelers – Formerly had branches in NY,
        Florida, Texas and California
Moose McGillycuddy's – Las Vegas and California
Red Dirt Shirt Company – Utah
Sheila Donnelly and Associates – Tuscon, L.A. and
        New York
Tony Group – Los Gatos Honda (California)

Gone, But Not Forgotten

BUSINESSES CLOSE FOR ALL KINDS OF PERSONAL AND financial reasons. In Hawaii, they face a triple whammy of high shipping costs, high taxes, and high lease rents. Add to that a state government that mandates excessive fees, regulations, and costs, and the mixture translates into many more companies shutting their doors than would elsewhere. Here are 200+ companies that have closed, merged, sold, or left Hawaii since 1990.

Adtech
Akasaka Marina Restaurant
Alex Drive-in
Alfred's Restaurant
Aloha Flea Market
Altillo's European Menswear
American Hawaii Cruises
American Movers
Andrade
Andrew's
Andy's Drive-in
Angelica's Gallery Cafe
Annabelle's at the Top of the I
Apartment Appearance
Arakawa's
Bagwells 2424
Bank of America
Bank of Honolulu
Barber's Point NAS
Barbizon
Beacon Restaurant
Bea's Drive In
Benetton
Bernard's N.Y. Deli
Bishop Trust
Black Orchid
Blue Hawaii
Blue Zebra
Bon Appetit
Bobby McGee's Conglomeration

Byron II
Carol & Mary
Castagnola's
Chi-chi's
Chicken Alice's
Chock's TV and Appliance
Chocolates for Breakfast
Cielo
Cinerama Theatre
Coco Palms
Coffee Manoa
Columbia Inn
Computer City
Cornet
Craig's Bakery
Danny's At Manoa
Digital Island
Dillingham Construction
Dutch Girl Pastry Shoppes
Eagle Hardware
East-West Bank
El Crab Catcher
Elephant & Castle
Ethel's Dress Shoppe
Excel Electrical Supply Co.
First Federal Savings
First Interstate Bank
Fishmonger's Wife
Flamingo Chuckwagon
Florence's Restaurant

Following Sea
Forty-Niner Cafe
Frankie's Drive-In
Fronk Clinic
Garden House
Gas 'n Glo
Gee...a Deli
GEM
Gibson's Department Store
Greek Island Taverna
Grocery Outlet
H. Hamada Store
Hajibaba's
Hanatei Bistro
Hartfield's
Hauoli
The Haven
Hawaii Baking
Hawaiian Bagel
Hawaiian Trust
Hilo Macaroni Factory
Holiday Mart
Home Improvement Warehouse
HonFed
Honolulu Bookstore
HonSport
House of Adler
House of Music
Iida's
Il Fresco
IMAX Theatre
India Imports International
International Savings
J. C. Penney
Ja-Ja
Jacques Bakery
Jeffrey Barr
Jetour Hawaii
Jolly Roger
Joyce-Selby Shoes
KC Drive Inn

Kahala Moon
Kailua Drive-in
Kam Drive-in
Kam Bowl
Kapiolani Theatre
Kelly's Coffee Shop
Kilgo's
Kim Chow Shoes
King's Bakery
Kinney Shoes
Kodak Hula Show
Kona Surf Hotel
Koolau Ranch House
Kuhio Theatre
Kuni Dry Goods
Kyotaru
Kyoya
La Paloma Mexican Cafe
L'Auberge Swiss Restaurant
Liberty Bank
Liberty House
Lindy's Foods
Lyn's Delicatessen
L'Uraku
McCully Chop Suey
McInerny
Mahalo Air lines
Maharaja's
Maile Restaurant
Mama's Mexican Kitchen
Marina Twin Theatres
Masu's Massive Plate Lunch
MicroAge Computers
Mid-Pac Lumber
Ming's
Mongolian Bar-B-Q
Musashiya
Nicole
Nicholas Nickolas
Oahu Constuction
Oahu Lumber

Orson's Seafood Restaurant
Otaheite Shoppe
Palomino
Pau Hana Inn
Pay Less
Pay 'n Save
Pats at Punaluu Restaurant
Pearl City Tavern
Peck Simms Mueller
People's Bank
Pihana Pacific
Pioneer Federal
Plush Pippin
The Pocketbook Man
Pomegranates in the Sun
Pottery
Red Baron Pizza
Rose City Diner
Ross Sutherland
The Round House
Sada's
Salerno
Sato Clothiers
ScooZees
The Secret (Third Floor)
Sei's Family Restaurant
Security Diamond & Conrad
  Jewelers
Shakey's Pizza
Shishido Manju Shop
SIDA Taxi
Software Plus
Something Special!
Spaghetti! Spaghetti!
Spats
Spindrifter
Square USA
Studabaker's

Strawberry Connection
Suda Store
Suehiro
Sunset Grill
Sweet Thoughts
Swiss Inn
Stadium Bowl-O-Drome
Tahitian Lanai
Taipan on the Boulevard
Taj Mahal Nite Club
Ted's Drive-in
T.J. Maxx
Thom McAn
Thrifty Drug Store
Touch The East
Trattoria
Tripton's American Cafe
Tusitalia Bookstore
Uniden
Uptown Hardware
VeriFone
Waikiki Theatres
Waiohai Hotel
Waltah Clarke's
Wildflowers
Wally Wok
Washington Saimin Stand
What's Cookin'
Wisteria
Wong's Okazu-ya
Woodland Potsticker
  Restaurant
Woolworth's
Yacht Harbor Restaurant
Yick Lung
Yong Sing
Yum Yum Tree
Zack's Frozen Yogurt

Upcoming Anniversaries

CONGRATULATIONS TO THE FOLLOWING COMPANIES for providing goods and services to the Hawaii public for so many years.

Anniversaries in 2007

25 years .... Auntie Pasto's, Windward Mall, Kukui Grove Center

50 years .... McCully Chop Suey, Fred's Produce, Paradise Cruises, Hilo Seaside Hotel, Crouching Lion Inn

60 years .... Outrigger Hotels, McKinley Car Wash, Tamashiro Market, Torkildson & Katz

70 years .... Beretania Florist, SPAM

75 years .... Kalapawai Market, Grace Pacific, Honolulu Police Department

80 years .... St. Francis Healthcare System, Maryknoll Schools, Star Markets, Royal Hawaiian Hotel (in Waikiki), Haleakala Motors, Malolo Beverages and Supplies

90 years .... Consolidated Theatres, Ah Fook Supermarket

100 years .... Halekulani Hotel, Suisan, University of Hawaii, Tripler Hospital, Fort Shafter

125 years .... Star Bulletin, Matson, Iolani Palace

150 years .... Carlsmith, Ball, Wichman & Ichiki

345 years .... Shirokiya

Anniversaries in 2008

25 years .... The Ultimate You, Brennecke's Beach Broiler (Kauai), Mauna Lani Bay Hotel, Sanford Saito, DDS, Pegge Hopper Gallery

50 years .... Maui Divers, Sizzler, American Trust Company of Hawaii

60 years .... Charley's Taxi, HMSA, Longs Drug Stores, Wilcox Health System, Kaimuki Super-Market, Dairy Queen

75 years .... Sure Save Super Market (Big Island), Gouveia Portuguese Sausage Factory

80 years .... Pacific Insurance, Kona Inn, Kahua Ranch (Kohala), Ala Wai Canal completed, Sumida Watercress Farm, first Lei Day

90 years .... Hirano Store (Glenwood)

100 years............... Mid-Pacific Institute, Outrigger Canoe Club, Ameron Hawaii, Pacific Fleet arrived at Pearl Harbor, Schofield Barracks

125 years .... Hawaiian Telcom (Mutual Telephone)

150 years .... First Hawaiian Bank, Macy's

Anniversaries in 2009

25 years .... Compadres Mexican Bar and Grill, Ba-Le

50 years .... Ala Moana Center, Reyn's, Pleasant Holidays, Chuck's Steak House, Nishimoto Trading Co., Kilani Bakery, Dee Lite Bakery

60 years .... Times Supermarket, Hawaii Stationery, Yori's Happy Valley Tavern (Maui), Koa Trading Co. (Kauai), Redondo's

70 years .... Fletcher Pacific, Island Insurance, Tamura Super Market, Easy Music Center, Honolulu Sign Co., Kramers Mens Wear, Fukuya Delicatessen, Kona Community Hospital

75 years .... Stanley Ito Florist, Hawaii Motors (Hilo)

80 years .... Hawaiian Airlines, Waikiki Lau Yee Chai, Koehnen's Interiors (Hilo), Teshima's Restaurant (Kona)

90 years .... Servco Pacific, Fujikami Florist

100 years............... C. S. Wo, Sacred Hearts Academy, Maui Land and Pineapple, Kemoo Farms, Kula Hospital

125 years .... Moanalua Gardens, Kamehameha Schools, Maui Memorial Medical Center, Kiewit Pacific

150 years .... The Queen's Hospital

Anniversaries in 2010

25 years .... Bubbies, Kona Brewing, Oceanit
50 years .... Hawaii National Bank, KNDI, Princess Kaiulani
Fashions, Hawaiian Host, Molokai Drive Inn,
Chaney Brooks & Co., Hy's Steak House,
Hawaiian Rent-All, Kona Seaside Hotel,
Marian's Catering
60 years .... Liliha Bakery, Tin Tin Char Sut, Aloha Tofu Factory, Trade Wind Tours, Flamingo Restaurants
70 years .... Barbecue Inn (Lihue), Naniloa Hotel, Dot's in
Wahiawa, Elsie's Fountain & Diner (Hilo)
75 years .... Honsador Lumber
80 years .... Victoria Ward Ltd., Hawaiian Bitumuls, R.M.
Towill Corporation, Holy's Bakery (Kapaau)
90 years .... Fisher Hawaii, Grace Pacific, Fukuda Seed,
Ebisuzaki Fishing Supply (Hilo)
100 years .... Hasegawa General Store (Hana), Sugai Kona
Coffee, Ishigo Bakery & Store (Honomu)

Anniversaries in 2011

25 years .... Yummy Korean Bar-B-Q, Hale Vietnam
50 years .... Rainbow Drive-In, Violet's Grill, Chart House
60 years .... Matsumoto Shave Ice, Young's Fish Market,
KIKI radio
70 years .... Robert's Hawaii
90 years .... Straub Clinic and Hospital, Territorial Savings
& Loan, HPM Building Supply, Diamond
Bakery, Natsunoya Tea House
100 years .... Eki Cyclery, First Insurance
110 years .... Moana Hotel, Dole, Hosoi Mortuary
120 years .... Hawaiian Electric, Bishop Museum
140 years .... Original Royal Hawaiian Hotel built
downtown, Kapiolani Park dedicated
160 years .... Castle & Cooke, Love's Bakery, Pacific Club
165 years .... Saint Louis School, Washington Place
170 years .... Punahou School
175 years .... Royal Hawaiian Band
175 years .... C Brewer

Answers to the Quizzes

How Well Do You Know Hawaii Companies? Answers:

1. Robert's Hawaii's rabbit is waving goodbye to the **Greyhound dog**. 2. The Pope picked the name "Order of St. Francis" indirectly naming **St. Francis Hospital**. 3. HAPCO (Hawaiian Pineapple Co.) was founded by **James Dole** and is now **Dole Foods**. 4. The Dairyman's Association is now **Meadow Gold**. The Waialae Country Club occupies the site of the original dairy. 5. A nurse at Queen's founded **HMSA** in 1938. 6. **Ilikai** means the "surface of the sea." 7. **Shirokiya** was founded in 1662. 8. **Famous Amos** sold his company only to realize he also had sold his name. 9. **The Queen's Medical Center's** logo has two intertwined "E's" with a crown on top. 10. The **Royal Hawaiian Hotel**. 11. Originally **Ricky's Crazy Shirts**, founded by Rick Ralston. 12. **Aloha Airlines** was originally named Trans Pacific Airways, or TPA. 13. Waialua Garage became Service Motors and then **Servco**. 14. **Mountain Apples** fell on Jon de Mello's home in Tantalus. 15. The song *Quiet Village* was written at the **Hilton Hawaiian Village** Shell Bar. 16. Roy Kelley scooped Sheraton Hotels out of the lease on the old **Outrigger** Canoe Club. 17. The **New Otani Kaimana Beach Hotel** is the "best hidden secret in Waikiki."

How Well Do You Know Hawaii Retailers? Answers:

1. **ABC Stores** stumbled into having locations close to each other accidentally. 2. Brothers Joe and Tom opened **Longs Drug Stores** in California in 1938. 3. Heinrich Hackfeld started what became **Liberty House**. 4. Wook Moon founded **Ming's** in 1939. 5. C.K. Ai founded **City Mill**. 6. Retail guru Glenn Kaya brought **GEM** to Hawaii in 1958. 7. Seventy-five years ago, **Musashiya** was known as Hawaii's best shirt maker. 8. **Maui Divers** started as a Lahaina dive shop and is now the largest coral jewelry manufacturer in the state. 9. **Reyn's** was known as "The Brooks Brothers of the Pacific."10. John **Nordstrom** struck it rich in the Alaskan Gold Rush and saved enough money to start a shoe store in Seattle in 1901. 11. **Sears** was the original anchor tenant at Ala Moana Cen-

ter. 12. **RadioShack** takes its name from the wooden room that houses a ship's electronic equipment. 13. **Old Navy** used to be called the Gap Warehouse. 14. "The big store in the little lane" was **Arakawa's**. 15. **Sedona** is named for a mystical, northern Arizona town with beautiful, red mountains. 16. **Samuel Kramer** founded Kramer's Naval Uniforms in 1939. 17. The well-known Hawaiian entertainer from the 1950s was **Hilo Hattie**. 18. **Chun-Hoon** was at Nuuanu and School for almost 50 years. 19. **Harry's Music Store** is in Kaimuki. 20. **Costco** "stacks it high and sells it cheap." 21. **Matsumoto's Shave Ice**. 22. **Wyland** is the "Marine Michaelangelo." 23. **S.H. Kress & Co**.

How Well do you Know Hawaii Restaurants, Drive-ins and Food Establishments? Answers to part 1

1. **Anna Miller's** has a Pennsylvania Dutch theme. 2. **KC Drive Inn** was the first drive-in in town. 3. Brothers Frank and Tosh Kaneshiro opened the **Columbia Inn**. 4. **Don the Beachcomber** pioneered the South Seas village style bar and restaurant. 5. **Pearl City Tavern** was famous for its Monkey Bar. 6. The "Best Restaurant Any Country in World" was **Waikiki Lau Yee Chai**. 7. Tony and Peaches Guerrero's three restaurants were named **The Tropics**. 8. **Ba-Le** means "Paris" in Vietnamese. 9. "La Infanta de Castille" was misunderstood as **"Elephant and Castle."** 10. Zippy's owner Francis Higa helped **Alan Wong** get started in his own restaurant. 11. Hilo's **Café 100** is home to the Loco Moco. 12. **Spencecliff** once had 50 restaurants. 13. **La Mariana** is one of the last South Sea's style restaurants on Oahu. 14. **Lyn's Delicatessen**.

How Well do you Know Hawaii Restaurants, Drive-ins and Food Establishments? Answers to part 2

1. Restaurateur Francis Tom built the **Wailana Coffee House** 2. Frank Sinatra's touring chef founded **Matteo's Italian restaurant.** 3. **Liliha Bakery** sells 5,000 Coco Puffs a day. 4. The Japanese consulate spy watched from **Natsunoya Tea House**. 5. **The Flamingo restaurant** took the name of a Las Vegas hotel. 6. An old name for a golf club is a **Niblick**. 7. The Salvation Army operates the **Waioli Tea Room**. 8. **Baskin-Robbins** created a different flavor

for each day of the month. 9. **Angelo Pietro** is a famous Italian fairy tale. 10. **Benihana Restaurant** began as a four-table Japanese restaurant. 11. A sign-maker misunderstood Yoshio Hori's name and painted "**Holy's Bakery.**" 12. **Wo Fat** is the oldest restaurant in Honolulu. 13. **The Willows** is known for its fabulous curries and mile-high pies served in a Polynesian thatched roof setting. 14. **Dot's in Wahiawa** was once the finest place for dining and entertainment in Central Oahu. 15. **Chez Michel** also started in Wahiawa.

How Well Do You Know Fast Food? Answers

1. **McDonald's** started in San Bernardino, California. 2. Colonel Harlan Sanders started **Kentucky Fried Chicken**, now KFC. 3. Robert Peterson's favorite childhood toy was a **Jack-in-the-Box.** 4. The Zip Code inspired **Zippy's** name. 5. The Raffel Brothers started RB's, now **Arby's.** 6. Glen Bell started **Taco Bell.** 7. **Bob's Big Boy** invented the double-decker hamburger. 8. "Grandpa" McCullough founded **Dairy Queen**. 9. Roy Allen and Frank Wright opened **A&W Root Beer.**

How Well Do You Know Hawaii Schools? Answers

1. **Lahainaluna** is the oldest school in Hawaii. 2. **Punahou** means "new spring." 3. **La Pietra** occupies Dillingham's estate. 4. **Iolani** began in Lahaina. 5. The Chiefs' Children's School is now **Royal School**. 6. **Saint Louis School** gave College Walk its name. 7. **Hawaii Pacific University** has the most international student body. 8. **McKinley High School** was once the Fort Street English Day School and Honolulu High School. 9. **Waldorf School** uses an arts-based curriculum. 10. A baby was lent each year to **Kamehameha Schools** from 1925 to 1962. 11. **Chaminade** was named for a French priest. 12. Buf 'n Blu refers to the colors of the **sand and the sea**. 13. The College of Agriculture and Mechanic Arts is now the **University of Hawaii**. 14. **Waipahu High School** was the first high school on the Leeward side. 15. **Hanahauoli's** name means "joyous work." 16. **Damien Memorial** occupies the former Houghtailing estate in Kalihi. 17. **Kalani High School** was originally going to be called Waialae High School. 18. The minor rebellion at U.H. was over wearing **aloha shirts** instead of coats and ties.

Answers to How Well Do You Know Punahou School?

1. **Queen Kaahumanu** encouraged Liliha to donate the land for Punahou. 2. Punahou means **"new spring."** 3. The spring forms a famous **Lily Pond** on campus. 4. The **Reverend Hiram Bingham** founded the school. 5. **Hiram Bingham III** discovered Machu Picchu. 6. Buf 'n Blu refer to the colors of the **sand and sea.** 7. From 1857 until 1934, Punahou was called **Oahu College.** 8. Lettermen earn an **"O" for Oahu College.** 9. Dole Street is named for the **Reverend Daniel Dole**, father to Sanford Dole. 10. The Chief's Children's School is now called **Royal School.** 11. The cactus hedge is a **Night-blooming Cereus.** 12. The **Army Corps of Engineers** occupied the school during World War II.

How well do you know Hawaii Radio and TV Stations? Here are the answers:

1. Before it was called KSSK and K59, it was **KGMB** radio. 2. **KCCN** is "All Hawaiian, All the Time." 3. K-POI's **Poi Boys** entertained us with pranks and "thons." 4. **Bob Sevey** was widely considered to be Hawaii's Walter Cronkite. 5. **Hal Lewis (J. Akuhead Pupule)** was famous for his nonexistent Second Annual Easter Parade on April 1, down Kalakaua Avenue. 6. **Paul Udell and Barbara Tanabe** co-anchored the KHON 2 News before Joe Moore. 7. KHVH was short for **Kaiser's Hawaiian Village Hotel.** 8. Kamasami Kong was the original host of the **Hawaiian Moving Company.** 9. **KGU**, the "Voice of Hawaii" was the first on the air in 1922. 10. **KIKU** means chrysanthemum in Japanese. 11. **Hawaii Calls** was broadcast from "beneath the Banyan Tree" at the Moana Hotel. 12. KGMB radio and KPUA radio in Hilo formed a **"Coconut Wireless."** 13. KQNG was inspired by **King Kong.** 14. Michael W. Perry was referred to as **"Uncle Mikey"** at KKUA. 15. **KNDI** had all-girl DJ lineup in the 1970s. 16. **KZOO** is the largest and oldest Japanese language radio station outside of Japan. 17. DJ Mel Medeiros' nickname is **Mynah Bird.** 18. KKUA and Habilitat put out three **Homegrown** albums. 19. **Lucky Luck** was a top morning DJ opposite Aku in the mornings. 20. **Joe Moore** was a sports reporter with Bob Sevey at KGMB TV.

How Well Do You Know Hawaii's Royalty? Answers:

1. Kamehameha V and Kalakaua helped start the **Royal Hawaiian Hotel.** 2. The Chiefs' Children's School is now **Royal School.** 3. **Bernice Pauahi Bishop** was the last of the Kamehameha line. 4. Princess Ruth's home later became **Central Intermediate School.** 5. Princess Victoria Kaiulani was born in a home that is now the **Pacific Club.** 6. William Lunalilo left money to care for elderly Hawaiians in **Lunalilo Home.** 7. Queen Emma founded **St. Andrew's Priory** and **Iolani School.** 8. Queen Liliuokalani lived in **Washington Place.**

What Was There Before? Answers:

1. Bishop Museum – Kamehameha Schools
2. Don Quijote (Honolulu) – Kapiolani Drive-In, Holiday Mart, Daiei
3. Tamarind Park/Pauahi Tower - Alexander Young Building
4. Neil Blaisdell Center – Ward Estate ("Old Plantation")
5. Sports Authority (Ward) – GEM
6. TGI Friday's (Ward) – Trader Vic's
7. Zippy's (Kahala) – Jolly Roger Drive In
8. Academy Art Learning Center (Victoria St) – Linekona School (and, before that, the University of Hawaii (1907) and, before that, McKinley High School, and, before that, the Maerten's residence)
9. Hard Rock Café – Coco's, Kau Kau Korner before that
10. Ala Moana Hotel – Tropics Restaurant, Universal Motors
11. City Mill (Waialae) – Chico's restaurant, P&P Supermarket
12. K-Mart (Nimitz) – Home Improvement Warehouse, Del Monte Cannery before that
13. First Hawaiian Bank (Moiliili) – Chunky's Drive-In
14. McDonald's (Haleiwa) – Haleiwa Theatre
15. Hawaii Prince Hotel Waikiki – Kaiser Hospital
16. 3660 on the Rise – Kaimuki Theatre
17. Wasabi Bistro (Kapahulu) – Alex Drive-In
18. First Hawaiian Tower (Fort Street Mall) – S. H. Kress
19. Convention Center – Aloha Motors
20. Central Intermediate School – Honolulu High School (later McKinley HS), and, before that, Princess Ruth's Palace.

How well do you recall Hawaii slogans - answers:

1. Wings of the islands – Hawaiian Airlines
2. Thank you *very* much – Lex Brodie's Tire Company
3. One of the good things about Hawaii – KGMB
4. Look at all the things we are – Oceanic Cable
5. All Hawaiian, all the time – KCCN
6. And away we go – Creative Holidays
7. The pulse of paradise – Honolulu Star-Bulletin
8. We'll make a believer out of you – Windward Honda
9. The power of yes – First Hawaiian Bank
10. We make you shine – McKinley Car Wash
11. If you're not buying your diamonds from the House of Adler, you *are* paying too much.
12. Two distinctive campuses – one great university – Hawaii Pacific University
13. Giving you the power – Hawaiian Electric
14. Entertaining Hawaii since 1917 – Consolidated Theatres
15. Hawaii's newspaper – Honolulu Advertiser
16. Hawaii's center – Ala Moana Center
17. Hawaii's radio station – KSSK
18. Hawaii's bank – Bank of Hawaii
19. Pink Palace of the Pacific – Royal Hawaiian Hotel
20. Creative Italian and Chinese cuisine – Ciao Mein
21. Doing our best for you – Foodland
22. Meet you beneath the banyan tree – Moana Hotel
23. An oasis in the heart of Honolulu – Pagoda Hotel
24. Walk in, hula out – Waltah Clarke's
25. You're going to find it at Kilgo's

Formerly Known As - answers:

1. Hawaiian Pineapple Co. is now **Dole**
2. Horatio's is now **Kincaid's**
3. Kahala Hilton is now **Kahala Mandarin Oriental**
4. Inter-Island Airways is now **Hawaiian Airlines**
5. Waialua Garage is now **Servco**
6. Mister K Stores is now **ABC Stores**
7. H. Hackfeld and Company became **Liberty House** and is now **Macy's**
8. Kapiolani Drive Inn is now **Wailana Coffee House**
9. Trans-Pacific Airways is now **Aloha Airlines**
10. Bullwinkle's is now **Moose McGillicuddy's**
11. KGMB radio is now **KSSK**
12. Oahu Railway & Land Co. became **Dillingham**
13. Japanese Hospital is now **Kuakini Medical Center**
14. Kuilima Hotel is now **Turtle Bay Hilton**
15. Dairyman's Association is now **Meadow Gold**
16. Bishop and Company is now **First Hawaiian Bank**
17. The British Club is now **the Pacific Club**
18. Olympic Grill is now **Flamingo**
19. GTE Hawaiian Tel is now **Verizon**
20. The Crater Hotel is **Volcano House**

Schools
21. Oahu College is now **Punahou**
22. Chiefs' Children's School is now **Royal School**
23. Ahuimanu College is now **Saint Louis School**
24. Luaehu School is now **Iolani School**
25. Honolulu High School is now **McKinley High School**
26. College of Agriculture and Mechanic Arts is now **the University of Hawaii**
27. Saint Louis Junior College is now **Chaminade University**
28. Church College of Hawaii is now **Brigham Young University Hawaii**

Bibliography

The following books and sources were used in the writing of this book.

The Aloha Shirt: Spirit of the Islands, Dale Hope.
Aloha Waikiki – 100 years of pictures from Hawaii's most famous beach, Desoto Brown.
Artifacts of the Pomare Family, Karen Stevenson.
A century of public education in Hawaii 1840–1940, Benjamin Wist.
The Chief's Childrens' School, Mary Atherton Richards.
50 Years of Aloha – The story of Aloha Airlines, Bill Wood.
Firsts and Almost Firsts in Hawaii, Robert C. Schmitt.
Hawaii Business magazine.
Hawaii's Glamour Days, Maili Yarley.
Hawaii Looking Back – an illustrated History of the islands, Glen Grant.
Hawaii Tropical Rum Drinks & Cuisine by Don the Beachcomber, Phoebe Beach, and Arnold Bitner
Hawaiian Street Names, Rich Budnick and Duke Kalani Wise
History of Bank of Hawaii - Chronology 1897 - 1975, Dorothy L. Newman, Research Librarian, Business Research Library
The Honolulu Advertiser
Honolulu Magazine
The Honolulu Star-Bulletin
Kahala – The Hotel that could only happen once, Ed Sheehan
Kapiolani Health, Hackler and Yardley
Legacy: A portrait of the Young Men and women of Kamehameha schools, 1887-1987, Sharlene Chun-Lum and Leslie Agard
Malamalama – A history of the University of Hawaii, Robert Kamins and Robert Potter.
On Bishop Street, Kenneth L. Ames
Pocket Place Names in Hawaii, Mary Pukui, Samuel Elbert, Esther Mookini
Stepping into time, A guide to Honolulu's Historic Landmarks, Jeannette Murray Peek.
The Story of C. Brewer and Company, Limited, Scott C. S. Stone
The Story of Mid-Pacific Institute, Helen Gay Pratt
Straub – Four Generations of Excellence, Carol Chang

Glossary

For those *malihini* readers, here are some definitions of Hawaiian and Japanese words and concepts that are used in the book.

Ahupuaa – A land division or area, usually extending from the mountains to the ocean.

Alii – Hawaiian royalty and nobility.

Big Five – The largest and most powerful sugar producers: C. Brewer & Company, Castle & Cooke, Alexander & Baldwin, Amfac, and Theo. H. Davies & Company.

Geta – Japanese wooden slippers.

Haole – Caucasian.

Hapa – literally "half." It cannotes someone of mixed race.

Heiau – A Hawaiian temple used as a place of worship, offering, and/or sacrifice .

Hui – a group that gets together to financially support something, usually a business.

Imua – To move forward, or lead.

Issei – 1st generation Japanese immigrant.

Kamaaina – Person of the land. Refers to someone who has been in Hawaii a long time.

Kahuna – Hawaiian priests.

Kanji – A Japanese written language using Chinese characters.

Madam Pele – The goddess of the volcano.

Makai – Towards the sea.

Malihini - Newcomer.

Manapua - A baked or steamed bun, usually containing pork. From the Hawaiian "mea'ono pua'a" meaning "tasty pig."

Mauka - Towards the mountains.

Nissei – Second generation Japanese.

Ohana – Family.

Sansei – Third generation Japanese.

Sumotori – Sumo wrestlers.

Tatami – Floor mats made from rice straw or rush grass.

Yukata – Japanese robe.

Chapter Twelve

Follow Up - Book Orders

DO YOU KNOW OF A GREAT STORY WE OVERLOOKED? We know that thousands are out there. Send it to us and we'll post new stories to our web site at www.CompaniesWeKeep.com.

There are over 3,000 facts and stories in the book and, despite our best efforts to check them, some may be incorrect. In some cases we found two sources that had slightly different sets of facts. If you know of an error or if you have a great story we overlooked or have interesting photos, send us an e-mail.

Book Updates

Would you like a reminder when the book's web site is updated with new material and stories?

The print in a book cannot be changed, but a web site can. If you'd like to know when new material has been added to the web site, send us an e-mail at: CompaniesWeKeep@Yahoo.com.

Put "Book Updates" in the subject line of your email. We'll send you an e-mail whenever new information is posted on the site.

Send us your comments

We'd love to hear your reaction to the book and its stories. Did it bring back old memories, or remind you of something? Send us an e-mail at: CompaniesWeKeep@Yahoo.com.

Book Orders

The book is a perfect gift for business people and those who appreciate interesting stories about Hawaii's well-known companies.

Copies can be sent anywhere in the world, and volume discounts are available.

In the Company of Aloha

A second book of amazing stories about Hawaii people and companies is due in late 2007 or early 2008. The working title is *In the Company of Aloha*. Here's a look at some of the stories it will include.

Who was Hawaii's first visitor from Japan?
In 1844, five young fishermen were shipwrecked off Japan. An American whaling ship brought them to Hawaii. One, "John" Manjiro, ended up advising and translating when Commodore Perry arrived in Japan, and was made a samurai for his service.

Four major sports have ties to Hawaii residents
Captain Cook found Hawaiians surfing when he arrived here, but can you guess the other three sports that were created or influenced by people who lived in Hawaii?

Don Ho and Kui Lee
Kui Lee wrote many of Don Ho's hits. Who was Kui Lee referring to when he wrote *I'll Remember You*? What did Don Ho say he'd name the White House when he was elected the first Hawaiian U.S. President?

Whose idea was Magic Island?
In 1955, one man suggested two large islands be built in addition to the peninsula he called Magic Island. He wanted to build water ways, bridges and 6 hotels on them. Who was this Hawaii visionary?

Other stories you'll find in this fascinating book:
- Which other names were considered for Aloha Stadium?
- How Elvis Presley helped build the Arizona Memorial.
- When Babe Ruth played baseball in Hilo.
- The plan to extend the Ala Wai Canal to Pearl Harbor.
- How an Aiea girl became the Divine Miss M.
- How Shirley Temple met her future husband in Hawaii.
- Which U.S. President visited Papakolea?
- How the Polynesian Cultural Center began in Waikiki.
- Who Duke Kahanamoku was named for.

Look for it at your favorite book store

Mahalo to All My Students

For 10 semesters, students in my HPU Integrated Marketing 6500 class interviewed the owner or president of one well-known Hawaii company. How did they get their name, slogan and logo? What was their company history? The assignment was designed to get them off campus to meet members of the business community.

After reading several semesters of their reports, it became clear that they had uncovered so many interesting stories that they should be published.

Mahalo to all my students from those 10 semesters!

Summer 1998
Jeannie Chan
Johnny Chen
Regina Cheng
Susanna Fong
Yoshi Hatanaka
Seila Hui
Mary Jiony
Edward Lee
Kai Lehmus
Mark Masterson
Tsuyoshi Niiro
Yukari Nishio
Irwan Prayogo
Eric Rita
Vanessa Tai
Christine Wong

Fall 1998
Fernando Bastos
Ernie Fukeda
Uli Haeske
Andrian Karjadi
Getrude Kitia
Chee Hong Lee
Kobi Lui
Sisi Maw
Seeto Yih Chieh
Twu Yong Tan

Spring 1999
Pratim Banerji
Doris Chen
Amelia Chen
Sharon Choong
Jack Chung
Diana Di Silvestro
Suzanna Galiza
Susan Goh
Andreas Gstoll
Penny Ho
Larson Kiyabu
Jarnett Lono
Suherman Menurung
Jack Mekworawuth
Karen Mirikitani
Suda Ngamvilai
Sujin Park
Rocky Ramirez
Seung-koon Seo
Vivek Sharma
Hsiao-hui Sheng
Vera Sunanto
Stephanus
  Suryaatmadja
Melissa Tsai
Hung-ming Tseng
Oguz Ulucayli
Jack Yu

Summer 1999
Kathryn Acorda
Veysel Bayam
Lian Chang
Grace Chen
Hui Chin Chua
Remy Cremers
Raquel De La Garza
Irena Deisinger
Tony Doddair
Delores Fung
Mark Griffin
Fehmi Gumusel
Maria Heljegard
Emily Huang
Joanne Huang
Dan Izawa
Aaron Lum
Malkawi Ahmed
Robb Orsuwan
Kev Perkins
JT Thames
I-Jen Tsai

Fall 1999
Angel Arias
Adriana Camara
Salig Chada
Birdie Chen

Johan Hedin
Karen Kaisan
Karla Legaspi
Marcus Lindstrup
Tiffany Liangkobkij
Yuki Moromizato
Jane Ng
Grace Nguchu
Glen Peterson
Alexandre Pires
Susanne Prosser
Norhidayah Rahman
Mari Sawamukai
Marcela Solera
Rasel Taher
Nunzio Taranto
Rainer Villa
Mikio Watanabe
Nicola Whistler

Spring 2000
Ray Chan
Lin Chaiwilai
  Siriporn
Ken Chen
Davilyn Costa
Frank Chua
Ohm Dhomasaroj
Christian Ekander
MJ Quenga
Ilima Guerrero
Calvin Huang
Carol Lai
Carrie Lin
Kyung-Hee Ma
Kelly Nguyen
Steve Risi
Jawd Saelin
Ahmad Samsudin
William Sheh
Blago Stephanov

Summer 2000
Faisal Abdulla
Ed Calvo
David Chang
Tina Chen
Allen Fu
Patty Hsu
Neil Illane
Janet Lin
Gloria Liu
Miho Mahler
Gabe Pangilinan
Su Hsiu-Chang
Maria Tani
Nelia Visitacion
Madeleine Wadelius
Vicky Wen

Fall 2000
Flaco Aguirre
Alec Chan
Bruce Chen
Daniel Chong
Chih-Fang
Jack Chou
Joy Crawford
Holly Kaneko
David Kwong
Natalie Lau
Effie Lin
Yvonne Mia
Dave Nazareth
Giuseppe Regina
Trevor Thompson
Chutima Tivattanasuk
Charlie Wang

Spring 2001
Richard Andermyr
Leo Bimbuain
Nicholas Chen

Jackie Chu
Keh-yi Hsu
Moon-Sun Kang
Kenson Kuboyama
Rachel Leber
Derek Leung
Mandy Liew
Michelle Liu
Karen Mirikitani
Christine Mizuno
Jonas Moen
Tini Mohtar
Joe Ruangronghiranya
Elie Sauma
Jane Ting
Celia Tso
Ryu Tsuji
Bernie Ye
Susan Yeh

Summer 2001
Laura Askew
Nicholas Anjos
Nadia Bakdash
Mike Gene Beckner
David Cho
Michael Fukutomi
Michael Gross
Gary Hamilton
Crystal Hinzy
Meng-Han Lin
Marissa Matsuda
Katsuyuki Nishikawa
Al Rodrigues
Nadav Scheinbach
Boris Solecki
Kathleen Severini
Chia Hui Tseng
Marina Tyan
Khawar Waheed
Dwight Walker
Kong Nam Yip

Index

Photo credits

Photographs were collected from dozens of sources for this project. Most pictures were cropped or cleaned of dust and other marks. Those modified more are listed below.

The following pictures came from the Hawaii State Archives, Bishop Museum of the Hawaiian Historical Society, except as noted. All other photographs are either from the individual or company pictured, or from the author's collection. If there is more than one picture on a page, the first is listed as "a," the second as "b," etc.

Hawaii State Archives

Cover – Dole Pineapple (colorized), Queen Emma, Diamond Head, Royal Hawaiian Hotel, Lurline; China Clipper, Kau Kau Korner sign; and ships in the harbor.

Page 1, 3, 4a, 14, 22, 23, 24, 25a, b, 26a, b, 27a, b, 28, 30, 33b, 57, 66, 67, 74, 79, 83, 85, 90 102b, 117, 118, 129 (Camera Hawaii), 135a,b, 136b, 137, 138, 139, 147, 148, 152 (Photo Hawaii), 166, 167, 169, 173, 176, 177, 178, 185, 192, 201, 209, 210, 219, 225, 226, 232, 234, 238, 244, 245, 257 (Camera Hawaii), 278, 282a, b, 283, 284, 285a, b, 289, 320, 329, 330a,b, 331, 332, 335a, 336, 337, 338a, 339, 340, 341, 342b, 343a, b, 344a,b, 345, 350.

Hawaiian Historical Society

Page 3, 6 (C. Burgess engraving), 36a, b, 47, 136, 157, 174, 175 (Camera Hawaii), 248, 249, 250, 258, 259, 287, 333

Bishop Museum

Cover – Coco's (Name is lightened for easier viewing).
Page 193, 264, 266, 277,

Cover – Hawaii Theatre Marquee from Lowell Angell.
Page 58 – Kinko's drawing by University of Southern California. p. 112 – Junior Achievement; p. 136a – Bank of Hawaii photo; p. 145 – Eki photo (composite); p. 149 – Consolidated Theatre's photo; p. 303 Mary Ann Chang photo. p. 313 - Mel Ah Ching.

About The Author

BOB SIGALL IS A LIFE-LONG ENTREPRENEUR. He started his first business in intermediate school, over 30 years ago, filing IRS tax returns for his friends so they would get refunds. For six years in high school and college, he had his own window washing business.

Bob has had several businesses since getting his Masters degree from the University of Hawaii in 1975.

He has been a business consultant since 1978 and has owned his own firm, Creative-1, since 1985. Over the years he has offered marketing and management consultation to over 1,000 Hawaii businesses.

In 2005, he launched Management Magic, which provides a mentor to work one-on-one with mid-level managers and supervisors. He also writes a column on marketing for *Hawaii Business* magazine.

Bob teaches marketing at Hawaii Pacific University and this book evolved out of an assignment he gave his students to interview the president of any well-known Hawaii business.

He's a director of Small Business Hawaii and was chairman of their Legislative Action Committee from 1992-2000. In 1997 he co-founded the Business Legislative Coalition.

Bob has been married since 1986 to Lei Honda-Sigall, a parish nurse with St. Francis Healthcare System.

Looking for a speaker for your group?

The author gives fun talks to community groups about several of the topics in the book. Contact him at CompaniesWeKeep@Yahoo.com.